Doomsayers

EARLY AMERICAN STUDIES

Daniel K. Richter and Kathleen M. Brown, Series Editors

Exploring neglected aspects of our colonial, revolutionary, and early national history and culture, Early American Studies reinterprets familiar themes and events in fresh ways. Interdisciplinary in character, and with a special emphasis on the period from about 1600 to 1850, the series is published in partnership with the McNeil Center for Early American Studies.

A complete list of books in the series is available from the publisher.

Doomsayers

Anglo-American Prophecy in the Age of Revolution

Susan Juster

PENN

University of Pennsylvania Press
Philadelphia

10   9   8   7   6   5   4   3   2   1

Published by
University of Pennsylvania Press
Philadelphia, Pennsylvania 19104-4011

Library of Congress Cataloging-in-Publication Data

Juster, Susan.
   Doomsayers : Anglo-American prophecy in the age of Revolution / Susan Juster.
      p.   cm. — (Early American studies)
   Includes bibliographical references and index.
   ISBN 0-8122-3732-3 (acid-free paper)
      1. Prophets—United States—History. 2. Prophecy—Christianity—History. 3. United States—
Church history. 4. Prophets—England—History. 5. England—Church history. I. Title. II. Series.
BR520.J87 2003
231.7'45'097309033—dc21   2002043044

Contents

Preface

Prophets are messengers. They listen to frequencies few others can or want to hear, for warning signs—signs that things are not what they seem, that trouble is coming. More often than not, they are lonely figures, their advice ignored and mocked by those who most need it. The "company of prophets" who visited Anglo-America in the war-torn years of 1765–1815 was, I think, particularly good at conveying certain messages, though not always the ones intended. They certainly taught me a lot about the nature of public life in the late eighteenth century, about the meaning of categories like "the Enlightenment," rational religion, imposture, authenticity, and revelation.

The popularity prophets enjoyed in the late eighteenth century, the celebrated "age of reason," may seem puzzling at first. How, we might ask, did eighteenth-century believers reconcile their newfound scientific and intellectual convictions with a religious practice as ancient as the Old Testament itself? Is prophecy best understood as a relic—an archaic remnant of some premodern religious sensibility lurking below the surface of a rapidly modernizing culture, as a living adaptation of a traditional practice to a new set of cultural and intellectual imperatives, or as something else entirely? Who believed in these messengers of doom, anyway, and why? Did prophets appeal to the most traditional members of Anglo-American society, those for whom the promises of economic and social advancement held out by a liberal commercial and political order failed to materialize, or did they draw their converts across a wide spectrum of social and political groups? Did a belief in the kind of savage justice promised by prophets undercut the liberal humanitarian ethos which seemed to be ascendant in the public culture of Anglo-America, or did prophets adjust their fire-and-brimstone message to the more delicate sensibilities of their modern-minded audience?

All of these questions, as phrased, presume an essential tension or incompatibility between religious faith and the enlightenment, between the ancient need to mortify the self and the newer desire to ennoble it. That these two impulses were in tension throughout the eighteenth century is, I think, beyond dispute; that they represented fundamentally alien ways of living in and with the world is less clear. Historians such as Phyllis Mack, Leigh Eric Schmidt, David Hall, Jon Butler and others have argued forcefully and persuasively that the old binaries (faith versus reason, primitive versus modern, orality versus literacy, magic versus science) are inadequate to capturing the full complexity of Anglo-American religious culture as it evolved in the century and a half following the chaotic violence of the English Civil War and the conciliatory gestures of the Restoration era. Phyllis Mack's most recent work, in particular, has helped me to see the myriad connections between the enlightened ideal of self-realization and the evangelical campaign to contain, control, and redirect the self and its appetites. Rather than offering a counternarrative of self-abnegation and political loss, the rise of evangelical Protestantism to a position of cultural authority in both England and North America after 1750 provided, she argues, a highly sophisticated and effective set of emotional and intellectual disciplines by which the enlightened ideal (shorn of its most arrogant presuppositions) could be realized. There was not, it now seems, a bloody war of attrition between two fully articulated and incompatible visions of the human condition vying for supremacy over the course of the eighteenth century, but a far more messy entanglement of ideas in which the discrete strands are often impossible to distinguish, let alone meaningfully disentangle.

Neither an archaic remnant nor a novel practice, prophecy in the revolutionary era (defined by most historians as the half-century from the onset of the American Revolution to the conclusion of the Napoleonic Wars in 1815) was a cultural hybrid, rooted both in the primitive worldview of the Old Testament and in the vibrant intellectual environment of the philosophes and their political allies, the republicans. Even to phrase its genealogy in these terms, however, is misleading, for the notion of a "hybrid" suggests a coming together of two things, and what I propose is that we stop seeing the enlightenment and religious enthusiasm as distinct and antagonistic forces. Believers like John Wesley certainly found no contradiction in being both a man of science and a man of intense faith, and we can learn from his example. Prophets, too, rarely felt the need to declare their allegiance to one worldview or another: Richard Brothers's visions of becoming the Prince of the Hebrews did not prevent him from cultivating the persona of a refined gentleman; Joanna Southcott spoke regularly with spirits who directed her to compile these conversations into pamphlets that sold thousands of copies; David Austin organized "concerts of prayer" and other expressions of the bourgeois public sphere while declaring his own immortality; Jemima Wilkinson defended her mission in the pages of the republic's newspapers even as she sought refuge in a secluded community of believers. There is no bright line separating fanaticism from rationality in the lives of these men and women, only a stubborn refusal to think and act in terms of the binaries we historians continue to erect as fences around the intellectual and cultural terrain of the eighteenth century.

Writing history is not nearly as lonely, or heroic, an undertaking as making it. I wish to thank the many friends and colleagues who helped me along the way. Phyllis Mack, Ruth H. Bloch, Michael Meranze, Cornelia Hughes Dayton, Elizabeth Reis, John Carson, and Dena Goodman commented generously on earlier drafts of chapters presented at seminars and conferences. Kathleen Brown suggested links among white, Native, and African American prophets that helped me to define more precisely the "Anglo" parameters of Anglo-American millenarian culture. Mike Zuckerman invited me to talk about the project at his Early American seminar several years ago when the book was in its formative stage. Jeremy Popkin allowed me to test out my ideas about the different discursive strategies of male and female prophets at the "Millenarianism and Revolution" seminar organized in 1998 by the UCLA Center for Seventeenth- and Eighteenth-Century Studies and the William Andrews Clark Memorial Library, a conversation I was able to continue at the University of Minnesota with the participants in Kirsten Fischer's gender and politics seminar. And I wrangled an invitation from Laura Kalman to visit the University of California at Santa Barbara in November 2000 to talk about angels and other supernatural visitors to the northern frontier in the early republic; thanks to Laura, Pat Cohen, and Ann Marie Plane for pushing me to think in more psychological terms about the meaning of spiritual power to women's lives. At the eleventh hour, Bill Miller encouraged me to make one final round of changes; his impatience with academic cant and cheerful irreverence helped make the book clearer and more readable.

Other friends contributed in less formal ways. Laura Lee Downs, Ken Lockridge, Michael MacDonald, and Leslie Pincus, great talkers all, helped me to see past the particularities of my story to larger truths, the mark of true friendship. Amanda Vickery and John Styles provided a home away from home, and their daughters a reminder of what I was missing on repeat visits to London. Jim Sidbury went so far as to indulge my fondness for country music and chicken-fried steak during my stint in the Joanna South-cott Papers at the University of Texas Library in Austin. Rachel Weil gener-ously shared her apartment and love of British police dramas while I tracked Jemima Wilkinson's whereabouts in Ithaca and the surrounding Finger Lakes region. Susan Thorne, a comrade in arms since our days as graduate students and a true visionary in her own way, listened patiently to the saga of Joanna Southcott, offering moral support and wisdom in equal measure. Ellen Hartigan-O'Connor deserves special thanks for her expert research assistance; over the years I came to rely on her sharp eye for sources and judi-cious criticism. The expert staff at the British Library, the American Anti-quarian Society, the Penn Yann Historical Society in New York, the Clements Library at the University of Michigan, the Harry Ransom Research Center at the University of Texas, the Friends' Library and Dr. Williams' Library in London, and the Western Reserve Historical Society in Cleveland made my work both much easier and far more enjoyable.

Various sections of the book have been published in article or chapter form, and I thank the publishers here for permission to reprint this material: much of Chapter 3 appeared in the April 2000 issue of the *William and Mary Quarterly* as "Mystical Pregnancy and Holy Bleeding: Visionary Experience in Early Modern Britain and America," and Chapter 4 has its origins in "Demagogues or Mystagogues? Gender and the Language of Prophecy in the Age of Democratic Revolutions," which appeared in the *American Historical Review*'s special forum on millennialism in December 1999. A portion of Chapter 6 has been taken from "'Neither Male Nor Female': Jemima Wilkin-son and the Politics of Gender in Post-Revolutionary America," in *Possible Pasts: Becoming Colonial in Early America*, ed. Robert Blair St. George (Ithaca, N.Y., 2000). A fellowship grant from the National Endowment for the Hu-manities in 1998–99 gave me the time and intellectual space to turn what was originally a series of essays about individual prophets into a story about the public shape of millenarian culture.

Two friends have lived with this book for almost as long as I have. Nei-ther one is a specialist in early American history, and one isn't (formally, at least) even a historian. But they read carefully and more times than I care to remember every draft of each chapter, commented extensively on the sub-stance and style of the argument, and spent hours with me talking about the politics and poetics of religious belief in past cultures and in our own. Val Kivelson pushed me to think about the relation of gender to religious prac-tice from the perspective of other orthodoxies, and kept asking me what the point of the whole thing was when I (and the manuscript) wandered aimlessly. Don Herzog, an incomparable anatomist of language, first suggested to me that I was really writing a book about the politics of cultural conflict, and refused to let me get away with sloppy formulations or easy generalizations. Their friendship and intellectual comraderie have meant more to me than I can say. A simple thanks will have to do.

I have been lucky in my choice of subject matter. The prophets whose stories are told in this book made excellent companions over the years. They—like the friends and colleagues acknowledged above—were funny, shrewd, sharp observers of their culture, and at times inspirational. We, my prophets and I, have been fortunate to have an editor like Peter Agree and a reviewer like Mike Zuckerman, both of whom are all these things and more, to shepherd us through the final stages of the process. It's probably time to stop calling them "my" prophets, a silly pretense they would utterly scorn. But old habits die hard.

Introduction

Noah White was no one's idea of a prophet, not even his own. A simple farmer from Massachusetts, he became an unlikely participant in the wars over religious enthusiasm that consumed as much cultural energy as the more famous constitutional battles of the late eighteenth century. "Since I first thought of prophesying, which was in January 1799," he explained in his rambling treatise *Visionary Thoughts, or, Modern Prophecy*, "I have had many other dreams, and visions, concerning severe frosts, and snow in the summer; and of seeing the trees, and the grass dry, and of seeing people cutting up their green corn; and foddering their cattle in September; and seeing the trees covered with worms, and other insects, and grasshoppers." From these rather unremarkable scenes of natural disturbances, White progressed through more ominous visions of divine retribution to active conversations with angelic messengers about the state of his own and America's soul. "I soon began to receive, not only other things, but in a different manner, for before I received them in dreams, but since that time, I have received many things in what may more properly be called a trance, or vision, in which a scene was spread before me, and words were frequently spoken explanatory of what I saw; and then suddenly it left me."

White was a reluctant prophet, doubtful both of the meaning of the messages he received and of the manner in which he received them. He confessed that he "frequently doubted myself whether there was any thing in the revelation which I pretended to or not." Vague premonitions came into his mind by some unseen agency, only to be "catched away" before he could understand their meaning. "I heard much said by invisible beings," he explained, "but forget it mostly as soon as I heard it." One time, after persuading himself that "the angels have not spoken to me as I have immagined," he "fell into a kind of a trance as I frequently did; and this question was asked, *Will you have bread and milk for supper, or baked pudding?* This made me the more think I was right in what I had said: for I thought it was very unlikely an angel would ask such a question as that." Even the timely appearance (and in prophetic interpretation, timing was everything) of an innkeeper who posed the same question to White that very night was not enough to dispel his suspicion that God was merely toying with him.

Embarrassed by the pedestrian nature of these visions, White was understandably nervous when told by the angels that he must go public with his revelations. It was "with the utmost difficulty that I could prevail to tell one word, either by writing or by word of mouth," he admitted. "And I found by sad experience, that to hear things, and not to be able to tell them, was much worse than nothing." His visions, he feared, were nothing more than infantile fantasies. "I saw one of the papers which I had written held up to view in a vision, and this word was spoken, *Babies*. But when I came to look over them again, they appeared so foolish that I said, *truly if they are babies, they are abortions*. Therefore I buried them; for which there were sensible tokens of Divine displeasure."

Finally yielding to the spirits' commands, White published his first book of visions in 1806 out of his own pocket. The response was hardly gratifying. "Sometime after I published the former things," he complained, "as I was going to a place where I left some books to be sold, it was signified in a vision that, *they had shamefully abused the books which I left there*. When I came to the place, I found written on the margin of one of them words to this purpose, *In my opinion the author of this pamphlet is deranged, and is full of notions as a horse is of hay, and I think he had better keep his dreams to himself than to publish them to the world*." White himself was "displeased" that he had been "sent to publish such foolishness" and determined never to write again. But, once more, the reluctant prophet found he could not escape so easily. "Soon after that I had an involuntary motion, in the middle finger of my right hand, which lasted a day or two, which I considered as a sign that I ought to write. I was also further encouraged to write by these words being spoken by an angel, *I must write*, not *you* must write." "He that is disposed to laugh," he concluded defiantly, "let him laugh."[1]

It is hard not to sympathize with Noah White's unorthodox journey from farmer to prophet. At every step of the way he faced the derision of strangers and his own considerable doubts. But the way of a servant of God was never easy ("that is hard work," he admitted after wrestling with the meaning of yet another obtuse vision), and White persevered. Even if in the end he benefited little from his labors—calculating at one point that he had

---

[1] Noah White, *Visionary Thoughts, or, Modern Prophecy* (Greenwich, Mass., 1806), pp. 17–18, 19, 20, 25, 43–44.

lost more than twenty dollars from his publishing ventures—he had fulfilled what he and many others saw as a noble calling. It was a calling, moreover, that took him out of his provincial world of cattle and crops and into the very hub of Anglo-America's thriving "republic of letters," where men like him often felt uncomfortable. His determination to make a public offering of his private visions is noteworthy in an era in which the parameters of the "public" were being debated and contentiously redrawn in the aftermath of the revolutionary war.

Noah White's account is almost a parody of more respectable forms of millenarian belief in the "age of revolution." Behind his tentativeness we can hear the snickers of a large but invisible audience of readers and writers, those who made it a popular pastime in Britain and the United States to satirize religious enthusiasm as an embarrassing holdover from a more primitive age. And yet, in White's earnest puzzling out of the often confusing messages he received and his dogged persistence in publicizing God's Word despite the ridicule of printers and readers alike, we can see something of the intellectual and moral stamina required of prophets. Prophets wrote and spoke against the grain of much of what passed for public discourse in the revolutionary era, and this lent a defiant tone to their pronouncements. They knew the rest of the world—at least, all but the devoted few—thought they were crazy, and they made their peculiarity the very cornerstone of their authority as holy men and women.

There were hundreds, possibly thousands, of Noah Whites in Britain and North America in the late eighteenth century. "As the world has seen an age of Reason, and an age of Infidelity, so also shall the world see an age of Prophecy," lamented one pamphleteer.[2] Some of these prophets and prophetesses are familiar figures, at least within the small circle of millennial scholars: Richard Brothers, the self-declared "Nephew of Christ" whose antics landed him in a private asylum for over a decade in the 1790s; Ann Lee, the unlettered visionary from England's industrial North who led the Shaker migration to America in the 1770s; Joanna Southcott, the matriarch of British millenarianism whose "mystical pregnancy" in 1814 captivated the London press; Jemima Wilkinson, the American Quaker who abandoned her sect and her female identity to preach as the "Publick Universal Friend" during the revolutionary war. Others are less well known: the New Englander Nat Smith who stitched the title "GOD" on his cap in the 1780s; the slave

---

[2] [A Convert], *The Age of Prophecy! or, Further Testimony of the Mission of Richard Brothers* (London, 1795), p. 7.

woman known only as Clarinda who warned sinners of the wrath to come in the streets of Charleston, South Carolina; the Scottish farmwife Elspeth Buchan who promised her followers spiritual "translation" as they awaited the Second Coming; the scattered remnants of the early eighteenth-century Camisards, like the prophetess Mary Plewit whom John Wesley visited in London in the 1730s. Most were as earnest and likeable as Noah White, but a few were simply cranks, impostors who exploited the immense interest in millenarianism in the 1790s and early 1800s for personal gain.

"Prophet" was a fairly elastic term in the late eighteenth century, a handy label to be applied liberally to a variety of exegetical practices. At the most basic level, anyone could be a prophet, for the signs God provided were everywhere—in simple everyday occurrences such as the rumble of thunder, the streak of a falling star in the night sky, the birth of a malformed animal, or in catastrophic natural disasters such as an earthquake or crop failure. Nature provided many clues, but so too did less transparent fields of study such as astrology, mathematics, and history. At its most arcane, prophetic calculation involved knowledge of dead languages and of obscure texts, skills available only to a select few. Even at its most sophisticated, however, true prophecy required a leap of faith—an exercise of vision, not intellect. The elusive element that transformed dry scholastic calculation into inspired prediction carried many prophets out of the realm of the natural world and into the supernatural one, where, like Noah White, they heard voices, had strange dreams, fell into trances, were guided by angels to celestial realms, and saw ghostly apparitions.

In keeping with the permissive categorization of the time, I use the term "prophecy" in its broadest possible meaning, to encompass all the shades of millennial interpretation from simple fortune-telling to formalized theories of Christ's return and the end of time. The common element is the conceit that biblical references and current events form a single providential history, a history for the most part of horrors unleashed and finally vanquished. Prophets spoke largely in the tragic mode, though not without traces of the comic and the ironic. Wherever they looked, they saw a bloody cycle of sin and retribution, endlessly repeated until God intervened to end time altogether.

Millenarian visions offered a dystopic reading of the truly world-shaking events of the 1780s and 1790s. John Wesley, the warrior of early Methodism, was annoyed by those irresponsible provocateurs—"prophets of evil," he called them—who were frightening gullible Christians with tales that England teetered on "the brink of destruction." "For near seventy years," Wesley complained in 1788, "I have observed that, before any war or public calamity,

England abounds with prophets, who confidently fortell many terrible things. They generally believe themselves, but are carried away by a vain imagination. And they are seldom undeceived, even by the failure of their predictions, but still believe they will be fulfilled some time or other."[3] Wesley's irritable dismissal of these "prophets of evil" carries a faintly mocking tone, and I intend to convey the irony if not the condescension implicit in this characterization of eighteenth-century millenarians as hapless doomsayers. Prophets offended evangelical sensibilities, which were more apt to see compassion in God's dealings with his children than retribution. Wesley's God was a God of love and mercy, not terror. But the God of the Old Testament patriarchs, however tamed by the liberalizing effects of humanitarian sympathy and evangelical sentimentality, was not dead. Speaking evil and, to an influential segment of the English reading public, personifying evil, was the elemental task of prophets.

This book is about the place of millenarian thinking in the public culture of Britain and the new American republic in what historians call the "age of revolution"—the half-century from 1765 to 1815. Framed on either end by war, and encompassing the remarkable rise of evangelical religion to a position of cultural power, these decades saw the resurgence of a latent millenarianism that both fed on and repudiated the evangelical ethos represented by men like John Wesley. Tom Paine's oft-quoted boast in *Common Sense* that "the birthday of a new world" was at hand in 1776 was echoed, in darker tones, by a generation of Anglo-Americans less sanguine than Paine and his republican friends about what a "modern" world might look like. Speculation about the "final days" as foreshadowed in the prophetic texts of the Bible, always a favorite pastime of biblical scholars and armchair intellectuals, reached perhaps farther and deeper in the late eighteenth century than at any point since the chaotic days of the English Civil War.[4]

Anglo-American prophets during the eighteenth century inherited a

[3] Nehemiah Curnock, ed., *The Journal of the Rev. John Wesley, A.M.*, standard ed., 8 vols. (London, 1910), 6:222, 7:459.

[4] For a sampling of the rich literature on millennialism in eighteenth-century Anglo-America, see Ruth Bloch, *Visionary Republic: Millennial Themes in American Thought, 1756–1800* (New York, 1985); Nathan Hatch, *The Sacred Cause of Liberty* (New Haven, 1977); James West Davidson, *The Logic of Millennial Thought in Eighteenth-Century America* (New Haven, 1977); W. H. Oliver, *Prophets and Millennialists: The Uses of Biblical Prophecy in England from the 1790s to the 1840s* (Auckland, 1978); J. F. C. Harrison, *The Second Coming: Popular Millenarianism, 1780–1850* (London, 1979); and James K. Hopkins, *A Woman to Deliver Her People: Joanna Southcott and English Millenarianism in an Era of Revolution* (Austin, Tex., 1982).

tradition of apocalyptic thinking that was highly sophisticated. Surging British nationalist pride underwrote much of the millennial writing of the early modern era, which tended toward triumphalist visions of a strong Protestant state reigning serene at home and unchallenged abroad. Prophetic history was Whig history translated into the peculiar idiom of the Books of Daniel and Revelation. The "imperial" school of British prophecy had its roots in a strong historicist tradition and a burgeoning interest in the new sciences of mathematics, astrology, and chronology, all of which seemed to provide abundant evidence of Britain's providential role as an "elect nation."[5]

By the early seventeenth century, the apocalyptic tradition had become, in the words of Katharine Firth, "too top-heavy, weighed down by too many theories attempting to cover too much material." The "hypersophisticated" minds who continued to calculate with ever greater precision the exact chronology of the four beasts, the seven vials, and the seven trumpets threatened to turn a vital, living tradition into a dead science.[6] The injection of a new spirit of millenarianism during the English Civil War reinvigorated this atrophied genre and gave new meaning to the apocalyptic scenarios that had previously been of largely academic interest to the reading public. Millennial calculation (the intellectual exercise of reading and interpreting signs) was transformed into millenarian zeal (the active anticipation of and preparation for the final battle between the forces of good and evil). New sects and new leaders emerged who promised to bring "fire from heaven." Thanks to the inspired work of Christopher Hill, Phyllis Mack, and Keith Thomas, we have vivid portraits of these millenarian sects and their utopian visions. In the heated atmosphere of revolutionary England, scholars became prophets, vague apprehension became urgent appeals for change, and thousands of men and women responded to the spiritual call to arms issued by "mechanick" preachers and others seemingly on the lunatic fringe of English sectarianism.[7]

The prophets of the Civil War era were a distinctive generation of spiri-

---

[5] Paul Christianson, *Reformers and Babylon: English Apocalyptic Visions from the Reformation to the Civil War* (Toronto, 1978); Katharine Firth, *The Apocalyptic Tradition in Reformation Britain, 1530–1645* (Oxford, 1979); Christopher Hill, *Antichrist in Seventeenth-Century England* (London, 1971).

[6] Firth, *Apocalyptic Tradition*, pp. 202–3.

[7] David Underdown, *Fire from Heaven: Life in an English Town in the Seventeenth Century* (New Haven, 1992); Christopher Hill, *The World Turned Upside Down: Radical Ideas During the English Revolution* (New York, 1972); Phyllis Mack, "Women as Prophets During the English Civil War," *Feminist Studies* 8 (Spring 1992), pp. 19–45, and *Visionary Women: Ecstatic Prophecy in Seventeenth-Century England* (Berkeley, Calif., 1992); Keith Thomas, "Women and the Civil War Sects," *Past and Present* 13 (1958), pp. 46–62.

tual virtuosos—filled with holy indignation over what they saw to be the unredeemable corruption of the British political and economic order, an order that consigned the mass of ordinary peasants and laborers to poverty, political invisibility, and social humiliation. Fired with a reforming zeal that translated the abstract symbols and ideals of Revelation into concrete realities, the Civil War prophets turned millennial speculation—vague, allegorical, sublime—into the art of politics—pointed, concrete, concerned not with the hereafter but with the here and now. This creative fusion of prophecy and politics had explosive consequences, as Ranters, Levellers, and Quakers stormed the bastions of British public life, haranguing magistrates and ministers and daring local constables to arrest them so they could continue to preach from the local jails.

During the "age of revolution," however, being a prophet meant something more and less than what the term had meant to earlier generations of Anglo-American visionaries. After the Restoration, and especially with the establishment of partial legal and practical toleration for dissenting religions in the calmer atmosphere of Hanoverian England, the political edge of radical prophecy was blunted. As Christopher Hill writes, "what had looked in the Ranter heyday as though it might become a counter-culture became a corner of the bourgeois culture whose occupants asked only to be left alone."[8] Prophets in the days of Richard Brothers and Joanna Southcott may have found themselves on the wrong end of the government's campaign to enforce public order on occasion, but they did not mount systematic attacks on the economic and political structures that sustained the church-state nexus. Spiritual reform, of a very personal and private kind, was their primary object—not wholesale political repudiation.

On the other hand, the prophets of the 1790s and early 1800s had a greater visibility than their Civil War counterparts despite their muted political rhetoric. The creation of a vigorous public sphere of coffeehouses, newspapers, corresponding societies, voluntary associations, and penny pamphlets in the eighteenth century transformed the sacred theater of the 1640s into something of a national culture in the 1790s. For every person who joined a millennial sect or heard an inspired prophet in the 1640s and 1650s, hundreds of men and women read a millennial tract, followed the careers of itinerant prophets in the daily newspapers, or attended large open-air assemblies where obscure men and women warned of the dangers to come in the 1780s or 1790s. The general diffusion of millennial expectation reached further

---

[8] Hill, *World Turned Upside Down*, p. 371.

into the reading public during the "age of revolution" even as its message became less distinct, more enmeshed in a wider web of cultural anxieties and political interests whose parameters were shaped not by scripture or the hermeneutic tradition of biblical exegesis but by the demands of the marketplace. Prophecy was no longer just the art of applying biblical passages to contemporary events (though it remained that as well); it was now the business of selling both terror and reassurance to eager buyers.

The commodification of prophecy in the late eighteenth century did not rob it of its ability to stir passions and harness discontent to larger social and political ends, but it did blur the theological and stylistic boundaries of a genre whose potency in the past had always derived from its ability to manipulate the extraordinary biblical literacy of Anglo-American Protestants. The consumer of prophetic literature in the 1790s did not need an extensive knowledge of the Bible and its tropes, or an intense interest in experiential religion. He or she merely needed to know how to read and to have the economic and cultural wherewithal to take advantage of the popular offerings of religious entrepreneurs, who staged prophetic dramas and hawked millennial literature at a cheap price.

The political stage of prophecy was broader as well in the decades between 1765 and 1815, because politics itself had been redefined to encompass more than parliamentary debate and ministerial maneuvering. The Civil War prophets wanted to destroy the monarchy and create a holy commonwealth in its place; the prophets of the "age of revolution" wanted to create a new world order defined not by the old polarities (republican versus monarchist, Catholic versus Protestant, metropole versus colony, Whig versus Tory, lord versus peasant) but by a single overarching polarity: that separating the saved from the damned. They did not align themselves with particular parties or interests, they did not (for the most part) contribute to the political debates of their day, they disdained the very idea of politics as outmoded, ungodly, and irrelevant. They denounced the sectarian jealousies and scholastic carping that had so distorted Christianity in the seventeenth century, and offered in their place a new vision of spiritual community anchored in the idea of "public man."[9] Nonetheless, and with a certain irony, revolutionary era prophets participated in the reformulation of politics even while they sought to distance themselves from the partisan wars of the era. Increasingly, salvation from horrors past and future was contingent upon one's willing-

[9] Richard Sennett, *The Fall of Public Man* (New York, 1977).

ness to participate in an expansive public sphere: reading, writing, conversation, and the free exchange of ideas and goods. After all, as Noah White found "by sad experience," to "hear things, and not to be able to tell them, was much worse than nothing."

This public sphere reached across national, confessional, and ethnic boundaries to encompass the entire British empire. Theoretically, no one was barred from joining the community of the saved. Old animosities did not disappear overnight, of course. English prophets looked down upon their Scottish, Irish, and North American compatriots with the contempt bred of centuries of colonial rule, while on the other side of the Atlantic, white Anglo-American prophets had to contend with the vibrant eschatological traditions of Indian and African prophets who created their own scenarios of divine retribution for the miseries they continued to endure in the new republic. Despite the persistence of national and ethnic prejudices, it is still possible to speak of prophets (white Protestant ones, at least) as inhabiting a transatlantic world defined more by a shared cultural sensibility than political unity.[10] We increasingly speak of the peaks and valleys of Anglo-American religion in the eighteenth-century as topographical features of a common landscape: revivals which began in the remote hill towns of Scotland in the 1730s were brought to the North American colonies by enterprising itinerant preachers in the 1740s, the next generation of whom then returned the favor in the early 1800s by introducing new ideas and measures such as the camp meeting to British audiences in the next great wave of evangelical fervor. Religion, in fact, inverted the relationship of metropole to

---

[10] In this book, "Anglo" means white, Protestant, and English-speaking. Heirs to a rich biblicist tradition and the beneficiaries of a common political and cultural identity as Britons (an identity ably described by Linda Colley in *Britons: Forging the Nation, 1707–1837* [New Haven, 1992]), white Protestant millenarians in England and America inhabited a common universe of historical memory and textual referents from which Indian and black prophets were largely excluded. This is not to deny that there were multiple lines of congruence and intersection connecting Anglo millenarians to their Indian and black counterparts, especially on the margins of white settlement in North America where a thriving multiracial society continued to exist well into the nineteenth century. Historians have just begun to explore this shared spiritual terrain; see, in particular, Sylvia R. Frey and Betty Wood, *Come Shouting to Zion: African American Protestantism in the American South and British Caribbean to 1830* (Chapel Hill, N.C., 1998); Mechal Sobel, *The World They Made Together: Black and White Values in Eighteenth-Century Virginia* (Princeton, N.J., 1987); and Jane Merritt, "Dreaming of the Savior's Blood: Moravians and the Indian Great Awakening in Pennsylvania," *William and Mary Quarterly* 3d ser. 54 (Oct. 1997), pp. 723–46. There is a book yet to be written on the spiritual and cultural affinities linking white, Native, and African American prophets in the formative years of the American republic.

colony in the first empire, as revivals created a "pincer movement" in which spiritual renewal spread from the periphery toward the center.[11]

The links connecting this far-flung evangelical empire were both personal and material. Preachers such as John and Charles Wesley, George Whitefield, Nancy Towle, Lorenzo Dow, and Dorothy Ripley criss-crossed the Atlantic Ocean in search of new souls to harvest, and along the way helped forge networks of evangelical preachers who were the foot soldiers of the transatlantic revival. Whitefield was the premier example of this kind of cross-cultural itinerancy, a man equally at home in the Georgia backcountry and in the urban haunts of London or Edinburgh. A true "citizen of the world," Whitefield pioneered the model of the field preacher whose field stretched from the Celtic fringe to the metropolitan centers of the first empire. Perhaps of even greater importance than these ocean-hopping preachers in creating a transatlantic religious culture was the circulation of printed material throughout the empire: sermons, accounts of revivals in far-flung places, memoirs and journals penned both by preachers and lay men and women, polemical essays, political satires, epistolary dialogues, and how-to manuals for conducting revivals and camp meetings. The journals of John Wesley, for instance, were widely distributed on both sides of the Atlantic, making the man himself and his particular brand of experiential religion intimately known to a generation of Anglo-American believers, along with a large and eclectic literature detailing the spiritual biographies of many lesser-known preachers. Much of this literature was personal rather than instructional, aiming to acquaint people separated by thousands of miles with the spiritual travails of fellow Christians. These biographies functioned as extensions of the preachers themselves who were the living embodiment of the evangelical ethos.

While it is fashionable now to speak of religion in the long eighteenth century as rooted in a larger Atlantic world rather than in particular national contexts, the transatlantic connections evident in the revolutionary era were

---

[11] Harry S. Stout, *The Divine Dramatist: George Whitefield and the Rise of Modern Evangelicalism* (Grand Rapids, Mich., 1991), p. 134. On the transatlantic connections linking British and American evangelical culture in the eighteenth and early nineteenth centuries, see Frank Lambert, *Inventing the "Great Awakening"* (Princeton, N.J., 1999); Marilyn Westerkamp, *Triumph of the Laity: Scots-Irish Piety and the Great Awakening, 1625–1760* (New York, 1988); Leigh Eric Schmidt, *Holy Fairs: Scottish Communions and American Revivals in the Early Modern Period* (Princeton, N.J., 1989); Michael Crawford, *Seasons of Grace: Colonial New England's Revival Tradition in Its British Context* (New York, 1991); Richard Carwardine, *Transatlantic Revivalism: Popular Evangelicalism in Britain and America, 1790–1865* (Westport, Conn., 1978).

not the same as those forged earlier in the eighteenth century. In the 1730s and 1740s, men like Whitefield and the Wesleys personally brought the evangelical revival home to thousands of Anglo-American Protestants by the sheer force of their wills and by their astute mastery of the nascent print culture of the empire. Direct, personal contact between these lions of British Methodism and ordinary men and women created something of a cult of personality which made them larger-than-life figures. In the case of Whitefield, the veneration generated by his numerous trips to the American colonies extended past his own lifetime to embrace his corpse as well, as devotees made pilgrimages to his grave and took bits of his clothing as holy relics. When a Freewill Baptist preacher visited the tomb in 1834, he found that souvenir seekers had left little, just a few bones and some dirt.[12] In the case of Wesley, his towering presence in the fledgling Methodist movement made him an object of adoration as well as veneration. "Big Daddy" Wesley, as his American and British preachers called him, evoked the kind of erotic desire customarily reserved for icons of popular culture.[13] Together, these two men symbolized the very direct and personal kind of connection that bound far-flung saints of a sprawling empire into a cohesive spiritual fraternity. True, revivals were spread as much by printed accounts, published in the new evangelical periodicals that sprang up in Edinburgh, Glasgow, and Boston to further the cause of reformation as by the individual efforts of Whitefield and Wesley, but these narratives carried the unmistakable stamp of personality as well. In them, preachers inspired by the example of the British evangelists used colloquial language and homey metaphors to create a bond with their listeners beyond that of author and reader, to capture for a wider audience the ephemeral moment of spiritual connection created in field revivals.

The kind of congregations called into being by the heroic efforts of these itinerants did not yet resemble the anonymous public sphere of political theorists, but remained within the traditional model of dissenting societies—local, intimate, bound by ties of blood as well as affinity. The mid-eighteenth-century revivals were a "transatlantic" event, in other words, in the sense of being carried on by men who literally were agents of empire—men who took it upon themselves to connect a dispersed population into a

---

[12] Quoted in Jon Butler, *Awash in a Sea of Faith: Christianizing the American People* (Cambridge, Mass., 1990), p. 188; see Butler's discussion of the cult of personality among eighteenth-century revivalists on pp. 182–91.

[13] Henry Abelove, *The Evangelist of Desire: John Wesley and the Methodists* (Stanford, Calif., 1990).

living, organic whole by the power of personal example. The model of community remained the local congregation, multiplied a thousandfold in a thousand locales.

The transatlantic community of saints envisioned in the late eighteenth century by a new generation of itinerants was altogether different. In the days of resurgent imperial structures, domestic convulsion and international war, prophets spoke not as members of particular communities—as Nonconformists or Methodists, Glaswegians or Bostonians, Englishmen or Irishmen—but as representatives of a universal religious sensibility that transcended national and confessional (if not racial) boundaries. Their tools of persuasion were no longer their own charismatic personalities, though many were compelling speakers with fascinating stories to tell, but the tools of mass culture: cheap pamphlets and broadsides, newsweeklies and periodicals, urban assemblies, the "penny-post." They spoke not only as one saint to another, in the idiom of friendship, but as salesman to consumer, in the idiom of the market. They instructed their followers, not in the ways of communal worship, but in the ways of consumer culture—to read their literary offerings at home, in the privacy of their own chambers, and to imagine themselves as part of an invisible, anonymous collective of other readers. They proposed "concerts of prayer" (moments when Christians everywhere, all strangers to one another, would stop at the same time and offer the same prayer) rather than organizing new churches. Their chapels were virtual rather than actual representations of community: subscription lists and correspondence circles, not brick-and-mortar structures. For all the affection lavished on itinerant preachers who braved bad weather and worse roads to visit isolated settlements in the American and English countryside, the ties forged between this new breed of preachers and their followers were less intimate, more fleeting than those that bound Whitefield and Wesley to an earlier generation of seekers. Itinerants, especially those in the Methodist discipline, were actively discouraged from creating close, personal bonds with the societies they organized; their biographies were circulated in place of their actual persons in part to ensure some measure of distance between the man and the message.[14]

This description of the transatlantic community of saints in the revolutionary era clearly resembles one of the most influential formulations of the

[14] Dee E. Andrews, *The Methodists and Revolutionary America, 1760–1800: The Shaping of an Evangelical Culture* (Princeton, N.J., 2000), p. 215.

public sphere available in contemporary scholarship, that penned by the German political theorist Jürgen Habermas more than thirty years ago. Habermas's account of the democratic or bourgeois public sphere created in the reading rooms, coffeehouses, literary societies, and salons of eighteenth-century Europe has great heuristic value for early American historians interested in the rise of alternative notions of the "public" in the interstices of empire over the course of the eighteenth century. At the center of Habermasian theory is the nexus between form and expression, between the institutions of liberal democracy and the practice of critical public discourse. A generation of political historians has described how new publics came into being and were exposed to new modes of scrutiny by ordinary citizens empowered by an ethos of publicity and transparency.[15]

Together, these two principles transformed not only the practice of politics but the very idea of politics itself. Politics had until the late eighteenth century been conceived of as a gentleman's game, a contest of skill among contestants who shared a similar pedigree and a classical education. The spoils of politics were the private perks of power—the fees, sinecures, and patronage that were regarded as a form of private property belonging not to the office but to the officeholder. The public (that is, the vast majority of Britons who had no public voice and no civic identity beyond that of subject) viewed the workings of government as a spectator sport in which they were not invited to participate, except in sporadic "rebellions of the belly" in E. P. Thompson's famous mocking phrase. Knowledge was a privileged commodity, and its dissemination beyond the privileged ranks carefully guarded through censorship of the press and the expert exercise of social condescension. The "patrician hegemony" of England's old order was maintained not by force or crude economic pressure, but by the effective sequestering of the poor and disenfranchised behind the barriers of ignorance and civic inability.[16]

---

[15] Jürgen Habermas, *The Structural Transformation of the Public Sphere: An Inquiry into a Category of Bourgeois Society*, trans. Thomas Burger (Cambridge, Mass., 1989; orig. pub. 1962). For a useful introduction to contemporary uses of Habermasian theory, see the essays in *Habermas and the Public Sphere*, ed. Craig Calhoun (Cambridge, Mass., 1992). Two superb though very different studies of the discursive institutions which shaped the public sphere in early Anglo-America are David Shields, *Civil Tongues and Polite Letters in British America* (Chapel Hill, N.C., 1997), and James Van Horn Melton, *The Rise of the Public in Enlightenment Europe* (New York, 2001).

[16] The phrase "patrician hegemony" comes from J. C. D. Clark, *English Society, 1660–1832*, 2d ed. (Cambridge, 2000).

These barriers were widely breached only in the late eighteenth century by the proliferation of new associations and new forms of print that made censorship impractical if not illegal, and by successive challenges to the authority of Church and Crown from dissenters and political radicals which pierced the facade if not the foundations of patrician hegemony. Simply put, politics was no longer just a gentleman's game, even if the landed and commercial elite continued to dominate the sport, but a popular form of entertainment open to all who could afford the low price of admission—as little as the cost of a daily newspaper. To defenders of the old order, the advent of mass media and a new style of communication meant the vulgarization of politics, not its progressive liberalization. "Excluded from Westminster, the lifeblood of popular politics coursed through the propaganda media of newspapers, handbills, ballads, posters and cartoons, through tavern and coffee-house debate, and spilt into the streets."[17] The admission of the lowly and the servile into public life entailed a broad-gauge reevaluation of the institutions and mores of the public sphere as the category of the "genteel" was successively widened until the term was rendered meaningless by the incorporation of mechanics, artisans, shopkeepers, and laborers into its ranks. Eventually, the practice of politics was sundered definitively from the concept of gentility, but until that happened (sometime in the nineteenth century) there was a bitter and protracted struggle over the norms of public association and discourse on both sides of the Atlantic.[18] As Gordon Wood has described it in the American context, during the late eighteenth century "gentility was republicanized." Everyone was, or could become, a gentleman; "To be a gentleman was to think and act like a gentleman, nothing more." By the 1830s, gentility was irrelevant to the exercise of power. No one in the materialistic, driven world of Jacksonian America was or wanted to be a gentleman.[19]

What did this reinvention of politics have to do with the art of prophecy? Prophecy was never a gentleman's game. Its association with the poor and

---

[17] Roy Porter, *English Society in the Eighteenth Century*, rev. ed. (London, 1991), p. 103. See also Kathleen Wilson, *The Sense of the People: Politics, Culture, and Imperialism in England, 1715–1785* (New York, 1995) on the popularization of politics in the eighteenth century.

[18] For two treatments of these debates on the British side, see Don Herzog, *Poisoning the Minds of the Lower Orders* (Princeton, N.J., 1998); H. T. Dickinson, *The Politics of the People in Eighteenth-Century Britain* (New York, 1994). On the American side, see Richard Gildrie, *The Profane, the Civil, and the Godly: The Reformation of Manners in Orthodox New England, 1679–1749* (University Park, Pa., 1994).

[19] Gordon Wood, *The Radicalism of the American Revolution* (New York, 1991), p. 195.

dispossessed had always been one of its strongest theological virtues, as prophets across the social spectrum declared their allegiance to the christological model of holy poverty and ignomy. To be a prophet was, ipso facto, to be ignored and despised by the high and mighty. Living in a state of righteous alienation, prophets from apostolic days to the English Civil War era had felt emboldened to attack the very foundations of church and state. The ultimate political outsiders, prophets enjoyed considerable freedom as holy men and women to criticize without fear of contradiction or rebuttal. But a curious reversal of status took place over the long eighteenth century. As politics became less and less the preserve of gentlemen and scholars, prophecy (within the Anglo-American ecclesiological mainstream) became more genteel. Only on the fringes did prophecy retain its millenarian, antipolitical edge. It was easy for churchmen and intellectuals to treat figures like Joanna Southcott with undisguised contempt, for she represented the kind of alienation no longer fashionable within millennial circles. The splintering of the prophetic tradition into two streams, one respected and respectable, the other defiantly part of the "radical underworld" of sectarians and pornographers that Iain McCalman has identified in late eighteenth-century London, left millenarians in a cultural and political wilderness.[20] Full of sound and fury, they signified little as the reassertion of imperial and domestic authority quieted the political storms of the 1790s. With the death of Joanna Southcott in 1814, an era of uneasy parallelism and cultural synergy in the worlds of high politics and popular religion came to an end.

There is something counterintuitive, of course, about examining prophecy through a Habermasian lens. Habermas himself saw the public sphere as antithetical to religious belief, as constituted in large part by the *rejection* of a religious worldview in favor of a secular language of human rights and opportunities. The institutions and forms of the bourgeois public sphere present a sharp counterimage to the biblical world of kings, prophets, and believers. Emptied of soteriological content and purged of the traditional authority of monarchs who ruled by divine right, the public sphere took shape under an aggressively secular set of imperatives. Religious man subordinates his own opinions to a higher power whose authority he takes on faith; public man looks to himself and his peers for truth and knowledge.

---

[20] Iain McCalman, *Radical Underworld: Prophets, Revolutionaries and Pornographers in London, 1795–1840* (Oxford, 1993).

This book works *within* that sense of counterintuition rather than against it, in the hopes of illuminating some of the more recessed corners of the bourgeois public sphere—those barely visible spaces (makeshift chapels, street corners, peddlers' bags, print shops, market stalls, the back rooms of inns and taverns, prisons, insane asylums) where faith and reason met, not to vanquish one another but to jostle energetically for the soul of the believer. The contest may have been unequal, but the outcome hardly preordained. Faith more than held its own in the intellectual battles of the revolutionary era, proving a resilient and resourceful foe to those who would exterminate religious passion in the name of the public good. A series of seeming oxymorons appear in these pages: visionary republic, republican prophet, mystical knowledge, illiterate eloquence, enlightened inspiration—all coined (by myself and others) to capture the elusive admixture of primitive occult desires and modern intellectual conceits that is a more accurate description of the phenomenon we simplistically call "the Enlightenment."

Millenarian movements continued to flourish in Victorian England and antebellum America, and prophets appeared with striking regularity to sound the apocalyptic alarm, but their sphere of influence was now that of popular culture rather than politics. The prophets of the nineteenth century are considerably better known, at least on the American side of the Atlantic, than those of the revolutionary era. William Miller and Joseph Smith, in particular, have earned a place in the popular retellings of Jacksonian America as exemplars of the spiritual eclecticism and robust populism of antebellum culture. The millenarian movements they organized (Seventh-Day Adventists and Church of Jesus Christ of Latter-Day Saints) survived the death of their founders and continue to thrive into the present day. Mormons, Gordon Wood tells us, were the quintessentially "American" sect in an era of unbridled sectarian innovation and expansion; their theology mirrored the surge in cultural nationalism then gripping the republic, while their organizational structures offered Americans fearful of the market a comforting vision of rural pastoralism in which fathers ruled over peaceful and productive communities.[21] In Britain, would-be successors to Joanna Southcott, the last of the revolutionary-era prophets, appeared throughout the 1820s and 1830s and, briefly if spectacularly, gathered thousands of devotees who were pre-

---

[21] Gordon Wood, "Evangelical America and Early Mormonism," *New York History* 61 (October 1980), pp. 359–86; and "Religion and the American Revolution," in *New Directions in American Religious History*, ed. Harry S. Stout and D. G. Hart (New York, 1997), pp. 173–205.

pared to follow them into spiritual exile.[22] Scattered groups of Southcottians exist in England and America today; one such offshoot makes its home not far from where I write, in Benton Harbor, Michigan.[23] But their stories, like those of Miller and Smith, belong more to the nineteenth than to the eighteenth century: to an age of rampant consumerism rather than genteel politics, of spiritual mediums and homeopathic remedies rather than itinerant preachers and "concerts of prayer." Little exists to connect them to a transatlantic network of spiritual providers, let alone a shared culture of sensibility, even if they did sometimes reach across national borders for recruits and money.

Revolutionary-era prophecy deserves its own chapter in our histories of Anglo-American religion, distinct from both the radicalism of the English Civil War sects and the eclecticism of Victorian millenarians. Late eighteenth-century prophets lived in an era acutely aware of itself as a definitive moment in the evolution of a modern political culture, and this awareness shaped their every move. A running quarrel with modernity—with what it meant to be a knowing, active subject in control of one's destiny—gave the public culture of prophecy a jagged rhetorical edge that cut in several directions: toward a more democratic understanding of human achievement and a more authoritarian understanding of power, away from coercion and the secrecy of hegemonic institutions and yet away from toleration and inclusion, the putative values of dissenting societies, too. At once quintessentially modern and thoroughly steeped in Old Testament values, prophets offer an ideal vantage point from which to survey the political, cultural, and intellectual transformations of the "age of revolution."

In order to best grasp millenarian culture in all its complexity, I have organized the chapters that follow as a series of steadily narrowing concentric circles, each of which probes more deeply into a particular facet of millenarian culture. From the debates over religious enthusiasm waged by

[22] Harrison, *The Second Coming*; Oliver, *Prophets and Millennialists*; G. R. Balleine, *Past Finding Out: The Tragic Story of Joanna Southcott and Her Successors* (New York, 1956).

[23] The House of David, which relocated to Benton Harbor from Ohio in 1903, enjoyed a brief moment of public renown in the 1910s and 1920s as the sponsor of a popular traveling baseball team and other cultural attractions. Today the society consists of a handful of members who work and plan for the Second Coming, which they expect to occur soon, if not in their lifetime. The founder of the House of David, Benjamin Purnell, is considered the seventh in a line of prophetic messengers that began with Southcott, and runs through George Turner, William Shaw, John Wroe, and James Jazreel. My thanks to Ron Taylor of the House of David for his generosity in sharing details of the community's history with me.

churchmen and the literati to the epistemological and expressive challenges facing ordinary men and women who believed they spoke for God, the book tracks the cultural process by which prophetic claims were formulated, challenged, tested, advanced, and abandoned. I am more interested in what might be called the atmospheric than the cognitive side of millenarian culture, the swirl of emotions, ideas, images, and arguments that encircled prophets and their critics. The content of revolutionary-era prophecy—the who, what, when, and where of millennial speculation—has been ably explored by historians and literary scholars alike. My aim here is to listen to the stories prophets told, and the stories others told about them. However much they wished to represent themselves as privileged outsiders, prophets could not escape the culture that surrounded them. Nor did they entirely wish to. For all their illusions (delusions?) of grandeur, prophets inhabited a remarkably ordinary world devoid of miracles and other supernatural interventions. Their skills and talents were those of Anglo-America's commoners writ large. This was their virtue, and their burden.

Their very ordinariness has made it difficult for scholars to take this generation of prophets seriously. More exotic examples of religious fanaticism can certainly be found (think of those medieval saints who drank pus and wept tears of blood).[24] Compared to the spectacular feats of self-mortification or miracle-working performed by past visionaries, the exploits of a Noah White seem tame indeed. But however mundane their lives, prophets in the revolutionary era raised exactly the same problems of transparency and authenticity that plagued medieval and early modern seers. The problem of distinguishing true from false prophets was a perennial one: millenarians knew that one of the signs of the coming apocalypse as foretold in Revelation was a proliferation of false prophets, and they were acutely aware of the possibilities for fraud and deception inherent in such a subjective enterprise as eschatological prediction.

Our challenge as historians is somewhat different. On the one hand, we risk consigning an entire class of people, for the most part deprived and despised within their own culture, to historical oblivion if we choose to interpret millenarian movements as chiliastic or delusional responses to real social and historical problems that demand other, less naive solutions. On the other hand, madness is a historical as well as a clinical category of analysis, and early modern Anglo-Americans certainly recognized religious fanati-

---

[24] See, for example, Caroline Walker Bynum, *Holy Feast and Holy Fast: The Religious Significance of Food to Medieval Women* (Berkeley, Calif., 1987).

cism as a distinct type of mental debility.[25] Some of the men and women whose stories are told below probably were clinically insane by any modern definition of the term. A few were eloquent in their madness: when the rural Maine prophet, William Scales, told the General Court in 1790 that "Insanity, or a fracture of the intellect, makes no odds, as to reason in a petition, or, the reasonableness of a petition of the people," he was making the point that a "fracture" of the mind was sometimes necessary to see beyond the corruptions of the man-made world.[26] Others, more problematically, were deadly sane. Mary Bateman, the "Yorkshire witch," was executed in 1808 after a lengthy career swindling the poor and credulous, and Jacob Weber met the same fate in South Carolina a half century earlier for murdering two men who challenged his claims of immortality—two of the many false prophets whose venality was exposed in the revolutionary era.[27]

My own position on the legitimacy of the prophets examined here is agnostic. I am curious about the cultural and political implications of the public performances of Anglo-American visionaries, while remaining sympathetic if undecided about their private beliefs. In some cases I feel reasonably certain that no deception was intended or fraud committed; in other cases, I suspect that the motives of these peddlers of paranoia were as much mercenary as spiritual. In each case my opinions will probably be clear to the reader. The full pathologization of religious enthusiasm can be credited to a later generation of reformers, but the century preceding the revolutionary era saw the beginnings of a sustained intellectual attempt to separate true spiritual enlightenment from spurious fanaticism. When we label some prophets visionaries and others impostors, we are participating in a process of cultural identification and validation begun by the very people we are studying.[28] To a large extent, their diagnostic language is our own.

Prophets like Brothers and Southcott may seem like throwbacks to an

---

[25] For one example of an historical treatment of religious enthusiasm that applies contemporary definitions of mental illness to the past, see Alfred Cohen, "Prophecy and Madness: Women Visionaries during the Puritan Revolution," *Journal of Psychohistory* 11 (1984), pp. 411–30.

[26] The case of William Scales is discussed in Alan Taylor, *Liberty Men and Great Proprietors: The Revolutionary Settlement on the Maine Frontier* (Chapel Hill, N.C., 1990), p. 150.

[27] *The Extraordinary Life and Character of Mary Bateman, The Yorkshire Witch* (Leeds, 1809); the case of William Weber can be found in *The Carolina Backcountry on the Eve of the Revolution: The Journal and Other Writings of Charles Woodmason, Anglican Itinerant*, ed. Richard Hooker (Chapel Hill, N.C., 1953), pp. 79–80.

[28] For a recent survey of the evolution of diagnostic language to differentiate types of religious enthusiasm, see Ann Taves, *Fits, Trances, and Visions: Experiencing Religion and Explaining Experience from Wesley to James* (Princeton, N.J., 1999).

earlier age when people still believed in witches and demons, in miracles and cunning folk, in the unexpected and dramatic intrusion of the supernatural world into daily life. We shouldn't be so quick to judge. Every generation has its "prophets of evil" to remind us of our vulnerability in the face of real horror, even if we dispute the provenance or meaning or the very existence of the evil they tell.

Chapter 1

The Making of a Prophet

In June 1781, the Methodist itinerant Freeborn Garrettson wandered into a small church in Virginia. "I saw a man in the pulpit dressed in black," he recorded in his diary. As he listened to the man speak, Garrettson became concerned. "I soon perceived he was a man bereft of his reason. I went into the pulpit and desired him to give over." Declaring that he was "a prophet sent by God to teach the people," the man rebuffed Garrettson's plea to "give over" and that night, after returning home, told his family that "at such an hour, he would go into a trance; and that they must not bury him till after such a time, should he not come to." To the astonishment of all, the man then fell into a deep trance from which he could not be awakened. The next day Garrettson visited the man and found his followers "weeping around the bed. He lay like a corpse, for I could not perceive that he breathed."[1]

Garrettson gives us no more details than this, other than to speculate about the devil's role in the whole sorry affair. "What was the cause of this?" he wondered. "Satan prompted him to think more highly of himself than he ought." Historians interested in other explanations might ask other questions. Did the man dressed in black recover from his "trance," as so many eighteenth-century visionaries did, to tell of whirlwind journeys to the spirit world and conversations with angelic guides? Was his trance similar to a dream, a tried and true means by which God traditionally communicated with his believers on earth, or a more unsettling visionary experience in which a radical dissociation of body and soul took place? What exactly did he prophesy, in the pulpit or while in trance? Did he foretell the imminent end of the world in apocalyptic terms, or speak more vaguely of sins committed and terrors to come? Did he speak to a small circle of intimates, or to a larger audience of Christians and countrymen? Did he link the biblical narrative of revelation to the revolutionary war then tearing apart the

---

[1] Robert Drew Simpson, ed., *American Methodist Pioneer: The Life and Journals of the Rev. Freeborn Garrettson, 1752–1837* (Rutland, Vt., 1984), p. 117.

American South? And what of the men and women who sat in the meeting-house that spring morning and listened to this unnamed prophet? Did they accept him as an authentic prophet—a man chosen by God, for reasons known only to God, to deliver a spiritual call to arms? If so, what convinced them that he was a true and not a "false" prophet, since false prophets abounded in these years of crisis: his words? his style of delivery? or his ability to suspend all bodily functions and appear "like a corpse"? Were they alarmed, amused, bemused, or indifferent?

In this brief encounter between the Methodist preacher and the man in black we can see many of the motifs and patterns that would shape Anglo-American prophecy during the long eighteenth century. Throughout the period, but with accelerating urgency in the decades after 1780, men and women of all ages and conditions called themselves prophets of God. A natural by-product of the religious enthusiasm which swept the Atlantic world in the late eighteenth and early nineteenth centuries, prophets were born in an era of mass revivals, grew up in camp meetings and love feasts, and came of age in the sectarian offshoots of the Wesleyan Methodists and Calvinist Baptists in the early 1800s. Some of these prophets made a brief appearance on the public stage of Anglo-American religious culture, their fame as fleeting as their sanity, while others staked more enduring legacies as oracles with impressive if unorthodox intellectual credentials and devoted followers numbering in the thousands. Their claims were always contested, either by rival prophets or by the clerical establishment, and much of what we know about them comes from their competitors. Men like Freeborn Garrettson—preachers with a strong visionary bent and considerable powers of persuasion—recognized in these fly-by-night prophets a serious threat to their own authority, as prophets appropriated many of the dramatic methods and marketing techniques of the flourishing evangelical subculture. A bitter Methodist itinerant complained that these "insane enthusiasts" could "manufacture more fanatics, and in a shorter time, than twenty good, sound, Gospel ministers can turn five sinners from the error of their ways."[2]

A contest between orthodox and heterodox understandings of spiritual power lay at the heart of these internecine battles, a battle that the evangelical establishment would win by the early nineteenth century—only to lose the larger war as visionary experience spiraled beyond the control of organized religion in the Victorian era. Rather than falling silent, as many en-

---

[2] Peter Cartwright, *Autobiography of Peter Cartwright, the Backwoods Preacher*, ed. W. P. Strickland (New York, 1856), p. 274.

lightened rationalists had hoped, God was speaking in a profusion of tongues. "God had more prophets, tongues, and oracles than ever before," observes Leigh Schmidt; "thus, the modern predicament actually became as much one of God's loquacity as God's hush."[3] More and more people were seeing and speaking to God directly, without the mediating influence of preachers or churches, and all that men like Garrettson could do about it was scoff.

Was the man in black a true or a false prophet? In the end, this was the only question that really mattered to Anglo-American believers. The tension between authenticity and imposture which structured accounts of religious enthusiasm was part of a larger dilemma which gripped the reading public on both sides of the Atlantic in the aftermath of the American and French Revolutions. As the frantic terror of war receded and the magnitude of the political and social disorder wrought by the "age of revolution" began to sink in, the need to separate the true from the false in all spheres of public life took on a desperate quality. The early Enlightenment fascination with "imposture"—a scholarly investigation into the historical roots of state and church corruption—became in the 1790s and early 1800s a rallying cry for a variety of disaffected Anglo-Americans, from coffeehouse radicals in London to farmer-preachers in the American backcountry.[4] Impostors were everywhere, in the halls of government and the pulpits of the established church, and their arrogance and disdain for the common people threatened to vacate whatever political and civil liberties had been gained by the bloodshed of patriots. Revolutionary-era prophets both fanned the flames of popular fears of imposture in their attacks on the church and its hireling ministers, and were burned by the heat of populist anger when they were exposed, as some inevitably were, as cheats and liars.

An overwrought and overdetermined discourse of authenticity and imposture, in other words, surrounded the public performances of Anglo-American prophets in the years from 1765 to 1815. A sophisticated conceptual

[3] Leigh Eric Schmidt, *Hearing Things: Religion, Illusion, and the American Enlightenment* (Princeton, N.J., 2000), p. 11.

[4] Peter Harrison argues that "the imposture theory was the most popular of all seventeenth and eighteenth century accounts of religion"; *"Religion" and the Religions in the English Enlightenment* (New York, 1990), p. 16, and Nathan Hatch call the early republic the "golden age" of impostors and counterfeiters in the United States; *The Democratization of American Christianity* (New Haven, 1989), p. 36. See also Frank Manuel, *The Eighteenth Century Confronts the Gods* (Cambridge, Mass., 1959); and Michael Heyd, *"Be Sober and Reasonable": The Critique of Enthusiasm in the Seventeenth and Early Eighteenth Centuries* (Leiden, 1995).

vocabulary was developed by Christian commentators keen to distinguish true from false prophets in an era that featured plenty of both. Observers looked for signs of legitimacy in the external appearance of prophets, in the language they used in both their oral and written performances, and in the response they inspired in their audiences. The focus in this chapter is largely on what critics had to say about the nature and perils of religious enthusiasm, though prophets themselves contributed to this discourse of authenticity as they faced a bewildering array of spiritual competitors whose legitimacy they attacked with all the righteousness of the persecuted. Certain criticisms they rejected outright, some they grudgingly conceded, and some they unwittingly reinforced by their own words and deeds. Charges and countercharges flew across the pages of newspapers, letters, journals, and the penny press in Britain and the United States, allowing us to reconstruct with some confidence the process by which prophets were made in revolutionary Anglo-America.

The Camisard Invasion: Setting the Stage

Anyone living in the 1780s or 1790s would have known exactly where to look for the nearest historical example of a "false prophet." Despite the still fresh memory of the political chaos wrought by the Civil War sects, eighteenth-century Britons tended to trace the peculiar features of religious enthusiasm in their own day back to the infamous French Prophets who invaded London in 1706. The arrival of the three Camisards (Elie Marion, Durand Fage, and Jean Cavalier) in the British capital sparked a heated debate about the evidence of true inspiration and imposture, the ripples of which continued to spread in ever wider circles of learned and popular discussion throughout the religious awakenings of the ensuing century. The antihero of the transatlantic revival, against whom real saints measured their own experience, was the Camisard prophet.

The victims of brutal repression in Catholic France, the Camisards brought a worldview shaped by violence into exile with them. Beaten, maimed, enslaved, even killed for their faith, they saw the world through a manichean perspective of absolute good and pure evil. But such moral absolutism was harder to sustain in the freewheeling atmosphere of Restoration London, where a proliferation of chapels and enterprising preachers offered urban residents a plethora of religious options. Upon their arrival in England, the French Prophets completed a transformation from flesh-and-blood rebels to cultural icons that would have lasting consequences for the future history of Anglo-American millenarianism. In their native land they had battled the king's armies in a devastating war of attrition that lasted for more than a decade and left thousands dead or imprisoned. In England, they faced a different enemy: the journalists and ecclesiastics who delighted in unmasking the pretensions of religious enthusiasts with the weapons at their disposal—satire and ridicule.

At first, the Camisards stumbled. Finding it difficult to persuade their fellow Huguenots to open their homes or churches to them, and lacking the cultural savvy necessary to combat their numerous critics on their own terrain, the three prophets floundered for several years in obscurity. The low point came with their arrest on charges of blasphemy and sedition. As described in the warrant for Jean Marion, the Camisard was a "pseudo-prophet, an abominable, detestable and diabolic blasphemer, a disturber of the peace, heretic and imposter, publisher of false, scandalous and seditious trials." After a trial that dragged on for months, the three prophets were convicted and sentenced to stand on a scaffold in Charing Cross and at the Royal Exchange.[5] Not death, but the kind of public shaming meted out to rogues and petty criminals was their punishment.

By the close of 1708, however, the Camisards and their English followers (now numbering more than four hundred prophets) had outlasted ignomy and government repression to constitute a significant presence on the British millenarian scene. In recognition of the new terrain on which the battle for authenticity would be waged, they adopted a more overtly theatrical style of performance and joined the war of words in the London press with their own narratives of sacred history. They staged miracles as well as delivering prophetic pronouncements in front of large audiences—John Lacy, the foremost English prophet, began to speak in tongues and to practice faith healing; 20,000 gathered around a gravesite to watch Lacy attempt to raise a believer, Dr. Thomas Emes, from the dead. Never diligent readers of the Bible, living as they did in the rapture of the moment, the prophets began to educate themselves and their followers in the prophetic scriptures and to enact different scenes from the Bible in their meetings, including some that were considered scandalous or indecent. (The title of one opposition pamphlet advertised itself as a *True and Comical Account* of a *Pretended French Prophetess, who on Sunday the 16th of November, did in a very Immodest and*

---

[5] Hillel Schwartz, *Knaves, Fools, Madmen, and that Subtile Effluvium: A Study of the Opposition to the French Prophets in England, 1706–1710* (Gainesville, Fla., 1978), p. 18.

Indecent manner (being inspired with a pretended Spirit) undress herself stark Naked at the Popish Chapel in Lincoln's-Inn Fields, and forced her self through the Crowd up to the Altar, in order to preach her new doctrine.) Their performances offered a kind of "mimetic violence" in which the terrible judgments promised in Revelation were staged in makeshift chapels. Such extreme behaviors were not new to the Camisards (in France there were reports of newborns who spoke fluent Latin, men walking barefoot over burning coals, and women who wept tears of blood), but in England, as Hillel Schwartz notes, the miracles the Prophets performed "were not broadly social and public, but private, personal, and explicitly physical."[6] Stripped of political content, the antics of the Camisards took on the appearance of an elaborate charade.

A new kind of "sacred theater," in other words, replaced the old culture of public prophecy for which the Camisards had been noted in France.[7] Highly physical, rooted in a conception of the symbiotic relationship of body to soul, the "labors" of the French Prophets (or *convulsionaires*, as they were known in France) represented a disturbing trend in religious experience toward the vulgar. The Camisards took the physicality of earlier sectarians like the Quakers to new extremes, including in their repertoire of sacred practices speaking in trance, uncontrollable shaking, and strange facial and verbal contortions. Samuel Keimer, a long-time supporter of sectarian causes, recalled the "very violent and strange Agitations or Shakings of Body, loud and terrifying Hiccups, and Throbs, with many odd and very surprizing Postures" that greeted him upon his first visit to a London chapel to see these odd preachers. Keimer's fascination soon turned to disgust, as he witnessed such bizarre enactments of inspired behavior as that of the prophetess Dorothy Harling, who urinated upon sinners after whipping them in a parody of spiritual cleansing.[8] Keimer was no neutral observer—he came to deeply regret his early flirtation with the French Prophets—but his descriptions of their devotional exercises are supported (in less sensational terms) by the memoirs of the Prophets themselves. John Lacy recalled how the Spirit took over the operation of his body, part by part: "[first] my Head

---

[6] Schwartz, *Knaves, Fools, Madmen,* pp. 19–20.

[7] Clarke Garrett, *Spirit Possession and Popular Religion: From the Camisards to the Shakers* (Baltimore, 1987). See also Hillel Schwartz, *The French Prophets: The History of a Millenarian Group in Eighteenth-Century England* (Berkeley, Calif., 1980).

[8] Samuel Keimer, *Brand Pluck'd from the Burning: Exemplify'd in the Unparallel'd Case of Samuel Keimer* (London, 1718), pp. 1, 6, 39.

came to be Agitated or Shaked Violently, and forcibly, and with a very quick Motion horizontally, or from Side to Side; then my Stomach had Twitches, not much unlike an Hickup; afterwards my Hands and Arms were violently shaken; at length a Struggle or Labouring in the Wind-pipe and sometimes a Sort of Catching or Twitches all over my Body."[9]

To those who witnessed their performances, the twitches, convulsions, and verbal tics for which the French Prophets became best known resembled nothing so much as the physical symptoms of lunacy. Critics from the right and the left attributed the French Prophets' agitations to natural rather than diabolical causes, though they disagreed about the degree of culpability to assign. The deist pamphleteer John Trenchard suggested that "the poisonous and melancholy Vapours streaming from an enthusiast, cause Distraction and Raving as well as the Bite of a Mad Dog."[10] Forced to defend their sanity, the prophets and their supporters tried to turn critics' arguments around, to argue that they enjoyed a more lucid relationship with the divine mysteries than those still mired in the darkness of carnal reasoning. John Morphew, in a 1708 pamphlet that would find a new audience in the 1790s, countered that he found the prophets to be "not only rational between their extatic fits, but even in those very fits (when they are mostly supposed to be mad) to argue with brighter reason, than out of them; [to] deliver discourses very elegant and long, ask, or answer questions, with wonderful propriety and wisdom, even exceeding their natural capacity." It was "the highest injustice in the world to charge them with madness," he concluded.[11] This defense, however, conceded too much to the prosecution. Acknowledging that human ideals of excellence would be the measure of authenticity, rather than the ineffable marks of inspiration, Morphew implicitly endorsed the idea that prophets were men and women of ordinary, not supernatural, ability whose pronouncements would be judged by conventional standards of gentility. Reason, not revelation, was to be tested in this debate.

A heated pamphlet controversy over the competing claims of reason and revelation had been simmering since the Civil War era, to which the Camisards and their opponents contributed new fuel. Between 1707 and

---

[9] John Lacy, *The Prophetical Warnings of John Lacy, Esq.* (London, 1707), preface; see also Lacy's memoir, *A Revelation of the Dealings of God to his Unworthy Servant, John Lacy* (London, 1708).

[10] John Trenchard, *The Natural History of Superstition* (London, 1709), pp. 19–20.

[11] John Morphew, *An Impartial Account of the Prophets* (London, 1708; reprinted 1795), p. 13.

1710, some ninety books, pamphlets, and journal and newspaper articles appeared opposing the French Prophets.[12] When critics analyzed the prophets' performances they saw a chain of malignity originating in the disordered body and overactive mind of the prophet and radiating outward, either through the hidden influence of "some natural Magic, Fascination or Magnetism" (in George Keith's words) or via the deliberate efforts of practiced impostors. "That there is an Efflux of Spirits, Particles, or Atoms, from one Body to another, is undeniable, in Fevers and Infectious Diseases," argued one critic. "And seeing there are such Spirits Immaterial as Material, why may we not conceive an *Effluvium* of some Immaterial Spirits from the *Mind* of one Man, as of Material from the *Body*! And as the one prevails to the affecting another's Body with these Fits and Agitations, so may the other to the affecting the Soul with the same Passions, Belief, and Imagination."[13] The question of responsibility remained undecided. Were the French Prophets victims or culprits? The more violent the exercises, the more likely they were to be excused as frenzies of the brain or symptoms of hysteria. Whether "forced or preternatural," the agitations of the Camisards are "no more than what happens many times to Women in Hysterick Fits, arising from the strength of their Fancies and Passions."[14] Those who saw method rather than madness in the performances of the Camisards emphasized their skill in feigning the symptoms of lunacy to ensnare the weak and naive. "These Prophets have learned their Extatick Motions, just as Men learn to dance upon the Ropes. Since these Men have been in London, there are several who can exactly imitate 'em."[15]

Whatever the specific diagnosis, the thrust of critical commentary was to redefine the problem of religious enthusiasm in terms of individual pathology rather than supernatural agency. Overrunning the channels of respectable piety, enthusiasm operated like a contagious disease spreading pathogens through the body politic. "There is no Pestilence more dangerous, or Poison more mortal, than to give Attention to Visions and Prophecies,"

[12] Schwartz, *Knaves, Fools, Madmen*, p. 40.

[13] George Keith, *The Magick of Quakerism, or, the Chief Mysteries of Quakerism Laid Open. To which are added, A Preface and Postscript relating to the Camisars, in answer to Mr. Lacy's Preface to the Cry from the Desart* (London, 1707), p. 37; John Humphrey, *An Account of the French Prophets, and Their Pretended Inspirations* (London, 1708), p. 8.

[14] Benjamin Bragg, *Observations upon Elias Marion, and His Book of Warnings, Lately Publish'd. Proving this Elias to be a false Prophet and a Dangerous Person* (London, 1707), p. 8.

[15] *Clavis Prophetica; or, A Key to the Prophecies of Mons. Marion And the other Camisars, With Some Reflections on the Characters of these New Envoys* (London, 1707), p. 3.

warned one writer.[16] Anthony Ashley Cooper, third earl of Shaftesbury, in his *Letter concerning Enthusiasm* spoke of the "Panic" of enthusiasm, a phrase that conjured up images of commercial speculation and political ambition run amok. Though there is little evidence that the prophets intended a political rebellion of comparable magnitude to that launched by the radical sects of the Civil War era (those who did propose sweeping political or social programs of reform were quickly disowned), the rhetoric of infection or invasion summoned up fears of a "world turned upside down."[17] "There is not a better State-Engine in the World, than Prophecy, when it is in hands that know how to play it skillfully," declared an influential pamphlet.[18]

As a social disease, enthusiasm needed a social cure, which the literati were more effective at delivering than the clumsy agents of state repression. Although some critics advocated an institutional response—John Tutchin, editor of the *Observer*, proposed the construction of a special asylum (the Royal Bethlehem lunatic hospital) for the French Prophets and their counterparts—most preferred, like Shaftesbury, the antidote of "*cold, dead Reasonings.*"[19] This response could take the form of either pity or ridicule. One anonymous author regarded the prophets as "Objects of Pity, not Fury, tricked by the Devil and his Agents into unheard-of Delusions."[20] Mockery, however, was by far the preferred counterpunch. Mounting an effective campaign of verbal harassment and literary satire, the opponents of the French Prophets moved the debate over the authenticity of revelation out of the religious and into the cultural realm, where it would firmly remain for the rest of the century. Henceforth discussions of true and false prophets

[16] Mark Vernous, *A Preservative Against the False Prophets of the Time; or a Treatise Concerning True and False Prophets with their Character* (London, 1708), p. 32.

[17] As Hillel Schwartz argues, there were hints that the French Prophets envisioned a broader political insurgency. Jean Marion predicted that soon there would be "Overturnings of whole States, I tell thee. I will overturn them upside down." The renegade prophet Abraham Whitrow advocated a widespread charitable program for the poor, a program that his wealthy patron Sir Richard Bulkeley began to implement in the summer of 1708 with funds from his own estate. Yet the Camisards consistently kept the "metaphors of destruction within the realm of personal spiritual transformation; Marion never once acted upon his prophecies as a guerilla leader initiating political warfare, and the French Prophets very quickly and publicly expelled Abraham Whitrow as a false prophet." *Knaves, Fools, Madmen*, p. 60.

[18] *Clavis Prophetica*, n.p.

[19] Shaftesbury, *A Letter Concerning Enthusiasm* (London, 1708); Schwartz, *Knaves, Fools, Madmen*, p. 51. See also John Brydall, *Non compos mentis; or the Law relating to Natural fools, Mad folks and Lunatick Persons* (London, 1700).

[20] Quoted in Schwartz, *Knaves, Fools, Madmen*, p. 44.

would conform to a common pattern: dissection of the physical and mental capacity of candidates, examination of their demeanor and language for signs of corruption, and disarming of the visionary's spiritual powers through the calculated use of ridicule. There was not much room for the soul in all these debates. Skeptics were interested only in what could be seen and interrogated by the eyes and ears of a discriminating public, not in what was visible only to God.

Critics, no less than the Camisards themselves, thus conceived of prophecy as a form of stagecraft. One of the French Prophets' major publications was entitled *Théâtre sacré des Cevennes*, and marionette shows and at least one full-scale production, Thomas D'Urfey's 1709 play *The Modern Prophets*, were part of the opposition's literary arsenal. The theatrical simile made a good deal of sense to both sides. As Hillel Schwartz notes, the Camisards were now centered in a city where public theater was a social reality, not just a literary metaphor. London was "a place where perforce strangers met, and they had to have a public language of gesture and a public rhetoric of emotions so that each in turn could be audience to the other's tale."[21] It was the genius of the Camisards to recognize the inherent theatricality of urban life and to craft their "cosmic playlets" to take full advantage of the opportunities for display afforded in the streets, markets, and civic spaces of the metropolis.[22]

Analogies with the theater, a staple feature of Anglo-American cultural criticism since the Elizabethan era, were a form of moral critique as well as social commentary. Moralists equated religious fanatics with the boundlessness of (in Jean-Christophe Agnew's words) the "placeless market." Like the traveling players and peddlers who clogged the roads and towns of Anglo-America, the Camisards were the moral peers of the much-despised itinerant classes—those who embodied in their very persons the "crisis of representation" that accompanied the spread of market relations throughout the first empire.[23] "They travel up and down," complained Samuel Keimer, "more like Strolling Players in their Behaviour, than the Messengers of the Living God."[24] Though prophets did not charge admission to their performances, this made them more, not less dangerous. "These Mock-Prophets set up

---

[21] Schwartz, *The French Prophets*, pp. 252–53.

[22] The phrase "cosmic playlets" is Clarke Garrett's; *Spirit Possession*, p. 53.

[23] Jean-Christophe Agnew, *Worlds Apart: The Market and the Theater in Anglo-American Thought, 1550–1750* (New York, 1986). For another view of the relationship between religious fanaticism and the dangers of itinerancy, see Timothy D. Hall, *Contested Boundaries: Itinerancy and the Reshaping of the Colonial American Religious World* (Durham, N.C., 1994).

[24] Keimer, *Brand Pluck'd from the Burning*, p. 41.

their Stage; acting as publickly, and almost as constantly as their Brethren of Drury-Lane or the Hay-Market; of whom they had this peculiar Advantage, that all People were admitted gratis to the Shew . . . so these Actors never wanted an Audience."[25]

The critique of the French Prophets as conniving actors registers an important shift in the cultural calculus of proof and demonstration that distinguished real from spurious prophets. Throughout the century, the Camisards would serve as a reminder and warning of the perils of counterfeit piety. By making faith the object of subjective evaluation, critics expanded the range of diagnostic tools available to discerning Christians who hoped to distinguish true from false prophets. Voice, language, dress, gesture, bodily deportment, all were open to scrutiny. If the immediate effect was to externalize the process—to direct attention to the outward signs of lunacy or imposture—the long-term effect was to make the mind of the prophet the ultimate source of his credibility. The effort to psychologize the internal experience of faith, to search out motives, ambitions, emotional and sexual needs and anxieties, was both a logical consequence of the theatrical analogy which shaped the discourse of authenticity and a new departure. Like theatrical productions, the emotional and physical displays of the prophets were contrived out of some calculus of cause and effect that took into account the psychological vulnerabilities of the audience and the skill of the performers. But, unlike the stage, the prophets' productions sought to transform the inner life of spectators, to change spectators into actors. The reciprocal nature of the relationship between prophet and audience was predicated on the ability of the actors to change hearts and souls, not just elicit sympathy or horror. The subjective dimension to the Camisards' peculiar stagecraft was not lost on their critics, who used the debate over revelation to construct a psychological model of the false prophet that helped move the entire discussion on to a new intellectual plane. In fact, Frank Manuel argues that the historical origins of the English discipline of psychology lie precisely in the urgent need of early eighteenth-century Christians to understand the source and appeal of aberrant religious experience.[26] The task of distinguishing false prophets was thus one freighted with lasting moral, cultural, and intellectual consequences.

After 1715, the French Prophets largely disappeared from the British religious scene. Small groups of *inspirés* continued to appear in London and other urban centers, and a series of schisms (all involving female prophets

---

[25] *Clavis Prophetica*, n.p.
[26] Manuel, *The Eighteenth Century Confronts the Gods*, p. 71.

who chafed under the sacerdotal restrictions imposed on women within the community) kept the flames of religious controversy flickering.[27] Unlike their closest sectarian peers, the Quakers, the Camisards were unable to make the transition from cultural gadfly to organized community of saints. But if largely extinguished as an active cultural force, their influence continued to be felt in evangelical circles for years to come. From small remnants of mystical believers like the Philadelphians and the Shakers to the large evangelical movements of the mid-eighteenth century, the impact of the Camisards on Anglo-American religious life was far greater than their brief public history would indicate. Within the fraternity of itinerant preachers who carried the fire of revival to every corner of the British empire, the connection between the behavior of religious fanatics and the example of the *inspirés* was clear. Surveying the wreckage of orthodox religion in mid-century, churchmen like Charles Chauncy condemned the Camisards for setting in motion a disastrous chain of enthusiastical disorders which would culminate in the excesses of the First Awakening. "Enthusiasm spread itself like a Flood, and with such a Torrent, that a Conflagration blown with a Wind, doth not spread faster from House to House, than this flew from Parish to Parish."[28] His theological opponent John Wesley concurred. Having seen firsthand the "convulsive motion[s]" of one of the last remaining French prophets, Mary Plewit, Wesley used Plewit as a barometer to measure the spiritual labors of other enthusiasts whom he encountered in his travels. Mrs. Cooper, "the supposed prophetess," imitated the French Prophets in her convulsions, though "her agitations were nothing near so violent as those of Mary Plewit are."[29] One pretend prophet after another paraded before the Methodist leader over the long course of his illustrious career, and all met the same response. True prophets did not flaunt their spiritual virtuosity in such indecent fashion but waited patiently and humbly for the Spirit of God to speak to them in proper ways.

The image of a true prophet constructed in the pamphlet wars of the 1700s continued to resonate nearly a century later when Britain faced a new onslaught of *inspirés*. A "True Prophet behaves himself in all that he says, with a clear and regular understanding," counseled Mark Vernous; "he preserves a decent Gravity in his Comportment, appearing with a just Modera-

---

[27] Hillel Schwartz narrates these schisms in *The French Prophets*, pp. 134–36.

[28] Charles Chauncy, *A Wonderful Narrative: or, a Faithful Account of the French Prophets, their Agitations, Extasies and Inspiration* (Glasgow, 1742), p. 3.

[29] Nehemiah Curnock, ed., *The Journal of the Rev. John Wesley, A.M.*, standard ed., 8 vols. (London, 1910), 2:214–15.

tion, Sobriety, and Modesty of Mind. This is otherwise in a False Prophet. 'Tis his peculiar Mark of Distinction to be disordered in Mind, to suffer the Violence and Necessity of obeying the Power of a Spirit, which draws and agitates him after such a manner as makes him appear distracted."[30] Summarizing the widely held consensus that the strange bodily and verbal agitations of the exiled Camisards violated the expressive rules of authentic Christian prophecy, Vernous' pamphlet highlighted the link between body and mind, extravagance and moderation, language and gentility, that would come to dominate revolutionary-era discussions of true and false prophets.

True and False Prophets in the Revolutionary Era

What set a prophet apart from other religious believers in the late eighteenth century? The critique of prophecy offered by churchmen, physicians, and intellectuals in the revolutionary era recycled the phrases and images of earlier critics of enthusiasm, but with a noticeable damping down of the temperature of the rhetoric. Insanity, hysteria, imposture, greed, all were invoked to explain the bizarre behavior of prophets and the gullibility of their followers. The stakes, however, were not as high, and consequently the rhetoric less charged. In fact, we can detect a subtle shift in tone that threatened to turn critique into caricature, as older images of transgression (the raving fanatic, the holy fool, the cunning peasant) became translated into the modern idioms of cosmopolitan social commentary.

We can, for the sake of convenience, break down the act of prophecy into three distinct stages, each of which elicited a range of responses from skeptics and believers. As messengers, prophets first *heard* God's word; then *interpreted* the meaning of what they had heard; then *delivered* the message to the appropriate audience. At each step, they faced hard questions about their legitimacy.

The quickest way for eighteenth-century religious leaders to attack the authority of prophets was to challenge the very possibility of revelation itself. Since the Reformation, it had been accepted wisdom in the Church of England that direct communications from God had ceased after the apostolic age. The "age of Pentecost" ended with the death of the apostles, and future generations had only the Word of God contained in the scriptures to guide them. As Edward King, the author of several millennial tracts in the 1790s,

---

[30] Vernous, *Preservative Against False Prophets*, p. 15.

put it, "The word of Prophecy is sealed for ever."[31] God's will could be providentially discerned in the movements of the heavens or the ravages of nature, but these signs were part of the created world and not supernatural interventions. Radical spiritualists appeared in every age who rejected this consensus—Anne Hutchinson defied the magistrates of Massachusetts in 1637 to claim that God spoke directly to her "by the voice of his own spirit to my soul," and the Quakers and French Prophets gave dramatic witness to the living presence of the Holy Spirit in their lives.[32] By and large, however, most Anglo-American Protestants accepted the idea that God's voice was no longer heard by human ears—a conclusion even some prophets were willing to advance, as they sought to fend off rivals. Two seventeenth-century prophets insisted that the era of direct revelation ended with *them*, not the apostles, and that all subsequent claims were therefore spurious. "John Reeve and Lodowick Muggleton are the last witnesses that God will ever send," Muggletonians insisted to a steady stream of challengers who came forward in the century following the death of the original "witnesses."[33] A modern-day prophet who claimed direct revelation opened up a theological Pandora's box that the established church and prior generations of millenarians alike had been trying to reseal since the 1640s.

When John Wesley encountered a young prophet in 1740 named Betty Bush, he rejected her spiritual authority because she "set her *private revelations* (so called) on the self-same foot with the written Word."[34] Wesley is a good barometer of shifting views on the reality of direct spiritual revelations, as he insisted on the continued presence of witches and other demonic forces in the world even while he doubted that God spoke in audible ways in the present age. No passive admirer of Enlightenment philosophy, Wesley thought long and hard about the leading scientific advances of his day and carefully weighed their empirical claims against the duty of a Christian to defend the truth of the Bible against secular inroads.[35] His conclusions, while

[31] Edward King, *Remarks on the Signs of the Times* (Philadelphia, 1800), p. 28.

[32] "The Examination of Mrs. Hutchinson at the Court at Newtown," 1637, in *The Antinomian Controversy, 1636–1638: A Documentary History*, ed. David D. Hall (Middletown, Conn., 1968), pp. 336–37.

[33] George Hudson to Martha Collier, n.d., Muggletonian Archives, Add. MSS 60168, British Library. Collier was one of several Muggletonians who split from the main body of believers in the 1770s and 1780s to claim a new revelation; all were rebuffed with the same argument.

[34] *Journal of John Wesley*, 2:381–82. Wesley noted that another young woman, Susan Peck, had similar "vain imaginations."

[35] Phyllis Mack provides a good overview of Wesley's scientific interests in "Religious Dissenters in Enlightenment England," *History Workshop Journal* 49 (2000), pp. 1–23.

not always tidy, are consistent with our emerging historiographical sense of eighteenth-century popular culture as a creative blend of old and new elements—a growing familiarity with the scientific principles that governed the natural world layered over a thriving quasi-magical sensibility. The world, in this hybrid or syncretic view, operated according to natural laws of cause and effect—crops thrived or failed depending on the weather, people sickened or recovered according to the balance of humors—but on occasion supernatural forces irrupted to disturb these laws, usually in dark ways. Wesley tended to credit accounts of demonic possession (providing his readers with several absorbing case studies) but rarely divine possession: the devil had a free hand in disrupting the lives of eighteenth-century believers, but God was constrained to work through the accepted channels of scripture and providence.

This distinction between the efficacy of demonic and divine intervention had a long pedigree in Reformed Protestantism. The fact that it was easier (or, rather, more likely) for the devil to make an appearance than for God made the task of discerning true from false prophets all the more tricky. The classic seventeenth-century treatise on prophecy, John Smith's *Select Discourses* (1660), warned "how easie a matter it might be for the *Devils Prophets* many times, by an apish imitation, to counterfeit the *True Prophets* of God."[36] Demoniacs had an uncanny ability to mimic the language and biblical literacy of prophets: a woman "long afflicted by the devil" told the Primitive Methodist leader Hugh Bourne that "the Lord was making a new Jerusalem out of the damned, and that the damned were to be saved by her sufferings."[37] Wesley himself was sometimes surprised by the power of demoniacs to "counterfeit" true prophecy. He recounted a conversation he had with the daughter of a weaver in 1758 who told him that "the devil had possession of her body and soul; that she had been taken to heaven and hell by angels; that future events had been revealed to her." Wesley recognized the signs of possession when he saw them ("words came from her mouth, without any motion of her lips") and interrogated the girl.

"Can you tell us those things that are to come?"
"I must not; no one could bear to hear them."
"Will the troubles that are coming be in part of the kingdom or all of it?"
"They will be all over England." . . .

---

[36] John Smith, "On Prophecy," *Select Discourses* (London, 1660), p. 190.
[37] John Walford, *Memoirs of the Life and Labours of the Late Venerable Hugh Bourne* (London, 1855), 1:294.

"Will they come soon?"

"A part of them will. Jesus Christ told me of the trouble to come; but the angels told me not to reveal what he said."

Wesley did not know what to make of the case. "Many acknowledged it must be the work of God; others were sure it was all a cheat."[38]

Dismissing prophetic claims of direct revelation as diabolically inspired was the first (and least creative) recourse of debunkers. The potential for Satan to confuse and even mislead ignorant believers incapable of properly discerning divine from diabolical revelations was apparent to even the most sympathetic Christian. Freeborn Garrettson recorded the tragic tale of one Mrs. W. of Vermont who "thought the Lord revealed it to her, that all her children would die unless she threw herself six times in the river, which she attempted in the night." After a desperate plunge into the icy waters, her "enthusiasm carried her farther." She and her sister, whom she had recruited by "infus[ing] strange notions into her head," "went into the water and sat chin deep till they received (as they said) a sign from the Lord that they were as pure as Angels in heaven. Now they concluded that the place was full of witches, and wizards, they were in the cats, dogs, and every part of the house."[39] The two women proceeded to kill every animal in sight, a sure sign of Satan's handiwork in Garrettson's opinion. Such tales of apocalyptic violence were few but made a deep impression on wary evangelicals. John Colby retold the story of Captain John Parringon of Maine who in 1806 "cruelly butchered" his family "in cold blood, under a mistaken frenzy, or notion, that every body would be saved, and the sooner they got out of this troublesome world, the better."[40]

The most famous case was probably that of Jacob Weber of South Carolina, who called himself the "Most High" and was executed in 1761 for the murder of two men who challenged his authority as a prophet. As the crusty Anglican missionary Charles Woodmason described the affair, with typical

[38] *Journal of John Wesley*, 4:251–52. Wesley presented another case of a prophetic demoniac, that of Elizabeth Booth, who as a child "stripped herself naked" and "ran up and down the house." While in a "trance," Booth "said she saw many visions—sometimes of heaven or hell or judgement, sometimes of things which she said would shortly come to pass." Booth later married John Oliver, a noted Methodist preacher, and settled into an otherwise unremarkable career as a "Mother in Israel." *Journal of John Wesley*, 4:71.

[39] Simpson, *American Methodist Pioneer*, p. 299.

[40] John Colby, *The Life, Experience and Travels of John Colby, Preacher of the Gospel. Written by Himself* (Rochester, N.Y., 1827), entry for July 8, 1806, p. 256.

hyperbole, Weber and his followers "kill'd a Travelling Person, and cut Him into Atoms singing Hymns . . . offering up this inhuman Sacrifice to the Deity."[41] But where Woodmason attributed the brutality of Jacob Weber to the devil's influence, later commentators saw only derangement—a natural rather than supernatural tragedy. Francis Asbury's account of the Weber affair, written fifty years later than Woodmason's, is less lurid if no less damning: "Here once lived that strange, deranged mortal, who proclaimed himself to be God: report says, that he killed three men for refusing their assent to his godship: he gave out his wife to be the Virgin Mary, and his son Jesus Christ; and when hanged at Charleston, promised to rise the third day."[42]

Over the course of the long eighteenth century, the devil disappeared from accounts of religious fanaticism—to be replaced by the clinical language of mental or physical weakness. The process by which *all* supernatural presences came to be exiled from the human world as phenomenological realities or explanatory mechanisms was, we now know, a long and circuitous one that had no clear endpoint. What one historian calls "Enlightenment fantasies of disenchantment" were often just that—fantasies, in which the desire of scientific and philosophical thinkers to strip the world of its magical qualities was never matched by their ability to banish witches, demons, ghosts, and other spiritual phenomena from the literary and imaginative landscape of eighteenth-century villagers.[43] Nevertheless, despite the tenacious hold of the supernatural on the minds of ordinary believers, pathological explanations of spiritual revelation did effectively displace demonic ones by the last decades of the eighteenth century. "Ghosts are not lawful," was William Blake's lament.[44] While some nineteenth-century prophets like

[41] Richard Hooker, ed., *The Carolina Backcountry on the Eve of Revolution: The Journal and Other Writings of Charles Woodmason, Anglican Itinerant* (Chapel Hill, N.C., 1953), p. 78. South Carolina had a checkered history of religious fanaticism; another infamous case involved the Dutartres, an old Huguenot family whose prophetic claims also led to bloodshed in the 1720s; see "Tragical Effects of Fanaticism," *American Museum* 6 (July 1789).

[42] Elmer T. Clark, ed., *The Journal and Letters of Francis Asbury*, 2 vols. (Nashville, Tenn., 1958), 1:507.

[43] Schmidt, *Hearing Things*, p. 3. The historiography on the "disenchantment of the world" under the reforming disciplines of the Enlightenment is rich and complex; see Walter Ong, *The Presence of the Word: Some Prolegomena for Cultural and Religious History* (New Haven, 1967); Michel de Certeau, *The Practice of Everyday Life*, trans. Steven Rendall (Berkeley, Calif., 1984); Mircea Eliade, *Myths, Dreams, and Mysteries: The Encounter Between Contemporary Faiths and Archaic Realities* (Chicago, 1969), and *The Sacred and the Profane: The Nature of Religion* (New York, 1959).

[44] Quoted in Roy Porter, *Mind-Forg'd Manacles: A History of Madness in England from the Restoration to the Regency* (Cambridge, Mass., 1987), p. 73.

Elspeth Buchan and Joanna Southcott were accused of witchcraft, such charges reflected more the desire to disparage their simple followers than to demonize the prophet herself.[45] More common was the response of men like Freeborn Garrettson to the man in Virginia—that false prophets were simply "bereft of reason." By the eighteenth century, insanity had replaced the devil as the medical establishment's diagnosis of choice for aberrant religious behavior.

Accusations of mental instability first surfaced in the sectarian wars of the 1640s and 1650s, when extreme behaviors which seemed to border on the "irrational" were, in truth, not uncommon. During the century following the English Civil War, the idea that religious enthusiasts were the "victims and carriers of mental disease" became, in Michael MacDonald's words, "a ruling-class shibboleth."[46] The Methodist movement of the mid-eighteenth century, with its exuberant physical and emotional behaviors, helped revive the association between mental instability and religious fanaticism; even John Wesley reported numerous cases of insanity associated with his ministry. Bethlehem Hospital in London (better known as Bedlam) admitted ninety patients between 1772 and 1795 who were alleged to be suffering from "religion and Methodism."[47] As a special breed of fanatics, prophets were well-represented among the inmate population of British and American asylums, including the famous Samuel Best, or "Poor-Helps," who "excited the attention and gratified the curiosity of many" in the 1780s, and Mary Pratt, who

[45] Elspeth Buchan, a Scottish prophetess, was presumed to profess "a proficiency in the *black art*," a critic wrote. But, he went on, this was merely folk superstition. "At the time they appeared in Ayrshire, the belief in witchcraft not being totally eradicated from the minds of the people, the singular tenets of this sect were attributed to the influence of demoniac agency, rather than to distempered organisation." Joseph Train, *The Buchanites, from First to Last* (London, 1846), p. 2. Southcott, too, found herself labeled a witch; R. Hann charged that her "cunning devised plan ought to be called the black arts, for by it, she acts the part of a witch." R. Hann, *The Remarkable Life, Entertaining History and Surprising Adventures of Joanna Southcott the Prophetess* (London, 1814), p. 32.

[46] Michael MacDonald, *Mystical Bedlam: Madness, Anxiety, and Healing in Seventeenth-Century England* (New York, 1981), p. 225; and MacDonald, "Insanity and the Realities of History in Early Modern England," *Psychological Medicine* 11 (1981), pp. 11–25. See also Porter, *Mind-Forg'd Manacles*, pp. 62–81, for a discussion of the shift from demonic to pathological explanations of religious enthusiasm. For contemporary attacks on enthusiastic madness, see Meric Casaubon, *A Treatise Concerning Enthusiasme*, ed. Paul J. Korshin (Gainesville, Fla., 1970); George Hickes, *The Spirit of Enthusiasm Exorcised* (London, 1680); Edmund Gibson, *A Caution Against Enthusiasm*, 7th ed. (London, 1751).

[47] Michael MacDonald, "Religion, Social Change, and Psychological Healing in England, 1600–1800," in *The Church and Healing*, ed. W. J. Sheils, vol. 19 of *Studies in Church History* (Oxford, 1982), pp. 101–25.

complained to Henry Brooke in 1792 that "my relations put me in a mad house privately."[48] Richard Brothers, the grand prince of British prophecy, was incarcerated in a mental asylum at the height of the political repression of the 1790s—a fate that his American counterpart, David Austin, narrowly escaped after a bout with scarlet fever in 1796 left Austin delusional.

Fears of incarceration invaded the dreams of late eighteenth-century visionaries. Sarah Richards, a disciple of the American prophetess Jemima Wilkinson, recorded a vision in her daybook in which men bearing warrants "declared me to be a delerious person and that some place of Confinement should be provided for me to secret me from all human Eyes and that I should run no more at Large."[49] So commonplace was the association between religious enthusiasm and mental debility by the end of the eighteenth century that, beginning in the 1780s, prophets routinely included ritualized disclaimers about their mental status in their published pronouncements. Nathan Barlow, who published his visions in 1803, wanted "to inform the readers what reason I have to think it is a real Vision, and not an imagination, delusion, or merely a dream."[50] The British prophetess Dorothy Gott admitted that "if any body had told me what God has shewn me, I very likely might have thought them mad, or deluded."[51] From the prison cell where he had been incarcerated (unfairly, he said) for petty crimes, the American Nimrod Hughes foresaw the destruction of the world on June 4, 1812, and warned his readers not "to say that this vision was the effect of a crazed or disturbed imagination. It is no such dream, nor effect of melancholy, or any other distemper of the mind or body, but an awful message from the Lord God."[52]

Other prophets took a different tack altogether and embraced the persona of a holy fool. As J. F. C. Harrison notes, "madness was not part of the

[48] On Samuel Best, see John Martin, *Imposture Detected: Or Thoughts on a Pretended Prophet, and on the Prevalence of his Impositions* (London, 1787), quote on p. 3. Best was described more sympathetically by Thomas Langcake; the "poor disordered man" quoted liberally from the "Book of Sensations," wrote Langcake. Letter to Henry Brooke, Nov. 30, 1782, Brooke Letterbook, pp. 37–38, Walton MSS I.1.43, Dr. Williams's Library. For Mary Pratt, see Pratt's letter to Henry Brooke in 1792, Brooke Letterbook, p. 344.

[49] Sarah Richards's Day Book 1789–1803, n.p., Jemima Wilkinson Papers, 1771–1849, Department of Manuscripts and University Archives, Cornell University Library.

[50] Nathan Barlow, *A Vision, Seen by Nathan Barlow* (Greenfield, Mass., 1802), p. 7.

[51] Dorothy Gott, *The Midnight Cry, "Behold the* BRIDEGROOM *comes!" or, An Order from God to Get your Lamps Lighted* (London, 1788), p. 90.

[52] Nimrod Hughes, *A Solemn Warning to All the Dwellers Upon the Earth*, 2d ed. (New Jersey, 1811), p. 21.

popular understanding of millenarianism—or rather, charges of madness did not diminish but only confirmed the truth of the claims" of millenarian prophets.[53] Prophets inhabited a parallel universe to the world of respectable religious culture, one with its own definitions of sanity and rules for personal behavior. Joanna Southcott embraced the idea that her prophecies were the product of a "disordered brain." If it was "madness to believe," she argued, then "I was born mad, and so was my mother before me."[54] Because the itinerant preacher and sometime prophet James Horton was so bellicose in his "exercises" ("I hallooed so loud it would frighten the devil's children"), he was labeled "crazy" even by his fellow Methodists. Horton did not dispute the diagnosis but countered that he was "as rational and as happy as a little angel."[55] The self-described "wild man," John Granade, made a name for himself by "howling, praying, and roaring in such a manner that he was generally reputed to be crazy." Satan took advantage of his reputation and "tempted him to believe that he was deranged," his biographer notes.[56] Lorenzo Dow was proud to be called "crazy," as was Joseph Thomas; "it was reported for a very serious fact, that 'Thomas had lost his senses and had run *crazy*'; hence I obtained the name of *crazy Thomas*."[57] The very terms in which prophets defended their sanity make clear just how far the diagnosis of spiritual possession had receded from the religious to the medical realm.

If this was madness, it was "a very methodical kind of madness."[58] To the medical profession, prophets seemed to suffer from a classic case of melancholia—in which, according to the eighteenth-century physician Alexander Crichton, the sufferer "conducts himself like a man of sense, in every respect but in one particular circumstances; but in that, his thoughts and actions are in such opposition to those of other men, that he appears to them to be evidently deranged." Crichton apparently had the prophet

[53] J. F. C. Harrison, *The Second Coming: Popular Millenarianism, 1780–1850* (London, 1979), p. 215.

[54] Joanna Southcott, *The Strange Effects of Faith; With Remarkable Prophecies, Made in 1792, &c of Things Which Are to Come. Fifth Part* (Exeter, 1801), p. 193.

[55] James Horton, *A Narrative of the Early Life, Remarkable Conversion, and Spiritual Labours of James P. Horton* (n.p., published for the author, 1839), pp. 24–25.

[56] Richard Price, *Holston Methodism: From Its Origins to the Present Time* (Nashville, Tenn., 1906), pp. 5–6.

[57] Lorenzo Dow, *History of Cosmopolite; or the Four Volumes of Lorenzo's Diary* (New York, 1814), pp. 47–48; Joseph Thomas, *The Life of the Pilgrim, Joseph Thomas* (Winchester, Va., 1817), p. 267.

[58] Joseph Moser, *Anecdotes of Richard Brothers, in the Years 1791 and 1792, with Some Thoughts upon Credulity* (London, 1795), p. 17.

Richard Brothers in mind when he wrote his treatise on melancholia. Brothers's contemporary, the prophet Henry Hardy, was described in similar terms as a partial lunatic: he was not "an idiot, a lunatic, or a madman; but only . . . entertained an extravagance of opinion on one particular subject."[59] Women, too, suffered from this affliction, though melancholia was typically considered a classic male disorder in the eighteenth century. The American prophetess Jemima Wilkinson was "perfectly rational" most of the time, "but upon religion she was a wild enthusiast, a monomaniac."[60] The label of "melancholia" was a fitting one for revolutionary-era millenarians given its connotations of abortive genius. This was a very different kind of melancholy than that suffered by past generations of religious enthusiasts, whom the Anglican cleric Robert Burton had described in his influential 1621 treatise *The Anatomy of Melancholy*. "Religious melancholy," according to Burton and other seventeenth-century clinicians of the spirit, was a kind of deep and soul-destroying despair, leading often to suicide or other violent acts.[61] Revolutionary-era Anglo-American melancholics, as Catherine Kaplan has shown, exhibited a much milder form of mental debility: they were men of great ambition but fragile temperament whose claims to intellectual precocity rang increasingly hollow in the late eighteenth century.[62] The bursts of maniacal energy for which melancholics were famed, which in an earlier age might have signaled either divine inspiration or real genius, were more likely to be regarded as temporary illness or weakness of character (as effeminacy, for instance). Such a state of not-quite-lunacy seemed to capture perfectly the emotional and mental instability of religious fanatics.

Over time, diagnoses extended well beyond general descriptions of mental derangement to embrace all sorts of nervous disorders, from epilepsy to gluttony, as the organic source of religious visions. Since the pioneering work of the physician George Cheyne on the "English malady" in the 1730s, English writers had linked religious fanaticism to diseases of the nervous

[59] Alexander Crichton, *An Inquiry into the Nature and Origin of Mental Derangement*, 2 vols. (London, 1798), 1:381. John Barrell suggests that Crichton wrote this description of melancholia with Brothers as a model; *Imagining the King's Death: Figurative Treason, Fantasies of Regicide, 1793–1796* (New York, 2000), p. 533. For Hardy, see John Martin, *An Account of the Proceedings on a Charge of High Treason against John Martin* (London, 1795), p. 10.

[60] Rev. Israel Wilkinson, *Memoirs of the Wilkinson Family in America . . . 1645–1868* (Jacksonville, Ill., 1869), p. 424.

[61] MacDonald, *Mystical Bedlam*; see also John Owen King III, *The Iron of Melancholy: Structures of Spiritual Conversion in America from the Puritan Conscience to Victorian Neurosis* (Middletown, Conn., 1983).

[62] Catherine O. Kaplan, " 'We Have Joys . . . They Do Not Know': Letters, Partisanship, and Sentiment in the New Nation, 1790–1812," Ph.D. diss., University of Michigan, 1998.

system. Cheyne—a mystic and friend of John Wesley—believed that nervous distempers were caused by a clogged digestive tract, which produced the "*Spasms, Convulsions,* and violent *Contractions*" that the ignorant often mistook for visionary fancies.[63] The emergence of nerve physiology in the seventeenth and eighteenth centuries directed attention away from the humors to the delicate structure of nerve fibers connecting body and mind as the source of organic disorders, including religious enthusiasm. Charles Chauncy cited "the learned Dr. Casaubon" in concluding that "Persons subject to the Epilepsy, are naturally liable to see Visions and Apparitions; which Phrensies of their Brain they are apt to take for Realities."[64] John Wesley compared the "convulsive motion" of saints under the power of the Spirit to "hysterical" and "epileptical fits."[65]

In the language of debates over revelation, false prophets had "disordered brains" or diseased imaginations, a malady with roots in both physiology and psychology. In the seventeenth century, the imagination had been accorded a place—albeit a lowly one—in the prophetic arts. John Smith's treatise "On Prophecy" distinguished four degrees of authentic revelation, ranging from the base to the sublime, depending on the mix of fancy and reason in the prophet's judgments. In the lowest degree, "the *Imaginative* power is most predominant, so that the impressions made upon it are too busie, & the Scene becomes too turbulent for the Rational facultie to discern the true Mystical and Analogical sense of [the prophetic texts] clearly."[66] Such turbulence could actually be a good thing for visionaries interested in escaping the constraints of rationality; the mystic John Pordage argued that "the strength and vehemence of Imagination, Phantasie, or Phan'sie will, sometimes, carri forth the Reason and Judgment to make new Worlds of discoveries, excite both to take such Circuits and Travels in the contemplation of *Eternal Entities,* til the very Soul is readi to be vertiginous, to swim and grow giddi."[67] But by the eighteenth century, there was no room for even so limited a role for the prophet's imagination, which was now dismissed as a

[63] George Cheyne, *The English Malady; or, A Treatise of Nervous Diseases of All Kinds, as Spleen, Vapours, Lowness of Spirits, Hypochondriacal, and Hysterical Distempers &c.* (London, 1733), p. 218. See Anita Guerrini's recent biography of Cheyne, *Obesity and Depression in the Englightenment: The Life and Times of George Cheyne* (Norman, Okla., 2000).

[64] Chauncy, *Wonderful Narrative,* p. 67; Meric Casaubon, *A Treatise Concerning Enthusiasm* (London, 1655).

[65] *Journal of John Wesley,* 2:221–22.

[66] Smith, *Select Discourses,* p. 180.

[67] John Pordage, *Theologia Mystica, or The Mystic Divinitie of the Eternal Invisibles* (London, 1683), p. 97.

"receptacle for vapours," as one critic of the British prophetess Joanna Southcott put it. Such "fumes," R. Hann concluded, are "doubtless the cause of all her dreams and visions."[68]

Once the question of the origins of a prophetic revelation was dispatched, skeptics turned their attention to the manner in which the prophet interpreted the words he or she claimed to have received. This was in many ways a far more interesting and contentious issue to eighteenth-century men and women ever suspicious of the exercise of untested and arbitrary power. If few learned observers doubted that false prophets had mistaken their own "vain imaginings" for divine impressions, there was less agreement on what the rules of interpretation should be in discerning God's intent—whether expressed in scripture, nature, or the (spurious) claims of direct revelation. The enigmatic nature of the scriptures themselves had always placed a special hermeneutic burden on would-be prophets, testing their analytical and verbal agility to the utmost. Prophets had to be skilled decoders of arcane symbolism, capable of discerning subtle shades of meaning in the apocalyptic texts that might mean the difference between life and death in the here-and-now. To offer oneself up as a prophet was to enter into sophisticated epistemological debates about the relationship of words to things currently engaging the most learned minds in Europe. It was a heady, and foolhardy, task.

Probably the most recognizable biblical figure from the prophetic scriptures was the whore of Babylon, on whose forehead was engraved the inscription MYSTERY BABYLON THE GREAT, THE MOTHER OF HARLOTS AND ABOMINATIONS OF THE EARTH. This vivid image, evoked so often in the political and religious controversies of the eighteenth and early nineteenth centuries as a symbol of political corruption and female depravity, was a fitting symbol for prophecy itself. Prophetic interpretation was, inescapably, a matter of mystery—as Paul Boyer reminds us, the word "apocalypse" is a Greek word meaning "an unveiling of that which is hidden."[69] The act of enlightenment was itself a moment of high drama in the apocalyptic scenario: the "unsealing" of the mysteries of the Bible was one sign, perhaps the most important, that the final chapter in human history was unfolding. Peeling away the "types and shadows" (to use the language of the prophetess Joanna Southcott) that were enfolded into the prophetic texts, readers found in Revelation one final enigma

---

[68] Hann, *Remarkable Life . . . of Joanna Southcott*, p. 31.
[69] Paul Boyer, *When Time Shall Be No More: Prophecy Belief in Modern American Culture* (Cambridge, Mass., 1992), p. 23.

that tested their interpretive powers: the identity of the witness who was to liberate the Christian world from mystery itself. As an expert on prophetic interpretation put it in 1795, "All prophecies are neither more nor less than true genuine enigmas, in which the meaning is so nicely and artificially enveloped by ambiguity of sense and of expression, that until we be furnished by the inventor himself, with the proper clue to unravel them, they are calculated to appear as a tissue of the most incongruent absurdities."[70]

One man's absurdity is, of course, another's wisdom. What irritated critics was not just that prophets claimed to have found the "proper clue" to unlock the mysteries of the Bible, but their insistence that they alone were in possession of this vital information. Dorothy Gott declared that she "spake, as with a mighty power, things which they could not at all comprehend."[71] Most prophets did not dispute the notion that the apocalyptic scriptures were hard to read and harder to understand: in fact, they celebrated the Bible's "mysteries" as proof of their own exalted powers of discernment. The conceit of singularity was a badge of honor to prophets and a red flag to their critics. Mary Pratt proudly told the mystic writer Henry Brooke that "There is no book extant that speaks my experience; because I am the first, who ever had the honor to have the seventh seal opened to them: the time was not *come*, till it *came* to me; be not staggered, dear sir, at my saying so."[72]

The prophet's singularity was a variant on the celebrated English penchant for oddity, which by the 1790s had made eccentricity into a public vogue. The Methodist itinerant and sometime prophet Lorenzo Dow advertised himself as an "eccentric genius" in the American newspapers; his fellow American Simon Hough was proud to be known as "a strange creature."[73] Like its more sober cousin, melancholy, eccentricity was a form of mild mental disorientation that signaled not real instability but a harmless character trait, often cultivated, mostly by people of modest ability. Eccentricity, Paul Langford notes, was "intrinsic, rooted in a fundamental misapprehension of the real world."[74] Though religious fanaticism was not the most common form of Anglo eccentricity, which tended to take the form of quirky personal

---

[70] Nathaniel Halhed, *Testimony of the Authenticity of the Prophecies of Richard Brothers* (London, 1795), p. 9.

[71] Dorothy Gott, *The Midnight Cry*, p. 53.

[72] Mary Pratt to Henry Brooke, Aug. 25, 1792, Brooke Letterbook, p. 341.

[73] *Salem Gazette*, 1805 (quoted in Dow, *Cosmopolite*, p. 231); Simon Hough, *The Sign of the Present Time: Or, A Short Treatise Setting Forth What Particular Prophecies are Now Fulfilling in the Author's Judgment* (Stockbridge, Mass., 1793), p. 19.

[74] Paul Langford, *Englishness Identified: Manners and Character, 1650–1850* (New York, 2000), pp. 302–3.

habits, prophets would have been easily recognizable as inhabiting the cultural zone of mannered eccentricity which in the eyes of many outsiders defined the very essence of the British national character in the eighteenth and early nineteenth centuries.

Prophets, of course, did not cultivate eccentricity in order to amuse foreign observers or charm their fellow countrymen. Their peculiarity was in the service of a far more deadly mission. The "holy ambition" of prophets must have seemed overbearing to even their most devout followers. Richard Brothers, who wrote "in the style of a peasant exalting himself above the mightiest of princes," was both "preemptory and dictatorial," his most prominent supporter admitted.[75] His rival Sarah Flaxmer, a minor player on the crowded British prophetic scene of the 1790s, could be equally hectoring toward the high and mighty; when she saw in a vision the royal family "in the greatest distress, wringing their hands and weeping bitterly," she scolded them for their lack of faith—"I replied, that if they had sent for me sooner, and would have followed my advice, I could have helped them, but now it was too late."[76] Nimrod Hughes took grim satisfaction in the sight of thousands of damned souls flying past him on their way to hell, all crying, "O! now I know that Hughes was right. He declared the truth, but we would not believe it."[77] Prophecy was not for the meek or mild. "The prophet," explained Thomas Everard, is "commanded to smite with his hands, and to stamp with his feet, and to speak on certain occasions with bold reproof."[78]

The ethos of singularity, which so easily bred arrogance, thus erected a wall of knowledge and insight between a prophet and his followers. As in all "works of interpretation," Frank Kermode observes, "there are insiders and outsiders, the former having, or professing to have, immediate access to the mystery, the latter randomly scattered across space and time, and excluded from the elect who mistrust or despise their unauthorized divinations."[79]

[75] Halhed, *Testimony*, pp. 6–7; the phrase "holy ambition" comes from Joseph Thomas, *The Life of the Pilgrim*, p. 115.

[76] Sarah Flaxmer, *Satan Revealed; or the Dragon Overcome* (London, 1795), p. 5. A fascination with royalty appears in the writings of many British prophets, even those of republican sympathies, many of whom fantasized (as did Brothers) of being crowned themselves or of besting kings and queens with their superior wit or intelligence.

[77] Hughes, *Solemn Warning*, pp. 21–22.

[78] Thomas Everard, *Some Plain Scriptural Observations and Remarks on what is Denominated Shouting, Comprehending High and Loud Praises Exerted on Extraordinary Occasions. Taking notice of some things mentioned in a late publication, entitled Methodist Error* (Philadelphia, 1820), pp. 40–41.

[79] Frank Kermode, *The Genesis of Secrecy: On the Interpretation of Narrative* (Cambridge, Mass., 1979), p. xi.

Such a hermeneutic practice could seem deeply authoritarian, concentrating power in the hands of a single figure who, moreover, lorded his power over those less favored. The Enlightenment posture of suspicion, so deeply implicated in all eighteenth-century discussions of political and religious power, thus cast prophecy in the unflattering light of other historical arts of deception. The British writer Henry Drummond, in an essay on *False Prophets* published in the 1830s, made the connection between tyranny and prophecy explicit. False prophets "come in secretly"; they do not "begin by proclaiming their doctrines publicly in the open streets, in the places of greatest concourse," he complained. Unlike "true preachers," who "proclaim from the house-tops, in the market-places, in the great assemblies, and concourse of the people," false prophets "*creep into houses, and lead captive silly women laden with sins, led away with divers lusts.*" Many are "radicals in politics; despisers of the powers that be . . . flatterers of the people; abettors of insubordination in all classes."[80] Whatever their political persuasion, false prophets exercised an authority that was despotic, singular, and highly seductive.

To many conservative writers for whom the political chaos wrought by past generations of millenarians was still a fresh memory, Ann Lee of the Shakers epitomized the tyranny of religious fanaticism. Lee was widely criticized (especially by American writers smarting under British arrogance) for her dictatorial control of the Society of Believers. "To be a body of more than two thousand people, having no will of their own, but governed by a few Europeans conquering their adherents into the most unreserved subjection, argues some infatuating power; some deep, very deep design at bottom," warned Amos Taylor. "The Mother, it is said, obeys God through Christ; European elders obey her; American laborers obey them."[81] In similar language, the American prophetess Jemima Wilkinson was accused of fleeing into the wilderness of up-state New York in order to isolate her deluded followers from the virtues of enlightened society. "To emigrate with her followers into an entire wilderness, where, as she supposed, they would remain for a long time without the means of ordinary instruction, and in a great measure cut off from a constant intercourse with an enlightened community," David Hudson argued, "seemed more likely to perpetuate her dominion."[82] The power that a prophetess (in this case,

---

[80] Henry Drummond, *False Prophets* (London, 1834), pp. 4, 6.
[81] Amos Taylor, *A Narrative of the Strange Principles, Conduct, and Character of the People Known by the Name of Shakers* (Worcester, Mass., 1782), pp. 3–5.
[82] David Hudson, *History of Jemima Wilkinson, A Preacheress of the Eighteenth Century; Containing an Authentic Narrative of Her Life and Character, and of the Rise, Progress, and Conclusions of Her Ministry* (Geneva, N.Y., 1821), p. 50.

Joanna Southcott, the woman most often compared to Ann Lee) exercised over her followers smacked of the "black art," another critic complained, for "by it, she acts the part of a witch, fascinates her friends, and makes them do what she pleases, submit to what she pleases, and believes what she pleases." The prophet-witch "destroys the human understanding" of her devotees through her own "cunning."[83] Such mental tyranny was nothing short of slavery, "more lamentable" even, than African slavery—"a slavery which enchains the human mind, perverts the best of religions, and stifles the noblest pursuits of nature."[84]

The prophet's "dominion" extended beyond politics to encompass the commercial realm as well. Henry Drummond in a felicitous analogy compared false prophets to unscrupulous traders who "merchandize" faith, no better than the peddlers pushing shoddy wares on unsuspecting customers in the markets of London.[85] Anglo-Americans who had watched the "empire of goods" expand at an exponential rate alongside the political machinery of empire in the eighteenth century were accustomed to seeing parallels in the workings of government and the market, of course, but prophetic writers also had ready to hand the biblical example of Babylon as a site of conjoined political, economic, and sexual license to explain the source of the religious tyrant's peculiar power. "Credit" underwrote the expansion of both the state and the commercial economy, and credit was metaphorically figured in the literature of the eighteenth century as a creature of enormous appetite and ruthless ambition—a figure uncannily like that of the religious fanatic.[86] William Huntington encountered one such pretend prophet, a "hawking peddlar," in London in 1804 who managed to fool the simple-minded by tossing around "a few scraps of Scripture," making herself "the formidable object of their fear."[87] Millenarians

[83] Hann, *Remarkable Life . . . of Joanna Southcott*, pp. 31–32.

[84] "Some Account of Joanna Southcott, the Pretended Prophetess," *Observer*, Aug. 28, 1814, p. 2.

[85] Drummond, *False Prophets*, pp. 7–8.

[86] T. H. Breen, "An Empire of Goods: The Anglicization of Colonial America, 1690–1776," *Journal of British Studies* 25 (1986), pp. 467–99; Breen, " 'Baubles of Britain': The American and Consumer Revolutions of the Eighteenth Century," *Past and Present* 119 (1988), pp. 73–104; John Brewer, "Commercialization and Politics," in *The Birth of a Consumer Society: The Commercialization of Eighteenth-Century England*, ed. Neil McKendrick, John Brewer, and J. H. Plumb (Bloomington, Ind., 1982), pp. 217–62; Carole Shammas, *The Pre-Industrial Consumer in England and America* (New York, 1990); and *Of Consuming Interests: The Style of Life in the Eighteenth Century*, ed. Cary Carson, Ronald Hoffman, and Peter J. Albert (Charlottesville, Va., 1994).

[87] William Huntington, *The Cry of Little Faith Heard and Answered* (London, 1804), pp. 28–33. This "mumping hypocrite" met a fitting end—Huntington reported with satisfaction that "the Lord smote her with convulsions and horrors of mind; and at the same time being struck dumb, she was not permitted to tell what she felt, or what she feared . . . and so she died."

like Huntington were always quick to sniff out the mercenary aims of their rivals: Joanna Southcott charged Huntington himself with "making a merchandize of the people that come to your chapel" by selling tickets to his performances (Figure 1).[88]

Prophets sold false terrors just as merchants sold cheap goods at inflated prices and harlots sold their bodies, and for the same end—the selfish gratification of illicit desires. A scatological attack on Abigail Daton—"a Fool by Birth and a Prophetess by Profession"—published in the Philadelphia newspaper *Freeman's Journal* played with the multiple meanings of sexual and commercial corruption contained in the image of prophets as modern "Jezebels." Adopting the language of courtship, the writer professed his devotion to Daton ("My Dear Abby, you are a charmer; I believe in you, and you shall be my prophetess forever") while condemning her as a "public" woman. "You must know," he scolded upon observing the prophetess entering an apothecary's shop, "this disgusts me a little as a lover of yours, and makes me imagine you are not quite so cleanly as I would wish you to be. . . . I must suppose it was some nasty stuff which must have made you smell rather disagreeable.—Fie, my dear, a pretty woman ought never to anoint her body with drugs, or if she does it, she ought never to tell it to any body, and much less to the *impartial public.*"[89] Taking a less subtle approach, Charles Woodmason gleefully recounted the story of a "notable She Saint" who under the cloak of divine revelation pursued an adulterous relationship with a local preacher. "This Devotee was highly celebrated for her extraordinary Illuminations, Visions, and Communications," Woodmason wrote. "It is the same who in her Experience told a long story of an Angel coming to visit her in the Night thro' the Roof of her Cabbin—In flames of Fire too! It was very true that she was visited in the Night . . . and that it came to her all on Fire. Yes! But it was in the Fire of Lust; and this Angel was no other than her Ghostly Teacher, to whom she communicated a Revelation that it was ordain'd He should caress Her."[90]

The image of the prophet as sexual predator was less common, however, than one might suppose. Woodmason's eagerness to equate religious fa-

---

[88] Joanna Southcott, *An Answer to Mr. Brothers's Book, Published in Sept. 1806, And Observations on his Former Writings; Also, a Letter sent to Mr. Huntington* (London, 1806), pp. 33–34.

[89] "To the Most High Sybil, Abigail Daton, a Fool by Birth, and a Prophetess by Profession," *Freeman's Journal* (Philadelphia), Aug. 29, 1787.

[90] *Carolina Backcountry on the Eve of Revolution*, p. 104. For another example of a woman who used her prophetic wiles to ensnare a reluctant lover, see the account of Eliza Niles ("an old maid with but one leg") in the *Bethlehem Star* 1 (Jan. 1824), p. 20. Such stories linking prophecy to illicit sexuality were as rare at the end of the revolutionary era as at the beginning.

Figure 1. "The Relics of a Prophet; or, Huntingdon's Sale." Department of Prints and Drawings, British Museum.

naticism with unbridled sexuality was not shared by most critics. (The contrast with the chorus of bawdy criticism that surrounded the French Prophets of the early 1700s is telling; behind every twitch of the Camisards, critics saw raw sexual energy.)[91] Even the infamous "mystical pregnancy" of the British prophetess Joanna Southcott at the highly suspect age of sixty-five was more often caricatured as an unscrupulous plot to defraud her followers than an example of illicit or unnatural sexual desires. A satirical play published in London after Southcott's death in 1814 featured a trio of petty crooks who set out to swindle the public: Jezebel Gammonall, "a pretended prophetess," Maria Weakwit, "her dupe, residing with her," and Lathrend, "a preacher of Jezebel's." As "Jezebel" swills gin and counts the day's take, Lathrend's clerk marvels that "This prophet-trade is vastly good, Better by half than chopping wood."[92] It was money and fame, not sex, that prophets wanted, and their ability to manipulate the flourishing consumer culture of Anglo-America's urban centers to inflate their public worth was the real secret behind their success.

The critique of prophets as avaricious was another variation on the "imposture thesis," the idea that corruption was traceable to the deliberate actions of selfish people acting in their own, rather than in the people's interest. Appropriately for such a highly commercialized society, prophets were routinely criticized for making a fortune out of their art. "As the love of money . . . hath spread itself so widely through the hearts of the present generation," Nimrod Hughes acknowledged, "it can be no matter of surprise that this work should be considered by such sordid minds as a mere scheme, devised for the purpose of making money."[93] The *Times* explicitly contrasted the luxurious life supposedly enjoyed by Joanna Southcott with the aesceticism of true prophets. The ancient prophets "fasted often . . . lived coarsely, and were more coarsely clad," but Joanna "passed much of her time in bed—in downy indulgence—ate much and often—and prayed—never. She loved to lodge delicately and feast luxuriously."[94] Suspicion of prophets as fortune-

---

[91] See, for example, Samuel Keimer, *Brand Pluck'd from the Burning*. Tim Hitchcock reviews the uncoupling of radical religion from sexual anxieties over the course of the eighteenth century in *English Sexualities, 1700–1800* (New York, 1997).

[92] Peter Pindar, Esq., *Physic and Delusion! or, Jezebel and the Doctors! A Farce, in Two Acts* (London, 1814), p. 10.

[93] Hughes, *Solemn Warning*, p. 10.

[94] *Times*, Jan. 12, 1815, p. 3. Southcott was routinely accused of selling her "seals" for profit, a charge she vigorously denied, and most historians dismiss; see, for an example, the article in *Bell's Weekly Messenger*, Sept. 4, 1814, p. 6, which voices the popular suspicion that Southcott was hawking these "*passports to Heaven.*"

hunters seems to have flourished wherever market relations were transforming agrarian villages into capitalist societies. The backcountry settlements of northern New England were home to a number of prophetic movements in the 1790s and early 1800s that combined religious seeking with treasure-seeking in illuminating ways. The well-publicized case of Nathaniel "Priest" Wood in 1800 shows just how entwined religious and economic anxieties were in these decades. Sporting a divining rod he named "St. John's rod" for its prophetic powers, Wood gathered a group of desperate farmers around him, promising to reveal all manner of hidden riches during the winter months of 1800–1801. As retold by a contemporary observer, the rod was used for a variety of purposes both sacred and profane: to predict whether the sick "would live or die," to designate the chosen people of God (the so-called "Jews" of America, most of whom were unaware of their true identity), and—most suspiciously—to locate deposits of gold and silver which would be used to "pave the streets of the New Jerusalem." With the help of a local diviner (later unmasked as a fugitive forger), Wood soon had his followers busily digging away in the stony soil of Vermont for the promised treasure which, somehow, never materialized.[95] That so many people were so quick to credit "St. John's rod" with the power to find both salvation and wealth speaks to the power of fantasies of supernatural deliverance in an era of rapid economic change.[96]

Whether quacks or cheats, "false" prophets spoke in a distinctive dialect that was the final, and most definitive, mark of imposture in revolutionary Anglo-America. The preoccupation with deceit in all its guises was certainly not new in the revolutionary era; the preoccupation with the *language* of deceit, however, took a new turn. In the fiercely partisan political wars of the 1790s and early 1800s, language was a key battleground as conservatives and republicans vied over the verbal norms of the new public sphere which had first emerged earlier in the century in the social interstices of the Anglo-American civic landscape—the coffeehouses, reading rooms, lyceums, and debating societies. Each of these venues represented not just a place for would-be political actors to congregate and exchange ideas, but also a distinctive "discursive

[95] Wood's story is told in a nineteenth-century account; Barnes Frisbie, *History of Middletown, Vermont* (Rutland, Vt., 1867), pp. 44–46. Stephen Marini provides a good overview of the religious seeking common to the northern backcountry after the Revolution in *Radical Sects in Revolutionary America* (Cambridge, Mass., 1982).

[96] Alan Taylor, "The Early Republic's Supernatural Economy: Treasure Seeking in the American Northeast, 1780–1830," *American Quarterly* 38 (1986), pp. 6–34.

institution," in David Shields's words, with its own rules for talking (and occasionally writing) about politics. The emergence of new modes of communication alongside new sites and new topics for public discussion politicized language to an unprecedented degree, to the point where citizenship itself—the ultimate mark of public standing—became as much a "linguistic concept" as a political one in the late eighteenth and early nineteenth centuries.[97]

Prophecy had always been a "discursive institution" as well as a form of exegesis. From medieval times on, the manner of prophetic expression had been as varied and disputed as the content of the prophecies themselves: some visionaries spoke in verse, some in foreign tongues they did not pretend to understand; many switched pronouns, from first to second to third person, with bewildering ease; some sang or chanted; others spoke with altered voices, in a deep monotone or high-pitched squeak. The more varied the expression, the greater the interpretive license of the speaker, and hence the greater the potential to mislead or confuse one's listeners. The polyphonic voice of late medieval and early modern prophecy posed interpretive challenges that stumped even the most determined opponent.[98]

By the eighteenth century, the discursive range of prophecy had narrowed considerably. Few prophets spoke in trance, for instance, as did the French Prophets of the early 1700s. Fewer still spoke in verse, although there were exceptions (Joanna Southcott being the most notable). Most affected a variant of the "plain speaking" then being aggressively promoted by Methodist itinerants and radical republicans alike, in which the speaker sought to avoid flowery modifiers and convoluted analogies in favor of the simplest expression available.[99]

[97] David Shields, *Civil Tongues and Polite Letters in British America* (Chapel Hill, N.C., 1995), p. xiv; Olivia Smith, *The Politics of Language, 1791–1819* (Oxford, 1984), p. xii. In the American context, see Christopher Grasso, *A Speaking Aristocracy: Transforming Public Discourse in Eighteenth-Century Connecticut* (Chapel Hill, N.C., 1999); Kenneth Cmiel, *Democratic Eloquence: The Fight over Popular Speech in Nineteenth-Century America* (New York, 1990); and Michael Warner, *The Letters of the Republic: Publication and the Public Sphere in Eighteenth-Century America* (Cambridge, Mass., 1990).

[98] On the eclectic linguistic styles of medieval visionaries, see Elizabeth Petroff, *Medieval Women's Visionary Literature* (New York, 1986); Laurie Finke, "Mystical Bodies and the Dialogics of Vision," in *Maps of Flesh and Light: The Religious Experiences of Medieval Women Mystics,* ed. Ulrike Wiethaus (Syracuse, N.Y., 1993). Michel de Certeau traces the reformulation of the "baroque" tradition of visionary writing in the seventeenth century in *The Mystical Fable,* vol. 1, *The Sixteenth and Seventeenth Centuries,* trans. Michael B. Smith (Chicago, 1992).

[99] On the tension between the prophetic and the plain-speaking voice in early Methodism, see Christine Krueger, *The Reader's Repentance: Women Preachers, Women Writers, and Nineteenth-Century Social Discourse* (Chicago, 1992).

While the emphasis on "plain speaking" was not uncontested, as we shall see in Chapter 4, there was a noticeable diminution in the more arcane rhetorical flourishes that had distinguished medieval and early modern visionary writing by the mid-eighteenth century. Prophets who continued to use extravagant language risked being labeled "false" prophets.

Political conservatives led the way in developing the critique of the language of religious enthusiasm as vulgar and undisciplined.[100] Plebian millenarians like William Huntington were favorite targets of abuse for their coarse language, described by one critic as "the loathsome spout of peevish rancor . . . unmannerly, absurd, and illiterate."[101] A popular satire on the Swedenborgians made fun of their peculiar love of elliptical expression. As "Jack Honesty" complains that "I was lately overtaken with a storm of *esses, truths, and falses*, and such outlandish gibberish as made my poor ship pitch so violently," his friend "Captain Condescension" advises him, "Less metaphor, Jack, and more plain English."[102] An anti-Shaker pamphlet criticized the Believers' peculiar mode of worship for its promiscuous blend of expressive styles. "When they meet together for their worship, some will be singing, each one his own tune; some without words, in an Indian tone, some sing jigg tunes, some tunes of their own making, in an unknown mutter, which they call new tongues . . . till the different tunes, groaning, jumping, dancing, drumming, laughing, talking, and fluttering, shouting, and hissing, makes a perfect bedlam; this they call the worship of God."[103] It is no surprise to find Charles Woodmason poking fun at the "New Tongues" of the New Lights, whom he said spoke "In a barbarous Dialect—A constant Menotomy A squeaking, untuneable, unintelligible Jargon. Neither Verse nor Prose, Singing or Speaking."[104]

But it is surprising to find that so many evangelicals agreed with Woodmason. Here again, John Wesley—the Methodist champion of the poor—proves a helpful guide to popular eighteenth-century notions of the expressive boundaries of godly speech. He visited another pretend prophet in April

---

[100] Sandra Gustafson, *Eloquence Is Power: Oratory and Performance in Early America* (Chapel Hill, N.C., 2000).

[101] William Huntington, S.S., *A Feeble Dispute with a Wise and Learned Man* (London, 1793), pp. 10, 16.

[102] Amicus Veritas, *Dialogue Between Captain Condescension and Jack Honesty, Two British Tars, Concerning the Doctrine of Baron Swedenborg* (Colchester, 1813), p. 3.

[103] Valentine Rathbun, *An Account of the Matter, Form, and Manner of a New and Strange Religion Taught and Propagated by a Number of* EUROPEANS . . . (Providence, R.I., 1781), pp. 11–12.

[104] Woodmason, *Carolina Backcountry on the Eve of Revolution*, p. 114.

1746, and gave this assessment: "I could not at all think that he was sent of God: (1) Because he appeared to be full of himself, vain, heady, and opinionated. (2) Because he spoke with extreme bitterness, both of the King, and of all the bishops, and all the clergy. (3) Because he aimed at talking Latin, but could not; plainly showing he understood not his own calling."[105] Wesley was particularly irritated by what he considered the stylistic bombasity of "antinomian" speech—speech, that is, uttered by religious enthusiasts who disdained the literary and moral conventions of Christian society.[106] Listing his objections to the "mystic writers" (among whom he included Jacob Boehme, William Law, and Emanuel Swedenborg) in 1764, Wesley singled out their peculiar style of writing for special contempt. Their "whole phraseology" is "both unscriptural and affectedly mysterious," he charged. Boehme's *Mysterium Magnum*, a canonical text in mystical circles, was "the most sublime nonsense, inimitable bombast"; Swedenborg's *Theologia Coelestis* was composed of nothing but "ravings." "St. John speaks as high and as deep things as Jacob Behmen," Wesley complained; "Why then does not Jacob speak as plain as him?"[107] Like Wesley, Huntington was disgusted by the affectation of classical learning that despoiled modern visionary writing; "Paul never tells young coxcombs to stuff their noodles with scraps of Greek, crumbs of Hebrew, and incoherent shreds of dog Latin," he protested.[108]

Mystic writers were not unaware of the criticism that they used unintelligible or inappropriate language. But, they believed, strange and wonderful revelations needed a strange and wonderful language to fully convey God's message to a deaf world. God's work in these "latter days," the Shaker prophet Ann Lee said, was "*a strange work . . . even a marvellous work and a wonder.*"[109] William Law, the influential eighteenth-century popularizer of

---

[105] *Journal of John Wesley*, 3:239.

[106] The original "antinomian," Anne Hutchinson, was likewise criticized for her "canting Harangue" and "vapouring Talk," in the words of Charles Chauncy (*Wonderful Narrative*, p. 80). On the verbal dimensions of Hutchinson's challenge, see Gustafson, *Eloquence Is Power*, pp. 29–33; on the connection between religious dissent and ungodly speech, see Jane Kamensky, *Governing the Tongue: The Politics of Speech in Early New England* (New York, 1997).

[107] *Journal of John Wesley*, 5:46, 5:440. Francis Asbury, his American lieutenant, shared Wesley's disdain for the linguistic excesses of so-called "antinomians," one of whom "gabbled strangely" and another used "a few pompous and swelling words." Asbury, *Journal of Francis Asbury*, 1:600, 1:188. Michel de Certeau explains how mystical language became a synonym for jargon by the end of the seventeenth century in *The Mystic Fable*.

[108] William Huntington, *The Modern Plasterer Detected, and his Untempered Mortar Discovered* (London, 1787), p. 33.

[109] *Testimony of Christ's Second Appearing*, p. 9.

mystical theology, spelled out the connection in a letter advising a new translation of Jacob Boehme's classic texts for a modern audience. "A new Translator of J.B. is not to have it in his intention to make his author more intelligible by softening or refining his Language," he explained. "His stile is what it is strange, & uncommon, not because he wanted learning and skill in words but because what he saw & conceived was quite new & strange, never seen or spoken of before and therefore if he was to put it down in writing, words must be used to signify that which they had never done before."[110] And after all, truth was truth—however badly expressed. "Should Sir Isaac Newton's system only appear to us undigested, in bad rhyme and bad English, ought we to reject it on that account?" queried another defender of the sometimes uncouth language of prophecy.[111]

Even mystic writers like Henry Brooke recoiled from the indiscriminate use of florid language among some of his contemporaries; he reprimanded Ralph Mather (who feared being thought a "mystic babbler") in 1779 for his "wild and extravagant letter." "You have been woefully captivated in the *Turba* of those spirits, among whom you are . . . and with the *horns of ye Lamb can now speak the Language of the Dragon.*" The Muggletonians, one of the last holdouts among the radical Civil War sects, chastised one of their own for her "subtil and misterius" language which, they charged, she used to "baffel and perplex Ignorant people."[112] By the conclusion of the Napoleonic Wars in 1814, few prophets were still "afflicted" by the "vein of flightiness" that Mather and other visionaries had succumbed to earlier in the century. Some went so far as to argue that the power of divine revelation made prophets more—not less—articulate. Though the fifteenth-century Cheshire prophet Robert Nixon "was a driveller, and could not speak common sense when he was uninspired," one writer noted, "yet in delivering his prophecies, he spoke plainly and sensibly."[113]

These, then, were the distinguishing marks of "true" as opposed to "false" prophets in the revolutionary era: an unwillingness to claim direct revelation beyond the parameters laid out by the church fathers; an ability to interpret the mysterious prophetic texts without recourse to "vain imaginings" or fan-

[110] Law to Mr. Penny, Apr. 8, 1747, Brooke Letterbook, p. 175.

[111] F. Lewis, *Why Should We Not ALL Take up Arms?* (London, 1803), p. 17.

[112] Henry Brooke to Ralph Mather, 1779, Brooke Letterbook, p. 75; Mather to Brooke, May 16, 1776, Brooke Letterbook, p. 150. For the Muggletonians, see George Hudson's letter to Martha Collier, n.d., Muggletonian Archives.

[113] *Past, Present and to Come: The Prophecy at Large, of Robert Nixon, the Cheshire Prophet* (London, 1810), p. 19.

ciful delusions; a clear head and stable nervous system; a becoming modesty; and, not least, a preference for plain over extravagant language. It is not surprising that so few contenders passed these multiple tests of legitimacy, for the rules of debate were drawn up to seriously disadvantage those who rejected the prevailing assumptions of public discourse itself. Prophets always flirted with anachronism—this was their special charm, and their greatest vulnerability.

But some did prevail.

Chapter 2

Varieties of Prophecy: Fortune-Tellers, Visionists, and Millenarians

We can think of revolutionary-era prophecy as spanning a continuum ranging from simple folk practices to learned exegesis. On the lower end of the spectrum are the cunning people, folk healers, and "second-sighted" whose ability to see into and manipulate the future was limited in kind and scope. Their prophetic powers rarely reached beyond the personal and the immediate: unexpected deaths, sudden reversals in fortune, warnings from beyond the grave to reform now or pay later. The world of peasants and common laborers was still a world of magic, despite the best efforts of Protestant reformers and Enlightenment popularizers who had worked so tirelessly since the sixteenth century to root out all vestiges of popish superstition and primitive occult beliefs. A robust if untheorized collection of magical and quasi-magical practices continued to arm Anglo-Americans against the exigencies of life, death, and random misfortune well into the nineteenth century.[1]

Elizabeth Hobson told John Wesley in 1768 that "From my childhood, when any of our neighbours died . . . I used to see them, either just when they died, or a little before; and I was not frightened at all, it was so common."[2] Wesley was fascinated by such folk beliefs, which he refused to dismiss as superstitious nonsense; his journals are full of stories of men and women who spoke to angels, dreamed of buried treasure, foretold their own and others'

---

[1] Keith Thomas, *Religion and the Decline of Magic* (New York, 1971); David D. Hall, *Worlds of Wonder, Days of Judgment: Popular Religious Belief in Early New England* (Cambridge, Mass., 1990); Jon Butler, *Awash in a Sea of Faith: Christianizing the American People* (Cambridge, Mass., 1990); John Wigger, *Taking Heaven by Storm: Methodism and the Rise of Popular Christianity in America* (New York, 1998); Erik R. Seeman, *Pious Persuasions: Laity and Clergy in Eighteenth-Century New England* (Baltimore, 1999); John L. Brooke, " 'The True Spiritual Seed': Sectarian Religion and the Persistence of the Occult in Eighteenth-Century New England," in *Wonders of the Invisible World, 1600–1900*, ed. Peter Benes (Boston, 1995), pp. 107–26.

[2] Nehemiah Curnock, ed., *Journal of the Rev. John Wesley, A.M.*, standard ed., 8 vols. (London, 1910), 5:267.

deaths, and healed the sick using folk remedies—all recounted without a hint of condescension. Bridget Bostock, an "elderly woman," healed "blindness, lameness, and many diseases" by "stroking the part chiefly affected, and sometimes applying a little spittle."[3] Daniel Car, an apothecary's apprentice, told a strange ghost tale to a curious Wesley, who obviously plied him for details. One night Car heard "strange noises in our house" and saw "a man standing in the middle of the chamber, in light-coloured cloths and a green velvet waistcoat, with a lighted torch in his hand." The apparition told Car, "I am the spirit of Richard Sims, who died here in the year 1702" and pleaded with the young apothecary to warn his niece and nephew that they must "turn to God, for he will die on the 26th of next month, and she will die on the 30th." The ghost even dictated a letter for Car to write to his nephew, "word for word," and singed a corner of the paper with his burning torch as tangible proof of his visitation.[4] Wesley was frankly agnostic about these supernatural appearances, at one point telling two young men who wondered whether the specters who visited them in the night were "good or bad spirits" that he "could not resolve" the question.[5]

Not all evangelical preachers (from whose diaries and memoirs much of our knowledge of lay religious practice comes) were as willing as Wesley to credit these stories of ghostly visits and occult powers. Yet despite their skepticism they were reluctant to dismiss out-of-hand such evidence, perhaps because they themselves often experienced unaccountable gifts of the spirit. Dreams and visions, many of a prophetic nature, were commonplace occurrences in the lives of most evangelicals. God often communicated with his people through such means, even if it was sometimes difficult to tell the difference between a vision sent by God and mere fancy. Nancy Towle, the most noted female preacher of her day, was "certain that God has not infrequently spoken to me, in dreams, and in visions of the night," and most sectarian preachers agreed.[6] The messages that God sent by way of dreams were usually intimate ones, intended for the personal knowledge of the dreamer himself. Freeborn Garrettson, who often found himself, as he put it, "in a kind of visionary way," had "a most remarkable vision of the night" in which "it was revealed to me what I was to suffer; and that the Lord would stand by me, so

[3] *Journal of John Wesley*, 8:157.
[4] Ibid., 4:148.
[5] Ibid., 5:587.
[6] Nancy Towle, *Vicissitudes Illustrated in the Experiences of Nancy Towle, in Europe and America. Written by Herself* (Charleston, S.C., 1832), p. 108.

that my enemies should not injure me."[7] Joseph Thomas, known as the "White Pilgrim" for his distinctive dress and vow of poverty, recalled one dream in which he was visited by "Isaiah the Prophet," who told him to "rise up and I will give thee something which came from heaven." The prophet showed Thomas a piece of wood, "deeply stained all over with blood," and a loaf of bread—the former signifying the suffering he was to endure and the latter the timing and manner of his death: "this loaf will last forty-eight years and six months," Thomas was told, "about which time, for the sake of what thou dost carry, *strangers shall kill thee*."[8] Another Old Testament figure, the prophet Nathan, made a visit to Lorenzo Dow in a dream, and when asked by Dow "how long I should live? SAID HE, UNTIL YOU ARE TWO AND TWENTY."[9]

Dreams that predicted future events rather than simply revealing one's spiritual condition always carried a whiff of the black arts about them that preachers found difficult to countenance. As always, clerical opinion was divided between those who hewed closely to the orthodox line relegating direct revelation to a bygone biblical era and those who believed that God continued to communicate with his people in direct ways. Francis Asbury, the ascetic leader of American Methodism who in general abhorred religious extravagance as the devil's handiwork, could not deny that several people he met on his travels had accurately prophesied their own deaths. Rachel Selby "dreamed that within three weeks she should die of the smallpox," he noted in 1783; soon after she "died triumphantly."[10] Freeborn Garrettson encountered a woman in 1779 who "told me many things that seemed strange to me. She said she knew when she was to dye and what death she was to dye. She told me she was to be put to death by false witnesses and that in a short time."[11] An oft-reprinted pamphlet told the story of an English clergyman,

[7] Robert Drew Simpson, ed., *American Methodist Pioneer: The Life and Journals of the Rev. Freeborn Garrettson, 1752–1837* (Rutland, Vt., 1984), pp. 101, 95.

[8] Joseph Thomas, *The Life of the Pilgrim, Joseph Thomas* (Winchester, Va., 1817), p. 20.

[9] Lorenzo Dow, *History of Cosmopolite; or, the Four Volumes of Lorenzo's Diary* (New York, 1814), p. 10. Dow went to live a long if not robust life, a discrepancy explained by another vision. On board the ship that would carry him to England he dreamed that "I died and was buried—I stood and looked at my body, and behold it began to putrefy and moulder. I was then a mystery to myself, to see my body in one place and I standing in another . . . a voice seemed to answer, I will explain this mystery to you: If you had tarried in America, you would have died as the prophet predicted, and your body would have been mouldering as you now see it; but now you are preserved for future usefulness" (*Cosmopolite*, pp. 85–86).

[10] Elmer T. Clark, ed., *The Journal and Letters of Francis Asbury*, 2 vols. (Nashville, Tenn., 1958), 1:443.

[11] Simpson, *American Methodist Pioneer*, p. 154.

Thomas Chamberlain, who was visited by "one like a Husbandman (tho' he seemed more like an Angel)" and told to preach the next Sunday with "his shroud on and coffin before him." After delivering "the Message [the Angel] had given him to warn the inhabitants of the earth," the minister dropped dead in his pulpit.[12] Theophilus Gates recounted the "melancholy" case of a man who ignored a warning to avoid communion; "A few days before the sacrament was to be administered, he was warned as by a voice, not to partake of it; by reason, it is supposed, of something he had done. He, however, did partake of it, and was found hung on a tree not many days afterward."[13] Like many preachers, Gates was careful to distinguish such warnings from "mere imagination or a visionary fancy," though in practice it was hard to tell the difference.[14]

Less common, though certainly more unsettling, were dreams that predicted the fate of a third party. Nancy Towle freely admitted that she herself was privy to supernatural premonitions. In bed one night, she saw "a 'deathlike shadow of a human being,' or the form of a man (as it seemed) [standing] erect before me. My blood chilled, as I gazed for a moment." Four months later she learned that a man who had scoffed at her visions "accidentally fell from the wharf; and so was seen no more!"[15] Hugh Bourne was "filled with the most fearful apprehensions" when told by Mary Dunnell, "a great visionist," that "she had seen his two bosom-friends, Clowes and Alcock, quite on the background, their trumpets laying idle, and their heretofore overflowing cups nearly empty."[16] Benjamin Abbott had a disturbing dream about a man he trusted. "In a dream I thought I saw the preacher under whom I was awakened, drunk, and playing cards, with his garments all defiled with dirt. . . . In about three weeks after, I heard that the poor unfortunate preacher had fallen into sundry gross sins, and was expelled from the methodist connection: Thus I saw my dream fulfilled."[17]

[12] England's Timely Remembrancer, *The Minister Preaching his own Funeral Sermon. Being a Warning from Heaven to all vile Sinners on Earth. With a particular Relation of many Wonderful Things seen by the Rev. Mr.* THOMAS CHAMBERLAIN, *in a Vision just before his Decease, the precise Time of which was shewn unto him,* 10th ed. (Boston, 1791), pp. 4–6.

[13] Theophilus Gates, *The Life and Writings of Theophilus R. Gates,* 2d ed. (New York, 1818), pp. 178–79.

[14] Ibid., p. 116.

[15] Towle, *Vicissitudes Illustrated,* p. 112.

[16] John Walford, *Memoirs of the Life and Labours of the Late Venerable Hugh Bourne,* vol. 1 (London, 1855), p. 336. Mary Dunnell was a source of constant friction in the Primitive Methodist community until she was finally disowned in 1811.

[17] Benjamin Abbott, *The Experience and Gospel Labours of the Rev. Benjamin Abbott,* ed. John Firth (New York, 1805), p. 21.

An exchange between William Smythe Babcock, a Freewill Baptist preacher in Vermont, and one of his parishioners reveals the ambivalence many evangelicals felt about such occurrences. After he saw an apparition who resembled a woman in his congregation, Babcock "told Mrs. Bates this afternoon that if I saw any appearance last Saturday evening, it was an appearance of herself. . . . I told her I had not been in the habit of believing such kinds of stories, as appearances of people to others either before or after death. She said, she believed that many had been warned of approaching death in such a way—And thought it was likely, it was a warning to her. She said she thanked me for telling her so."[18] Premonitions of this nature were dangerous in the wrong hands, and evangelicals were careful to couch their prophecies in strictly contingent terms.

With these revelations we are getting closer to the elusive world of popular prophecy. For the most part these premonitions of death and disaster were private messages to believers about their own fate, or occasionally the fate of others. They warned of immediate dangers that would befall individuals rather than collective judgments of biblical proportion. It is perhaps not fair to classify them as prophecies at all, though they contained the critical element of prediction. On occasion, though, ordinary men and women were visited by spirits who carried messages of wider import that more clearly belong in the category of prophecy. Eliza Thomas, who published her vision in a cheap pamphlet in 1800, told of a nighttime visit by the ghost of an old school friend who had recently died. "I am come not to terrify you," the ghost (somewhat disingenuously) reassured Eliza, "but to discourse on the great and important realities of the external world." After then warning her friend that "you must soon, ah very soon, die," the ghost spelled out for Eliza the "dreadful and lamentable situation of many of the people of this Country;—they are deluded;—believing that God is not a being who will punish the transgressions of their children." The "age of depravity has now arrived," she concluded with a flourish, and "soon will a change take place."[19] The allusion to Revelation is unmistakable in the final phrase, even while the first part of the vision resembles more an ordinary exercise in fortune-telling. Jeremiah Palmer, a member of William Babcock's church, was favored with a visit from an apparition who resembled his dead wife. He asked "whether she came in the name of Jesus, she answered Yes—she then delivered

---

[18] William Smythe Babcock Diary, Aug. 7, 1802, Babcock Papers, American Antiquarian Society, Worcester, Mass.

[19] Eliza Thomas, *A Vision; Tending to Edify, Astonish, and Instruct: Experienced by Miss Eliza Thomas* (Stonington, Conn., 1800), p. 6.

three messages to him to deliver to as many different persons." When pressed by Palmer to explain the Millennium, "she said the great reformation which we called the Millennium had already begun before your day or mine, & when arrived to its meridian Christ would appear & reign a thousand years with his saints."[20] Glimpses of natural disasters seen in nightmares often led to larger apocalyptic visions: a young man who dreamed that he saw "the world on fire—at a distance saw the fire flashing over the rocks and mountains, and fast approaching to him," inspired the Freewill Baptist preacher Abel Thorton to contemplate the end of time. "When I lay down on my bed and shut my eyes, it appeared as though the judgment-day was fast approaching—I could view the great conflagration, and I thought this would be the last opportunity I should have to repent."[21]

Certain key phrases and images link these visions to the wider ambit of Anglo-American prophecy. Visions did not need to reference the entire scenario of Revelation to qualify as prophecies. They might hint at awful calamities to come using the language of vials or seals; they might speak of judgment with a capital "J" or refer in passing to key sites of millennial geography—the cities of Babylon and the New Jerusalem, the Euphrates River, the "wilderness" into which the "Woman" flees in the twelfth chapter; they might enumerate in vague terms the "signs of the times" or lament the proliferation of false prophets. The casual insertion of images drawn from the Books of Daniel and Revelation in common visions of judgment, punishment, and redemption testifies to the widespread familiarity of large segments of the Anglo-American populace with the more learned traditions of prophetic exegesis.

Popular exposure to this tradition came largely from the efforts of itinerant preachers to spread God's Word throughout the British and American countryside. Though literacy rates were relatively high in the Anglo-American world, especially in the former colonies, contact with a living witness was more important than access to printed texts in generating a broad popular awareness of prophetic possibilities. Simple statements such as William Babcock's journal entry for February 19, 1802—"Evening, had considerable conversation with Br. & Capt. Hubbard upon the present fulfilling of the Prophecies by the Commotions of the Nations the last 25 Years"—testify to the easy familiarity of most Anglo-Americans with the prophetic meaning

---

[20] Babcock Diary, Sept. 20, 1802.

[21] Abel Thornton, *The Life of Elder Abel Thornton, Late of Johnston, R.I., A Preacher in the Free-will Baptist Connexion. Written by Himself* (Providence, R.I., 1828), p. 16.

inherent in the events of the day.[22] Evangelical preachers routinely read the prophetic texts and jotted notes to themselves on their present significance in their journals; they took their sermons as often from the Book of Revelation as from any other biblical text; they counseled their followers to study and heed the "signs of the times" and to prepare themselves for the Day of Judgment. In inns, private homes, and meetinghouses they spoke of warnings, punishments, and retribution to people who knew exactly what they were talking about. And sometimes they crossed the line from preacher to prophet themselves. A vague reference to unsealing "the mystery which hath been hid from ages" inserted by Benjamin Abbott in one of his sermons led his listeners to conclude rashly "that I was going to prophesy, and would tell how the [revolutionary] war would terminate." Abbott obliged, despite his ordinary reluctance to venture into the murk of prophetic prediction.[23] In the case of John Granade, "extraordinary zeal" produced "extravagance"; "at one time," his biographer confessed, the blustery itinerant "assumed the role of a prophet; but his prophecy signally failing to come to pass, he was suspended from the functions of the ministry for about three months."[24]

The excesses of the Methodist Awakening, in particular, were a fertile breeding ground for self-made prophets.[25] Methodist practices often flirted with the magical, including faith healing, the discernment of spirits, and sudden, overpowering conversions common in the early years of the movement. Rural audiences were quick to smell trickery when scores of stricken saints fell under an itinerant's spell; "Some said [John] Granade had some kind of powder to throw over the people; some said he had some secret trick by which he threw them down."[26] In Britain, an offshoot known as the "Magic Methodists" flourished in the Delamere Forest in northwest England under the charismatic leadership of James Crawfoot in the early 1800s, though "what the world ascribed to magic," Hugh Bourne explained, were in reality "visions and trances which frequently occurred among them."[27] It was a small step from faith healing and speaking in tongues to pretensions of

[22] Babcock Diary, Feb. 19, 1802.

[23] Abbott, *Experience and Gospel Labours*, pp. 69–70.

[24] Richard Price, *Holston Methodism: From Its Origins to the Present Time* (Nashville, Tenn., 1906), pp. 18–19.

[25] Methodism's unique stress on the mystical relationship between believers and Christ, Cynthia Lynn Lyerly has suggested, "made each a prophet." *Methodism and the Southern Mind, 1770–1810* (New York, 1998), p. 9.

[26] Price, *Holston Methodism*, p. 15.

[27] *Memoirs of Hugh Bourne*, p. 141.

prophetic sight. Peter Cartwright traced the rise of prophecy directly to the overheated revivals he himself organized in the American backcountry in the early 1800s. A "great evil arose from the heated and wild imagination of some," he lamented. "They professed to fall into trances and see visions . . . and when they came to, they professed to have seen heaven and hell, to have seen God, angels, the devil and the damned; they would prophesy, and, under the pretence of Divine inspiration, predict the time of the end of the world, and the ushering in of the great millennium. This was the most troublesome delusion of all," he argued, for "it made such an appeal to the ignorance, superstition, and credulity of the people, even saint as well as sinner."[28]

To listen to Cartwright, one would think that the hardworking Methodist itinerancy—the heart and soul of the evangelical movement on both sides of the Atlantic—was being overrun by a motley assortment of prophets, visionaries, and vulgar enthusiasts. He exaggerated, but not by much. Combing through evangelical memoirs, pamphlets, newspapers, denominational records, and local histories, we can identify some three hundred men and women who were recognized (by themselves or others) as prophets in England and North America in the period 1750 to 1820. The following section offers a composite profile of these individuals, 60 percent (189) of whom lived in Britain, 40 percent (126) in the United States or Canada. The total figure surely underrepresents the actual number by a considerable margin; it is based on a survey of published sources (pamphlets, broadsides, newspapers, literary journals, and evangelical memoirs), sources which do not capture the full range of unorthodox religious activity but only those individuals and practices thought noteworthy by churchmen and the educated elite. If the published memoirs of evangelical preachers are at all representative of the experiences of those who did not keep journals, or who did not offer their journals for public consumption, millenarian prophecy was a widespread and persistent feature of popular religious culture throughout the late eighteenth and early nineteenth centuries. We can probably multiply our figure of 315 by a significant factor and still be reasonably confident that we have underestimated the total number of prophets and prophetesses in Anglo-America during the revolutionary era.

We can further divide this number into two groups—those who gathered followers into loose millenarian movements, and those who confined

---

[28] Peter Cartwright, *Autobiography of Peter Cartwright, the Backwoods Preacher*, ed. W. P. Strickland (New York, 1856), pp. 51–52.

their prophetic efforts to written interventions. Among the former we would find some of the best-known public figures of the day (Joanna Southcott, Richard Brothers, Ann Lee, David Austin, Jemima Wilkinson), as well as hundreds of obscure individuals whose names have barely survived the vagaries of history and intellectual fashion. Among the latter we would include the dozens of millennial writers, almost all men, who made prophecy such a potent political genre during the crises of the American and French Revolutions. For a select few, prophecy was a lifelong calling; for most, a temporary detour through the thickets of enthusiasm. Together these millenarian prophets and millennial authors formed a powerful counter-public to the Anglican churchmen, dissenting societies, republican literary clubs, and patrician elites who shaped learned opinion in revolutionary Anglo-America.

Millenarian Prophets

Most prophets could identify a single moment of revelation, an epiphany in which they first realized their status as a chosen one. These epiphanies ranged from the dramatic to the mundane—from deathbed conversions to quiet convincement. On the more dramatic side were men and women who escaped ignomy, illness, starvation, even death, through the miraculous intercession of God or one of his spiritual emissaries. A period of physical debility (whether natural or self-induced) was a good way to prepare the mind to receive a divine summons to serve. Jemima Wilkinson, the ex-Quaker who founded a millenarian sect at the very outbreak of the revolutionary war in America, was literally caught from death to life as she lay ill with a "fatal fever" in October 1776. "The heavens were open'd and she saw too Archangels descending from the east bringing a Sealed Pardon from the living God. . . . And then taking her leave of the family between the hour of nine and ten in the morning, [she] dropped the dying flesh & yielded up the Ghost. And according to the declaration of the Angels, the Spirit took full possession of the Body it now Animates."[29] Her fellow American, David Austin, dated his prophetic powers from the bout with scarlet fever that almost killed him in 1796. A severe emotional shock could sometimes be as effective as bodily illness in awakening a prophet. Incarceration inspired prophetic visions in a number of Anglo-Americans, including Nimrod Hughes and the Shaker founder, Ann Lee.

---

[29] "A Memorandum of the Introduction of the Fatal Fever," undated, Jemima Wilkinson Papers 1771–1849, Department of Manuscripts and University Archives, Cornell University Library, Ithaca, N.Y. (hereafter JW Papers).

Yet these cases of miraculous recovery from severe distress are rare. For the most part, prophets discovered their unique powers in remarkably ordinary circumstances. A vision in the night, a barely perceptible impression of a voice whispering in one's ear, a chance encounter on the streets or in a shop with an angel disguised in human form, a moment of illumination while reading the Bible or listening to a sermon: these were the more common forms of enlightenment in the revolutionary era. Joanna Southcott received the first sign of her exalted status while sweeping the store in which she worked as an upholsterer in 1792. Tucked in a corner was a ring with the enigmatic inscription "I. J.", which Southcott (through a vision) interpreted to refer both to Jesus Christ and herself. "From this moment she bid adieu to the shop, and commenced a prophetess."[30] William Huntington, S.S. (the initials stand for "Sinner Saved," though one wit rechristened him "Sorry Scribbler"), received the call to serve out of the blue; one day, he "heard the Lord call to me, with a very shrill, distinct voice, saying *Son of man, son of man, prophesy! Son of man, prophesy! I answered, Lord, what shall I prophesy?* The voice came again, saying, *Prophesy upon the thick boughs.*" Huntington took this as sign to move to London and "preach in the great metropolis."[31] James Birch, a former Muggletonian, had a similar experience. "I was in no sleep or Dream but perfectly awake when the Spirit came upon me and all Nature struck senseless or inactive, and was taken in Spirit unto the high mountain of Faith and saw the Kingdom of Heaven and God in his Glory and heard his Voice speaking unto my Soul . . . therefore I do declare myself a Messenger, or Prophet."[32] Such dreams, as we have seen, were commonplace in the evangelical world of the eighteenth century. Nothing in these particular visions stands out as extraordinary or singular, and yet on the basis of such thin evidence men and women were emboldened to "declare" themselves prophets of God.

The experiences of Dorothy Gott offer a good illustration of the ordinariness of Anglo-American prophecy in the eighteenth century. Gott, a Quaker who endured a bad marriage and deepening poverty in London, was "awakened in a morning about one or two o'clock (as near as I can remember) and received as a new breath passing through my body; it gave me a

[30] *Bell's Weekly Messenger*, Sept. 4, 1814, p. 6; the author notes, tongue-in-cheek, that "it is not stated whether or not she had a miraculous broom."

[31] William Huntington, S.S., *The Sinner Saved; Or, Memoirs of the Life of the Rev. W. Huntington, the Coal Heaver* (London, 1813), p. 20. A review of Huntington in the *Critical Review* 8 (August 1793), p. 230, referred to him as a "Sorry Scribbler."

[32] James Birch to Joseph Coal, Feb. 10, 1778, Muggletonian Archives, Add. MSS 60168, British Library.

strength in all my limbs, and enlightened my understanding." From this small beginning grew a suspicion that she was destined to be the figure foretold in the twelfth chapter of Revelation (the woman "clothed with the sun and with the moon under her feet," who will give birth to the "man-child," the savior of the Jews). Gott's spiritual visions have a homey quality to them, a feeling of familiarity with the spiritual world that is almost domestic in tone. "Then my eye was carried over the world, as from one end to the other. Then God asked me if I would accept all people to be my *friend* and *neighbour*. I was happy at that sound." Gott enjoyed an increasingly intimate relationship with the "voice" she had first heard in bed at night, and grew in both scriptural knowledge and confidence. "The voice spoke to me, calling me by my name; it was as if he walked by my side, and we talked together. . . . And as I got strength, I was much enabled to pray for the people; for when I came to town, it was said, 'Look the people full in the face, and pray for them:' which was not usual with me, for I had been used to hang my head down like a bulrush." In keeping with his cozy appearance as a friend and counselor, God made use of the little things of the world to reveal cosmic truths. Gott was "ordered" by the Spirit to keep certain items—"a pack of cards, and a child's ragged dirty shirt"—as a reminder of man's corruption. A shopping expedition to purchase "a little coarse cloth, to pack a box" was the occasion for another dramatic revelation.[33]

This catalogue of events, signs, and portents is striking only in its focus on the mundane details of a servant's life in Hanoverian London.[34] It was a truism of biblical history that God chose the ordinary to reveal the extraordinary, but revolutionary-era prophets made a special case for the sacred meaning of everyday life. This celebration of the quotidian could be seen as another victory for the common man in an age of democratic possibility. The intrusion of commoners into politics, literature, and the arts by the closing decades of the eighteenth century was accompanied by a "vulgarization" of public life—a new willingness to incorporate details once thought private or shameful into accounts of public doings. Yet it is also possible to see this celebration of the common as parodic, an ironic comment on the depths to

---

[33] Dorothy Gott, *The Midnight Cry, "Behold the* BRIDEGROOM *comes!" or, An Order from God to Get your Lamps Lighted* (London, 1788), pp. 21, 29, 58, 48.

[34] Anna Clark argues that Gott's writings describe a "typically plebian female experience;" Clark, "The Sexual Crisis and Popular Religion in London, 1770–1820," *International Journal of Labor and Working Class History* 34 (1988), pp. 56–69 (quote on p. 59). For a broader discussion of the role of women in plebian millenarianism, see Clark, *The Struggle for the Breeches: Gender and the Making of the British Working Class* (Berkeley, Calif., 1995), pp. 107–11.

which God had sunk in an age of diminishing expectations. Even prophets sometimes wondered, as did Noah White (whom we met in the Introduction), whether they were truly meant to "spiritualize" the everyday detritus of their lives. David Austin's wife reprimanded him when his prophetic musings "seemed to extend to the whole house . . . considering the house as an emblem of the present state of the Christian church, or of our country in general." Was "*the state of the floor*" really "an emblem of what needed to be done in respect to those who lived upon it," he wondered? An "ingenious mind might spiritualize any thing," was her tart response.[35]

This struggle to comprehend the spiritual value of the unexceptional would bedevil millenarian prophets, living as they did on the cusp of a cultural transformation in attitudes toward commoners and common life. A striking feature of the eighteenth-century mental universe, Frank Manuel has observed, was "an overwhelming tendency to become matter-of-fact, to eschew wonder, to reduce the fantastic to a commonsense narrative. There was a general movement to de-allegorize, to perceive the ordinary where previous generations had sought occult connotations. The world was obvious, the cloud of past obfuscations had lifted, things were to be seen and described as they were and as they should appear to reasonable people not possessed by romances or religious enthusiasm."[36] The Enlightenment campaign against all forms of "wonder," including the miraculous, left little room for the kind of spiritual virtuosity exercised by prophets.[37] Prodigies were more likely to be found in the natural than in the supernatural realm, and more likely to demonstrate nature gone awry than providential favor. Late eighteenth- and early nineteenth-century literary journals served up a steady fare of human and animal freakery to customers eager for novelty and the spice of transgression—albinos, white Africans, hermaphrodite cows, talking pigs. By the end of the Napoleonic era, prophets found themselves sharing literary and cultural space with these unnatural wonders: R. S. Kirby included Joanna Southcott in his *Wonderful and Eccentric Museum; or Magazine of Remarkable Characters* side by side with "white negroes," bearded women, and the "hare-faced girl," while Robert Southey considered Southcott to be one of

[35] David Austin, *The Voice of God to the People of the United States, by a Messenger of Peace* (Elizabethtown, N.J., 1796), p. 40.

[36] Frank Manuel, *The Eighteenth Century Confronts the Gods* (Cambridge, Mass., 1959), p. 26.

[37] Lorraine Daston and Katharine Park, "The Enlightenment and the Anti-Marvelous," chapter 9 in *Wonders and the Order of Nature, 1150–1750* (New York, 1998).

the wonders of the age along with the "Wild Indian Woman," the "Wandering Jew," and the "Learned Pig."[38]

But for most of the revolutionary period, prophets were neither natural prodigies suffering from deformity nor holy fools blessed with supernatural powers. They were ordinary men and women, undistinguished in appearance and of average aptitude. Their outsized ambitions embodied the problem of ego in an age that was struggling to redefine the parameters of human achievement. The political attack on prescriptive measures of status (lineage, titles, wealth) and the elevation of individual merit as the ultimate mark of distinction in republican circles certainly opened the door to new ways of identifying remarkable men and grand deeds, but there was really no clear consensus on what constituted greatness in a democratic society. The classical language of heroism was no help, tainted as it was by aristocratic privilege. Nor was the modern psychological language of subjectivity (egotism, megalomania) available yet to describe the inflated pride of ordinary people. And, as we have seen, the effort to despiritualize the phenomenon of charisma left religious enthusiasts scrambling to find a substitute to fill the void left by the disappearance of the supernatural. If God (or the devil) was no longer directly responsible for the inspired words and actions of prophets, who or what was to be credited for their deeds? A kind of rustic cleverness found in peasants everywhere? The shrewdness of producers and consumers who had learned to bargain well in the flourishing labor and commodity markets of Anglo-America? A heightened sensory receptiveness to the signals God continued to transmit to the human world, albeit in more limited frequencies? Dumb luck? Commentators were left to cobble together an awkward vocabulary of the matter-of-fact and the grandiose that sounds bombastic and slightly silly to us, as it did to many of them. Prophets fortunate enough to live a generation later, in the "Age of the Common Man," would have an easier time convincing their contemporaries of their own capacity for greatness.

If the call to serve came unbidden and unheralded, it did at least open new vistas and confer new powers on its recipients. Prophets received a number of spiritual "gifts" for their labors, tokens of God's appreciation of the

---

[38] *Kirby's Wonderful and Eccentric Museum: or Magazine of Remarkable Characters* (London, 1820), 1:370, 376, 2:frontispiece, 3:frontispiece; Robert Southey, Letters 55, 70, on "English Credulity" and "Joannah Southcott," in *Letters from England*, ed. Jack Simmons (London, 1951; orig. pub. 1807), pp. 337–41, 433–46. See also the comparisons of Southcott with the "pig-faced woman" in the *Times*, Feb. 17, 1815, p. 3.

burdens they had agreed (sometimes reluctantly) to assume. Freedom from bodily needs and sufferings was a natural prize for those who had renounced the world of the flesh for a higher spiritual purpose. Since the 1750s, circles of "perfectionists" had been a thorn in the side of respectable dissenters with their claims to have overcome both sin and death through sanctification. The Baptist leader Isaac Backus encountered one such "immortalist" in 1753 who told him that "this night 2 months ago She passed thro' a change in her Body equivalent to Death, so that She had been intirely free from any disorder in her Body or Corruption in her Soul ever Since; and expected she ever should be So; and that her Body would never see Corruption, but would Live here 'till Christs personal coming."[39] Shadrach Ireland, the Massachusetts prophet, told his followers not to panic when he lay ill in 1778, for God had told him he would not die. "I am going, but don't bury me," he was reported to have said, "for the time is short; God is coming to take the church." Six weeks later, the unbearable stench from Ireland's decomposing body compelled even his most faithful followers to bury their leader hastily, and in secret.[40] The leader of the Buchanite sect in Scotland claimed to be "the third person in the Godhead, or, in other words, the Holy Ghost, and therefore could not die." She instructed her followers not to be "discouraged" if she should appear as dead, "for she would only sleep; and if their faith were pure without alloy, she, at the end of six days, would return for them." In an odd throwback to late medieval tales of sanctity, the prophet's body "emmitted an odiferous perfume" after death which lingered on the hands of her disciples.[41]

For those whose renunciations of the flesh did not extend to immortality, fasting and other regimes of self-denial were another route to sanctification. Some prophets boasted of their ability to live without food or drink: Hugh Bourne encountered one such woman in 1810 and "was led to believe her a saint."[42] Another told Freeborn Garrettson that "he did not eat a

---

[39] *The Diary of Isaac Backus*, ed. William McLoughlin (Providence, R.I., 1979), 1:141, 1:294.

[40] Ireland's story is retold in Isaac Backus, *A History of New England with Particular Reference to the Denomination of Christians Called Baptists*, 2d ed. (Newton, Mass., 1871), 2:462; and in Thomas Hammond's manuscript history of the Harvard, Mass., Shaker Church; see Harvard Shaker Church Records, octavo volume, pp. 11–12, 255, American Antiquarian Society. Stephen Marini gives a brief history of the Irelandites in *Radical Sects in Revolutionary New England* (Cambridge, Mass., 1982), p. 51.

[41] Joseph Train, *The Buchanites, from First to Last* (London, 1846), pp. 161–62.

[42] "A woman was then living at Tutbury, professedly without meat or drink of any kind. This wonderful phenomenon excited curiosity in the minds of many. Hundreds went to see her, and no doubt by her well-managed imposture she reaped a pretty good harvest." *Memoirs of Hugh Bourne*, pp. 297–98.

mouthful of victuals during forty days, and only drank water and a few times a little small beer. He likewise told me that nothing went through his body for forty days."[43] Ann Lee claimed that while imprisoned for blasphemy she was without food or drink for fourteen days—"four days longer than they could reasonably expect that any one could live without food," she noted.[44] Henry Brooke and his circle of correspondents were fascinated by the story of the "entranced maid" of Wales who was "as cheerful as a little baby, & chirrupping & crowing as one would do on its Mothers lap" while she fasted. As Ralph Mather enthused, this was not an isolated case: "book hunters" had found two other examples in their perusal of the foreign press—"one lived in Germany for three months and another in France for seven yrs. without any manner of food. I believe some niggardly scanty souls have been with the Welsh maid who I am told allways lies in bed, understands little of what she says; but this I do not wonder at."[45]

These stories of fasting saints had a long pedigree in Anglo-American religious history (not to mention western Christendom more generally). The prophets of the Civil War era were renowned for their physical asceticism. As Diane Purkiss argues, protracted fasts were an "example of bodily weakness as a signifier for prophetic empowerment."[46] We will explore in the next chapter the larger significance of the body and physical debility in the world of eighteenth-century Anglo-American prophecy, but it is worth noting here an important contrast with these earlier manifestations of prophetic power through bodily renunciation. To seventeenth-century Puritans, fasting represented not only personal self-denial but "an act of quasi-magical efficacy" grounded in the symbiotic relationship of body and soul: depriving the one of sustenance was a way of releasing the other to join in metaphysical union with Christ. The metonymic chain linking food, word, and flesh in Puritan theology made fasting an act of high devotional purpose as well as a practical exercise in self-control. By the eighteenth century, the devotional meaning

---

[43] Simpson, *American Methodist Pioneer*, p. 270.

[44] *Mother's First-Born Daughters: Early Shaker Writings on Women and Religion*, ed. Jean M. Humez (Bloomington, Ind., 1993), p. 32.

[45] Ralph Mather to Henry Brooke, 1777, Brooke Letterbook, Walton MSS I.1.43, Dr. Williams's Library, p. 156. See also Mather to Brooke, 1778, Brooke Letterbook, p. 121. The maid told Mather, "there was some other in Scotland much lead as she is."

[46] Diane Purkiss, "Producing the Voice, Consuming the Body: Women Prophets of the Seventeenth Century," in *Women, Writing, History, 1640–1740*, ed. Isobel Grundy and Susan Wiseman (London, 1992), p. 145. On the fasting of medieval saints, see Caroline Walker Bynum's influential work *Holy Feast and Holy Fast: The Religious Significance of Food to Medieval Women* (Berkeley, Calif., 1987).

of food and of rituals of abstinence was eclipsed by a more instrumental view of eating (and other bodily functions) as components of human subjectivity. Fasting, or its opposite, gluttony, defined a person's capacity for self-discipline, not his or her incorporation into the mystical body of Christ.[47]

To rationalists, conversely, fasting signified one's capacity for self-destruction. For every fasting saint who was extolled as an example of God's power in the revolutionary era, many more were pitied as victims of self-delusion. Mrs. B.—"a woman of strong sense and a lively imagination" but "given up to a strong delusion (whether natural or diabolical I know not)"—told John Wesley's society that "the day of judgement would begin that evening" and that they must fast for forty days and nights in imitation of Christ. "So for three weeks they took no sustenance but three gills of water per day," Wesley recorded, "and three weeks more they took each three gills of water-gruel per day. What a mercy that half of them did not die in making the experiment!"[48] Others were not so lucky. A disciple of the American prophet Abel Sargent "worked himself up into the belief that he could live so holy in this life, that his animal nature would become immortal, and that he would never die; and he conceived that he had gained this immortality, and could live without eating." The man refused to eat for sixteen days and "then died a suicidal death."[49] For Anglo-Americans increasingly suspicious of all extreme forms of religious enthusiasm, including the penitential or ascetic, self-denial was a mark of a diseased imagination and not a redemptive act.

This suspicion of somatic forms of supernatural power carried over into a general distrust of such spiritual "gifts" as faith healing and speaking in tongues. Some prophets, to be sure, did claim the gift of healing. Ann Lee, the Shaker founder, was remembered by her followers to have extraordinary powers to heal emotional and physical wounds by the mere touch of her hand. The *Testimonials of the Life and Character of Mother Ann Lee*, published some years after her death, recounts numerous examples of Believers who credited Lee with fixing broken bones and broken hearts.[50] Lee's contemporary Elspeth Buchan used less orthodox methods, including "breathing"

---

[47] As Phyllis Mack argues, "For eighteenth-century religious seekers, spiritual enlightenment was experienced, not in the ecstasy of the purified body, but in the dominance of mind *over* body." Mack, "Religious Dissenters in Enlightenment England," *History Workshop Journal* 49 (2000), pp. 1–23 (quote on p. 7).

[48] *Journal of John Wesley*, 8:72.

[49] Cartwright, *Autobiography*, 1807, p. 102.

[50] See the stories recorded in *Testimonies of the Life, Character, Revelations and Doctrines of Our Ever Blessed Mother Ann Lee* (Hancock, Mass., 1816).

on afflicted followers, as well as touch.[51] George Bell reportedly healed a young woman of breast cancer in 1761, and a Quaker visionary in Philadelphia "got so high an opinion of his Gifts & Qualifications as to undertake, by stroking or some such manual performance, to heal Diseases & cleanse from internal Pollutions."[52] But most prophets maintained a healthy distance from the world of physical miracles, preferring instead to exercise their spiritual powers through the less dangerous channels of intellectual discernment and prophetic foresight.

The ultimate test of a prophet was, of course, his or her ability to predict the end of the world and Christ's Second Coming. Most avoided the temptation of date-setting that had ensnared so many would-be prophets over the years, preferring to offer indeterminate estimates of proximate events. "When men pretend to fix the day, the hour, the times, or years, which God has put in his own power, they are to be suspected," warned William Huntington.[53] But a few brave souls did venture to attach specific dates to the apocalyptic script. George Bell, a one-time follower of John Wesley, made quite a stir when he predicted that the world would end on February 28, 1763: thousands of people waited anxiously in their homes and fields that night, including many Methodists who returned sheepishly to a bemused Wesley the next day.[54] Elspeth Buchan gathered her entire flock on a mountaintop on an autumn day in 1784 to await "translation" (the ascension of the entire body of believers) into heaven. The American David Austin told all who would listen to expect the Second Coming on May 15 or 16, 1796, and spent the next decade trying to explain away the failure of the Messiah to materialize as promised. Nathaniel Wood's divining rod pointed to January 14, 1801,

---

[51] The poet Robert Burns said of the Buchanites: "Their tenets are a strange jumble of enthusiastic jargon; among others she pretends to give them the Holy Ghost by breathing on them, which she does with postures and gestures that are scandalously indecent." Quoted in *Dictionary of National Biography*, ed. Leslie Stephens and Sidney Lee (Oxford, 1937–38), 3:178–79.

[52] *Journal of John Wesley*, 4:481–82; Henry Tukes to Isaac Jacob, Feb. 9, 1807, Portfolio 17/32, Library of the Society of Friends, London.

[53] William Huntington, S.S., *The Lying Prophet Examined, and His False Predictions Discovered; Being a Dissection of the Prophecies of Richard Brothers* (London, 1795), p. 3.

[54] Wesley recounts the Bell heresy in his *Journal*, 5:4–9. Bell and his followers were arrested on a mound near St. Luke's Hospital and committed to prison. Robert Southey traced his subsequent life: "Passing from one extreme to another, the ignorant enthusiast became an ignorant infidel, turned fanatic in politics, as he had been in religion, and . . . died at a great old age a radical reformer." Robert Southey, *The Life of Wesley and Rise and Progress of Methodism* (London, 1846), 2:344–45.

as the date on which an avenging angel would pass over the earth and destroy all unbelievers—an event that his contemporary Nimrod Hughes believed would occur on June 4, 1814. As these dates came and went, prophets showed a remarkable ability to recover from the stigma of failed predictions ("error," Hughes explained, "is calculated to make mystery more mystical").[55] Some persuaded their disappointed followers that their own lack of faith was to blame, while others returned to the drawing board to review and recalculate on the basis of new revelations. Prophecy was a tricky business, and few believers held prophets personally responsible for misreading the signs of the times.

Still, it was better to avoid the quagmire of date-setting altogether if possible. Prophets were more likely to market themselves as skilled exegetes than as fortune-tellers, as oracles who enjoyed access to some special source of illumination necessary to understand the enigmatic texts of the Bible. The quintessential eighteenth-century metaphor of "enlightenment" is an apt one to capture the prophet's spiritual awakening from the darkness of ignorance and inability to the light of truth and power. Dorothy Gott repeatedly used the image of a "solar microscope" to explain the enlargement of perception she experienced as a prophet: "the solar microscope," she explained, "represents Christ enlightening our dark hearts by fresh objects being brought to our view, as through a glass, by the power of the sun." In a letter to John Murray, she described how, despite the disadvantage of illiteracy, she was enabled to pen the visions that appeared to her in the night. "When I sit down to write, it appears but a few sentences; but, like the solar microscope, it enlarges as I write: for I never know what I have wrote till I read it."[56] All of the prophets' senses—hearing, taste, sight—became "enlarged," as did their powers of communication. Their voices swelled, their vocabulary expanded, their command of foreign tongues grew (Ann Lee was said to be able to speak fluently in seventy-two languages), their vision became razor sharp.[57] Prophets lived more fully in the sensory world mapped so diligently by Enlightenment philosophes than most of their contemporaries. Cornelius Cayley described the feeling of God's power within as a "resurrection from the

[55] Nimrod Hughes, *A Solemn Warning to All the Dwellers Upon the Earth*, 2d ed. (New Jersey, 1811), p. 23.

[56] Gott, *Midnight Cry*, pp. 66, 92.

[57] For Lee, see Hannah Adams, *An Alphabetical Compendium of the Various Sects which have Appeared in the World from the beginning of the Christian Era to the present Day* (Boston, 1784), p. lviii; and Valentine Rathbun, *Account of the Matter, Form, and Manner of a New and Strange Religion Taught and Propagated by a Number of* EUROPEANS . . . (Providence, R.I., 1781), p. 6. Dorothy Gott "received great power to sing"; *Midnight Cry*, p. 66.

grave of my wither'd self. . . . This life I experience, begins to send up fresh sap into my dead earth; the blind in me begins to see, the deaf to hear, & the dumb to speak."[58]

The first sign that one had been chosen was usually the ability to understand the Bible in a new light. Prophets awoke from their dreams and visions with a particular text fixed in their minds, or a newfound ability to discern the true meaning of a difficult passage. The Vermont prophet Caleb Rich explained that the "medium of the holy spirit" had "open[ed]" his "understanding" to the revealed word.[59] Some even found, to their amazement, that they had mysteriously learned to read while entranced. Black visionaries, from the population in Anglo-America most deprived of formal access to learning, were most likely to enjoy the miracle of instant literacy, but prophets of all backgrounds described the gift of literacy (the ability to read in a *new* way) as the first and most precious token of God's favor.[60] No miracles were needed for the most part, just a fine-tuning of the normal channels of perception and understanding. Those who could already read found they could now read faster or with greater insight; those who could already write (and some who couldn't) found the words spilling from their mouths faster than their pens could move. "Somehow Ideas have rolled like a flood into my Mind & words like the drops of rain for multitudes have flowed in profusion from my tongue," William Babcock confided.[61] Eunice Wyeth received what the Shaker chronicler Benjamin Seth Wells called the "gift of poetry" under inspiration: "lines flowed into her mind as fast as she could pen them." (According to Wells, these hymns came to Wyeth "in the darkest hours of the night suspended from the ceiling over her head written in letters of gold," which she then copied verbatim.)[62] The precocious child prophet Joseph

[58] Cornelius Cayley to Friends in Leeds, January 1771, "Collection of Letters, Dreams, Visions, and Other Occurrences of some of the People Called Quakers," 1788, p. 231, Library of the Society of Friends, London.

[59] *Candid Examiner* 2 (June 18, 1827), p. 201.

[60] John Jea and Rebecca Jackson both described the miracle of literacy in their memoirs; see John Jea, *The Life, History, and Unparalleled Sufferings of John Jea, the African Preacher* (Portsea, England, c. 1815), pp. 112–13, and *Gifts of Power: The Writings of Rebecca Jackson, Black Visionary, Shaker Eldress*, ed. Jean Humez (Amherst, Mass., 1981). Henry Louis Gates, Jr., analyzes the importance of literacy in the religious experience of African Americans in *The Signifying Monkey: A Theory of African-American Literary Criticism* (New York, 1988).

[61] Babcock Diary, June 26, 1801, p. 32.

[62] Testimony of Eunice Wyeth, 1807, Shaker MSS VI:A-5, Western Reserve Historical Society, Cleveland, Ohio.

Prescott enjoyed the gift of art, producing beautiful pen-and-ink drawings as well as watercolor paintings to illustrate his visions.[63]

Several prophets—all women—found it necessary to employ amanuenses so that God's message would not be lost because of their own insufficiency as writers, while others hired scribes to render their scrawl into legible prose. When Joanna Southcott's writings proved "illegibile to every one besides herself," she hired Jane Townley and Ann Underwood to transcribe the words of the Spirit. At first, Townley admitted to a friend, she found "the task [too] hard for me," though after two years she had learned to read Southcott's writing "with perfect facility."[64] Both Dorothy Gott and Elspeth Buchan confessed to being bad spellers who needed the help of outsiders to "copy over" their writing.[65] But these were minor obstacles, occasions even for God to toy with them. (Gott admitted that God "often shewed me that he could make me spell my own name wrong" to humble her.)[66] Good grammar and spelling were man's standards, not God's. True believers—those who had been enlightened by the spirit of God dwelling within—did not need the crutch of human learning to know and appreciate God's word.

An anti-intellectualism, in other words, hovered below the surface of much prophetic activity in the revolutionary era. "Enlightenment" did not mean what philosophers and scientists meant by the word; it had little to do with human reason or the attainment of learning. Learning, in fact, was a liability. "I have languages; I have philosophy; I have astronomy; am acquainted with the motions of the heavenly bodies; I have the arts and sciences, &c. &c.," Benjamin Abbott wrote, "and yet cannot obtain consolation and serenity of mind; but am harassed and wonderfully tormented by, I know not, in the silent watches of the night; I am alarmed with dreams, visions, and awful apprehensions."[67] One of Joanna Southcott's most learned followers lamented that for "more than thirty-seven years I have diligently searched the Scriptures in seven different languages," only to find that he

[63] James K. Hopkins recounts Prescott's career in *A Woman to Deliver Her People: Joanna Southcott and English Millenarianism in an Era of Revolution* (Austin, Tex., 1982), pp. 127–31. The Southcott collection at the University of Texas contains fourteen of Prescott's paintings, either originals or duplicates.

[64] Jane Townley, *A Letter from Mrs. Jane Townley to the Editor of the Council of Ten, in Answer to His Remarks and Misrepresentations Respecting the Mission of Joanna Southcott*, 2d ed. (London, 1823), p. 29.

[65] Like Joanna Southcott, Sarah Flaxmer used an amanuensis; for Elspeth Buchan, see James Purves, *Eight Letters*, p. 47; for Dorothy Gott, see *Midnight Cry*, p. 33.

[66] Gott, *Midnight Cry*, p. 33.

[67] Abbott, *Experience and Gospel Labours*, p. 215.

could not understand the Bible unless guided by "the finger of God."[68] Southcott herself proudly acknowledged her profound ignorance of what the world considered knowledge. "What a proud, conceited fool must I be, to say of myself, I have more knowledge than the learned, and can tell them better than they know from my own wisdom.... Shall I say I had the spirit of wisdom given me, when I never had any talents to boast of in my life, and was considered by all my worthy wise brothers and sisters the simplest of my father's house?"[69] Only the presence of God's spirit within could lift the darkness from man's soul—a "living spirit" that was explicitly counterposed to the "dead letter" of human invention.

To speak with the living spirit was to speak with grace and power as if God himself was present. The evangelical movement of the eighteenth century had pioneered the technique of extemporaneous speech as the preferred mode of public oratory, and prophets extended this critique of scholastic, formal language to include any language that was not immediately inspired. By the early nineteenth century, the denigration of eloquence had been extended so far that some evangelicals feared they were making a fetish of the vernacular; Hugh Bourne admitted that "Appearing to be illiterate, when I am not illiterate seemed to be quite wrong.... O Lord, if thy will be that I should use fine language, give me a fine flow of eloquence—touch my lips with a live coal from off the altar."[70] Speaking in trance was the logical outgrowth of this emphasis on direct inspiration, but for the most part revolutionary-era prophets did not pursue this path (popularized by the French Prophets of the early 1700s). They continued to speak in their own voice, not God's, even if the words they uttered were not always their own.

Not passive vessels of divine speech, eighteenth-century prophets were conversationalists. They conversed with God or his spirit and conveyed the essence of these communications in a variety of conversational guises to their audience. Readers should not be "astonished nor scandalized," a supporter

[68] Rev. Hoadley Ash to Southcott, Sept. 28, 1807, in Alice Seymour, comp., *The Voice in the Wilderness: The Gospel of the Holy Spirit As Given to Joanna Southcott by the Spirit of Truth* (Ashford, Middlesex, 1933), pp. 78–80.

[69] Joanna Southcott Collection, 340, June 3, 1802, f. 61, Harry Ransom Research Center, University of Texas at Austin.

[70] On the rhetorical innovations of the evangelical movement, see Harry S. Stout, "Religious Communications, and the Ideological Origins of the American Revolution," *William and Mary Quarterly*, 3d ser., 36 (1977), pp. 519–41; Nancy Ruttenberg, *Democratic Personality: Popular Voice and the Trials of American Authorship* (Stanford, Calif., 1998); and Sandra M. Gustafson, *Eloquence Is Power: Oratory and Performance in Early America* (Chapel Hill, N.C., 2000); *Memoirs of Hugh Bourne*, p. 231.

admonished, "when we hear Mr. Brothers affirm that God speaks to him in plain direct words, as one man would to speak to another."[71] In this as in so much else, George Whitefield was the progenitor and master of the inspired style. His "mighty musical voice itself flowed easily as if in familiar conversation, and the fine deep tones were as distinct on the outskirts of the crowd where we stood as if he had been whispering in one's ear." Whitefield's voice made one young listener "feel more at home than any words since Mother's last prayer with me."[72] Even in their most polished publications prophets employed the conversational mode, trying to establish a personal bond with their readers that more formal modes of address made difficult. The modern-day "Prophet Nathan" asked his readers to "suffer me, as a friend, to converse with you (if not personally, yet with my pen), about your *difficulties*." Out of such easy familiarity with their listeners millenarians wove tales rather than delivered sermons; "Preaching was with him talking—his discourses were as storytelling," wrote William Huntington in self-admiration.[73] Of course, by unmooring the act of communication from conventional standards of human excellence, prophets accentuated the problem of "false speaking" that plagued the enterprise. False prophets were exceptionally skilled at the art of verbal deception—the rural American prophet William Scales denounced the "fair, the beguiling, the enchanting speeches and conversations of false teachers," which seemed to drown out the voices of true believers.[74] But this was the price to be paid for opening up the channels of genuine spiritual communication.

Prophets reaped more tangible rewards for their labors as well—not least of which, of course, was fame. Dramatic role reversals were the common coin of prophecy through the ages as the inarticulate became eloquent and the lowly were raised to new heights. Sarah Richards, chief acolyte of the American prophetess Jemima Wilkinson, dreamed that she was invited by an angelic messenger to a great house and dressed in "the Riches Cloathing which nothing on Earth Could Esxel." There she saw "a great number of People all Richly Drest all in a very humble Posture Some Kneeling others Prostrate on the floor."[75] Dorothy Gott told her sister, with whom she boarded,

---

[71] Nathaniel Brassey Halhed, *Testimony of the Authenticity of the Prophecies of Richard Brothers* (London, 1795), p. 36.

[72] *Diary of Mrs. Kitty Trevylyan: A Story of the Times of Whitefield and the Wesleys* (New York, 1865), p. 53.

[73] Huntington, *Sinner Saved*, p. 32.

[74] William Scales, *The Confusion of Babel Discovered; or, An Answer to Jeremy Belknap's Discourse upon the Lawfulness of War* (1780), pp. vii-viii.

[75] Sarah Richards' Dream Book, Jan. 18, 1788, JW Papers.

that "I have looked upon myself as your servant, but now I have a great Master, and must do his work." From that point on she "withdrew and took no further notice of the household affairs."[76] Her fellow laborers from the industrial North, Ann Lee and Elspeth Buchan, became mistresses of thriving rural households. To the arrogance of prophets mentioned in the first chapter we might now add the element of social striving. Prophets were social malcontents (however much they disdained the perks of worldly distinction) who scrambled over the backs of their rivals to secure the undivided attention of the masses. Most were men and women of obscure origins, whose families were either at the bottom of the pecking order or fast descending the social scale. Joanna Southcott filled her prophetic pamphlets with tales of stolen inheritance and social slights. From his jail cell Nimrod Hughes wrote of the theft of his good name and his economic opportunities by those who had falsely accused him. Mary Pratt complained of a "persecuting" husband and an "infamous ungodly" son, who had conspired to defraud her of her last shilling.[77]

The keen sense of social deprivation felt by many prophets made them good grudge-bearers. "Few prophets," Henry Spencer observed in 1795, "have been deficient in the noble passion of revenge."[78] Prophets were neither sympathetic nor generous toward imitators. Their immersion in the apocalyptic world of calamities certainly colored their attitude toward competitors; living in daily expectation of imminent disaster led them to see danger everywhere, but the severity of their judgments is striking by the prevailing standards of public discourse. Sarah Flaxmer warned the prophetic community known as the Avignon Society, or that "Synagogue of Satan" as she preferred to call it, to disband or be "immediately destroyed and utterly consumed from off the face of the earth."[79] Jemima Wilkinson recorded numerous visions in which the "false teachers" and "painted Jezebels" who swarmed over the American countryside were brought to ruin. "Therefore will I number you to the Sword and you shall all bow down to the Slaughter," she threatened, "because when I called you did not Answer and when I Spake you did not hear but did evil before mine eyes. . . . Dogs & Sorcerers & Whoremongers and all Lyers shall have their part in the Lake that Burns with Fire & Brimstone."[80]

[76] Gott, *Midnight Cry*, p. 57.
[77] Pratt to Henry Brooke, Brooke Letterbook, p. 360.
[78] Henry Spencer, *A Vindication of the Prophecies of Mr. Brothers* (London, 1795), p. 31.
[79] Sarah Flaxmer, *Satan Revealed; or the Dragon Overcome* (London, 1795), p. 11.
[80] Diary of Abner Brownell, 1779–1787, 2:73, American Antiquarian Society; Publick Universal Friend to Sarah Richards, March 11, 1787, JW Papers.

Bible-wielding priests and religious impostors fall again and again to the apocalyptic sword in Wilkinson's allegories, vivid testimony to the violence that lurked beneath the surface of eighteenth-century religious discourse. With its bloody imagery and martial cadences, Wilkinson's oratory belongs in a well-established tradition of apocalyptic literature—a tradition, however, that was supposed to be in decline in the more refined climate of Georgian England, where a kind of pragmatic latitudinarianism prevailed. But eighteenth-century prophets inhabited the world of the Old Testament, not the New. They spoke of revenge and punishment, not mercy and redemption. They wanted to destroy, not save, their enemies.

Like his messengers, the God of prophecy was a figure to be feared and obeyed. Quick to anger and slow to forgive, God did not hesitate to visit horrific judgments upon his people. The litany of punishments that unbelievers could expect was well known—fire, earthquake, plague, war, famine—to which eighteenth-century prophets added the contemporary evils of revolution, insolvency, and excessive taxation. (One could argue, of course, that these latest evils [Figure 2] hardly compare in ferocity to the plagues visited upon the Old Testament Jews for their sins; the tax man doesn't quite cut it as a figure of terror.) While their reading of the fate that awaited infidels and apostates was relatively unimaginative, even mild, revolutionary-era prophets spoke in a language that jarred against contemporary sensibilities. The rise of a humanitarian ethos has been well documented in eighteenth-century discussions about the plight of the unfortunate (slaves, paupers, the mentally and physically weak, even criminals), but prophets displayed no such tenderness toward the spiritually disabled.[81] Sinners could expect no charity, no protective institutions or sympathetic ears. Only death (sudden and gruesome) awaited those who ignored the prophet's warning. The authority of the prophet's God was raw and untamed by the conventions of polite society or responsible government.

At its most basic, this was a primitive (in the sense that evangelical Protestants used the term in the eighteenth century) message of divine judgment and retribution. This message resonated in the remote reaches of the empire, where poverty and dependence ate into the fragile confidence of men and women already battling the demons of despair. Visionary experiences of an extravagant nature were more common in the American and

[81] Thomas Haskell, "Capitalism and the Origins of the Humanitarian Sensibility, Part I and Part II," *American Historical Review* 90 (April 1985; June 1985); Louis P. Masur, *Rites of Execution: Capital Punishment and the Transformation of American Culture, 1776–1865* (New York, 1989).

The Turbulent Mr. Fight-all   The Hon'ble Mr. Tax-all   The Worshipfull Mr. Take-all

THREE PLAGUES OF EUROPE.

Figure 2. "Three Plagues of Europe," ca. 1803. Department of Prints and Drawings, British Museum. Note the juxtaposition of archaic and modern images of evil.

British backcountry, a hardscrabble land of continuous subsistence struggles. In Vermont in the early 1800s, a Freewill Baptist community enjoyed the attentions of an angel of God who visited in a variety of guises over a period of five years. In a series of remarkably vivid conversations, recounted faithfully by the minister William Babcock in his diary, we can hear the voice of the prophet's God loud and clear. Infidelity and immorality were everywhere (Brother Sheppard was "double faced," "young John Johnson was a deceiver," Elder Putnam "had no religion & was a deceiver"), and if the people did not repent, retribution would follow: their crops would fail, or "God would be pleased to send the Spotted Fever among them & cut off the hypocrites & Opposers."[82]

The interjection of such a harsh and judgmental voice into the community of saints calls into question any easy assumptions about the populist nature of evangelical religion. While it may be less humiliating to be judged and found wanting by an angel of God than by a social superior or a governmental official, it remains true that lay men and women remained vulnerable to the sudden and arbitrary exercise of power that marginal people everywhere faced in their secular lives. Even on the Anglo-American frontier, authority, for all its tenuous institutional hold, was exercised in many ways—by charismatic seers who played on the emotional fears of their spiritually starved audiences, by counterfeiters and other con artists who persuaded desperate men and women that there was treasure buried in the ground, by patriarchs who governed their households free of interference from meddlesome kin or an inquisitive state. The kind of authority that the angel wielded over Babcock's congregation was that of an Old Testament patriarch, not a bourgeois gentleman or enlightened republican—highly personalized, rooted in the primal emotions of love and fear, and jealous of rivals.

In keeping with this primitive worldview, prophets presented themselves as martyrs who sacrificed their health, reputation, and fortune in the sacred cause. The memoirs of prophets are heroic tales of great suffering and little reward. Stories of persecution often overtake the narrative of spiritual labors; we hear more about the broken bones, verbal insults, and common indignities suffered by prophets than we do about the predictions fulfilled and souls converted. Many faced the anger of mobs who assaulted them and their followers for sport or revenge. Elspeth Buchan, who complained that

---

[82] Babcock Diary, Jan. 17, 1810; Jan. 19, 1810; July 3, 1810; Aug. 31, 1810; May 9, 1810. For a fuller discussion of the "Angel Delusion," see Susan Juster and Ellen Hartigan-O'Connor, "The 'Angel Delusion' of 1806–1811: Frustration and Fantasy on the Northern Frontier," *Journal of the Early Republic* 22 (Fall 2002), pp. 375–404. This and the following paragraph are taken from this article.

for ten years she had been "the very butt of the Devil's wrath," was attacked by a group of drunken revelers who subjected her to an impromptu chari-vari. "After dragging her through all the streets of the town, nearly in a state of nudity, many were for ducking her in the river, but the majority were for hounding her home to her husband, to the sound of an old tin kettle!"[83] The Shaker James Whittaker suffered a mock crucifixion at the hands of his tormenters. "I was whipped in the most cruel manner," he recounted, "being stripped and my two hands tied up being stretched up above my Head."[84] William Huntington complained (boasted) that he was "continually derided, abused, resisted, pelted while travelling, burned in effigy, and his life not seldom endangered."[85] When Joanna Southcott's "mystical pregnancy" ended in her death in December 1814, the prophetess was hung in effigy throughout England and copies of her books burned in public.[86]

Such acts of public violence were a constant feature of life in the evangelical circuits of Anglo-America. Methodist and Baptist preachers were attacked with clubs, horsewhips, and fists, driven from their pulpits and out of the homes of the faithful, sometimes imprisoned for sabbath-breaking or preaching without a license. A culture of martyrdom developed within the Methodist itinerancy, in particular, in which preachers boasted of the unparalleled persecution they faced. "I cannot easily describe the pain under which I shrink and writhe," Francis Asbury wrote near the end of his life; "mine are apostolic sufferings."[87] But their sufferings, while severe, were not quite apostolic. "It is perhaps as hard to be racked with the gout, or to burn several days in a fever on a sick bed, as you or I may be forced to do, as to be for a few minutes with Shadrach and his companions in a burning furnace, or to feel for a fleeting moment the anguish of bruised flesh and a fractured skull, with the triumphant martyr," the Methodist John Fletcher wrote somewhat defensively.[88] Gout and fever—the characteristic rewards of a hard life spent on

---

[83] Purves, *Eight Letters*, p. 36; Joseph Train, *The Buchanites*, p. 41.

[84] Whittaker to Jonathan and Ann Whittaker, Feb. 20, 1784, Shaker Mss. IV:B-3, Western Reserve Historical Society.

[85] Huntington, *Sinner Saved*, p. 30.

[86] Joanna Southcott, *The Fifth Book of Wonders* (London, 1814), p. 16.

[87] *Journal of Francis Asbury*, 2:715. For accounts of the violence faced by evangelicals, see Cynthia Lynn Lyerly, *Methodism and the Southern Mind, 1770–1810*; Dee Andrews, *The Methodists and Revolutionary America, 1760–1800: The Shaping of an Evangelical Culture* (Princeton, N.J., 2000). For a good discussion of the culture of martyrdom among early southern evangelicals, see Christine Heyrman, *Southern Cross: The Beginnings of the Bible Belt* (New York, 1997).

[88] "On the Spiritual Manifestation of the Son of God," *Arminian Magazine*, 16 (June 1793), p. 318. Phyllis Mack has likewise noted the tendency of Methodists to exaggerate their physical sufferings; "Religious Dissenters in Enlightenment England," p. 7.

the road—were one thing; the martyrdom of biblical saints was quite another. On the scale of heroic suffering, prophets were closer to their contemporary rivals, the evangelical itinerants, than they would have us believe. No prophet lost his life in this era; very few, in proportion to their total number, were incarcerated for their beliefs.[89] Their sufferings were, like their ambitions, overblown.

The hyperbolic quality of much prophetic writing in the revolutionary era was symptomatic of the paradox at the heart of millenarianism: the collision of the ordinary with the extraordinary. Prophets lived at the very center of this paradox—ordinary people caught up in cosmic dramas whose very claim to fame lay in the unremarkable nature of their lives and characters. As his most prominent supporter said of London's most famous prophet, "Mr. Brothers is certainly a most unexceptional character. . . . But he has written two very extraordinary books—Aye, Sir, there's the rub."[90] The intellectual climate of the late eighteenth century heightened rather than diminished prophets' anxiety over their reputations, as the democratization (or vulgarization) of public life made the ordinary both a political virtue and a cultural joke. Praised by republican writers like Tom Paine for their "common" sense, ridiculed by conservatives and the literati for their rustic manners and clumsy speech, ordinary Anglo-Americans were the object of a number of cross-cutting discursive projects whose purpose was to recalibrate the boundaries of the public sphere in order to defuse the threat of political insurgency from below.[91] The response to millenarianism—contempt, ridicule, medicalization, incarceration—was profoundly conservative at heart, whatever the political persuasion of those who encountered modern-day prophets. If religious extravagance was more likely to trigger gentler forms of coercion than mass hysteria or political repression, it still, as Roy Porter says, "struck real fear into the polite and propertied."[92] For prophets were never polite, and rarely respectable. They were John Bull at his most vulgar and confused.

[89] Porter, *Mind-Forg'd Manacles*, p. 80. Porter notes that some prophets were "by any standards dangerous, such as the Pentecostal Bannister Truelock, whose voices persuaded James Hadfield to shoot George III, or later Jonathan Martin, the divine arsonist of York Minster." But by and large the threat posed by millenarians was cultural, not political, and thus best defused by reason and ridicule rather than repressive measures (p. 77).

[90] Nathaniel Brassey Halhed, *A Calculation on the Commencement of the Millennium* (London, 1795), pp. 28–29.

[91] For a fascinating account of these discursive projects in England, see Don Herzog, *Poisoning the Minds of the Lower Orders* (Princeton, N.J., 1998).

[92] Porter, *Mind-Forg'd Manacles*, p. 77.

What was the response when prophets put away their swords and picked up their pens? Millennial writers were, by definition, a more respectable subset of the prophetic population than their millenarian brothers and sisters. Many, if not most, millenarians were illiterate and proud of it; millennial authors, by definition, had at least a rudimentary exposure to the world of print and high culture. Their enthusiasm took a different form— stylistic experimentation, verbal jousts with noted authorities, a literary playfulness that often stretched the boundaries of good sense and good taste. The lively argument with modernity that millenarian prophets embodied in their very person was carried on in the pages of millennial authors, albeit at a lower temperature.

Millennial Authors

In October 1795, the *Critical Review* reviewed some thirty or so publications on prophecy which had appeared that year in the wake of Richard Brothers's sensational appearance on the British literary scene. "We think we hear our readers cry out, Enough! enough! on only perusing the titles of these numerous pamphlets, on a subject which is now grown as stale as ever it was disgraceful to the boasted good sense of the nation." The reviewer's dismay at the insatiable appetite of the London press for "catch-penny" prophetic pamphlets was well placed, if not his optimism that the revelations of Brothers himself were "now almost forgotten."[93]

Despite the existence of a statute prohibiting seditious prophecy throughout the century, the more liberal licensing laws of the Georgian era made it difficult to stem the printing of prophecies concerning the fate of the monarch and the nation. And so prophecies flowed from the presses in stunning numbers from the 1790s through the 1820s and 1830s. Deborah Valenze, in a study of chapbooks issued in the eighteenth century, found that works on the supernatural were the second most commonly issued books after traditional fiction. "Judging from the popularity of these chapbooks," she concludes, "prophecy was a household word in the commoners' vocabulary."[94] A dictionary of works on prophecy, published in London in 1835, lists 274 publications in England and Scotland between 1775 and 1815. Considering that the output—sixty-five titles in all—of England's most prolific prophet,

---

[93] *Critical Review* 15 (October 1795), pp. 214–17.
[94] Deborah Valenze, "Prophecy and Popular Literature in Eighteenth-Century England," *Journal of Ecclesiastical History* 29 (1978), pp. 75–92, quote on p. 78.

Joanna Southcott, are not included, that figure is (as James Hopkins says) "woefully incomplete."[95] Ruth Bloch calculates that the pace of millennial publication in the United States, steady throughout the colonial period, quickened exponentially in the 1790s; between 1793 and 1796 alone the number of works on eschatology published by American printers increased tenfold over the considerable output of the previous thirty years.[96]

One significant stream of this literary flood was comprised of old prophecies, recycled and repackaged for a new audience. The writings of Christopher Love, Mother Shipton, Robert Nixon, and Mother Bunch continued to sell well into the nineteenth century, and every year brought to light previously unknown prophecies issued centuries before but only now reaching their fulfillment. A millennialist in Paris wrote excitedly to his friends in London about the discovery of a six-hundred-year-old prophecy "engraved on a flagstone, two yards square, in Hebrew characters," which supposedly predicted "a most glorious and universal revolution in 1800."[97] A Boston printer reissued *The Strange and Wonderful Predictions of Mr. Christopher Love* in 1759, after an earthquake rattled the good Puritans of the town who "*shrieked with Apprehension of its being the Day of Judgment.*"[98] A new genre made its appearance—the prophetic serial, a compendium of prophecies old and new.[99] Booksellers anxious to take advantage of the robust market for classic prophecies packaged them with popular fiction. An advertisement on the back page of Thomas Chamberlain's 1748 deathbed prediction, reissued for the tenth time by a Boston printer in 1791, assured "Country Shopkeepers, Travelling-Traders and others" interested in the pamphlet that "a Number of other curious and entertaining pieces" were also

[95] Joshua Brooks, comp., *A Dictionary of Works on the Prophecies* (London, 1835); Hopkins, *Woman to Deliver Her People*, p. xiv.

[96] Ruth Bloch, *Visionary Republic: Millennial Themes in American Thought, 1756–1800* (New York, 1985), p. 121.

[97] [R. Hawes], *A Remarkable Prophecy* (Portsmouth, N.H., 1794), pp. 3–5. Ruth Bloch notes that this pamphlet was extensively reprinted in America, as a separate publication and in almanacs and newspapers with wide regional circulation. "It is doubtful," she writes, "that many people took it seriously. Perhaps it was even intended as a spoof on contemporary credulity." At least one New Englander, however, cited "the Quarry-stone (if any such there be)" as proof of the imminent defeat of the Antichrist. Bloch, *Visionary Republic*, p. 163.

[98] Quoted in Paul Boyer, *When Time Shall Be No More*, p. 76.

[99] See, for example, George Riebau, *God's Awful Warnings* (London, 1795); Garnet Terry, *Prophetical Extracts* (London, 1795); the weekly periodical *The World's Doom; or Fate Unlocked* (London, 1795); and the edited volume *Prophetic Conjectures on the French Revolution*, which was published in London in 1794 and reprinted in Northampton, Philadelphia, and Baltimore. Riebau and Terry were well-known publishers of radical political material as well as millenarian tracts in the 1790s.

available, "and are to be sold exceeding cheap by Wholesale."[100] As a contributor to the *Gentlemen's Magazine* complained in 1812, "nothing written upon the subject of prophecy, rational or enthusiastic, now remains long upon the shelves, or even upon the stalls of the meanest bookseller." Readers were alarmingly undiscriminating in their choice of material, consulting respectable almanacs side by side with "the ravings of Johanna Southcott."[101] Indeed, almanacs were likely to include excerpts from prophetic pamphlets, as did Robin Goodfellow's *Poor Robin's Alamanc for the Year 1796*, which incorporated extracts from Richard Brothers's best-selling *Revealed Knowledge of the Prophecies & Times.*[102]

The ancient prophecies appealed because they touched a scarcely dormant collective memory of folk prophets and their predictions. When the American itinerant Lorenzo Dow toured England in 1806, he was astonished (and pleased) at the depth of British knowledge of their own prophetic history. "As I was passing *Moor*, I could not but reflect on *Nixon's* prophecy of a battle to be fought in this place, in which England should be won and lost three times in one day, whilst a miller with three thumbs should hold three kings horses; which I remarked in my discourse at *Newpale* at two o'clock; and was afterwards informed that a miller of the above description, now resided at the mill mentioned in the prophecy; and moreover, that 'in the neighborhood where *Nixon* (called the *Cheshire fool*) lived, it was received as a truth, that many things which he had prophesied, did really come to pass.' "[103] Modern-day versions of Nixon's prophecies were not simple reproductions; they often substituted contemporary personalities and events for the original characters, as in the case of the pamphlet *Past, Present, and to Come*, where readers were advised to insert the name "George" into verses predicting the defeat of Richard III.[104]

The transformation of folk heroes like Nixon into modern-day prophets entailed more than just the insertion of contemporary references into old

---

[100] England's Timely Remembrancer, *The Minister Preaching his own Funeral Sermon*, n.p.

[101] *Gentlemen's Magazine* 82 (April 1812), p. 328.

[102] Robin Goodfellow, *Poor Robin's Almanac* (Philadelphia, 1795), pp. 18–21; for other examples, see Nehemiah Strong, *An Astronomical Diary, Calendar, or Alamanck, for the Year of Our Lord, 1794* (Hartford, Conn., 1793); David Hale, *Father Abraham's Almanac for the Year of Our Lord, 1794* (Philadelphia, 1793); *Haswell's Almanack, and Register for the State of Vermont; for the Year of Our Lord 1793* (Bennington, Vt., 1795).

[103] Dow, *Cosmopolite*, p. 285.

[104] *Past, Present, and to Come: The Prophecy at Large, of Robert Nixon, the Cheshire Prophet* (London, 1810), p. 25.

dynastic stories. The figure of the prophet himself was transformed from that of a conjurer skilled in the ancient arts of divination to that of a rustic peasant whose predictive powers were more a matter of native cunning than true inspiration. An early account of Mother Shipton (Figure 3) published in the *Gentleman's Magazine* lampooned her reputation as a woman of supernatural origins and powers. "This *great Prophetess* came into the World, like her Brother Merlin, in a very extraordinary Manner, being begot by a *Damon* in Masquerade, on the Body of a *poor young Girl* whom He found bemoaning her Condition by the side of a River." Shipton's many "Pranks" included "setting Women upon their Heads, and transforming Men into horned Beasts." Beguiled by this she-devil, "Multitudes of all Ranks resorted to Her for the Knowledge of future Events, which she explain'd to Them in several *mystical prophecies*," none of which made any sense. The author "humbly propose[d]" in closing that the "*Ladies of Great Britain*" erect a statute in her memory "in some Place of publick Resort, with *Mother Bunch*, on one Side, as her *Prime Minister*, and *Mother Osborne*, as her *Secretary*, on the other."[105] Such articles poked fun at the credulity of England's popular classes while leaving no room for serious consideration of prophecy as a valid intellectual or political enterprise. Robert Nixon suffered a similar fate at the hands of late eighteenth-century popularizers. Born in 1467, the Cheshire prophet was noted for his "stupidity and invincible ignorance." A "short, squab fellow [who] had a great head and goggle eyes," he spoke "with so rough a voice that it was painful to hear him" and was, in the words of a local woodman, "extraordinarily surly." The reputation of this "famous idiot" was more an indictment of his foolish contemporaries than of Nixon himself, who after all only behaved as any simple peasant would when presented with such a golden opportunity to gull the high and mighty.[106]

If ancient diviners could be so easily discredited as fools and knaves, the classic literary foils of an enlightened age, how did millennial writers in the revolutionary era present their own qualifications to a skeptical readership? Most, mindful of the modern impatience for religious enthusiasm of any kind, were careful to distance themselves from the world of supernatural inspiration altogether. The prefaces to prophetic publications offered writers the opportunity to disarm critics, and most included fairly formulaic disclaimers of the type penned by James Bicheno in 1817: "I make no pretence to any extraordinary qualifications for the interpretation of Prophecy. . . . If I

---

[105] "Rachel Foresight to Mr. D'Anvers," *Gentleman's Magazine* 6 (Feb. 1736), p. 88.
[106] *Past, Present, and to Come*, pp. 3–4; Valenze, "Prophecy and Popular Literature," p. 78.

Long have I view'd thy troubles Fox,
Fear not for thou shalt yet controul.
And be great Britains chief —
England will sink without thy aid.
Take this Good Man be not afraid
And Guard its pudding & its beef.

SACRED
TO LIBERTY

MOTHER SHIPTON'S PROPHECY

Figure 3. "Mother Shipton's Prophecy," ca. 1784. Department of Prints and Drawings, British Museum. The ancient diviner is advising Charles Fox, the people's politician, to "guard" England's "pudding & its beef."

have any true light, and be not deceived by the illusions of fancy, it is derived from that source which is open to all."[107] The American Edward King, in his *Remarks on the Signs of the Times*, reassured readers that he was "no rash Enthusiast.—I desire to be exceedingly guarded against Error; and I have not the least presumptuous idea of intending to prophecy."[108] One of Richard Brothers's many defenders argued, "It needs neither the penetration of the eagle eyed divine, nor the critical acumen of the Goliah of literature" to be a prophet. "Any person possessing common sense, and a mind untainted with prejudice, may if he will examine for himself, descry in the Scriptures, a faithful account of modern revolutions, and the awful signs of the times, written as with a sun beam, in characters the most legible."[109] The American Benjamin Gale agreed. The prophecies are "so easy, clear, and intelligible, that it would be an affront to any rational intelligent *Revelationist* to attempt by any words to render [them] more intelligible."[110] Even a common farmer, fearful that the "Dark Day" of May 19, 1780, signaled the end of the world, refused the temptation to call himself a prophet. "Though I do not pretend to predict what will follow this, for I am no Prophet, nor do I pretend to any revelation, for I am no Enthusiast; yet we may rationally conclude, that some singular judgment will follow."[111] If any "rational" man could read the signs of the times, then reason itself was the real winner in the game of prophetic interpretation. "The author expects to be credited only in proportion as his calculations correspond to scripture, authentic history, and rational probability," Lewis Mayer wrote somewhat pompously.[112]

This chorus of praise to reason, common sense, and the transparency of the prophetic scriptures stands in stark contrast to the singular ambitions and twisted hermeneutics of millenarian prophets. Millennial authors fairly aggressively marketed themselves as real men of the Enlightenment, free of the superstitious attachment to "mystery" that had disgraced so many prophets in the past. They challenged the epistemological foundations of

[107] James Bicheno, *The Fulfillment of Prophecy Farther Illustrated by the Signs of the Times* (London, 1817), p. vi.

[108] Edward King, *Remarks on the Signs of the Times* (Philadelphia, 1800), p. 28.

[109] S. Whitchurch, *Another Witness! or Further Testimony in Favor of Richard Brothers with a Few Modest Hints to Modern Pharisees and Reverend Unbelievers* (London, 1795), p. 9.

[110] Benjamin Gale, *A Brief Essay or, An attempt to prove . . . what period of prophecy the Church of God is now under* (New Haven, 1788), p. 31.

[111] A Farmer in the State of Massachusetts-Bay, *Some Remarks on the Great and Unusual Darkness, that appeared on Friday, May 19, 1780* (Danvers, Mass., 1780), pp. 5–6.

[112] Lewis Mayer, *Lucifer, Gog and Bonaparte: and the Issue of the Present Contest between Great Britain and France, Considered according to Divine Revelation; with an Appeal to Reason* (London, 1804), p. 23.

prophecy as understood and practiced by generations of seers before them: that the Book of Revelation was a "sealed" book, unintelligible to all but a chosen few; that carnal reason alone was insufficient to understand the meaning of God's messages, whether encoded in scripture or in providential occurrences; that prophets had unique access to the world of revelation because of their special sensory receptiveness. Prophecy, to these enlightened authors, was the art of translation only—equivalent to rendering Greek into English, say. Their skills were those of the linguist, acquired through diligent study of the classical languages and applied in a conscientious manner to current events. Millennial authors were no less elitist than millenarian prophets, but their distinction was a matter of superior intellect and training, not miraculous spiritual discernment. They could be downright contemptuous of their less cultured peers; James Bicheno explicitly contrasted his own learned explications with the "effusions" of a "few crazy, or deluded people" who were passing themselves off as divine oracles. Bicheno—a republican in his political leanings—was a cultural snob at heart, promising not to "obtrude my own reveries" upon his readers.[113]

For all their pretensions of gentility, however, millennial authors did not entirely abandon the vulgarity that gave millenarian culture its vaunted bellicosity. Their classicisms, linguistic showiness, and scholarly allusions were often encased in a narrative structure that was more playful than pompous. The juxtaposition of bombast and humility that characterized the writings of those whom Catherine Kaplan calls "political melancholics" in the revolutionary era also characterized the productions of millenarians despite their greater distance from the norms and standards of the literary mainstream. Worlds apart in their relation to the "republic of letters" being constructed by publicists and politicians in late eighteenth-century Anglo-America, melancholics and millenarians nonetheless shared an essential identity as spurned prodigies competing for reputation and influence in the marketplace of public opinion with more adept practitioners.[114]

Millennialists engaged in a form of shadowboxing with their cultural critics, rejecting the argument that prophetic exegesis was circular, obtuse, and maddeningly indeterminate even while they flirted with incomprehensibility. Those furthest down the social scale had the least to lose, in terms of reputation and remuneration. Millennialists who hailed from the empire's

---

[113] James Bicheno, *The Probable Progress and Issue of the Commotions which have Agitated Europe since the French Revolution* (London, 1797), p. 8.

[114] Catherine O. Kaplan, " 'We Have Joys . . . They Do Not Know': Letters, Partisanship, and Sentiment in the New Nation, 1790–1812," Ph.D. diss., University of Michigan, 1998.

periphery (Scotland, Nova Scotia, the western fringes of North American settlement) came closest to capturing the eccentricity of millenarian prophets in print.[115] A dialogue conjured up by the western Massachusetts prophet Simon Hough with a fusty clergyman typifies the irreverence of millenarian culture.

Clergyman.   Then you think you are a Prophet, do you?
Simon.   My works show what I am; and yours what you are.
Clergyman.   Why what are you? and what am I?
Simon.   I am a poor old, despised creature: and you are a hireling, I think.
Clergyman.   I think you are a pretty blunt, saucy fellow.[116]

His fellow prophet from the New England backcountry, William Scales, played both ends against the middle in his manifesto *The Confusion of Babel Discovered.* Opening with a standard denial of personal ambition ("As to people's despising my person, I nothing regard that; I don't want to be much esteemed"), Scales urged his fellow commoners to "Read this piece with candor; and if you can answer it fairly without quibbling, carping, or wrestling reason and scripture, but in a rational scriptural way, I desire you would." While denouncing the clever words of those "criticks and quibblers" who were hiding scriptural truth behind "serpentine mazes," Scales proceeded to engage in some verbal dexterity of his own. "Some words I use are indeed something singular, and one or two of them I formed myself," he confessed. But it was sometimes necessary to fight fire with fire. "I know that I have as good a right to form words as others; especially when the words I form are expressive of the tricks of the deceivers," he argued cleverly. "The word bamboozlement I formed from the verb to bamboozle, which word means to deceive a man out of common sense by much fair speeches, by much insinuation, much sophistical argumentation and pretensions of friendship. . . . By the word cajolement, I mean the fair, the beguiling, the enchanting speeches and conversation of false teachers."[117] It's not clear who's bamboozling who here; when

---

[115] Ruth Bloch's survey of the social origins of millennial writers reveals that, though most were college-educated clergymen or lay professionals, "the authors of millennial works came from unusually modest social backgrounds and isolated rural milieus." Bloch, "The Social and Political Base of Millennial Literature in Late Eighteenth-Century America," *American Quarterly* 40 (Sept. 1988), p. 389.

[116] Simon Hough, *The Sign of the Present Time: Or, A Short Treatise Setting Forth What Particular Prophecies are Now Fulfilling in the Author's Opinion* (Stockbridge, Mass., 1793), p. 23.

[117] Scales, *Confusion of Babel Discovered*, pp. iv, vi, vii-viii.

all words are equally unreliable, who should readers trust? The implicit message, that language itself is an unstable medium of communication open to error and outright fraud in the hands of the wrong person, was conveyed in the form if not the content of much millennial writing in the revolutionary era.

Henry Alline, the charismatic Nova Scotian prophet, provides perhaps the best example of the studied eccentricity of millennial writing. Alline wrote much as he spoke—rapturously. Sounding every bit as inflamed as the most *outré* medieval saint, Alline's theological and devotional texts combined the erotics of mystical experience with the poetics of a venerable strand of visionary literature. One of his critics, a Methodist, scorned the heterogeneous brew that Alline served up in his printed journal and sermons. "He allegorized to such excess the plainest narratives and announcements of Scriptures, that the obvious and unsophisticated import of the words of inspiration were often entirely lost amidst the reveries of mysticism."[118] The charge is not entirely frivolous; Alline's theological works do in fact exhibit some extravagant tendencies, such as a reluctance to break up his visionary riffs on resurrection and the day of judgment into paragraphs or even sentences. A rhapsodic, though by no means extreme, passage wonders how the "Soul" can resist the biblical invitation to "view the ravishing Scene, glide the attracting Stream, feast on the living bread, and drink the essence of Angellic Cordials, without a friendly Warning, and an endearing Call to that wandering Soul, starving Stranger, benighted Mind, unfeeling Reader, wandering Jew, that never tasted of the clusters of Eshcol?"[119] The lush lyricism of Alline's prose probably sounded better in person than it does on the printed page; there's no question he was a powerful speaker, capable of rousing the emotions of Nova Scotia's Scots-Irish Calvinists—a notoriously dour bunch. Ecstasy was a hard sell, however, for a millennial author: such purple prose was deemed closer to spiritual intoxication than enlightenment. No wonder John Wesley dismissed Alline's "miserable jargon" as a consequence of his ill-considered "dabbling in Mystical writers."[120]

[118] Matthew Richey, *A Memoir of the Late Rev. William Black* (Halifax, 1839), p. 45; quoted in George Rawlyk, ed., *Henry Alline: Selected Writings* (New York, 1987), p. 10. Alline's clearest theological and literary debt was to the strand of mystical teaching represented by Jacob Boehme and his eighteenth-century disciples, including William Law: some of Alline's book *The Anti-Traditionalist* (Halifax, 1783) is, in fact, lifted directly from Law's *Spirit of Power* (*Henry Alline: Selected Writings*, p. 19); see also John M. Bumsted, *Henry Alline* (Toronto, 1971).

[119] Alline, *The Anti-Traditionalist*; quoted in *Selected Writings*, p. 214.

[120] John Wesley to William Black, July 13, 1783, in John Telford, ed., *The Letters of Rev. John Wesley* (New York, 1915), 8:182.

We have heard this critique before, and will hear it again when we delve more deeply into the murky politics of revolutionary-era prophecy in Chapter 4, but the effort to translate the "reveries of mysticism" into a respectable form of millennial discourse did not wither in the face of such unrelenting criticism. Rather, it continued to vex prophets well into the nineteenth century. Once committed to print, however, such reveries lost some of their power to dazzle and compel, and left their authors open to charges of delusion or (worse) bad taste. Alline's more formal writings on the millennium never enjoyed the popularity of his journal, which was first published posthumously in 1806. Other prophetic writers cut from the millenarian cloth limited themselves to one or two literary offerings, and their publications rarely reached the sales of more respectable authors such as James Bicheno and the American millennialist Samuel Hopkins.

Without exception, these millennial tracts were written by men. This should come as no surprise: few women had the classical training necessary to be prophetic linguists, and the intellectual emancipation promised by the Enlightenment was rarely extended to women, still considered the mentally weaker sex by most philosophes. Biblical explication, whether of the prophetic texts or of other scriptures, was traditionally the preserve of ministers and theologians, also an exclusively male fraternity. Women found it easier to navigate the public culture of millenarianism, rooted as it was (still, if problematically) in the promise of direct revelation. It is as close to a truism as historically possible that women were associated in western Christendom with the domain of the spirit rather than the mind: with revelation over the word, inspiration over education.[121] The farther the culture of millenarianism moved away from its supernatural origins, the more difficult women found it to assume the role of prophet; women were underrepresented among the population of millenarian prophets described earlier, and (with a few prominent exceptions) they tended to disappear from public view after 1800.[122]

[121] Marilyn J. Westerkamp explores the basic theological and devotional tension between (female) spirit and (male) word in Anglo-American religion in *Women and Religion in Early America, 1600–1850: The Puritan and Evangelical Traditions* (New York, 1999); Catherine Brekus examines the practical effects of this tension on women's opportunities for public expression in *Strangers and Pilgrims: Female Preaching in America, 1740–1845* (Chapel Hill, N.C., 1998). For a review of the historical literature on women and the spirit, see Susan Juster, "The Spirit and the Flesh: Gender, Language, and Sexuality in American Protestantism," in *New Directions in American Religious History*, ed. Harry S. Stout and D. G. Hart (New York, 1997), pp. 334–61.

[122] On both sides of the Atlantic male prophets outnumbered female prophets by a considerable margin. In Britain, 67 of the 189 prophets I have identified in the revolutionary era were female (35 percent), while in North America 45 of the 126 prophets were women (36 percent).

Gender was, however, always a second-order category of analysis for prophets and their critics. Women prophets may have occupied a special place as illiterate visionaries in the discourse of authenticity, but their primary virtue (or liability, depending on one's point of view) was their close identification with the "common": illiteracy was a marker of class position more than gender in the eighteenth century, and visionaries who claimed direct inspiration did so in the face of mounting cultural criticism of religious enthusiasm as undisciplined, disorderly, and unseemly—in a word, vulgar. As a subcategory of the vulgar, Anglo-American women in general and prophetesses in particular found themselves engaging the rhetorical wars over inspiration on a number of different fronts. Sometimes their gender worked against them, as when they tried to adopt the language and rhetorical forms of "civil millennialism."[123] Sometimes their gender worked in their favor, as when they used their sexuality to envision ever more intimate encounters with the divine. Always they faced the contempt of the learned and powerful, which was a disarmingly flexible weapon in the revolutionary era.[124] How, and at what costs, men and women prophets entertained the spirit of prophecy in the glare of relentless public exposure is the subject of the next two chapters.

[123] Nathan Hatch, in *The Sacred Cause of Liberty* (New Haven, 1977), coined the phrase "civil millennialism" to describe the fusion of political and religious aims in millennial publications in the American colonies during the French and Indian War.

[124] Don Herzog explores the varied political uses of contempt in British political culture in *Poisoning the Minds of the Lower Orders*.

Chapter 3
Body and Soul:
The Epistemology of Revelation

Three decades before the French Prophets made their dramatic entrance upon the British religious scene, a prophetess by the name of Jane Lead joined a small millenarian sect in London. Lead was a new breed of prophet from the fire-eaters of the Civil War era, who, convinced that the world would come to a bloody end in their own lifetime if not by their own hand, spoke with an urgency born of genuine panic. Lead was more a mystic than a red-blooded millenarian, drawing inspiration from the visionary rhapsodies of the German writer Jacob Boehme (or Behmen, as the English called him) while affecting a posture of quiet waiting for the Second Coming. Surveying the wickedness that surrounded her, she counseled patience and penitence, not immediate action. In her passivity and insistence that Christ's kingdom be renewed from within rather than imposed from without, she represents the chastened millenarian culture of the Restoration era. Escaping her own bodily infirmities into the exalted realm of the spirit, she spoke with celestial beings and translated their wisdom into human terms. She was also a bridge between two traditions of inspired behavior—the incorporated and the incorporeal. When she died in 1704, she left behind a corpus of mystical treatises that were widely read on the continent and a small but sturdy circle of adherents who would welcome the Camisard prophets in 1707 as fellow travelers. Straddling two centuries, her story allows us to see how the epistemology of revelation was reconfigured in the Anglo-American world in the century and a half between the Civil War and the "age of revolution."

Lead belongs to a long, illustrious tradition of spiritual prodigies who come from nowhere to speak with a mighty voice. No one could have predicted that this unassuming widow would become the leader of a small community of mystics whose influence would cross international borders by the 1690s. Frail, and without any visible means of support after her husband's death in 1670, Lead moved into the home of her spiritual father, Dr. John Pordage, four years later. Pordage, the foremost popularizer of Jacob Boehme's theology in England, was a noted visionary in his own right who had helped found the millenarian Philadelphian Society in the 1660s after being briefly imprisoned for "blasphemy and immoral conduct" during Cromwell's Protectorate. Lead soon surpassed her mentor, a rather anemic mystic whose "pale and bloodless" revelations (in the words of one historian) betray a certain "poverty of emotion and imagination" in comparison to the far more robust visions of his disciple.[1] Together Lead and Pordage transformed the Philadelphians from a private congregation into a public society, of which Lead was the undisputed head following Pordage's death in 1681.

Prophecy was never the focal point of Lead's ministry. She "always rejected the title of a prophetess when it was applied to her," according to her son-in-law and chief scribe Francis Lee, though she did "think herself to be conducted & taught by ye Holy Spirit, as really as ye Prophets under ye old, or ye Apostles under ye New Testament did themselves." Her prophecies, however, tended to be "of a more universal nature, or indeterminate as to persons & times" than English millenarians were accustomed to, Lee explained. Rather than issue pointed calls-to-arms, Lead advised her followers to await Christ's Second Coming in their own hearts and souls—"to retire into their centre, that they might find within them the living oracle."[2] Under her leadership the society became a center of mystical theology, publishing a monthly periodical and Lead's own writings, which by the 1690s were available in Germany and Holland, earning the prophetess an international reputation as an important and original thinker in the Behmenite tradition. By 1703, however, Lead's health was deteriorating and her final publication, written in haste and poorly edited, went nearly unnoticed in Britain. When she died in August 1704 after a long and debilitating illness, she left behind a dispirited group of believers whose millenarian hopes were buried with their leader.[3]

Lead's visions, profuse and sensual, are at the core of her unique theology. The full flowering of her mysticism began with a visit in April 1670 to the

[1] Nils Thune, *The Behmenists and the Philadelphians: A Contribution to the Study of English Mysticism in the Seventeenth and Eighteenth Centuries* (Uppsala, 1948), pp. 155, 158.

[2] Francis Lee, "Copy of Letter to Henry Dodwell," Lee Letterbook; Walton MSS I.1.35, Dr. Williams's Library, London.

[3] Modern treatments of Lead include B. J. Gibbons, *Gender in Mystical and Occult Thought: Behmenism and Its Development in England* (Cambridge, 1996); Catherine F. Smith, "Jane Lead: The Feminist Mind and Art of a Seventeenth-Century Protestant Mystic," in *Women of Spirit: Female Leadership in the Jewish and Christian Traditions,* ed. Rosemary Ruether and Eleanor McLaughlin (New York, 1979), pp. 183–204; and Catherine F. Smith, "Jane Lead: Mysticism and the Woman Clothed with the Sun," in *Shakespeare's Sisters: Feminist Essays on Women Poets,* ed. Sandra Gilbert and Susan Gubar (Bloomington, Ind., 1979), pp. 3–18.

"astral" regions where she met a woman in gold with flowing hair who pronounced herself to be "God's Eternal Virgin-Wisdom," a figure of central importance in Behmenist theology as the personification of the original, androgynous essence of the deity. The woman told Lead, "I shall now cease to appear in a Visible Figure unto thee, but I will not fail to transfigure myself in thy mind; and there open the Spring of Wisdom and Understanding."[4] From this original vision, Lead spun out an elaborate cosmology that combined alchemical, hermetic, and cabalistic elements. A contrast between the "terrestrial" and the "celestial" spheres anchored this cosmology. The former is dark, foul, full of loathsome matter and rank corruption: the world of human bodies and their gross materiality. The latter is light, airy, transparent: the world of God and his angels, of "translated" souls who have been liberated from the "Dark Root" of human nature and released into their true spiritual form. Imprisoned in the terrestrial sphere, the soul yearns to recapture the lightness and purity it once enjoyed as part of the cosmic oneness of all being. This yearning—powerful, at times erotic—drives the believer to declare war on the body, to mortify the flesh and literally "starve" its appetites into submission. This was, Lead confessed, "*Bloody* Work," since the "animal" part of human nature did not yield easily to the "Sacrificing Knife." But if vigilant in self-denial, the believer can "famish the life of low Mortal Sense" and overcome desire itself. The result of such "spiritual death" will be a new, "supersensual" body—"aiery, thin, and of a transparent purity."[5] Purified by fire (the alchemist's tool), or what Lead called the "burning Spirit," the carnal body of the saint is consumed from within in a slow, painful process of self-immolation: "the Furnace of everlasting Burnings must be fixed on necessity, and then diligently attended upon, till the dark black Matter become white, clear, and shining, as transparent Silver."[6]

The final and complete obliteration of the physical self will not be accomplished until death for most believers, of course, but God has provided an alternative route to "spiritual death" for those believers willing to explore the visionary realm. The "*Natural* and bodily sense" is "the great and only impediment to all Divine Vision, Prophecy, and Revelation," Lead argued; "no soul or Spirit can come to have a plain and open view of a Glorified Personality, as seen and known in the Heavenly Sphears, but as their sensible

---

[4] Quoted in Thune, *Behmenists and Philadelphians*, p. 175.

[5] Jane Lead, *The Heavenly Cloud Now Breaking; Or the Lord Christ's Ascension Ladder Sent Down* (London, 1682), pp. 6, 26.

[6] Jane Lead, *A Fountain of Gardens; or, A Spiritual Diary of the Wonderful Experiences of a Christian Soul, under the Conduct of the Heavenly Wisdom* (London, 1700), pp. 68, 258.

part is suspended, and laid as in a deep sleep." The body of the visionary must enter into a "Transical, Eternal Nothingness. Then it Knows, Hears, and Sees, as in God's Glance."[7] This was no easy task, given the coarseness of the material which the Spirit had to overcome. "The Spirit of our Lord Jesus hath a difficult and hard word to effect," Lead cautioned, "because he hath to do with a heavy gross, sluggish Body."[8] This suspension of all bodily functions was described as a "mystical death," the first step in the visionary's journey toward union with God. The next step ("resurrection") entails "the *restoring* of the *lost* Senses in a Supernatural way. For a risen Soul and Spirit have all the sensation of a Spiritual Body." Freed of the burdens of the terrestrial sphere, the visionary's spiritual senses are heightened and enhanced: she enjoys "crystalline *sight*," "supersensual *hearing*," an "all-penetrating" sense of smell, and "unutterable ravishing Pleasure."[9]

The final stage, which only a select few can hope to reach, is "ascension": the actual merging of the body of the visionary with Christ's spirit. In this exalted state a true "transubstantiation" takes place, a literal deification of the body of the saint in which the ontological "distinction of Body and Spirit shall cease."[10] Lead herself did not believe that she had achieved the final metamorphosis until her last illness. "The whole constitution of her body had been for some time before entirely infected and corrupted so that she compared it to a rotten sack," Francis Lee reported; "She was even wont to say that all that was put into it was just as if it had been thrown into a filthy receptacle, and that there was in her body a continual springing up of corrupt matter, which it was impossible to get rid of or entirely exhaust." But in her last days, she told her followers that she "was really about to be translated into the heavenly Society." As recounted by her son-in-law, "some who attended her saw her thus really hanging on the Cross. . . . She answered very readily that she not only hung on the Cross then, but had already done so for sixteen weeks. And after this, some of them observed that her feet were cold and dead."[11]

Lead's transformation into a supersensual being was a promise that she held out to all true Christians at the dawn of the millennium. The "Dying out of Creaturely Sensation, whereby a Vacancy of Place would be for the

[7] Lead, *Heavenly Cloud*, pp. 15–16.
[8] Lead, *Fountain of Gardens*, pp. 66–68.
[9] Lead, *Heavenly Cloud*, pp. 29, 41–42.
[10] Lead, *Fountain of Gardens*, p. 322.
[11] Francis Lee, "The Last Hours of Jane Lead, by an Eye and Ear Witness," 1704, Walton MSS C.5.30, Dr. Williams's Library, London.

Holy Ghost to rise, spring and move," was not a privilege given to prophets only, but "will be the manner of my Coming in this Latter Day," the Spirit of God told her. At the Second Coming, "each one [will] become a Christ (or an Annointed) from this Deified Root opening with their own Soul."[12] And only those who had experienced spiritual translation will be saved from destruction when the final battle with the Antichrist was joined; "in this last troublesome time that Fire-Ball will kindle throughout all Nations, whereby they shall consume and devour one another. But there will be given again the immaculate Body to some, for a distinguishing and sealing Mark over which the destroying Angels of Judgment will have no Power."[13] The conventional Protestant eschatology is here reversed; rather than the soul being released to merge with the mystical body of Christ at the millennium, Christ's divinity takes up residence in and transforms the body of the believer.

This powerful image of the resurrection of Christ's "Ethereal Body" in each of his believers would prove to be enormously appealing to a new generation of spiritual seekers who shared Lead's animosity toward the body and her desire for physical dissolution. In the memoirs of evangelicals and visionaries written in the century after Lead's death, believers struggle with and against their bodies, trying to rid themselves of the burden of physicality in order to reach the light of truth. They speak of being "crucified" in nature, of having their bodies dismembered and pulled apart. They long to feel God's love flowing through their veins and his breath filling their lungs, but instead find themselves invaded by sharp objects and scorched by hot flames and burning coals. The bodily representations of eighteenth-century visionaries—full of pain and the primal fear of evisceration—tell us that the role of the body in the epistemology of revelation had changed significantly between the revolutions of the 1640s and the 1790s. Late eighteenth-century prophets inherited this ambivalent relationship to the world of bodies and materiality, and they responded with a variety of representational strategies that only underscored how difficult it was to successfully dismember the body without destroying the soul.

[12] Jane Lead, *The Enochian Walks with God, Found out by a Spiritual Traveller* (London, 1694), p. 48.
[13] Lead, *Fountain of Gardens*, p. 57.

Crucifying the Flesh: Open and Closed Bodies

Hostility toward the flesh is, of course, a mainstay of Christian soteriology. The need to overcome the corruptions of the natural self in order to reach a higher spiritual level is present in Christian theology as far back as Augustine. But the nature of the body and its relation to spirituality has been understood differently in different confessional traditions and different time periods. By listening closely to the words of visionaries as they tried to describe what is at bottom an ineffable experience, we can begin to sketch a history of what we might call the epistemology of revelation—the various ways that human beings in the past have come to know God. This chapter explores the internal dynamics of supernatural encounters in the lives of eighteenth- and early nineteenth-century prophets and visionaries. The focus here, and in the following chapter, is on the shifting dialectic between body and language, experience and expression, that has shaped the spirituality of charismatic men and women: how exactly did visionaries experience God, and how did they communicate that experience to their followers? What do the answers to these questions tell us about notions of human subjectivity and the place of the body and gender in conceptions of the self in the eighteenth century? For all the bluster and drama of millenarian culture in the revolutionary era, prophets were astute readers of the psychological milieu in which they operated, and they responded to a variety of clues in their cultural environment about how best to capture the phenomenological experience of spiritual communion for their audiences. Their goal was always to persuade listeners predisposed to discount tales of spiritual prodigy that they had been truly touched by the spirit, and the burden of plausibility imposed certain rhetorical constraints on their autobiographical writings that reveal as much as they conceal for the discerning reader. We will hear echoes of the larger public discourse about truth and authenticity explored in Chapter 1; here, too, the broader evangelical community of which millenarians were a quirky subset provides much of the evidence for prevailing cultural attitudes about the relation of body to soul. Historians are fortunate that eighteenth-century evangelical Protestants left such a rich biographical and autobiographical literature behind for us to mine, albeit in ways that would surely have discomfited the men and women we study.[14]

[14] For recent examples of the use of religious memoirs to uncover structures of subjectivity, see Mechal Sobel, *Teach Me Dreams: The Search for Self in the Revolutionary Era* (Princeton, N.J., 2000); Phyllis Mack, *Visionary Women: Ecstatic Prophecy in Seventeenth-Century England* (Berkeley, Calif., 1992); Ann Taves, *Fits, Trances, and Visions: Experiencing Religion and Explaining Experience from Wesley to James* (Princeton, N.J., 1999).

Broadly speaking, we can discern three models of the human body that were formative in the experience of visionaries from the early modern period through the nineteenth century. The first model, operative from at least the late Middle Ages and continuing to shape religious behavior well into the eighteenth century, is that of the porous, unbounded body: a body constituted by the flow and balance of humoral fluids, open physically to the external world via an interlocking system of orifices and arteries and metaphorically by a cosmology that posited a fundamental congruence between the natural and the supernatural. Knowledge and sensation both flow through the unbounded body, allowing visionaries to experience God in a particularly intimate and material way. Visionaries within this paradigm speak of being saturated by the presence of the Spirit, of grace flowing through their very veins, of an ability to incorporate both the sufferings and ecstasies of Christ and his people into their own bodies.

In the second model, which became the dominant paradigm in the eighteenth century, the reciprocal relationship of nature and supernature is still maintained via the body of the saint, but the human body itself has become a "clogged" vessel rather than a porous one—defined not by openings and channels, but by bones and muscles and the ligatures that bind them. Spiritual encounters are just as somatic as in the early modern period, but access to the body takes different form: spiritual power pulsing through limbs and muscles in a jerky and often painful way rather than flowing through the veins and porous membrane of the skin. Visionaries within this paradigm no longer speak of being saturated by God, but of being "invaded" by the Spirit, of having their bodies attacked and even destroyed by the experience.

In the third model, which we can trace to the influence of Romanticism and the turn away from the more mechanical philosophy of the Enlightenment in the early nineteenth century, the supernatural is very much present in nature but not within the physical body of the believer. The external world, including the spiritual realm, is available to individuals in transparent and sublime ways, but in order to gain access to the supernatural, men and women must transcend their physical selves through mental or emotional transport. Romantic visionaries speak of "emptying" the self to form a spiritual connection with God; they experience this connection "insensibly," in a trancelike state or a state of sensory deprivation that approaches near death.

It is the second model—that of the "clogged" body and its bruising encounters with the Spirit—that most closely captures the spiritual experiences of revolutionary-era prophets and visionaries. Beginning with the Camisards and continuing through the many spiritualist movements of the eighteenth century, from early Methodism to the Shakers, a common pattern of "inspired" behavior began to manifest itself among a variety of believers. The French Prophets were particularly adept at this type of behavior, which we can conveniently label (as many contemporaries did) the "convulsive" model. The twitches, shakes, and verbal tics that struck skeptical observers as "hysteric fits" or demonic possession became generalized in the collective experiences of eighteenth-century evangelicals.[15] Like the inspired antics of the French Prophets, the sacred dancing of the Shakers and the physical convulsions of revival converts represent a form of localized somatic piety in which spiritual power energized particular bodily sites rather than flowing in and through the entire body. Legs jerking and arms flailing, Shakers and evangelicals more generally resembled puppets being manipulated by the strings of a divine puppeteer. As the Quaker Anne Moore described it, "the divine power seized me and made my flesh and bones to tremble."[16]

Paradoxically, the body remained the primary means of spiritual access in the long eighteenth century even while its more rigid and solid structures yielded less easily to the overtures of the spirit. Sarah Prentice, the wife of the Connecticut Separatist leader Solomon Prentice and a notorious immortalist, underwent a particularly jarring encounter with the Spirit: her "Nerves and Sinews contracted," and her tongue felt "like an Iron bar in her Mouth"—"At length her Stomach heaved, and She broke forth" in praise to God.[17] The British evangelist Dorothy Ripley "resisted the sacred influences of the Holy Ghost, till she sternly required of me her own; locking my jaw while I did comply with her request."[18] Susanna Anthony implored Christ "to enter the secret recesses of my soul, and divide between the joints and marrow" after suffering several harrowing encounters with the devil, during which she "twisted every joint, and strained every nerve; biting my flesh; gnashing my teeth; throwing myself on the floor."[19]

It was not until the revivals associated with the Methodist movement in

[15] The phrase "hysterick fits" is from Benjamin Bragg, *Observations Upon Elias Marion, and His Book of Warnings, Lately Publish'd* (London, 1707), p. 8; see the discussion of the French Prophets in Chapter 1.

[16] *Journal of Ann Moore*, Part II, 1778, in *Wilt Thou Go On My Errand? Journals of Three Eighteenth-Century Quaker Women Ministers*, ed. Margaret Hope Bacon (Wallingford, Pa., 1994), p. 371.

[17] "Solomon Prentice's Narrative of the Great Awakening," ed. Ross W. Beales, Jr., *Proceedings of the Massachusetts Historical Society* 83 (1971), pp. 130–47; quote on p. 135.

[18] Dorothy Ripley, *The Extraordinary Religious Conversion and Religious Experiences of Dorothy Ripley* (New York, 1810), p. 18.

[19] Samuel Hopkins, ed., *The Life and Character of Miss Susanna Anthony* (London, 1803), pp. 105, 20, 23–24.

Britain and North America that this particular model of somatic piety reached its full flowering. The journals of Methodist and other itinerant preachers are especially revealing on this score, as they record instance after instance of converts who roared out under the power of the Spirit, fell to the floor and writhed in convulsions. John Wesley encountered such behaviors everywhere he went in Great Britain, to his own discomfort. By necessity Wesley became an astute and largely sympathetic diagnostician of the workings of the Spirit, providing us with detailed, almost clinical descriptions of the bodily "exercises" of converts. Noting that his listeners were routinely "seized with violent pain" when he preached, he dissected with care the "different manners" in which their distress was expressed. "Some said they felt just as if a sword was running through them; others, that they thought a great weight lay upon them, as if it would squeeze them into the earth. Some said they were quite choked, so that they could not breathe; others, that their hearts swelled ready to burst; and others that it was as if their heart, as if their inside, as if their whole body, was tearing them all to pieces."[20] This sensation of being stabbed, choked, and torn by the Spirit led saints to insist they had been literally as well as metaphorically "crucified with Christ," a compelling metaphor for broken bodies.[21] Richard Clarke, a prolific writer of prophetic tracts in the 1760s and 1770s, declared that he had been "crucified" by "the *holy Fire . . .* which goes through and through the Joints and Marrow, with the *Jealousy* of an *Husband,* mortifying the Flesh, cutting asunder the Hardness and Adhesion of its Parts."[22]

American preachers took their cue from Wesley's influential journals, which they read avidly. The austere Francis Asbury worried that the "loud outcries, tremblings, fallings, and convulsions" common among revival converts made them appear "more like a drunken rabble than the worshipers of God."[23] But his less inhibited colleagues welcomed these "outcries" as powerful evidence of God's presence in their meetings. Benjamin Abbott recalled how "the word reached my heart in such a powerful manner that it shook every joint in my body"; when he took to his circuit he found his experiences replicated in the reactions of his listeners to his own preaching. A "quaker

[20] Nehemiah Curnock, ed., *The Journal of the Rev. John Wesley, A.M.,* standard ed., 8 vols. (London, 1910), 3:69.

[21] Testimony of Abijah Worcester, Shaker MSS VI:A-5, Western Reserve Historical Society, Cleveland, Ohio.

[22] Richard Clarke, *A Second Warning to the World by the Spirit of Prophecy* (London, 1760), p. 36.

[23] *The Journal and Letters of Francis Asbury,* ed. Elmer T. Clark (Nashville, Tenn., 1958), 1:213.

girl" was so "powerfully wrought upon, that every joint in her shook," while another woman "trembled in every joint in her body, and soon lost the use of her speech."[24] Like many itinerants, Joseph Thomas, the "White Pilgrim," was particularly struck by the strange behavior of congregations in the western theater of American evangelicalism. In Tennessee in 1810, he encountered "an exercise called the *jirks*. When it comes upon the subject he is deprived of his own power, and sometimes of his speech, as long as it continues on him. He is thus taken with an irresistible force, altogether off his feet and dashed to the ground or floor, and from one place to another, sometimes hours together."[25] The "jirks" were often accompanied by uncontrollable laughing, "screeching," "hallowing," and dancing.

The violence of these encounters—bodies flung to the floor, limbs "shaken as if . . . severed from each other"[26]—speaks to the hostility many saints felt toward their bodies in the eighteenth century. "My soul exults in the prospect of a separation from the polluted hell I live in; namely the body," the prophet Mary Pratt wrote in 1792 in language reminiscent of her forebear Jane Lead. "This foul body is like a *beast*, its appetites, its passions, its gratifications, are vile, unbecoming the loveliness of a celestial inhabitant who is always attended by a Host of Blessed Angels."[27] A natural consequence of this long and difficult process of yielding to the Spirit was the evangelical preoccupation with pain. Put most simply, it hurt to be saved. One of John Wesley's listeners felt "the very fire of hell already kindled in my breast; and all my body was in as much pain as if I had been in a burning fiery furnace." Benjamin Abbott's agony was so severe at one point that "I believe I could not have continued in the body, if God had not moderated the pain and anxiety that I was in."[28] Their bodies "torn asunder with pain," evangelical converts testified time and again that it was no easy thing to be born again.[29]

But their pain, as they recognized, was of a different order than the sufferings of medieval saints and martyrs. More pedestrian in origin and

[24] Benjamin Abbott, *The Experience and Gospel Labours of the Rev. Benjamin Abbott*, ed. John Firth (New York, 1805), pp. 43, 9–10, 14, 120, 125–26, 144, 105.

[25] Joseph Thomas, *The Life of the Pilgrim, Joseph Thomas* (Winchester, Va., 1817), pp. 162–63.

[26] Diary of Catherine Livingston Garrettson, transcribed by Diane Lobody in "Lost in the Ocean of Love: The Mystical Writings of Catherine Livingston Garretson," Ph.D. diss., Drew University, 1990, p. 279.

[27] Mary Pratt to Henry Brooke, Oct. 14, 1792, Brooke Letterbook, p. 366, Walton MS I.1.14, Dr. Williams's Library, London.

[28] Abbott, *Experience and Gospel Labours*, p. 13.

[29] Both quotes are from *Journal of John Wesley*, 3:60 ("very fire of hell") and 2:393 ("torn asunder").

less spectacular in nature, the everyday afflictions that seemed to torment eighteenth-century saints threatened to overwhelm rather than invigorate their faith. Aching heads, bruised limbs, intestinal disorders—these were occupational hazards for itinerant preachers who traveled thousands of miles in rough circumstances, and for their converts who immersed themselves in a punishing regime of self-denial and bodily mortification to conquer sin. Preachers often complained that they were "reduced to an emaciated state" by their pastoral labors, recounting in graphic detail the hardships they endured.[30] There was nothing "supernatural" or transcendent about these afflictions, for all their intensity: rather, eighteenth- and early nineteenth-century evangelicals suffered from a variety of self-described "nervous" ailments whose symptoms parody the physical ecstasies of medieval mystics. Whereas late medieval holy women bled from mysterious openings in their bodies in sympathetic imitation of the sufferings of Christ, their eighteenth-century counterparts suffered nosebleeds, bleeding lungs, and ulcerated wounds that were more likely to signal the onset of consumption than mystical union. Benjamin Randel "began to bleed from his lung, and continued bleeding all night" in 1807; "he remarked, that he left blood in a number of places in every town between Ashby and New-Durham."[31] "Crazy" James Horton reported, "When I sat down [after preaching], I felt a sudden warmth in my chest, and brought up a mouthful of blood . . . for a moment I thought I might bleed to death."[32] There is no hint of a divine origin or ecstatic release for the debilitating bleeding that afflicted so many eighteenth-century saints.

The Methodist preacher who drew "an analogy between a person sick

[30] *American Methodist Pioneer: The Life and Journals of the Rev. Freeborn Garrettson, 1752–1827*, ed. Robert Drew Simpson (Rutland, Vt., 1984), pp. 361, 401. For complaints of being "reduced to a skeleton" or "worn down to anatomy," see the following memoirs: John Oliver, *Arminian Magazine* 2 (Aug. 1779), p. 420; John Buzzell, *The Life of the Elder Benjamin Randel* (Limerick, Me., 1827), p. 49; *Memorials of Rebecca Jones*, comp. William Allinson, 2d ed. (Philadelphia, 1849), pp. 12, 14, 43; *Memoirs of B. Hibbard* (New York, 1843), p. 108; *Gifts of Power: The Writings of Rebecca Jackson, Black Visionary, Shaker Eldress*, ed. Jean M. Humez (Amherst, Mass., 1981), p. 76; and *Vicissitudes Illustrated in the Experiences of Nancy Towle, in Europe and America. Written by Herself* (Charleston, S.C., 1832), p. 17. The life spans of itinerant preachers were, in fact, shortened by the rigors of their travels. Nathan Hatch estimates that 35 percent of men who served as Methodist itinerants between 1780 and 1818 died before they reached age thirty, and another 27 percent died before the age of forty; Hatch, *The Democratization of American Christianity* (New Haven, 1989), p. 88. Catherine Brekus notes that many female preachers likewise died young; *Strangers and Pilgrims: Female Preaching in America, 1740–1845* (Chapel Hill, N.C., 1998), p. 255.

[31] *Life of Benjamin Randel*, p. 275.

[32] James Horton, *A Narrative of the Early Life, Remarkable Conversion, and Spiritual Labours of James P. Horton* (n.p., pub. for author, 1839), p. 86.

of a consumption and a sin-sick soul" was thus speaking directly to the experiences of his audience—and making an important cultural connection along the way.[33] Consumption seems to have been the archetypal disease for eighteenth- and early nineteenth-century evangelicals; almost without exception, itinerant preachers feared at one time or another that they were dying of the disease, a fear that, for some, became a reality.[34] Cultural historians like to note the tangled etymological roots of the term in the culture of eighteenth-century Britain and North America; falling prey to consumption was a social hazard of the emerging capitalist economy as well as a medical risk exacerbated by overcrowded and unsanitary living conditions. As consumption heated up in the economic sphere, the disease whose name it shared grew to dominate health concerns among doctors and laity alike.[35] For evangelicals as well as physicians, the term conjured up images of an overheated body turning on itself, becoming consumed from within by disease. In physiological terms, consumption is the inverse of sanctification: blood leaks into and clogs the lungs, contaminating rather than purging the body. The "holy bleeding" for which earlier saints were renowned was thus reduced to a pathological rather than a mystical experience.

As they slid into what they feared was a "consumptive" state, evangelicals felt their bodily and spiritual powers leached away: voices "shattered," throats "closed," stomachs "puked," "cankers" appeared, perspiration was "obstructed."[36] Disease, in fact, worked much like the spirit itself—"agitating," "seizing," and "invading" the body at its weakest points. Reading through these memoirs it is difficult to know where physical discomfort leaves off and spiritual enlightenment begins, for they are often described in exactly the

[33] Quoted in Lorenzo Dow, *History of the Cosmopolite; or the Four Volumes of Lorenzo's Journal*, 2d ed. (New York, 1815), p. 13.

[34] Christine Heyrman notes that "the early Methodist itinerancy seems to have drawn a disproportionate number of consumptives," whose "frail" and "feminine" appearance was as much a cause of concern as their uncontrolled bleeding; *Southern Cross: The Beginnings of the Bible Belt* (New York, 1997), p. 213.

[35] G. J. Barker-Benfield notes that "Consumption, denoting both the 'wasting' disease and the acquisition of new goods . . . took on fresh value in this century." *The Culture of Sensibility: Sex and Society in Eighteenth-Century Britain* (Chicago, 1992), p. 28.

[36] For "shattered voices," see *Memoirs of B. Hibbard*, p. 420, *Life of the Pilgrim Joseph Thomas*, pp. 51, 158: for "closed" throats, see Account of Thomas Olivers, *Arminian Magazine* 2 (Feb. 1779), p. 84; for "foul" stomachs and nausea, see Diary of William Smythe Babcock, Feb. 19, 1802, Jan. 3, 1804, Babcock Papers, American Antiquarian Society, Worcester, Mass.; and Dow, *Cosmopolite*, p. 60: for cankers and ulcers, see *Journals of Francis Asbury*, 1:146–47; Babcock Diary, Apr. 5, 1802; Dow, *Cosmopolite*, pp. 109, 261, 303: for obstructed perspiration, see Babcock Diary, Feb. 19, 1802; *Memoirs of B. Hibbard*, p. 232; *Journals of Francis Asbury*, 1:645, 2:429: for "a most violent fever," see *Journal of Elizabeth Hudson*, p. 142.

same language. The point is that for many saints, grace *felt* like illness; they were often hard pressed to distinguish between the two. If grace was experienced as a "spasm" of the arms and legs, so too was illness: William Smythe Babcock complained repeatedly of the "spasmodic affections" that induced lameness in his legs, and Lorenzo Dow was on several occasions "flung" into "spasms like convulsions" which "shook his constitution to the centre."[37] If the Spirit invaded the bones of converts, so too did disease: Alexander Mather's bones were "filled as with a sore disease," and John Haime's "very bones quaked" when he was "thrown into a bloody flux."[38] "Attacked again and again" by spiritual and physical torments whose meaning they could not decipher, evangelicals like Catherine Livingston were confused and disoriented; after months of recording such "cruel conflicts," Livingston stopped writing in her diary altogether for two years out of sheer frustration. "I know not what to think!—I am confounded!" she confessed in December 1788. "Seven months I have wandered in a strange land. . . . I have been afflicted! tormented! disappointed! deluded! I have been bewildered and almost distracted!"[39] She was not alone in her despair, as the demystification of pain led eighteenth-century saints to question why they continued to suffer afflictions that seemed to have no redemptive value. The "psychosomatic unit" of body and soul that late medieval saints found so empowering was disrupted if not shattered in the eighteenth century.[40]

[37] Babcock Diary, Jan. 3, 1804; *Cosmopolite*, pp. 261, 276, 300, 306.

[38] Account of Alexander Mather, *Arminian Magazine* 3 (Feb. 1780), p. 95; Account of John Haime, *Arminian Magazine* 3 (Apr. 1780), pp. 265–66.

[39] Lobody, "Lost in the Ocean of Love," pp. 152, 182–83, 197–99, 201–2, 209, 213, 239, 244–45.

[40] The phrase "psychosomatic unit" is Caroline Walker Bynum's; see "The Female Body and Religious Practice in the Later Middle Ages," in her *Fragmentation and Redemption: Essays on Gender and the Human Body in Medieval Religion* (New York, 1992), p. 234. As Phyllis Mack argues, pain had no "inherent spiritual significance" for eighteenth-century dissenters; Mack, "Giving Birth to the Truth: A Letter by the Methodist Mary Taft," *Scottish Journal of Religious Studies* 19 (1998), p. 24. On the eighteenth century as a pivotal moment in the history and discourse of pain, see Elaine Forman Crane, " 'I Have Suffer'd Much Today': The Defining Force of Pain in Early America," in *Through a Glass Darkly: Reflections on Personal Identity in Early America*, ed. Ronald Hoffman, Mechal Sobel, and Fredrika J. Teute (Chapel Hill, N.C., 1997), pp. 370–403.

Spectacle and Sympathy: Imagining the Body

The fear and pain that spiritual seeking brought was repressed or redirected away from the self toward the visionary realm in evangelical memoirs. Many dreamed of hell and its creatures in harrowing terms. Serpents repeatedly assaulted Hannah Heaton in her nightmares, rats sucked the blood of Lorenzo Dow while he slept, and frogs attacked Christopher Hooper "from head to foot and began to eat the flesh off my bones."[41] Several preachers were assaulted by the devil himself. Benjamin Abbott was "put into a vice, and tormented until my body was all in a gore of blood," while a fellow itinerant dreamed of "a large auger" being screwed into his heart. "The auger was turned two or three times, when I seemed to hear the bones and sinews crack, and it gave me terrible pain."[42] Probably the most graphic and disturbing account we have of spiritual night-terrors comes from the journal of Rebecca Jackson, a nineteenth-century black Shaker. Jackson dreamed one night that "a man" (later identified as the Methodist preacher Jeremiah Miller) cornered her in a room of the house in which she lived. After peeling the skin from her face "with a lance" until she was covered with a "veil" of blood, the man "took a long knife and cut my chest open in the form of the cross, and took all my bowels out and laid them on the floor by my right side."[43] These dreams of bodily invasion and mutilation, which brought "exquisite pain" in Hooper's words, convey the fear of evisceration that lurked at the margins of the spiritual journeys of eighteenth-century saints—a fear more safely expressed through fantasy than acknowledged in real life.

Small wonder, then, that so many evangelicals chose to describe their spiritual visitations as "out-of-body" experiences. For only by escaping their bodies altogether could they achieve some measure of relief. After a period of severe trials, Rebecca Jackson "came out of the body . . . with all ease

[41] "Spiritual Exercises of Hannah Heaton" (1740–1790), photocopy of manuscript journal, Connecticut Historical Society, Hartford; Dow, *Cosmopolite*, p. 313; Life of Christopher Hooper, *Arminian Magazine* 4 (Jan. 1781), p. 26.

[42] Abbott, *Experience and Gospel Labours*, p. 8; dream of "large auger" quoted in Donald E. Byrne, Jr., *No Foot of Land: Folklore of American Methodist Itinerants* (Metuchen, N.J., 1975), p. 60. The dreams recorded in eighteenth-century journals identify their authors as "dramatic narrators," in Mechal Sobel's terms, as individuals with some sense of the narrative possibilities of their life stories. Dreams do, for the most part, appear when Sobel suggests they would—at turning points in the spiritual development of the author. See Sobel, "The Revolution in Selves: Black and White Inner Aliens," in *Through a Glass Darkly*, pp. 163–205.

[43] *Gifts of Power*, pp. 94–95.

and without any suffering," but found, to her dismay, that her faith required her to return to her earthly state; "I now found i had this suffering to go through . . . I reentered my body." Jackson, atypically, did not leave the knowing, feeling self behind when she entered into these trances. "When my spirit left my body," she insisted, "I was as sensible of it as I would be now to go out of this house and come in it again. All my senses and feeling and understanding was in my spirit."[44] Most saints, in contrast, entered into trances insensibly, in passive submission to a higher power. The stripping of "agency", as the French Prophet John Lacy put it, or of will in the pursuit of spiritual communion sets these eighteenth-century visionaries apart from their medieval counterparts, as well as from the seventeenth-century Quaker prophets studied by Phyllis Mack, who were more likely to see themselves as active participants in their own spiritual dramas than as insensible vessels of grace.[45]

As she recorded one striking vision of mystical union after another in her diary, Catherine Livingston compared herself to "nothing more than a blank sheet of paper, not a thought, not an Idea that I can trace passed through my mind."[46] Others described losses of bodily function—of motor skills, of sensory perception, of the ability to speak. Nathan Barlow "was taken all at once with a strange kind of feeling, and laid me down; I began to grow stiff and to lose the power of moving by degrees, till I was totally unable to stir." Barlow was very insistent that he did not merely fall asleep, "for I was sensible at the time that I had left my body behind, and had no feeling of weight, but light as air."[47] The loss of cognitive and physical abilities that saints experienced in their visions was often compared to a state of death. Lorenzo Dow saw a "black woman" in Georgia who was "struck under con-

[44] Ibid., pp. 110–11. Cynthia Lynn Lyerly suggests that enslaved visionaries were less able to "transport" themselves entirely out of the physical world than their white counterparts because of the all-consuming labor demands placed on them by their masters; she gives the example of "Old Elizabeth," who recalled that "still I was required to do all my duty" while "my spirit was carried away to spiritual things." Lyerly, "Passion, Desire, and Ecstasy: The Experiential Religion of Southern Methodist Women, 1770–1810," in *The Devil's Lane: Sex and Race in the Early South*, ed. Catherine Clinton and Michele Gillespie (New York, 1997), p. 172.

[45] Mack, *Visionary Women*. Mack has made the contrast explicit in her most recent work, which carries the discussion of religious subjectivity into the eighteenth century; as she argues, "Eighteenth-century women lost the capacity to feel and express their religious insights with their bodies," though they "gained the capacity to perceive and articulate those insights with their intelligence." Mack, "In a Female Voice: Preaching and Politics in Eighteenth-Century British Quakerism," in *Women Preachers and Prophets Through Two Millennia of Christianity*, ed. Beverly M. Kienzle and Pamela J. Walker (Berkeley, Calif., 1998), p. 260.

[46] Lobody, "Lost in the Ocean of Love," p. 262.

[47] Barlow, *A Vision, Seen by Nathan Barlow* (Greenfield, Mass., 1802), p. 3.

viction, with the power of God: Her body was cold as a corpse, and laid aside sixteen hours as in a sweet sleep or state of insensibility; and no symptoms of life except a regular pulse."[48] The Free-Will Baptist preacher Nancy Towle noted in her journal the "striking" case of a young woman who "lay cold, breathless, and stiff, for the space of an hour or two: her eyes wide open . . . and not the least appearance of life in any part of her system." When the girl finally came to, "I asked Whether she was sensible, at the time, of any thing that passed. She replied in the negative; and that she knew nothing."[49]

Eighteenth-century saints thus swung between two opposing states—the hypersensitive and the insensible—that locate them firmly within a new paradigm of human physiology, the "sensible or reactive" body. From paroxysms of grace, they entered into deathlike trances that extinguished all traces of vitality in their bodies. Following the medical literature of the day, which categorized convulsions as a species of nervous disorder (and a peculiarly "English" malady at that) caused by clogged arteries and obstructed bowels, preachers turned to science as well as scripture to describe what was happening in their circuits. A "dynamic new typology of the body" had emerged from the relatively new discipline of physiology by mid-century which looked beyond the mechanics of the human body to the vital forces that animated it. Centering on the nerves (the fibers that connected heart, stomach, and bowels to the head) and their stimulation by external and internal agents, this new paradigm of the "reactive body" came to dominate learned and popular discussions of medicine, literature, aesthetics—and religion. In an era "acutely attuned to the ways that humans respond to stimuli," physiologists and philosophers alike provided a roadmap through the body's sensitive points that evangelicals eagerly followed in their spiritual journeys.[50]

It is rare to find such descriptions of sensory deprivation before 1800 in the literature on Anglo-American revivals. While a few converts in the

[48] Dow, *Cosmopolite*, p. 172.

[49] Towle, *Vicissitudes Illustrated*, pp. 165–66.

[50] Ann C. Vila, *Enlightenment and Pathology: Sensibility in the Literature and Medicine of Eighteenth-Century France* (Baltimore, 1998), pp. 5, 28, 180. See also G. S. Rousseau, "Nerves, Spirits, and Fibres: Towards Defining the Origins of Sensibility," in *Studies in the Eighteenth Century, III: Papers Presented at the Third David Nichol Smith Memorial Seminar, Canberra, 1973*, ed. R. F. Brissenden and J. Eade (Canberra, 1976), pp. 137–58. George Cheney, *The English Malady: or a Treatise of Nervous Diseases of all Kinds, as Spleen, Vapours, Lowness of Spirits, Hypochondriacal, and Hysterical Distempers, etc.* (London, 1733), was the standard work on nervous disorders in the eighteenth century, with its elaborate taxonomy and its diagnosis of luxury and excess consumption as the cause of the "English malady"; see G. S. Rousseau, "Medicine and Millenarianism: Immortal Dr. Cheyne," in *Millenarianism and Messianism in Enlightenment England*, ed. Richard Popkin (Berkeley, Calif., 1987).

mid-eighteenth-century awakenings did record lapsing into what Nathan Barlow called "a state of inanimation" (usually at the height of emotional distress or
the moment of ecstatic release), the experience of insensibility was relatively
widespread in the revivals of the early nineteenth century.[51] Preachers were baffled by these cases, which tested their pride as enlightened men of science while
confirming their belief that God works in mysterious ways in the modern day.
They prodded the entranced with their fingers, rolled them over to awaken
them, pried open their eyelids, even stuck pins in their flesh. When converts did
not respond, the preachers were amazed and sometimes frightened. Theophilus
Gates "had heard a great deal about persons being in trances in modern times,"
though he "could never before put full confidence in them." Then, in 1810, he
met a young girl in Virginia who "fell down, and was to all appearance dead for
six hours.... A doctor in the meantime being called in, thrust pins into her flesh
up to the heads, without any apparent sensation or signs of life." Gates was convinced.[52] Billy Hibbard had quite a scare when one of his converts stopped
breathing. "I started up and felt her pulse, but found she had none. I perceived
she had no symptoms of life, her eyes and jaws were set, and her head, neck, and
arms were cold." While her relatives massaged her legs and stomach, Hibbard
"rubbed her neck and jaws until I could open them, so as to blow down her
throat to inflate her lungs," but nothing worked. Two hours later Hibbard finally
succeeded in reviving the girl, to his immense relief.[53]

By the first decade of the nineteenth century, these episodes had become something of a cultural curiosity—promoted by an enterprising religious press and dissected by a skeptical medical community. Accounts of
ordinary men and women who fell into trances and were led by angels to
view heaven and hell (populated, often, by people they knew) were popularized in cheap pamphlets that began to issue from the presses in greater numbers in the last decade of the eighteenth century.[54] Some even preached while
insensate, to the amazement of their families and friends; Rachel Baker, the

[51] Barlow, *A Vision*, p. 8.
[52] Theophilus Gates, *Truth Advocated: or, The Apocalyptic Beast, and Mystic Babylon,
Clearly Delineated for the Serious Consideration of Christians Universally and Unbelievers of
Every Description* (Philadelphia, 1818), pp. 155–56.
[53] *Memoirs of B. Hibbard*, pp. 162–64.
[54] See, for example: Hezekiah Goodwin, *A Vision* (Norwich, Conn., 1776); *A New
Prophecy; or An Account of a Young Girl, not above Eight Years of Age: Who being in a Trance, or
lay as dead for the Space of Forty Eight Hours* (London, 1780); Sarah Alley, *Account of a Trance
or Vision of Sarah Alley* (Philadelphia, 1807); *A Wonderful Account of a Little Girl of nine years
old ... Also an Account of a Girl of twelve years of age ... Likewise an Account of the Vision or
Trance of a Young Woman* (Windsor, Vt., 1800); *The Pious Virgin: Or, Religious Maid ... who,
falling into a Trance, declared the wonderful Things she had seen ...* (London, 1780); Jane Cish,

"Sleeping Preacher," assumed a certain notoriety in 1814 as physicians and ministers alike puzzled through the medical and spiritual meaning of her prolonged catatonia. A respected medical journal took up the case, only to conclude that Baker's symptoms remained impervious to organic diagnosis.[55] These tales, formulaic and melodramatic though they were, provide an early glimpse of a new model of visionary experience (the romantic) that would become increasingly attractive to believers over the course of the nineteenth century. By 1850 the rise of spiritualism to a place of cultural prominence in both England and the United States marked the coming-of-age of the romantic or transcendental model.[56]

It was during these insensible states that evangelicals were most likely to experience the "ecstasy" of mystical union and not, as we might expect, when they were in the throes of spiritual convulsion. In fact, sexual language is almost entirely absent from eighteenth-century spiritual memoirs, in contrast to the visionary literature of the previous century. The feeling of being saturated with God's presence was often explicitly eroticized in seventeenth-century literature as a form of sexual union; just as suffering flowed through the entire body, so too did ecstasy. While eighteenth- and nineteenth-century evangelicals occasionally reached for erotic metaphors to describe the joy of sanctification, their accounts of bodily experience were more likely to register pain than pleasure. As Phyllis Mack notes, "the language of constriction and coercion is vastly different from the boundaryless, almost liquified eroticism of seventeenth-century Quaker language."[57] We can, from a scholarly distance, perceive erotic impulses in some forms of somatic piety that became popular in the revivals of the eighteenth century—in the frenetic jerking of the camp meeting, or the dancing of the Shakers. But whatever sexual feelings were unleashed by these exercises were so sublimated as to be nearly invisible to saints themselves, who spoke far more often of aching limbs and sore feet than sexual release. Ecstasy came when saints *imagined* Christ,

---

The Vision and Wonderful Experience of Jane Cish, Showing How she was Converted and How She Fell into a Trance on the Third of May, 1780 (Philadelphia, 1793).

[55] Charles Mais, *The Surprising Case of Rachel Baker, Who Prays and Preaches In Her Sleep* (New York, 1814). See also the broadside *A Wonderful Dream*, by "Miss Jemima Wilkinson, a Sleeping Preacher," published in 1810. *Kirby's Wonderful and Eccentric Museum: or Magazine of Remarkable Characters*, 3 vols. (London, 1820), lists several instances of "sleeping preachers," who are "no longer considered a novelty" in the present age; 1:184–85, 188, 262, 264.

[56] Braude, *Radical Spirits*; Robert S. Cox, "Without Crucible or Scalpel: A Sympathetic History of American Spiritualism," Ph.D. diss., University of Michigan, 2002.

[57] Phyllis Mack, "Religious Dissenters in Enlightenment England," *History Workshop Journal* 49 (2000), pp. 2–3.

when—in other words—they escaped their bodies and entered into the realm of fantasy. Visions of Christ as the heavenly bridegroom, or as a bleeding martyr, inspired "raptures" in men and women alike.[58]

The Christ of their dreams was the ethereal figure of mystical theology. John Engelbrecht saw in a trance an image of Jesus in "transparent body," with the souls of the saints figured as sparks of light moving through one another.[59] Leaving behind the intractable body of the natural self, visionaries were "translated" (to use Jane Lead's term) into a more sprightly form. Surrounded by angels "clothed in transparent Garments resembling Silver," a young British woman found herself transported to heaven. "On my being admitted into the *heavenly City*, I received, as I thought, a *Change of Nature* and seemed quite *Light* to myself."[60] Her experience was echoed in countless memoirs by visionaries who marveled at their spiritual selves, all "full of light," whose luminosity struck observers as preternatural. Billy Hibbard had a vision in which he "thought I was dead, and my soul had left the body, and appeared transparent in the perfect shape of my body, standing before me."[61] Nimrod Hughes recalled how his spirit returned to the cell where his body was imprisoned "by a strong whirling motion" and "entered again into my body, and those who were in the prison with me saw my body in a shining light."[62]

Evangelicals paid close attention to their dreams and visions, subjecting them to various tests of legitimacy from which we can learn much about what constituted authentic spiritual revelation in an era of shifting standards of knowledge and truth. Nighttime dreams were distinct from visions, which could occur either while asleep or awake, and inner visions were different from more tangible visitations in which the believer could see, hear, and sometimes touch the spiritual messenger.[63] While rejecting the notion that dreams were but "the shaking of the nerves," as a physician once told the mil-

---

[58] Cynthia Lynn Lyerly describes the sensual visions of southern Methodist women in "Passion, Desire, and Ecstasy," though her examples tend to the romantic rather than the erotic. Women like Sarah Jones and Sally Eastland describe "fainting away" during the "love visits" of Christ to their souls (p. 180) in terms that foreshadow the veiled eroticism of Victorian literature.

[59] Hans Engelbrecht, *The Divine Visions of John Engelbrecht* . . . (Northampton, Mass., 1780).

[60] *The Glory of the Heavenly City, and Blessedness of Departed Saints, Graciously Manifested in a Vision to a Young Lady at Bristol on the 10th of October, 1781* (Bath, 1782), pp. 5, 8.

[61] *Memoirs of B. Hibbard*, p. 224.

[62] Thomas, *Life of the Pilgrim*, p. 22; Nimrod Hughes, *A Solemn Warning to All the Dwellers Upon the Earth*, 2d ed. (New Jersey, 1811), p. 21.

[63] John Smith argued in 1660 that the distinction between a dream and a vision lay in "*Circumstantials* [rather] than in any thing Essential." Smith, "On Prophecy," *Select Discourses* (London, 1660), pp. 181–82.

lenarian William Sharp, evangelicals agreed that the more palpable the vision, the greater the suspicion that its source was not divine but pathological in some sense.[64] In general, visions should be *seen*—not felt or heard in any physical way—and seen by the "eye of faith" alone. At the height of the First Great Awakening, the Scottish minister James Robe had warned his congregation "in the expressest, strongest, plainest manner I could" that genuine visions were to be seen with the "spiritual" and not the natural eye: "Jesus Christ in the body cannot be seen by any with their bodily eyes in this life," he declared. To those who insisted Christ had appeared to them in person, he replied, "it was owing only to the strength of their imagination, to the disorder of their head, and of the humours of their bodies at that time; and that it was not real."[65] While some of the more zealous itinerants of the 1740s had indeed presumed a physical as well as spiritual connection to the supernatural—William Tennent, Jr., for instance, believed that he had lost the toes on one foot during a visionary battle with Satan—most quickly retreated from the kind of embodied spiritual encounters that had so distressed Robe.[66]

By the late eighteenth century, the effort to distinguish bodily from divine sensations and images had grown into a sophisticated intellectual project which drew on medical theory and natural philosophy as well as theology to argue for the primacy of the "spiritual" over the "animal" senses in genuine religious experience.[67] Lorenzo Dow, in his picaresque memoir *The Cosmopolite*, summarized the prevailing consensus in typically straightforward language. "There are but six ways to receive ideas," he lectured his readers, "which are by *inspiration* or one of the *five senses*. Deny inspiration, and there are but five ways; and matter of fact demonstrates, that a man by these outward sensitive organs, can neither hear, see, smell, taste nor feel God: How then can we know him but by a revelation in the inward sense?" In not denying the possibility of direct inspiration, Dow was in line with the more radical wing of the evangelical movement; but in insisting that inspiration was not an operation of the physical senses but an "inward" phenomenon only, he echoed larger concerns about the unruly nature of the human body as a

[64] William Sharp, *Sharp Answer to the World* (London, 1806), p. 43.

[65] James Robe, *Narratives of the Extraordinary Works of the Spirit of God at Cambuslang* (Glasgow, 1790), pp. 200–201.

[66] For the case of William Tennent, Jr., see Jon Butler, *Awash in a Sea of Faith: Christianizing the American People* (Cambridge, Mass., 1990), p. 185.

[67] Taves, *Visions, Fits and Trances*; Leigh Eric Schmidt, *Holy Fairs: Scottish Communions and American Revivals in the Early Modern Period* (Princeton, N.J., 1989), and *Hearing Things: Religion, Illusion, and the American Enlightenment* (Cambridge, Mass., 2000).

receptacle of spiritual power. Dreams were as likely to come from "a *disor-dered body*" as from God, he warned.[68]

Evangelicals were very careful in the language they used to describe their visionary experiences, always conscious of the porous line separating faith from superstition. They used words like "seemingly" and "by faith" to signal their awareness of the enormous potential of unorthodox spiritual experience to disrupt conventional channels of truth and knowledge. Listen to Hugh Bourne, the founder of Primitive Methodism in England, describe a vision he received in 1809: "It seemed as if Jesus Christ embraced me in his arms. After this he seemed to move to the church at Cloud, and there he sat as he is represented in Isaiah's vision; and he seemed to put his arms around me, and say that I should reign with him."[69] Freeborn Garrettson once found himself "in a lonely wood" where he "sensibly felt two spirits, one on each hand." Though "Carnal people" might misunderstand the experience, to him the spirits were "as perceptible . . . as if I had been conversing with the persons face to face."[70] Even when "sensible" to the touch, the existence of spirits was ultimately a matter of perception—of perceiving them *as if* they were real. Garrettson's fellow laborer James Horton, never one to shy away from experiences others would consider out-of-bounds, "seemingly" heard "a voice spake unto me" when he was suffering from severe pain, and "in that very instant I felt the power of the Lord to heal me, as sensibly as I ever felt the hand of a person upon any part of my body."[71] In these examples we can see the self-censoring of even the most ardent evangelicals at work: voices only "seem" to speak, the sight and touch of God are analogous to ("as perceptible as," "as sensible as"), but not identical with, ordinary human sensation.

The visionary's connection to Christ was thus depicted as one of sympathy rather than incorporation; that is, unlike earlier mystics who had reveled in the experience of being absorbed into the body of Christ, eighteenth-century visionaries were more likely to regard their spiritual "labours" as Christ-*like*. The "Sympathizing Body of Christ," in the words of one Shaker, allowed visionaries to claim Christ's sufferings for their own without inflicting upon themselves the kind of physical torture that late medieval saints endured.[72] The devotional imperative of *Imitatio Christi*—

---

[68] Dow, *Cosmopolite*, pp. 329, 307.

[69] Walford, *Memoirs of Hugh Bourne*, p. 196.

[70] Simpson, *American Methodist Pioneer*, p. 44.

[71] Horton, *Narrative*, p. 135.

[72] Letter from Elder Brother Seth [Wells] to Brother Issachar [Bates], Jan. 18, 1815, Shaker MSS, IV: A-77, Western Reserve Historical Society ("Sympathizing Body"). For a dis-

imitating the life and death of Christ—thus had a different meaning for eighteenth-century visionaries. John Church was "favored with a most solemn and affecting vision of the Saviour on the cross, apparently suspended between the roof of the chapel and the gallery opposite to where I stood; his sacred body appeared of a bluish hue, apparently with the bruises he had received; and the blood appeared to be fresh as it was shed from his hands, his head, his feet, and his side. This continued a few moments, clearly presented to me."[73] David Austin had a similar experience. Recovering from a near fatal bout with scarlet fever in 1796, Austin heard the voice of God calling him to the prophetic office. "I beheld the blessed Jesus as our *elder brother*," he recounted in his journal; "Here I seemed to stand, stripped of myself and of all self-dependence, looking faintly at the blood which seemed to have issued from the Saviour's side."[74] For both Church and Austin, Christ's blood was a devotional image to behold, not a penitential discipline to be imitated. The figure of Christ was often perceived through a "veil" of some kind which blocked the visionary's access to his material presence. In Lovisa Smith's words, "I seemed to be borne away to the world of spirits, where I saw the Saviour, as through a veil, which appeared to me about as thick as a spider's web."[75]

By distancing themselves from the physical reality of a bleeding and dying Christ, prophets could enjoy the glory of martyrdom without having to actually suffer; this, after all, was the purpose of "sympathy" as a theory of human relations. Sympathy was not the same thing as empathy, Jean-Christophe Agnew reminds us, but its opposite: as described by Adam Smith in his seminal *Theory of Moral Sentiments* (1759), sympathy was the act of impersonation whereby spectators coldly and deliberately imagined themselves in another's place. "As we have no immediate experience of what other men feel," Smith argued, "we can form no idea of the manner in which they are affected but by conceiving what we ourselves should feel in the like situation." Such an act of mental impersonation avoids any messy emotional entanglement with the weak and pitiable, and thus shields society from the disruptive effects of violent passion. "That imaginary change of situation . . . is but momentary. The thought of their own safety, the thought that they

cussion of the physical sufferings of medieval saints, see Caroline Walker Bynum, *Holy Feast and Holy Fast: The Religious Significance of Food to Medieval Women* (Berkeley, Calif., 1987).

[73] John Church, *The Foundling; or, The Child of Providence* (London, 1823), pp. 172–73.

[74] David Austin, *The Voice of God to the People of the United States, by a Messenger of Peace* (Elizabethtown, N.J., 1796), p. 36.

[75] Quoted in John L. Brooke, *The Refiner's Fire: The Making of Mormon Cosmology, 1644–1844* (New York, 1994), p. 84.

themselves are not really the sufferers, continually intrudes itself upon them; and though it does not hinder them from conceiving a passion somewhat analogous to what is felt by the sufferer, hinders them from conceiving any thing that approaches the same degree of violence."[76] Smith was describing an emotional economy predicated on the absence of real material suffering on the part of the prosperous middling classes, who were at least a generation removed from the acute privations endured by those most in need of their sympathy. A certain level of physical comfort was necessary for spectators to imagine, rather than feel, the pain of others.[77]

The distancing from the world of pain and suffering posited by Smith's theory of sympathy found expression in the new forms of literature produced in the eighteenth century, from the *Spectator* (whose aim was to take pleasure in observing life's calamities) to the sentimental novel. As Daniel Defoe wrote in the *Spectator*, "when we read of torments, wounds, deaths and the like dismal accidents, our pleasure does not flow so properly from the grief which such melancholy descriptions give us, as from the secret comparison which we make between ourselves and the person who suffers."[78] Revolutionary-era prophets performed just the kind of vicarious identification with Christ through their visions that Smith's theory proposed as normative for a society composed of autonomous, self-interested individuals. Their emotional isolation made it easier for them to project the gruesome plagues foretold in the prophetic texts onto their countrymen, who in turn were invited to imagine themselves as spectators to the misery unfolding around them. In this way both could enjoy the "secret pleasures" of the spectator.

A recursive cycle of vicarious identifications, always one step removed from the grim reality of death and destruction, thus gave revolutionary-era prophecy a peculiarly bloodless quality. For ultimately prophecy was a spectator sport for prophets and their audiences alike, a game of hide-and-seek

---

[76] Jean-Christophe Agnew, *Worlds Apart: The Market and the Theater in Anglo-American Thought, 1550–1750* (New York, 1986); Adam Smith, *Theory of Moral Sentiments*, quoted in Agnew, pp. 178, 180.

[77] Barker-Benfield, *Culture of Sensibility*, pp. xx–xxii; Peter Earle, *The Making of the English Middle Class: Business, Society, and Family Life in London, 1660–1730* (London, 1989); Peter Borsay, *The English Urban Renaissance: Culture and Society in the Provincial Town, 1660–1770* (Oxford, 1989); Lorna Weatherill, *Consumer Behaviour and Material Culture in Britain, 1660–1760* (London, 1988).

[78] *Spectator*, no. 418, 6:98–99; quoted in Barker-Benfield, *Culture of Sensibility*, pp. 62–63. On the emotional economy of sentimentalism, see Julia A. Stern, *The Plight of Feeling: Sympathy and Dissent in the Early American Novel* (Chicago, 1997), and Julie Ellison, *Cato's Tears and the Making of Anglo-American Emotion* (Chicago, 1999).

with the powerful forces of good and evil in the world. The "Prophet Nathan" admitted that "it is not expedient that I should go into every state, town, and family, and point with my finger to every one who hardens himself against God . . . and say, thou art the *man*." Rather he let his pen do the dirty work: "I direct the point of my *pen*, as an instrument to every stupid awakened conscience."[79] What's left unsaid here—what doesn't need to be said—is that the reluctance to confront evil head-on was mutual. Few sinners, after all, would welcome a visit from a self-styled prophet of evil.

Always dodging the proverbial bullet, prophets took their followers on an imaginative journey through the apocalyptic scenario that led, not to the actual Second Coming, but (as Jane Lead believed) to a new heart and a new self. Most millennial authors argued for a figurative rather than literal meaning of Christ's Second Coming. "Some have supposed that this passage is to be taken literally, as importing that at that time, Jesus Christ will come in his human nature . . . and reign visibly, and personally," the American Samuel Hopkins wrote. But "this important passage is to be understood in the figurative sense"—though, as he cleverly explained, "if he shall reign on earth in the hearts of men . . . he will reign as literally as if he were present on earth in his humanity."[80] As his colleague Theophilus Gates put it, the world will be saved by the coming of Christ "not in his visible person, as some for want of understanding the figurative language of certain prophecies have supposed, but by the invisible, yet enlightening and powerful operations of his holy Spirit in the hearts of many individuals."[81]

Women prophets did not always play by the same rules, however. Their visionary raptures were more embodied than men's, their descriptions of the apocalyptic terrors more palpable and their appreciation of suffering more empathetic. Women tended, for instance, to feel a visceral connection to the bleeding body of Christ; rather than just viewing the blood coming from Christ's wounds, they often experienced a physical reaction in their own bodies. A Shaker recalled the spots of blackened flesh on Ann Lee's arms, which the prophetess explained as "the marks of the sufferings of Christ." "I bear, in my body, daily, the marks of the Lord Jesus Christ," she is reported to have told her followers.[82] John Wesley was appalled at the visionary excesses

---

[79] *The Prophet Nathan, or, Plain Friend* (Hudson, N.Y., 1788), p. 9.

[80] Samuel Hopkins, *A Treatise on the Millennium* (Boston, 1793), pp. 43–44, 47.

[81] Theophilus Gates, *Observations on the Signs of the Times; or, Things as they are now in the world, and as they will be hereafter* (New York, 1818), p. 354.

[82] *Testimonies of the Life, Character, Revelations and Doctrines of Our Ever Blessed Mother Ann Lee* (Hancock, Mass., 1816), pp. 347–38. Hereafter 1816 *Testimonies*.

of some women in his congregation: "As to what some of them said concerning feeling the blood of Christ running upon their arms, or going down their throat, or poured like warm water upon their breast or heart, I plainly told them . . . that [these were] the mere empty dreams of an heated imagination."[83] But, as the magazine he edited until his death in 1791 shows, such visions were more commonplace than he wished to acknowledge. One woman felt "the Lord, as it were, put my fingers into the nail prints, and my hand into his side. . . . I cried out in raptures. . . . There I saw him by the eye of faith tortured, groaning, bleeding, and expiring!—for me! and my heart was melted like wax before the fire. How did I weep beneath the cross! With the same eye of faith, I saw my lovely *Jesus* taken down, the veins empty, the stretched out sinews, and the whole remains of my Saviour thus disordered! O the spectacle to behold, sufficient to rend my heart in twain!"[84] Even here, despite the graphic language of the description, the *spectacle* of Christ's sufferings was finally more striking than the *experience* of vicarious suffering.

Women did continue to express their attraction to and empathy for the suffering of others in metaphors of embodiment. Nancy Towle was struck by the "emaciated" appearance of London's destitute on her preaching tour in the 1820s. In every street of the metropolis she saw "pale looks, hollow eyes, and meager limbs," terms which parallel eighteenth-century visionaries' descriptions of their own debilitated state.[85] The "emaciated" saint served in the writings of many female visionaries as a trope for suffering in general, an evocative image of the deprivation and frailty under which the spiritually impoverished labored everywhere. The wasted appearance of so many saints was thus not a physical or typological projection of the "emaciated poor," as it might have been understood in a different epistemological context, but an exercise in sympathetic identification grounded in the expressive properties of the human body. Few women prophets took the notion of vicarious suffering to the extreme represented by Ann Lee, who "actually vomited up the sins of the people" according to one disciple, but there is clear evidence that women believed themselves to have a phenomenological connection to the physical sufferings of others that most men refused to entertain.[86] Perhaps men were too overwhelmed by their own exaggerated sense of vulnerability

---

[83] *Journal of John Wesley*, 3:44.
[84] *Arminian Magazine* 15 (Sept. 1792), p. 476.
[85] Towle, *Vicissitudes Illustrated*, pp. 72, 74.
[86] Clarke Garrett, *Spirit Possession and Popular Religion: From the Camisards to the Shakers* (Baltimore, 1987), p. 204. One exception to this general rule was the Avignon prophet William Bryan, who described his skill as a pharmacist in terms comparable to the empathy of

to feel much sympathy for the pain of others; on average, men complained more, lingered longer over descriptions of their aches and pains, felt themselves more often on the very brink of death, than their female counterparts. Theophilus Gates described himself as a "frail being . . . whose life in eight different illnesses has been despaired of."[87] Few memoirs match Lorenzo Dow's for its celebration of disease. *The Cosmopolite* is an exhaustive (and exhausting) narrative of Dow's unparalleled sufferings and mysterious physical ailments whose symptoms "baffled the skill" of the most renowned doctors in Europe and America. "I was taken very unwell of late with a convulsive affection of my belly," he noted in a typical passage in 1806, "and my Doctor said *he* had never before seen or heard of any person under the same affliction." While his own wife, Peggy, lay dangerously ill with a "convulsive disorder" from which she would never fully recover, Dow devoted page after page of his journal to cataloguing his own "extraordinary" sufferings. The grandiosity of his afflictions made him incapable of the act of sympathetic identification, which, as outlined in Adam Smith's *Theory of Moral Sentiments*, required a sense of both affinity and detachment, grounded in well-being.[88] Dow, unlike Towle, did not connect his own travails to the squalor and misery that surrounded him.

Despite these traces of an incorporative model of sanctity in the visions of female prophets, their public careers exhibit an eagerness to align themselves with the *voice* of God rather than his mystical body. Unlike the seventeenth-century Quaker prophets whom Phyllis Mack has written about—who aimed, she says, at "nothing less than the experience of a divine presence, or indwelling, in their own bodies"—eighteenth-century prophets believed, like Jane Lead, that their bodies were not a fit tabernacle for God's spirit.[89] They preferred to follow the lead of the French Prophets, who were famous (or infamous) for their spiritual ventriloquism, in which the Spirit of God spoke directly *through* them rather than *in* them. When speaking for God, the Camisards used the first person (the divine "I"), and when they slipped back into their natural selves they clearly marked the shift both by switching pronouns and altering the very timber of their speech. Under

---

female prophets for the suffering poor. "By his Holy Spirit I have at times been favoured to feel so much of that love as to enter into a sympathy of feeling with my patient, so that I could describe every symptom of their disease from *feeling it in my own body.*" Bryan, *A Testimony of the Spirit of Truth concerning Richard Brothers . . . with Some Account of the Manner of the Lord's Gracious Dealing with his Servant William Bryan* (London, 1795), p. 30.

[87] Gates, *Truth Advocated*, p. 304.

[88] Dow, *Cosmopolite*, pp. 276, 300.

[89] Mack, *Visionary Women*, p. 143.

inspiration, Hannah Wharton moved back and forth between these two modes during a speech in Birmingham recorded in 1732, declaring one moment that "ye are under the Government of my Voice . . . *my* Voice is not like the Voice of Man," and later resuming her natural voice, telling her audience that "*his* Voice may be heard, Come, my Beloved, enter, enter."[90] Mary Beer, in a prophecy recorded in Bristol in 1709, switched from the first- to the third-person within the space of two sentences. "God is now coming in a Manner extraordinary to Visit his People. . . . And now have I poured forth my Holy Spirit that every Soul may know his Coming is near."[91] Such grammatical maneuverings betray the extent to which the inspired behavior of the Camisards involved a splitting of the natural and the divine selves rather than a fusing of the two.

By the late eighteenth century, few prophets, male or female, claimed to speak *as* God rather than *for* God. With the exception of those few who had messianic ambitions (Ann Lee, Nat Smith, Jemima Wilkinson), revolutionary-era prophets were messengers, not oracles in the inspired tradition. Only Joanna Southcott continued to prophesy in the Camisard manner, and her earnest forays into spiritual ventriloquism in the early 1800s (which we will explore at greater length in Chapter 6) were perceived as clumsy and faintly ridiculous by the majority of the British reading public. No other prophet even made the effort. The Camisards' "divinized speech" seemed as remote a possibility as absorption into God's mystical body by the late eighteenth century.[92] Romantic visionaries would resurrect the practice of trance preaching in the nineteenth century as the epistemology of spiritualism was reconfigured once again, but revolutionary-era prophets rejected both the incorporative model of sanctity embodied by medieval visionaries and the ventriloquist model of inspired speech popularized by the French Prophets.

For women, the persistence of maternal imagery suggests that language and body could never be entirely severed in their visionary experiences. The Camisard Hannah Wharton likened her spiritual "labours" to childbirth; "I am big with Love," she declared, "the Word is come forth big with Love, the Travail of the Word does bring forth, it travails not in vain."[93] She invited her

---

[90] Hannah Wharton, *Divine Inspirations: Or, A Collection of Manifestations . . . by the Mouth of Hannah Wharton* (London, 1732), pp. 5, 8. My italics.

[91] *A Collection of Prophetical Warnings, Pronounc'd under the Operation of the Holy Eternal Spirit . . . By the following Persons, viz. Mary Beer, Mary Keemer, Ann Watts* (Bristol, 1709), p. 14.

[92] Garrett, *Spirit Possession*.

[93] Wharton, *Divine Inspirations*, pp. 23, 33. The clipped, elliptical cadence of these passages is typical of the French Prophets' writings, which purport to be direct transcriptions of their inspired speech.

listeners to suckle the "Word" that she delivered: "The Manifestation of the Word is as the Breast of the Mother to the weak Babe; and assuredly such that do feed upon the Milk of the Word, they shall grow therein."[94] When the prophet Mary Pratt spoke in the 1790s of feeling "the *Man*child born in me," she was speaking metaphorically; "the pain was the pains of hell," she clarified, not the pangs of childbirth.[95] Ann Lee represents the apogee of this form of linguistic maternalism, declaring herself to be "Ann the Word" and her followers "my epistles, read and known of all men." Following the death of all four of her children in infancy, Lee repudiated sexuality and the role of biological motherhood in order to become a "Mother in Israel" to her community. She ministered personally to the physical and emotional needs of her "children," offering her wisdom as spiritual milk, and allegorized the female experiences of pregnancy, birth, and lactation by, in Catherine Brekus's words, "encouraging men as well as women to labor in the 'world of spirits.' "[96] Not surprisingly, celibacy was endorsed, though not necessarily mandated, by other female prophets (including Jemima Wilkinson, Joanna Southcott, and Elspeth Buchan) who also felt estranged from the female world of sexuality and maternity.[97]

Ann Lee is a special case in many ways. The direct heir of Jane Lead and her Behmenist theology of an androgynous god, Lee does not fit easily into either the medieval or modern model of inspired behavior. On the one hand, her retrospective biography offers one of the most graphic descriptions of

[94] *Some Manifestations and Communications of the Spirit, in Forty Days Ministration in That Place London, By the Mouth of Hannah Wharton* (London, 1730), p. 60.
[95] Mary Pratt to Henry Brooke, Aug. 25, 1792, Brooke Letterbook, p. 341, Walton MSS I.1.43, Dr. Williams's Library, London.
[96] 1816 *Testimonies*, p. 26; Brekus, *Strangers and Pilgrims*, p. 109. See also Jean M. Humez, " 'Ye Are My Epistles': The Construction of Ann Lee Imagery in Early Shaker Sacred Literature," *Journal of Feminist Studies in Religion* 8 (Spring 1992), pp. 83–104, and Garrett, *Spirit Possession*, pp. 140–241.
[97] Celibacy has an honored place in Anglo-American sectarianism, especially in movements begun or led by women. For scholars interested in how early modern men and women inhabited different sex roles, celibacy is seen as offering women an opportunity to escape the constraints of patriarchy and domesticity in favor of spiritual autonomy; for those scholars more interested in the evolution of devotional language and imagery, celibacy is seen as the theological consequence of the mystical ideal of an androgynous God. See Erik Seeman, " 'It Is Better to Marry Than to Burn': Anglo-American Attitudes Toward Celibacy, 1600–1800," *Journal of Family History* 24 (1999), pp. 397–419; Seeman, "Sarah Prentice and the Immortalists: Sexuality, Piety, and the Body in Eighteenth-Century New England," in *Sex and Sexuality in Colonial America*, ed. Merril Smith (New York, 1998), pp. 116–31; and Tim V. Hitchcock, " 'In True Imitation of Christ': The Tradition of Mystical Communitarianism in Early Eighteenth-Century England," in *Locating the Shakers: Cultural Origins and Legacies of an American Religious Movement*, ed. Mick Gidley and Kate Bowles (Exeter, 1990), pp. 13–25.

spiritual rebirth as physical purification we have from any century. For a period of nine years, Lee suffered severe physical and mental torment. "In my travail and tribulation," her disciples remembered her saying, "my sufferings were so great that my flesh consumed upon my bones, and bloody sweat pressed through the pores of my skin, and I became as helpless as an infant. . . . I travelled in such tribulation, wringing my hand and crying to God, that the blood gushed out from under my nails, and with tears flowing down my cheeks, until the skin cleaved off." Reduced to mere bones from incessant fasting and weeping, Lee described her spiritual transformation as a literal rebirth in which her old skin was replaced with a new one: "Thus I labored day and night, till my flesh wasted away, and I became like a skeleton; and a kind of down came upon my skin, until my soul broke forth to God; which I felt as sensibly as ever a woman did a child, when she was delivered of it. Then I felt unspeakable joy in God, and my flesh came upon me, like the flesh of an infant."[98] There are many images layered together in this description, from the Christological to the maternal, but the image of the body consuming itself to reveal the skeleton beneath is one that we find in many other texts from the eighteenth century.

Reborn into physical and spiritual wholeness, Lee's body became a receptacle of holy power. Her "gifts" were legendary—speaking in tongues (she was said to be able to speak seventy-two languages fluently), frenzied singing and dancing, healing by touch. She attributed her gifts to the power of Christ's blood flowing through her body: "I feel the blood of Christ running through my soul and body, washing me." Blood played a central role in the spiritualist economy of the seventeenth century, as it had in late medieval Christendom, connecting the body's interior to the surface and providing a phenomenological point of access between the body of Christ (bleeding on the cross) and the body of the saint. The image of the holy woman as a spiritual "sponge," soaking up God's essence and distributing it through the arteries and internal organs (the "feminized" spaces of the body in early modern medical paradigms), is powerfully expressive of both the humoral tradition and the metaphorical importance of fluids like blood as the carriers of grace.[99]

Like those medieval mystics who came before her, Lee was depicted as so full of supernatural energy that her body could not contain it—blood seeped from her very pores. Yet while seventeenth-century prophets like Jane

---

[98] 1816 *Testimonies*, pp. 47–48.

[99] Marie-Christine Pouchelle, *The Body and Surgery in the Middle Ages*, trans. Rosemary Morris (New Brunswick, N.J., 1990; orig. pub. 1983), pp. 147–50.

Lead were praised for their spiritual "inebriation," Lee was widely and repeatedly castigated for being, in the words of one scoffer, "a drunken old
squaw." Tales of Lee's inebriation followed her all through her travels, dog-
ging her efforts to attract new converts and generating considerable negative
press.[100] However much she wished to resurrect the somatic model of spiritual ecstasy, Lee was unable to persuade most observers that her body had indeed been sanctified by the indwelling presence of God. Instead, she suffered
the indignity of having her body searched for signs of criminality and witchcraft. When a mob accused her of having been "cropped and branded" and
her "tongue bored through for blasphemy" in England, she "turned up her
cap and showed her ears, and said; 'see if my ears have been cropped; and see
if my forehead has been branded.' Then showing her tongue, she said, 'See if
my tongue has been bored.' " She was even forced to strip in front of a panel
of matrons who inspected her sex for evidence that she was, as rumor had it,
"a British emissary dressed in woman's habit."[101] The resistance Lee faced
was not new; holy women with pretensions to charismatic power have always provoked fear along with awe, and their bodies scrutinized for signs of
imposture or diabolical possession. But the signs themselves change along
with religious sensibility and cultural attitudes toward the body and its expressive properties. There was room in the late medieval paradigm for the
possibility of spiritual "inebriation," the condition of being saturated with
the presence of God. Saturation was an inappropriate metaphor for spiritual
empowerment in the eighteenth and early nineteenth centuries.

Ann Lee is unique in the annals of eighteenth-century Anglo-American
prophecy: no other figure ever claimed such extensive incorporation into the
mystical body of Christ. Other prophets like the American Jemima Wilkinson eschewed somatic models of charismatic authority altogether, claiming
to have been "reanimated" in spirit but not in body by the presence of
Christ.[102] Even Lee's own society sought to distance itself from the disorderly

---

[100] 1816 *Testimonies*, p. 34. The accusations of drunkenness are highlighted even more in
the 1827 version of the *Testimonies*, which was commissioned specifically to refute the grow-
ing body of published criticism of the society and its founder, written primarily by apostates.
Benjamin Seth Wells, *Testimonies Concerning the Character and Ministry of Mother Ann
Lee . . . Approved by the Church* (Albany, N.Y., 1827). Even some sympathetic scholars concede
that excessive drinking was in all likelihood part of Lee's repertoire of spiritual practices;
Stephen Stein, *The Shaker Experience in America: A History of the United Society of Believers*
(New Haven, 1992), pp. 26–31.

[101] 1816 *Testimonies*, pp. 140–41.

[102] "A Memorandum of the Introduction of the Fatal Fever," undated, Jemima Wilkinson Papers, 1771–1849, Department of Manuscripts and University Archives, Cornell University Library, Ithaca, N.Y.

aspects of her "labours" in the early 1800s. When the Shaker leadership first reviewed the testimonies of old believers collected in 1816, they were alarmed at what they read. "Many of Mother's labours were private & peculiarly adapted to the time place & circumstances" of her day, Seth Wells cautioned; "others again were never properly understood by those present, and much less perhaps by other persons." To protect the sensibilities of young believers and safeguard the honor of the Society, the Elders decided to restrict publication of the *Testimonies of the Life and Character of Mother Ann Lee* and limit access within the community until a more sanitized version could be compiled.[103] Whatever her original aspirations may have been, it is clear that in the years following Lee's death in 1782 her role as a prophet was deliberately suppressed by the Shaker leadership. Successive editions of the original *Testimonies* downplayed Lee's charismatic powers (the gifts of healing, speaking in tongues, communing with the spirits of the dead) and emphasized instead her nurturing role as "Mother Ann." In the process, Lee's status as the female godhead was transposed into a theological principle of dual divinity. Not Lee herself but the principle of "female divinity" became the cornerstone of Shaker theology and practice as the sect entered the nineteenth century.[104]

Yet, if not quite accepted as the female Christ she believed herself to be, Lee did possess real power as a spiritual leader that marks her experience as paradigmatic for the revolutionary generation of Anglo-American prophets. When John Bishop first met Ann Lee after he had traveled forty difficult miles on foot, the Shaker founder took him by the hand. "The effect was like the sudden operation of an electric shock; he was instantly released from all his weariness."[105] One of Lee's most determined critics, the apostate Valentine Rathbun, was duly impressed by the "extraordinary and uncommon power" which the Shaker prophet seemed to possess. "I found a power come over me different from what I had ever felt before and made me feel very weak and maugre, and in a little time it so affected my nerves that they gave a twitch, as sudden as a flash of lightning. . . . I can compare it to nothing

---

[103] Benjamin Seth Wells to Elder Benjamin Young, 1818, Shaker MSS, IV: 77, Western Reserve Historical Society. See also the letters of Feb. 22, 1819, IV: 77; and Apr. 25, 1822, IV: 78. Only twenty copies of the 1816 *Testimonies* were printed in the end, and these were to be read only by the Elders and the few Old Believers still living.

[104] See Jean Humez's introduction to *Mother's First-Born Daughters: Early Shaker Writings on Women and Religion* (Bloomington, Ind., 1993), for a discussion of how the character of Lee became transformed into the theological principle of "Holy Mother Wisdom."

[105] 1816 *Testimonies*, p. 216.

nearer its feeling than the operations of an electrifying machine."[106] The role of the prophet's body in transferring divine power from the inspired to the needy is reduced here to that of a conduit only; its physical properties are not implicated in the process. Unlike earlier saints who, say, ingested the sufferings of others by drinking pus from the sores of lepers, Lee did not offer her body as a vehicle of supernatural empowerment via the medieval model of incorporation. Instead she channeled the power of the Spirit by the electrifying touch of her hand.

Eighteenth-century physicians and preachers knew all about the healing power of electricity.[107] The search for effective ways to stimulate the reactive body led to new metaphors for describing spiritual power. For Methodists, God's grace was like an electrical surge. "Then, like a flash," recalled a slave convert, "the power of God struck me. It seemed like something struck me in the top of my head and then went on out through the toes of my feet. I jumped, or rather, fell back against the back of my seat." The very air at a Methodist camp meeting "seemed impregnated with electric fluid," and converts displayed the effects visibly on their bodies—some "had spots of purple and scarlet thick on their hands and in their faces, visible, through the Holy Power passing through them, which caused an extraordinary quick circulation to pass through the blood and fluids."[108] Caleb Rich, one of the many rural prophets who traversed the New England countryside in the years following the Revolution, "felt as it were a shock of electricity, my lips quivered, my flesh trembled, and felt a tremour throughout my whole frame for several days."[109]

Electricity was a particularly apt metaphor for spiritual power, given its

[106] Valentine Rathbun, *An Account of the Matter, Form, and Manner of a New and Strange Religion Taught and propagated by a Number of* EUROPEANS, *living in a Place called Nisqueunia, in the State of New-York* (Providence, R.I., 1781), p. 17.

[107] John Wesley, for one, was fascinated by the power of electricity, or "fire," to heal as well as spiritually wound; "Electricity is a thousand medicines in one," he enthused after reading Dr. Priestley's *History and Present State of Electricity* (London, 1767), "it is the most efficacious medicine in nervous disorders of every kind which has ever yet been discovered" (*Journal of John Wesley*, 5:247). In his later years he carried with him on his preaching tours a copy of Benjamin Franklin's "electrical machine" with which he treated himself and his patients on a regular basis.

[108] John Wigger, "Taking Heaven by Storm: Enthusiasm and Early American Methodism, 1770–1820," *Journal of the Early Republic* 14 (Summer 1994), pp. 167 (slave convert), 192 ("electric fluid"); Thomas Everard, *Some Plain Scriptural Observations and Remarks on what is Denominated Shouting* (Philadelphia, 1820), p. 37 ("spots of purple").

[109] Caleb Rich, "A Narrative of Elder Caleb Rich," *Candid Examiner* 2 (Apr. 30–June 18, 1827).

affinities to fire. As the element best suited to piercing the hard outer shell of the body and purifying the corruption within, fire was to eighteenth-century evangelicals what blood was to late medieval saints: the medium of spiritual regeneration. What blood washed away in the medieval spiritual economy, fire consumed—hence the centrality of metaphors of melting and burning in evangelical memoirs. "I burn, I melt, I blaze," Sarah Jones confided to a friend; "the fire of Jesu's love hath taken possession of all my soul."[110] The itinerant preacher and sometime prophet John Granade was "seized with a burning in his stomach," the first symptom of the "burning flame" which "ran through his whole being" for a period of two years in the late 1790s.[111] Like Jane Lead, the founders of the Primitive Methodist Connexion in Britain, Hugh Bourne and William Clowes, both felt a "spirit of burning" working in them. "William Clowes grows at a vast rate," Bourne noted with some envy in his journal; "He felt the spirit of burning . . . till it filled every part of his body at once, burning to his fingers."[112] Once the spirit of burning had gone through the body, nothing remained but the "bare bone" of the natural self, in the prophet Dorothy Gott's phrase, and sometimes not even that.[113] "I have neither heart, liver, nor lungs; nor any thing at all in my body, nor a drop of blood in my veins," declared an unnamed "gardener" who was incarcerated in an insane asylum for his fanaticism. "My bones are all burnt to a cinder."[114]

Being struck by lightning was thus a fairly common experience in the eighteenth-century evangelical world. And, like any other brush with fire, it could be a searing experience. Here we return, as eighteenth-century visionaries always did, to the elemental importance of pain and its enigmatic status in their spiritual lives. The convergence of the language of disease and the language of spiritual union gives us an important window into the troublesome violence of millenarian culture. The desacralization of the body made public violence gratuitous; stripped of its redemptive role, pain had an uncertain place in end-time scenarios despite the graphic nature of the suf-

---

[110] Quoted in Lyerly, "Passion, Desire, and Ecstasy," p. 179. A common metaphor compared sanctification to being in the refiner's fire, as Francis Asbury did: "I am in the furnace; may I come out purified like gold!" *Journal of Francis Asbury*, 2:42.

[111] Richard Price, *Holston Methodism from Its Origins to the Present Time* (Nashville, Tenn., 1906), pp. 5–6.

[112] Walford, *Memoirs of Hugh Bourne*, 1:109.

[113] Dorothy Gott, *The Midnight Cry*, "Behold the BRIDEGROOM comes!" or, An Order from God to Get your Lamps Lighted (London, 1788), p. 19.

[114] *Gentleman's Magazine* 85 (Dec. 1815), p. 503.

ferings foreshadowed. The evangelical subculture out of which millenarianism emerged was certainly a violent one, in language if not in deed. The
"military ethos" that Christine Heyrman argues pervaded Southern religious
culture by the early nineteenth century reached deep into evangelical homes
and churches, distorting relations of dominance and subordination from
marriage to slavery. Even when their ecclesiastical enemies retreated from
public confrontation, and infidelity and apathy were thoroughly routed,
evangelical preachers continued to hone their rhetorical weapons in verbal
duels with sinners and scoffers well into the nineteenth century.[115]

Millenarians shared the violent rhetoric of their evangelical rivals if not
the glory of public martyrdom, but their militancy was, oddly enough, less
purposeful.[116] With the disappearance of the devil as the literal embodiment
of evil and the redirecting of public sensibilities away from the spectacle of
punishment and repentance and toward the psychodrama of self-realization,
who exactly were millenarians fighting against? And what did they hope to
accomplish by weaving frightening tales of unspeakable suffering if pain was
no longer a salvific agent? Millenarian culture by 1800 promised violence
without redemptive meaning, a radical repudiation of mainstream Protestant soteriology that would, by the end of the nineteenth century, give birth
to the ruthlessly nihilistic form of millennialism known as dispensationalism
where only the damned would know the wrath of God firsthand. In premillennial dispensationalist theology, suffering was for fools only.[117]

There are hints that eighteenth-century millenarians understood the
temptation to denigrate pain as a sign of weakness rather than ennoble it as a
spiritual virtue. Unremitting and indeterminate, pain threatened not only to

[115] Heyrman, *Southern Cross*, p. 234; see pp. 225–52 for a general discussion of the aggressive masculinity of Southern preachers, especially after 1800.

[116] See Paul Johnson and Sean Wilentz's discussion of the grandiose militarism of one
antebellum prophet in *The Kingdom of Matthias: A Story of Sex and Salvation in Nineteenth-
Century America* (New York, 1994), pp. 106–7; in the case of Robert Mathews, millenarian
militancy was a matter of fashion more than substance—a desperate gambit for attention
rather than a theological position.

[117] On the shift from postmillennial to premillennial scenarios after the American Civil
War, see George Marsden, *Fundamentalism and American Culture: The Shaping of Twentieth-
Century Evangelicalism, 1870–1925* (New York, 1980); on dispensationalist theology, see Paul
Boyer, *When Time Shall Be No More: Prophecy Belief in Modern American Culture* (Cambridge, Mass., 1982), chapter 3. Dispensationalists believed that the elect would escape the
plagues foretold in the Book of Revelation by being miraculously transported to heaven before the troubles began, where they would watch—secure and unharmed—the terror unfolding below.

overwhelm their faith but to emasculate saints as well. Pain was understood by eighteenth-century anatomists as the result of excessive stimulation of the nervous system, a condition to which evangelicals (and women) were exceptionally prone through their hysteric fits and "nervous" behaviors. Francis Asbury carefully monitored his own spiritual state for any hint of enervation. "I find a degree of effeminacy cleaving to me," he confided to his journal in 1772, "but abhor it from my very heart." His efforts to suppress the feminizing tendencies of his faith, including regular readings of Wesley's journals and an ascetic lifestyle matched by few of his itinerant brethren, were not always successful: twenty-five years later, he was still complaining of being "subject to the greatest effeminacy" by "my gloomy and nervous affections." Asbury's concerns were shared by the Methodist itinerants whose labors he supervised. Theophilus Gates saw himself as "an effeminate, unimportant person," undone by his own frailness.[118] The physical debility and emotional transports that itinerant preachers suffered threatened to unman them at a critical juncture in their personal and professional lives, when they needed all the muscle they could muster to battle indifference and infidelity on the Anglo-American frontier. While "shrink[ing] and writh[ing]" under the pain inflicted by the Spirit, men like Asbury and Gates struggled to redeem their manhood by "work[ing] our bones and flesh" in the Lord's service.[119] Those millenarians who took denial of the flesh to the extreme of celibacy believed that true saints are "separated from all effeminate desires and sensual pleasures."[120]

Evangelical preachers may have had special cause to regret their embrace of nerve psychology, as they faced constant taunts about their manliness from the worldly and the profane, but they were not the only ones to make the connection between excessive stimulation and various forms of personal and collective debility.[121] The language of the human body (its anatomy, vital properties, and structural vulnerabilities) provided a powerful way to envision other "bodies" in the early modern period, from the celestial

---

[118] Gates, *Truth Advocated*, p. 301.

[119] *Journals of Francis Asbury*, 1:44–45, 2:132, 2:326.

[120] Letter of James Whittaker to "Natural Relation," undated, Copies of Letters, Shaker MSS, IV:B-3, Western Reserve Historical Society.

[121] For three excellent discussions of "evangelical manhood" in the American South, see Heyrman, *Southern Cross*, chapter 5; Janet Moore Lindman, "Acting the Manly Christian: The Construction of White Evangelical Masculinity in Eighteenth-Century Virginia," *William and Mary Quarterly* 3d ser., 57 (Apr. 2000), pp. 393–416; and Cynthia Lynn Lyerly, *Methodism and the Southern Mind, 1770–1810* (New York, 1998).

to the political. Political theorists were particularly adept at using bodily images to describe both healthy and diseased states. The Enlightenment view of the human body as an enclosed, self-contained, and self-regulating mechanism gained currency in economic and political theory in the eighteenth century because it fit with new ideas about self-regulating markets and self-governing polities. The architecture of the solidistic body with its connective joints and detachable parts provided a more conducive model for theorizing about the relationship of individuals to the state for Enlightenment thinkers than the unformed, spongy mass of the humoral body.[122]

But, as evangelicals like John Wesley and Francis Asbury knew all too well, the vitalist forces which powered the body could easily *overpower* the delicate balance between the members that a healthy body sustained. An excess of nervous energy, misdirected in the wrong channels, could derail the entire system, leading to political disorder as well as physiological distress. Political theorists feared the "convulsions" that the body politic could be thrown into by war and social unrest, having had some experience with both during the age of revolution. Urban riots, agrarian insurrections, slave rebellions, all were described as "spasms" of the discontented and dispossessed. Like evangelical converts, the urban crowd and the frontier regulators who erupted periodically in anger against their social and political betters were subject to a new construction of the civil body as one prone to "nervous disorders," especially in its lower parts.

"Nerves" played a crucial role as conductors of pathogens in the analysis of political disorder as well as disease in the late eighteenth century. "That the political body, like the animal, is liable to violent diseases" is "a truth which we all acknowledge," wrote a contributor to the federalist magazine the *American Museum* in 1787.[123] Lamenting the "sick disordered state" into which independence had thrown the former colonies, federalists in the United States complained bitterly of the "factions, seditions, convulsions, and fatal revolutions" that seemed endemic to the new republic in the 1780s and 1790s. Even a republican prophet like David Austin recognized that "so

---

[122] For a recent discussion of the intellectual and cultural linkages between anatomical renderings of the human body and political economy in eighteenth-century America, see Robert St. George, *Conversing by Signs: Poetics of Implication in Colonial New England Culture* (Chapel Hill, N.C., 1998), pp. 195–203. On the "solidistic" body, see Charles E. Rosenberg, "The Therapeutic Revolution: Medicine, Meaning, and Social Change in Nineteenth-Century America," in Morris J. Vogel and Charles E. Rosenberg, eds., *The Therapeutic Revolution: Essays in the Social History of American Medicine* (Philadelphia, 1979), pp. 3–25.

[123] *American Museum* 1 (Feb. 1787), p. 116.

convulsed is the national sea, and so vivid the tempest, that some of the
mariners fear for the safety of the federal ship."[124] The "volcano" that was
American democracy had its eruptions large and small: rebel farmers in
Massachusetts, fueled by "irritable passion," took up arms against the state in
1786, while ignorant "mechanicks"—their minds disordered by the "irritation" and "dilating" of the "nervous fibres"—dared to take up letters. "I have
known a cit to commence a poet," scoffed one disgruntled intellectual; "his
brain has been agitated and disturbed."[125] Meanwhile conservatives in England watched with horror as the Terror unfolded across the Channel. "My
heart is sick, my stomach turns; my head grows dizzy," Edmund Burke wrote
at a low moment. "The world seems to me to reel and stagger." Discouraged
radicals in Britain could be just as contemptuous of the "addled brains" of
the lower orders who had refused to follow them into rebellion in the 1790s:
wrote Henry Hunt from his jail cell where he was imprisoned after the Peter-
loo Massacre of 1819, "their heads had been so mystified, and their brains so
confused" that they sank into "hysteria."[126] From the New World to the Old,
the literature of political reaction after the revolutions of 1776 and 1789 reveals, in Anne Vila's words, a "profound fear" that the Christian world was
"in danger of succumbing to a kind of mass hypochondria—a collective
weakening of the nervous system, brought on by culturally induced overstimulation of everyone's sensibility."[127]

The worry that the English world was on the brink of a collective
nervous breakdown made prophecy a risky business in the late eighteenth
century. Prophets had to walk a careful line between arousing people's fears
to a healthy pitch and irritating their already frayed nerves to the point of
hysteria or paralysis. They accomplished this delicate balancing act by saying
one thing and doing another: by composing lurid end-time scenarios while
being purposefully vague about the when, where, and how; by agitating for
violent spiritual rebellion while denying that they intended any harm to

[124] David Austin, *The Dawn of Day, Introductory to the Rising Sun, Whose Rays Shall Gild
the Clouds* (New Haven, 1800), p. 15. His fellow republican Lorenzo Dow also feared that "the
whole world appears to be convulsed," which led him "to think the prophecies are fulfilling."
Dow, *Hints on the Fulfillment of Prophecy* (New York, 1815), p. 399.

[125] *Pennsylvania Gazette*, May 26, 1779; for "factions, seditions, convulsions," see *American Museum* 1 (Mar. 1787), pp. 205–6; for democracy as a "volcano," see "Letter from Dr. Rush
to Dr. Ramsay," *American Museum* 3 (1788), p. 419; for "passionate" farmers, see *American
Museum* 2 (Oct. 1787), pp. 3–17; for "cits" who become poets, see *American Museum* 1 (Apr.
1787), pp. 351–52.

[126] The quotes are from Don Herzog, *Poisoning the Minds of the Lower Orders* (Princeton, N.J., 1998), pp. 89, 533.

[127] Vila, *Enlightenment and Pathology*, p. 105.

monarchy, the republic, or capitalism; by speaking angrily about the corruption of hireling priests and greedy magistrates while repudiating politics as an unworthy pursuit for godly men and women; by insisting that destruction, total and final, lay just around the corner while doing nothing to impede its arrival. Here their studied eccentricity was a real asset, for, as Paul Langford notes, eccentrics were as a cultural type entirely benign. "The power to inflict real harm, let alone the inclination to do so, are alien to eccentricity, the essence of which is amiability. An eccentric cannot be sinister or malign."[128] Revolutionary-era prophets combined the clownish persona of the eccentric with the calculating ethics of Smithian sympathy, a combination unlikely to produce real terror in its audience.

Mainstream evangelicals recognized the danger of promising more than they could deliver before their millenarian cousins did. Tired of the abuse they had received for decades from the political and religious establishment and betrayed by an ethos that no longer recognized sacrifice as a virtue, Methodists decided in the first decades of the nineteenth century to trade the "hysterical" aspects of their culture for sentimentality. "The paroxysms and epilepsies of enthusiasm are now no longer heard among these people," Robert Southey observed with approval (if a bit prematurely) in 1807; "groaning and sobbing supply the place of fits and convulsions." What remained after the taming of Wesleyan Methodism were the sectarian offshoots (Primitive and Independent Methodists, the Welsh "Jumpers," the "Magic" Methodists of Delamere Forest) and an array of idiosyncratic prophets and visionaries.[129] Some prophets, mostly men, learned the lessons of overenthusiasm as well; some, mostly women, did not. In the end, whether they followed the evangelicals into respectability or remained stubbornly affixed to the vulgar edge of millenarian culture, revolutionary-era prophets came close to making a mockery of the very thing that sustained the enterprise in the first place: the fear, naked and raw, that Britons were going to hell.

---

[128] Paul Langford, *Englishness Identified: Manners and Character, 1650–1850* (New York, 2000), p. 301. Langford argues that the eccentric was not a revolutionary: "a revolutionary is one who by definition is hostile to eccentricity. He is the advocate of a code, not the bearer of a character" (p. 305).

[129] Robert Southey, *Letters from England*, ed. Jack Simmons (London, 1951; orig. pub. 1807), p. 327. On the splintering of Wesleyan Methodism, see Julia Stewart Werner, *The Primitive Methodist Connexion: Its Background and Early History* (Madison, Wis., 1984).

Chapter 4
Millenarian Politics:
Language and the Public Sphere

Joseph Thomas cut a distinctive figure in the American back-country, an area swarming with itinerant preachers and folk prophets, in the early 1800s. Known as the "White Pilgrim" for his white robe and monastic demeanor, Thomas traveled a familiar path from itinerant preacher to inspired prophet after an epiphany in 1812. Told that "I should esteem nothing on earth my own . . . and that I should deny the present fashion of dress, both as it relates to the *cut* and the *colour*, and particularly to refuse *black*," the Pilgrim set his course through the American backcountry in search of the millennial city, "NEW JERUSALEM." (A man whom he met along the way told Thomas he had "heard of that place"; "I believe, said he, this New Jerusalem stands on the banks of the Ohio River.") Despite his vow of apostolic poverty and his quite public repudiation of worldly concerns, the White Pilgrim did not entirely fit the model of otherworldly asceticism long associated with the itinerant lifestyle. Though he was careful to steer clear of direct intervention in the burning political questions of his day, fearful of offending those who believed religion and politics should not mix, his views nonetheless were decidedly democratic in tone. "It was observed by some," he noted in his journal, "that they thought from my preaching I was a Republican, and if they were sure of it, would drive me off. As to politics, I had said nothing neither on the one side nor the other, as I considered the subject unsuitable to the pulpit and too worldly for a preacher to engage in. But if my sentiments in a political point of view (without saying a word upon the subject) were taken, agreeably to my views on church government they would most certainly be republican throughout. For in the government of Christ, given to his people, I consider there is a perfect *equality* as it relates to power."[1]

Revolutionary-era prophets had not always been so cagy about their political sentiments. As imperial and domestic tensions mounted in the

---

[1] Joseph Thomas, *The Life of the Pilgrim, Joseph Thomas* (Winchester, Va., 1817), pp. 263, 268, 206.

1760s and 1770s in the colonies, few Anglo-Americans could avoid taking sides—millenarians included. Nathan Hatch and Ruth Bloch have made a persuasive case that millennialism was a potent strand of revolutionary political culture in America through the 1770s, one which added the critical element of eschatological urgency to the patriot cause and turned a war for colonial independence into a holy war against the British Antichrist. "Without this visionary dimension it is difficult—perhaps even impossible—to imagine the development of an American revolutionary ideology at all," Bloch argues.[2] Millenarians added their strident voices to the chorus of discontent swelling from the multitudes of disadvantaged and disaffected colonists who saw in the war a chance to punish sin, exact revenge, and establish America's proper place at the right hand of God. Apocalyptic warnings, a staple of colonial sermons for two centuries, reached a fever pitch in the early years of the war, offering wavering patriots a grim picture of the cataclysmic judgments that awaited those who thwarted God's plan for the "American Israel." Samuel Clarke's vision of the imminent pouring of "the first vials of God's Wrath" went into six editions between 1769 and 1776, and children prophesied doom in the streets of Philadelphia (America's "Sodom").[3] While prophets tended to see cities as breeding grounds for all manner of vice, those who hailed from the rural hinterlands believed the American West had a special eschatological role to play as the site of Christ's Second Coming. A class-inflected millenarianism fueled the agrarian rebellions, endemic in the American backcountry throughout the period 1760 to 1820, which fed revolutionary demands for a greater popular voice and an end to aristocratic tyranny.[4]

---

[2] Ruth Bloch, *Visionary Republic: Millennial Themes in American Thought, 1756–1800* (New York, 1985), p. 93. The summary that follows draws on the work of Bloch and Nathan Hatch, *The Sacred Cause of Liberty* (New Haven, 1977); Melvin Endy, "Just War, Holy War, and Millennialism in Revolutionary America," *William and Mary Quarterly* 3d ser., 42 (Jan. 1985), pp. 3–25; James West Davidson, *The Logic of Millennial Thought in Eighteenth-Century America* (New Haven, 1977); Jon Butler, *Awash in a Sea of Faith: Christianizing the American People* (Cambridge, Mass., 1990); Alan Heimert, *Religion and the American Mind* (Cambridge, Mass., 1966); and Ernest Lee Tuveson, *Redeemer Nation: The Idea of America's Millennial Role* (Chicago, 1968).

[3] [Samuel Clarke], *Blazing Stars: The Messengers of God's Wrath* (Boston, 1769); and [Clarke], *A Short Relation, Concerning a Dream* (Boston, 1769). For the child prophet of Philadelphia, see Bloch, *Visionary Republic*, p. 66.

[4] See, in particular, the writings of Herman Husband, a North Carolina Regulator and millenarian: [Herman Husband], *An Impartial Relation of the First Rise and Cause of the Recent Differences* (n.p., 1770); *A Continuation of the Impartial Relation of the First Rise and Cause of the Recent Differences in Publick Affairs* (New Bern, N.C., 1770); and *Some Remarks on Religion, with Author's Experience in Pursuit Thereof* (Philadelphia, 1761). The best treatment of the millenarian strain in agrarian radicalism is Alan Taylor, *Liberty Men and Great Proprietors: The Revolutionary Settlement on the Maine Frontier, 1760–1820* (Chapel Hill, N.C., 1990).

Millenarian militancy faded somewhat as the war effort wound down, with visions of a glorious future replacing warnings of divine retribution in the 1780s: victory had a soothing effect on the eschatological nerves of America's Christian citizens. A kind of popular secular optimism, defanged and latitudinarian in impulse, reigned as Americans looked benignly toward the future. Moments of doubt and despair certainly intruded into the national consciousness as Americans weathered the periodic economic and political crises of the decade, but overall the prophetic scriptures were understood to herald the eventual triumph of the United States as the leader of the "free" and the Christian world, which were assumed to be one and the same thing. By the time the new republic was firmly established in law and practice, a powerful fusion of millennial and political expectations that Mark Noll has termed "Christian republicanism" gave American politics the peculiarly evangelical flavor it has maintained to the present day.[5]

In Britain, the marriage of millennialism and politics was more stormy.[6] The heady events of the French Revolution had for a brief period provided a welcome opportunity for millenarians to recapture the political high ground they had vacated after the Restoration. The prophets of the Civil War era were as feared for their political aggression as for their otherworldly visions: "there is no better State-Engine in the World, than Prophecy, when it is in hands that know how to play it skillfully," one disgusted critic complained. "Let a serious People (such as the English are) be but once persuaded of a Man's Prophetick Character, and there is nothing so extravagant which he shall not be able to persuade them to afterwards. . . . He may come at last to tell us, how we shall continue the War with France, and who shall command

---

[5] Mark Noll, "The American Revolution and Protestant Evangelicalism," *Journal of Interdisciplinary History* 23 (1993), pp. 615–38. Bloch narrates the diminishing of political themes in millennial writing in the postrevolutionary era in *Visionary Republic*.

[6] British historians have, by and large, been less sympathetic to the notion that the worlds of radical politics and radical religion merged in the late eighteenth century than their American counterparts. Ever since the pioneering work of E. P. Thompson on the compensatory quality of early Methodism forty years ago (*The Making of the English Working Class* [New York, 1963]), studies of popular religion have remained under the shadow of a functionalist perspective that sees religion as the handmaiden of other, more important social forces. Even Thompson's later work on William Blake and the Muggletonian tradition, which posits an intimate if vague relation between sectarianism and urban radicalism, placed religion ultimately outside of politics, in the land of utopian visions rather than concrete political radicals; *Witness Against the Beast: William Blake and the Moral Law* (New York, 1993). Prominent exceptions to the Thompsonian perspective include Deborah Valenze, *Prophetic Sons and Daughters: Female Preaching and Popular Religion in Industrial England* (Princeton, N.J., 1986); and Deryck W. Lovegrove, *Established Church, Sectarian People: Itinerancy and the Transformation of English Dissent, 1780–1830* (New York, 1989).

our Fleets and Armies; and if any of the present Managers of the Publick Affairs be not approv'd, 'twill be the easiest thing in the World to Prophesie some Men out of Places and others into them."[7] While England's millenarians retreated from such overt political maneuvering for much of the eighteenth century, the 1780s saw the resurgence of the kind of political activism associated in popular memory with the 1640s. Rallying around the revolutionary attack on king and pope as the twin pillars of Satan's empire, British millennialists added their outraged voices to those of French prophets (the Avignon Society, Catherine Theot, Suzette Labrousse) calling for the violent overthrow of the ancien regime.[8] It was child's play (for a dedicated reader of the prophetic scriptures and Christian history, at any rate) to see in the events unfolding across the Channel the literal fulfillment of the apocalyptic sequence foretold in the Books of Daniel and Revelation. British millennialists had been long accustomed to identifying France and the papacy with the Antichrist, and they had been expecting both to meet a fiery end for several centuries. France's nightmare was a dream come true for most millennialists. But now Britain itself was courting annihilation by (depending on one's perspective) flirting with republicanism or conspiring with the forces of reaction to abort the Revolution before it could finish its eschatological work. As was the case in the United States, the French Revolution was a polarizing moment in millenarian politics—energizing those on the left *and* the right. While George Stanley Faber manipulated the prophetic scriptures to argue against free thinking and democracy, his contemporary James Bicheno defended both with equal certitude in his own millennial writings.

The arrest of the most outspoken prophet, Richard Brothers, for "unlawfully, maliciously, and wickedly writing, printing, and publishing various fantastical prophecies, with an intent to create dissensions, and other disturbances within this realm" in 1795, however, and the outbreak of the Terror in France scuttled the political fortunes of Britain's millenarians.[9] It is no accident, one historian argues, that the most eloquent and openly radical

---

[7] *Clavis Prophetica; or, a Key to the Prophecies of Mons. Marion, and the Other Camisars* (London, 1707), n.p.

[8] This and the following paragraph are drawn from Clarke Garrett, *Respectable Folly: Millenarians and the French Revolution in France and England* (Baltimore, 1975); W. H. Oliver, *Prophets and Millennialists: The Uses of Biblical Prophecy in England from the 1790s to the 1840s* (Auckland, 1978); and J. F. C. Harrison, *The Second Coming: Popular Millenarianism, 1780–1850* (London, 1797).

[9] Brothers was declared insane on March 27, 1795, and committed to a private asylum for the next eleven years. The "act against fantastical prophesies" under which he was prosecuted, Statute 5 Elizabeth c. 15, reads: "divers evil disposed persons, inclined to the stirring

millenarian of the age—William Blake—published no new illuminated works between 1795 and 1809. "To defend the Bible in this year 1798," Blake wrote following the incarceration of Brothers, "would cost a man his life."[10] The failure of literary and political malcontents to create a genuine revolutionary movement in the 1780s and 1790s essentially short-circuited the millenarian project, stalling its development at the moment when it was most shrill and divisive. Unable to make the transition from rebels to reformers, urban radicals labored in the political wilderness after the government crackdown of the 1790s, their proposals ignored and their aspirations to legitimacy mocked. The "radical underworld" of preachers, prophets, and pornographers that Iain McCalman has tracked in London from the 1790s through the 1830s was as culturally isolated as it was politically ineffective, mired in the reckless pursuit of eccentricity. Millenarians found it difficult to make their voices heard above the din of sedition, nihilism, and blasphemy that passed for critical discourse among this motley crowd.[11] The prospects for forging a distinctive political identity out of the shards of radical culture seemed dim indeed by the time Britain's last revolutionary-era prophet, Joanna Southcott, died an ignominious death in 1814.

Millenarians on both sides of the Atlantic thus had good reason to mask their true political feelings in the early 1800s.[12] By the first decade of the new century Anglo-Americans had endured a period perhaps unrivaled in the history of Anglo-American politics for the viciousness of its rhetoric and the harshness of elite responses to popular expressions of discontent. The 1790s has earned a reputation, richly deserved, as one of the most partisan eras on record in Britain and the new American republic: while Americans were struggling to contain the bitterness unleashed by the rushed (some would

---

and moving of factions, seditions, and rebellion within this realm, have been the more bold to attempt the like practices in feigning, imagining, inventing and publishing of such fond and fantastial prophecies . . . to the great disquiet, trouble and peril of the Queen's majesty, and of this her realm." The statute remained law until 1863. Morton D. Paley, "William Blake, The Prince of the Hebrews, and the Woman Clothed with the Sun," in *William Blake: Essays in Honour of Sir Geoffrey Keynes*, ed. Morton D. Paley and Michael Phillips (Oxford, 1973), pp. 260–93 (quote on p. 262).

[10] Paley, "William Blake," p. 267.

[11] Iain McCalman, *Radical Underworld: Prophets, Revolutionaries and Pornographers in London, 1795–1840* (Oxford, 1993).

[12] Ruth Bloch argues that millennial literature began to "markedly disengage from political commentary" around 1800 in the United States; "The Social and Political Base of Millennial Literature in Late-Eighteenth-Century America," *American Quarterly* 40 (Sept. 1989), p. 393.

say forced) ratification of the federal constitution and the first ugly stirrings of party politics, their old imperial masters were combating a wave of radical insurgency at home by issuing a series of repressive countermeasures which effectively protected the conservative alliance of church and state for another generation. The passage of the Alien and Sedition Acts at the end of the decade in the United States and the suspension of habeus corpus in Great Britain in 1794 highlighted a legislative offensive against "the democratic mob" that did not bode well for prophets and others who claimed to speak for the common man. Even the triumph of the Republican Party in the United States in 1800 did not decisively reverse the conservative attack on popular politics so much as it redirected populism into safer channels— away from riots and toward electoral politics, away from the demagoguery of self-appointed champions of the poor and toward collective petitions for relief, away from organized public demonstrations of popular discontent and toward what Kimberly Smith has called the "dominion of voice."[13]

On the cusp of a new century, prophets were well aware that they lived in a moment of high democratic possibility and danger. As did Joseph Thomas, they modulated their political opinions, sometimes beyond the point of recognition, to avoid the charge of sedition while finding new and creative ways to link political reform to the dawning of the millennium. Although their political dispositions spanned the entire spectrum from arch-monarchist to rabid republican, most prophets were reformers in one sense or another. They could hardly be otherwise, convinced as they were of the utter degradation of human society and its imminent destruction by an avenging God. The truly disturbing events of the day—the periodic crop failures of the 1790s and the early 1800s, the agrarian and urban insurrections which plagued both countries, and the Napoleonic wars and the constant postrevolutionary skirmishing between America and Britain which led to the War of 1812—provided more than enough evidence that the English world was in mortal peril, in desperate need of salvation by some heroic man or grand gesture. Prophets offered to supply both.

Despite its reformist manifesto, prophecy was an awkward addition to the expanding public sphere of the late eighteenth century. Francis Asbury's offhand admission that "I am a prophet of evil tidings, as it suits my cast of mind" suggests an instrumental, highly contingent approach to politics that

---

[13] Taylor, *Liberty Men and Great Proprietors*; Kimberly K. Smith, *The Dominion of Voice: Riot, Reason, and Romance in Antebellum Politics* (Lawrence, Kan., 1999).

was representative of millenarian culture more generally after the French Revolution.[14] Rather than comment directly on political issues, many prophets preferred to play a kind of shell game with their audiences, hiding their convictions under one or another rhetorical diversion. A quick detour through the history of ancient Babylon might hold lessons about the evils of commercial emporiums today, or it might signal divine disfavor with current tyrants (the pope, certain emperors, prime ministers who overreached) or with lower-class venality. The litany of disasters that typically comprised an apocalyptic sermon sometimes made it difficult to identify the primary danger facing today's Christians. Should the spiritually vigilant guard against external threats (as the Whigs and Republicans tended to urge) or against internal enemies (as Tories and Federalists contended)? It was safer to speak of evil in general rather than condemn specific individuals or acts. Nancy Towle, like many American itinerants, saw sin all around her when she visited London in the 1820s. "The blackness of darkness I saw, as a curtain, hanging over the nation. . . . The sin, I conceived, for which God was about to visit them, was a national sin, consequently must be punished with a national evil." But, Towle cautioned, "what that evil would be I did not pretend to say: whether the sword, famine, or pestilence."[15] Edward King was equally hesitant to name the evil that was menacing the American republic in the 1790s. While positive that "THIS IS THE YEAR 1798" in which "the WOE is now indeed come to pass," King backed off from making a detailed prognosis. "As, in my former commentaries, I stopped short at what appeared to be the precise description of the period in which we were *then* living," he explained, "so do I now, at the present dread Period."[16] References to specific events and personalities largely disappear from millennial tracts written after 1800, replaced by a generalized narrative of sin and retribution that created an atmosphere of terror rather than a blueprint for action. Francis Asbury knew that America would be punished for its "wickedness," whether by "pestilence, or civil discord, or internal plague," but could offer nothing more in the way of concrete diagnosis.[17]

Even the most brazen of revolutionary-era prophets, Richard Brothers, maintained he had left politics behind after his arrest for sedition. Writing

---

[14] Elmer T. Clark, ed., *The Journal and Letters of Francis Asbury*, 2 vols. (Nashville, Tenn., 1958), 1:376.

[15] Nancy Towle, *Vicissitudes Illustrated in the Experiences of Nancy Towle, in Europe and America* (Charleston, S.C., 1832), pp. 74–75.

[16] Edward King, *Remarks on the Signs of the Times* (Philadelphia, 1800), p. 21.

[17] *Journal of Francis Asbury*, 2:25–26.

from his cell, a chastened Brothers insisted, "I embrace all governments, whether kingdoms, republics, or principalities; all men, whether kings, princes, or republicans. . . . I openly, as well now as always before, disclaim any connection with the political events of the times, and all their concurrent transactions. . . . I have nothing to do with parties, politics, treasons, meetings, or associations of any kind whatever."[18] His supporters rejected the idea that he was "the *working tool* of a particular political party." Rather, they argued, Brothers was, and always had been, an equal opportunity doomsayer: "he fulminates destruction to all parties—dethronement to our present king—subversion to the present government both civil and ecclesiastical—a speedy termination to both Houses of Parliament, and violent threats are denounced against the whole British Nation."[19] Those who continued to write in a political vein were careful to separate an interest in public affairs from raw partisanship after the specter of global war became a reality in the 1790s: "the less we have to do with the squabbles of *party* politicians," James Bicheno wrote in 1817, "the better. We mean to take more holy ground."[20]

Beneath the diversionary tactics we can discern a few core convictions which anchored the millenarian political agenda, if we can call it that: a deep suspicion that politics was by nature a dirty game, corrupt both in the rules that governed participation and in the amorality of the participants; an equally firm belief that politics could not be avoided if the world was to be saved from its own sins; and a genuine commitment to the democratic premise that common men and women had something valuable to contribute to the formation of public opinion. The close, even symbiotic identification of prophecy with print culture in Anglo-America helped reconcile the apolitical nature of millennialism with its democratic aims; with so many publications eager to satisfy the public desire for eschatological narratives, millenarian

[18] Richard Brothers, *A Letter from Mr. Brothers to Miss Cott, the Recorded Daughter of King David and Future Queen of the Hebrews* (London, 1798), pp. 63–64.

[19] Henry Francis Offley, *Richard Brothers, Neither a Madman nor an Impostor* (London, 1795), pp. 30–31.

[20] James Bicheno, *A Word in Season: or, a Call to the Inhabitants of Great Britain* (London, 1795), p. 4. Bicheno was among the few prophets who continued openly to avow a political intent in his prophetic writings into the 1810s. While admitting that "there are some well-meaning Christians who think that religion and politics should be kept more apart than they are in the following pages," he argued that he was merely following in the footsteps of the Old Testament prophets whose writings were full of "*religious* politics." "How is it possible," he asked, "to watch the signs of the times . . . without comparing national occurrences with the sacred predictions; and how make this comparison, without interfering with political questions and public conduct?" *The Fulfillment of Prophecy Farther Illustrated by the Signs of the Times* (London, 1817), pp. vii–viii.

fever could be safely contained in the world of print rather than being transformed into action. The sheer *printedness* of so much millennial speculation
in the 1780s and 1790s stripped the apocalyptic scenario of much of its urgency and violence; Anglo-Americans could read about the coming battle
with the Antichrist and the establishment of the millennium without having
to act on their fears or hopes, secure in the knowledge that others were being
vigilant on their behalf. A kind of vicarious millenarianism thus lulled Christians into a posture of complacent expectancy, a sharp departure from the agitated paranoia of the Civil War era.[21]

We can see this dynamic at work in the transformation of one of the
most recognizable biblical figures, the "Woman of Revelation," into an allegory of American exceptionalism in the revolutionary era. While there were
few American candidates for this mysterious character, in contrast to the European prophetic scene, the figure of the "Woman" appears with some fre-
quency in millennial tracts—but not in reference to a flesh-and-blood
female prophet. Rather, it is America itself that assumes this persona in millennial writings. David Austin's 1794 compendium of millennial texts offers a
stirring image of America as the Woman of Revelation. "See, on the wings of
a bounteous providence, how she is wafted across the Atlantic, and settled in
these peaceful American abodes!" Victorious over the "Protestant Dragon"
who "vomited forth for the destruction of the woman in the American
wilderness" a "flood of troops, armies, and fleets," the Woman succeeds in
fulfilling the scriptural prophecy by giving birth to the "Man-child," the new
republic. "Behold the regnum montis, the kingdom of the mountain, begun
on the Fourth of July, 1776, when the *birth* of the MAN-CHILD—the hero of
civil and religious liberty took place in these United States. . . . Follow him, in
his strides across the Atlantic!—See him, with his spear already in the heart
of the beast!—See tyranny, civil and ecclesiastical, bleeding at every pore!"[22]
Bombastic and patriotic, Austin's prose is typical of the kind of overblown,
ready-to-hand millennial rhetoric that historians associate with the first,
most optimistic phase of the American Revolution.

[21] This retreat from action into rhetoric was characteristic of the kind of "armchair politics" practiced more generally in British political culture in the late eighteenth century, even
among radicals and reformers; see Eliga Gould, *The Persistence of Empire: British Political
Culture in the Age of the American Revolution* (Chapel Hill, N.C., 2000).

[22] David Austin, *The Millennium* (Elizabethtown, N.J., 1794), pp. 393–94, 413. For other
examples of this metaphorical association of America with the Woman of Revelation, see
Samuel Sherwood, *Church's Flight into the Wilderness* (New York, 1776); William Foster, *True
Fortitude Delineated* (Philadelphia, 1776), p. 17; [Wheeler Case], *Poems, Occasioned by Several
Circumstances . . . in the Present Grand Contest of America for Liberty* (New Haven, 1778), p. 21.

Women served the visionary republic, then, more as literary tropes than as flesh-and-blood participants. Invoked to represent the vulnerability of the American revolutionary experiment, the figure of the "Woman of Revelation" served a number of rhetorical and political purposes for millennial writers. It added the emotional power of outraged femininity to the patriot cause and allowed revolutionaries to portray the English crown (the Beast) as a sexual as well as political predator. It drove home the message of secular political addresses that the soul of America was imperiled as much by its own effeminacy as by the brutal overtures of the British "dragon," and urged America to transform itself from the fragile woman of the wilderness to the sturdy "man-child" she gives birth to. The dramatic plot of Revelation is telescoped in the American renditions of the millennial script, as America is portrayed as both the woman and the man-child, the former representing its colonial vulnerability and the latter its newfound strength as an independent nation. Politically, the rhetorical coupling of America with the Woman of Revelation accomplished the same ends as the secular impulse to portray Liberty as female: redefined as allegory, women's political usefulness could be safely contained in the realm of myth rather than action.[23] Readers found such allegorical maneuverings very reassuring.

To truly grasp the place of millennial thinking in revolutionary Anglo-America, then, we have to understand the politics of reading and myth-making. Prophetic writers were engaged as much in an extended critique of the culture of print itself as in scriptural exegesis. In this they have much to tell scholars who are interested in the revolutionary era as a pivotal moment in the history of print culture, a moment when the acts of reading and writing became politicized to an unprecedented degree and the nation itself constructed along textual lines.[24] Print was the primary medium of prophecy in

[23] On the use of female allegory in the early republic, see John Higham, "Indian Princess and Roman Goddess: The First Female Symbols of America," *Proceedings of the American Antiquarian Society* 50 (1990), pp. 45–79; Jan Lewis, " 'Of Every Age Sex and Condition': The Representation of Women in the Constitution," *Journal of the Early Republic* 15 (1995), pp. 359–88. As Lynn Hunt and Joan Landes have shown in the context of the French Revolution, the iconic presence of women in the symbols of revolution was a graphic reminder of their marginality in the political culture of the new republic; Hunt, *Politics, Culture and Class in the French Revolution* (Berkeley, Calif., 1984), pp. 113–19; Landes, *Women and the Public Sphere in the Age of the French Revolution* (Ithaca, N.Y., 1988), p. 83.

[24] On the American side, see Jay Fliegelman, *Declaring Independence: Jefferson, Natural Language, and the Culture of Performance* (Stanford, Calif., 1993); Michael Warner, *Letters of the Republic: Publication and the Public Sphere in Eighteenth-Century America* (Cambridge, Mass., 1990); and Richard D. Brown, *Knowledge Is Power: The Diffusion of Information in Early America, 1700–1865* (New York, 1989). On the British side, see J. H. Plumb, "The

the late eighteenth century, a fact of which prophets themselves were keenly aware as they sought to claim the privileges of authorship for themselves and instill the responsibilities of readership in their audience.

Commoners' access to the world of cheap print expanded exponentially in the decades after 1750 on both sides of the Atlantic. At the start of the eighteenth century, there were only four newspapers in all of the American colonies; one hundred years later that number stood at 370 and growing yearly. In Britain, a vigorous newspaper industry was already well established by mid-century and the trend was toward daily rather than weekly accessibility. On the eve of the French Revolution there were fourteen daily newspapers in London; by 1821, eleven million newspapers were sold each day in the capital. Periodicals, too, made rapid advances: the prototypical *Gentleman's Magazine* had debuted in 1731, and literary journals modeled on the British periodical first appeared in the American republic in the 1780s. While subscription rates remained relatively low in the new American republic (the most popular urban periodical, the *American Museum*, sold 1,250 copies a year), in Britain an enterprising journalist like William Cobbett could reach some 300,000 readers a week by 1817.[25] Those who did not bother or could not afford to subscribe could pick up a copy of these magazines at any local bookstore; as William Blake observed in 1800, London had "as many Booksellers as there are Butchers & as many Printshops as of any other trade."[26]

Within the pages of these papers and magazines, Anglo-Americans found more than just international news—the standard fare of the prerevolutionary press—but whole new categories of cultural and social interest: "domestic intelligence," amusing anecdotes, running exchanges between pseudonymous correspondents, book reviews, social commentary, announce-

---

Commercialization of Leisure in Eighteenth-Century England," in *The Birth of a Consumer Society: The Commercialization of Eighteenth-Century England*, ed. Neil McKendrick, John Brewer, and J. H. Plumb (Bloomington, Ind., 1982), pp. 265–85; and Bob Harris, *Politics and the Rise of the Press: Britain and France, 1620–1800* (New York, 1996).

[25] On the expansion of print culture and newspapers in Britain, see Michael Harris, *London Newspapers in the Age of Walpole: A Study in the Origins of the Modern English Press* (London, 1987); J. H. Plumb, *The Commercialisation of Leisure* (Reading, 1973); and Lucile Werkmeister, *A Newspaper History of England, 1792–1793* (Lincoln, Neb., 1967), pp. 19–41. On newspapers in America, see Charles Clark, *The Public Prints: The Newspaper in Anglo-American Culture, 1665–1740* (New York, 1994); on the rise of American periodicals, see Frank Luther Mott, *A History of American Magazines, 1741–1850* (Cambridge, Mass., 1930), and David Paul Nord, " 'A Republican Literature': Magazine Reading and Readers in Late-Eighteenth-Century New York," in *Reading in America*, ed. Cathy N. Davidson (Baltimore, 1985), pp. 114–39.

[26] Quoted in Don Herzog, *Poisoning the Minds of the Lower Orders* (Princeton, N.J., 1998), pp. 68–69.

ments of public events, gossip, satire, and, of course, advertisements selling everything from hair tonic to religious revivals. The heterogeneity of the late eighteenth-century newspaper was its most distinctive feature, a fact that publishers themselves celebrated. "It has been observed, that there is not so inconsistent, so incoherent, so heterogenous, although so useful and agreeable a thing as a public newspaper," argued the Philadelphia weekly *Freeman's Journal* in 1785; "the very ludicrous contrast in advertisements, the contradictory substance of foreign and domestic paragraphs, the opposite opinions and observations of contending essayists, with premature deaths, spurious marriages, births, bankruptcies, &c. form a fund of entertainment for a world, of which it is in itself no bad epitome."[27] The tone of the popular press was changing as well as its content, as journalists adopted a breezy, bantering style of writing more in keeping with the vulgar interests of their expanded audiences. It was natural that stories of religious prodigies (including prophets) would find their way into press, and natural, too, that these stories would be reported in the manner of *exposés*—tales of folly designed to expose the natural credulity of Anglo-America's popular classes.

When the American prophet Jemima Wilkinson visited Philadelphia in the early 1780s, she sparked a lively newspaper debate that outlasted her abrupt departure from the city in 1782. The British prophetess Mrs. S. Eyre was known only in the pages of the London daily *Oracle*, which published her prophecies over the course of several issues in 1795. Prophecy was the subject of serious (if cranky) discussion in the more respectable journals of the day as well. Both the *Critical Review* and the *British Critic* begrudgingly devoted substantial coverage to Brothers and his many imitators in the 1790s, and the Philadelphia-based *American Museum* and *Columbian Magazine* played leading roles in the war of words surrounding Jemima Wilkinson a decade earlier. The granddaddy of British periodicals, the *Gentleman's Magazine*, serialized an account of the famous Samuel Best (or "Poor Helps") in the late 1780s and regularly featured articles comparing the relative merits of miracles, prophecies, and other supernatural interventions in contemporary affairs.

The association between popular prophecy and the media went deeper still. Newspapers themselves were oracles of sorts in the revolutionary era, a fact captured in a 1798 cartoon (Figure 4). Broadcasting news far and wide to an ever-expanding audience of readers thirsty for the latest "intelligence," the urban press was an active participant in politics, not merely a passive spectator. Anticipating changes of policy, advocating certain positions through

[27] "Thoughts on a Newspaper," *Freeman's Journal*, Oct. 26, 1785.

editorials and selective reporting, championing one minister over his rival—all these practices, familiar enough in our own day, helped transform popular perception of the press from a peripheral organ of the state or party to an active shaper of events. Its ability to make news, not just report it, gave the press a reputation for prophetic vision that made it the natural medium for millenarian expectations.

The role of the fourth estate in shaping policy was still not universally accepted or respected, of course. It was impossible to escape the implications of political subversion that surfaced wherever commoners intruded into affairs of state, however sincerely millennial authors disclaimed any overt political agenda. The *British Critic* exposed the hidden ties that bound millenarians and radical republicans together in an unholy alliance. "The shops that sell the pamphlets of Eaton, deal also in the prophecies of Brothers. In many cases, it appears that the contagion of insanity has actually caught the friends of anarchy; how else has it happened, that a very eminent engraver [William Sharp], whose political opinions are but too notorious, has executed a fine print of Brothers?"[28] William Sharp's journey from radical to millenarian is illustrative, if not typical. A charter member of the Society for Constitutional Information, Sharp was among the earliest supporters of Richard Brothers and later transferred his allegiance to Joanna Southcott after Brothers's incarceration. His engravings of the two prophets gave both instant notoriety (Figures 5 and 6). The involvement of noted radicals like Sharp in the world of prophetic publishing meant that commoners wandering into one of the many bookshops that peddled penny literature may have been unwittingly lured into confusing the destruction of Babylon and the defeat of the Antichrist with the reformers' goal of purging the British commonwealth of commercial and political corruption. One cautious author seeking a publisher for his millennial writings refused to be "seduced" by those "bold adventurers," the radical printers, whose "seditious publications" had ruined the market for respectable prophecy.[29] Beyond any covert political message, however, the consumers of cheap millennial literature were exposed to a genre that celebrated vulgarity itself. Flimsy and cheap, these pamphlets mirrored the social origins of their customers—divine proof that truth comes in shabby packages. As the visionary Quaker Cornelius Cayley put it, "the Books which gave my Soul the most comfort, and spiritual Edification, were such, as I gather'd from Stalls in Moorfields, and other Streets in

---

[28] *British Critic* 5 (1795), p. 555.
[29] Gilbert Wakefield, *The Spirit of Christianity, Compared with the Spirit of the Times in Great Britain* (London, 1794), p. iii.

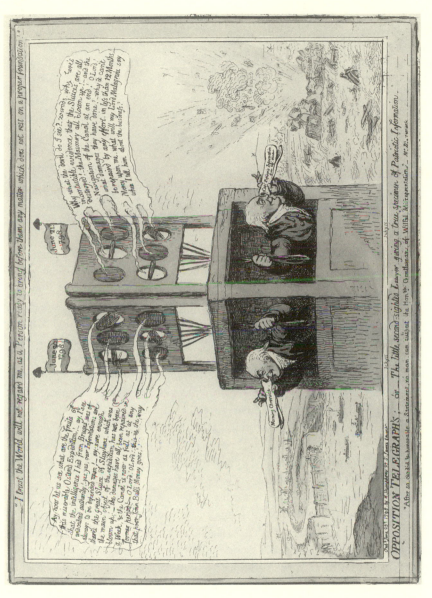

Figure 4. "Opposition Telegraphs; or The little second-sighted Lawyer giving a true specimen of Patriotic Information," 1798. Department of Prints and Drawings, British Museum. The telescope on the left, the *Morning Chronicle*, played a leading role in publicizing the deeds of London's prophets, including, most famously, the "pregnancy" of Joanna Southcott in 1814.

London; where several of them were exposed for Sale, with this Title over their Heads, PICK AND CHUSE FOR TWO PENCE, OR THREE PENCE, A PIECE. Poor old shabby looking Books, quite despicable to appearance, and the Authors chiefly Persons of low estate in Life . . . they contain the marrow of Christ's Gospel."[30]

But just how subversive were these prophecies? Were they really, as conservatives charged, millennial versions of radical fantasies? It is, in fact, extremely difficult to locate prophecy on the political map of late eighteenth-century Britain and America. On the one hand, prophets were traditionalists who reached backward to an archaic form of authority, to the "mystery" of monarchies with their secret societies and closed systems of knowledge. On the other hand, they were also democrats who shrewdly used the print culture of the new bourgeois public sphere to proclaim a message of spiritual equality. Some spoke in the arcane language of the Old Testament patriarchs, others in the modern tones of Painite republicanism. But whatever their own affinities, none could escape the widespread popular association of prophecy with political disorder. This association could run in two directions—toward demagoguery (the manipulation of the vulgar and uninformed by a glib appropriation of the language and symbols of democratic politics) and toward "mystagoguery" (the seduction of the weak and credulous through the exploitation of primitive religious passions). Whether one chooses to interpret revolutionary-era prophecy as the fulfillment or the betrayal of democratic political hopes depends in the final analysis on how we understand the prophets' own hermeneutic mission. Did prophets represent their exegetical forays into the historical and biblical past as practical lessons for the present or as timeless demonstrations of the universality of God's laws? Was the rule of God as preserved in the scriptures accessible to all, available to a select few, or entirely unscrutable by human means?

The answer to these questions depended largely on the gender of the prophet. Male and female prophets assumed different audiences for their texts, positioned themselves differently as divine oracles, and expounded radically different models of reading. Prophets and prophetesses, in other words, enacted different versions of spiritual "citizenship" that turned many conventional assumptions about the relationship between language and authority on their head. By making the act of interpretation itself a principal object of study, prophets and their followers contributed to broader political

---

[30] Cornelius Cayley, *The Riches of God's Free Grace, Display'd in the Life and Conversion of Cornelius Cayley* (Leeds, 1778), p. 53.

RICHARD BROTHERS
PRINCE OF THE HEBREWS.

Fully believing this to be the Man whom GOD has appointed; — I engrave his likeness, *WILLIAM SHARP.*

Published at N°8, Charles Street, Midd.ᵗ Hospital London April 16 1795 by W.Sharp.

Figure 5. "Richard Brothers, Prince of the Hebrews," 1795. Engraving by William Sharp. Department of Prints and Drawings, British Museum.

Isaiah Ch. LXV & LXVI.   JOANNA SOUTHCOTT   Jan. 1 1812.

Drawn and Engraved from life by Wm. Sharp

Published by Jane Townley, London.

Published according to Act of Parliament Jan. 1st 1812 by Jane Townley London.

Figure 6. "Joanna Southcott," 1812. Engraving by William Sharp. Department of Prints and Drawings, British Museum.

discussions about the rights of subjects to know and interpret the laws which bound them. The same question that animated prophetic discourse—who has access to truth?—was at the heart of the political controversies of the late eighteenth century in both Britain and America. These debates pitted reason against inspiration, literacy against experience, knowledge against secrecy, and, often, men against women.

Demagogues or Mystagogues? Prophecy in a Republican Mode

In an influential critique of E. P. Thompson's *Making of the English Working Class*, Joan Scott counterposes Thompson's celebratory treatment of Tom Paine—the quintessential "citizen of democratic revolutions"—with his caricature of Joanna Southcott. "Deluded yet charismatic," Scott writes, "[Southcott] evoked in her utterances the lures of sexuality and religion; fantastic prophecy was her mode of expression, in her hysterical pregnancy one sees the sterility of her revolutionary appeal."[31] Most observers of the British political scene in the 1790s and early 1800s would have endorsed wholeheartedly the notion that Tom Paine and Southcott stood at opposite ends of a political, religious, and aesthetic spectrum, and most would have concurred with Thompson that the Southcottian end of this spectrum was a political dead end. No group endorsed more emphatically the elevation of Painite reason over Southcottian mysticism than male prophets, for whom Paine served as a compelling literary model even while many disparaged his radical political sensibilities. Even among those for whom Paine's infidelity was inexcusable, the Painite literary style was the preferred mode of address.

Tom Paine's most celebrated pamphlets, *The Age of Reason* and *The Rights of Man*, introduced a new literary style to millions of readers. Earthy, grammatically uncomplicated and literal-minded, Paine's writings appealed directly to men's reason. He attacked the political and ecclesiastical establishment alike for deliberately shrouding the process of governance in the language of classical oratory, which the common man could neither understand nor reproduce. Writers like Edmund Burke he singled out as particularly grievous offenders of this art of mystification. "As the wondering audience, whom Mr. Burke supposes himself talking to, may not understand all this

---

[31] Joan Wallach Scott, "Women in the Making of the English Working Class," in her *Gender and the Politics of History* (New York, 1988), p. 78.

learned jargon," Paine wrote in the preface to *Rights of Man*, "I will undertake to be its interpreter."[32] To make a "mystery" of government or religion was to perpetuate the authority of learned gentlemen (the parasitical class) and exclude ordinary citizens from fully participating in the civic life of the nation. "A prophet is a seer, not an arbitrary dictator," counseled William Blake.[33]

This was a message that resonated with men whose political consciousness was being sharpened through the expansion of print culture and the diffusion of political debate through every level of society. The democratic or bourgeois public sphere which supposedly came into being in the reading rooms, coffeehouses, lyceums, and salons of eighteenth-century Europe and America was characterized above all by the qualities of transparency, universality, rationality, and the negation of the self. The Habermasian model of this public sphere contrasts the privatized authority of monarchical states, where sovereignty is maintained by "secrecy" and the suppression of ideas, to the impersonal rule of law in democratic societies, where the common good is promoted through public disclosure and the free circulation of opinions.[34] The ethos of publicity that Habermas identified as the guiding principle of bourgeois civic life demanded widespread literacy and the establishment of a "republic of letters," where printed texts—shorn of the personalized traits of their authors—circulated widely among anonymous individuals who collectively imagined themselves part of a community of "unknown and *in principle unknowable* others," in Michael Warner's words.[35]

The ideal public man was thus one who rose above the entanglements of family and community to engage other men in the disinterested pursuit of universal principles through the medium of print. As a group of "volunteers" from Belfast phrased it in their declaration of support for the French Revolu-

---

[32] Quoted in Eric Foner, *Tom Paine and Revolutionary America* (New York, 1976), p. 214. See also James T. Boulton, *The Language of Politics in the Age of Wilkes and Burke* (Westport, Conn., 1975) on the writings of Paine and Burke as two contrasting models of political language.

[33] Paley, "William Blake," p. 273.

[34] Jürgen Habermas, *The Structural Transformation of the Public Sphere: An Inquiry into a Category of Bourgeois Society*, trans. Thomas Burger (Cambridge, Mass., 1989; orig. pub. 1962). As Habermas notes, the specific form of the "public" in Britain was "the bourgeois reading public of the eighteenth century. This public remained rooted in the world of letters even as it assumed political functions" (p. 85). For recent studies of the discursive dimensions of the public sphere in eighteenth-century Anglo-America, see James Epstein, *Radical Expression: Political Language, Ritual and Symbol in England, 1790–1850* (New York, 1994), and David Shields, *Civil Tongues and Polite Letters in British America* (Chapel Hill, N.C., 1997).

[35] Warner, *Letters of the Republic*, p. 40.

tion, "We are men of plain and, we hope, sound understanding. We will disentangle ourselves from those bewitching bonds, with which an enticing and meretricious eloquence has of late vainly endeavoured to tie down the freedom and the strength of manhood; and, neither sophisticated by genius, nor rendered miserable by refinement and mystery, we will think and declare our thoughts, not as politicians, but as men, as citizens, and as volunteers."[36] That such a vision of enlightened citizenship was encoded male in the gendered discourse of republican theory is abundantly clear from the declaration of the Belfast volunteers, who found their "manhood" endangered by the eloquence and mysterious refinement of aristocratic society. As Joan Landes and Carole Pateman have argued, the public sphere as it took shape in Britain and France in the late eighteenth century was constructed via a series of ideological oppositions which associated the virtues of bourgeois civic life with manliness and the vices of aristocratic society with effeminacy.[37] To be manly was to be open and sincere, to use language to elucidate rather than obscure truth, to create a society where abstract reason and impartial appeals to scientific knowledge determined right from wrong. To be effeminate was to conceal and equivocate, to use artifice to deceive, to rely on superstition and primitive attachments to override the public good.

In such a semiotic universe, the world of religious prophecy was gendered female. Religious enthusiasm in general was derided by enlightened thinkers as a remnant of medieval superstition and fanaticism. Religious fanatics, like women, like the common people, were ruled more by their passions than their reason. If, in the republican critique, monarchies govern by the illicit powers of mystification and concealment, with the full complicity of their deluded and ignorant subjects, the same was true of populist preachers who used spiritual trickery to gull their credulous followers. The spirited and often scatological anti-Methodist literature of the eighteenth century drew on the long-standing association of religious passion with irrationality to depict enthusiasts as philandering "Mystagogues" who seduced their ignorant followers into error: "a *glib, deceitful Tongue, Wheedling, and Tricking, Impudence, and Lyes*. And *Subtlety,* with half-clos'd, owlish Eyes—These are the constant *Tabernacle-Tools*" of the itinerant preacher.[38] Moravians, too, were depicted as experts in the arts of mystification, their "cloudy, intricate,

---

[36] Reprinted in the Philadelphia periodical *American Museum* 10 (Sept. 1791), p. 153.

[37] Landes, *Women and the Public Sphere;* Carole Pateman, *The Sexual Contract* (Stanford, Calif., 1988); and Pateman, *The Disorder of Women: Democracy, Feminism, and Political Theory* (Stanford, Calif., 1989).

[38] *Fanatical Conversion; or, Methodism Displayed* (London, 1779), p. vii.

and Mysterious manner of writing" offering a convenient screen behind which to hide all manner of "gross Obscenities."[39] The charge of "mystagoguery" has a certain irony, considering the general charge of democratic leveling that conservative churchmen often directed against dissenters who insisted that anyone with an inner call, even those lacking special knowledge or formal training, could preach to the faithful. The powerful oratory of a John Wesley or a George Whitefield, both of whom were famed for reducing their audiences—men and women alike—to tears, was often decried as a form of demagoguery. Like radical democrats, evangelists in the Whitefieldian mode used simple but emotionally powerful words and images to elicit feelings of anger, disgust, and resentment against Satan's emissaries on earth (usually the standing clergy). As sketched by the urban press, the "character of a Demagogue" was suspiciously close to that of a religious fanatic or democrat: both were "moral monster[s]" who "would disorganize the world to obtain the huzza of a mob, or the plaudits of a tavern assembly."[40]

But whether described as demagogues or mystagogues, religious enthusiasts were condemned for using the unchecked power of language to lead true Christians (especially weak women) astray. In an essay on *False Prophets*, Henry Drummond castigated these enthusiasts for violating the ethos of publicity that was so essential to the maintenance of the public sphere. "They have come in secretly; they did not begin by proclaiming their doctrines publicly in the open streets, in the places of greatest concourse," he complained. Unlike "true preachers," who "proclaim from the house-tops, in the market-places, in the great assemblies, and concourse of the people," false prophets *"creep into houses, and lead captive silly women laden with sins, led away with divers lusts."*[41] Drummond's tirade, typical of many written after the prophetic frenzy of the early 1800s was spent, concisely summarized the antirepublican tendencies of radical religion. Though he himself was no democrat, he recognized in the form and language of enthusiastic religion a serious threat to the conventions of reasoned public discourse which kept a free society from collapsing into anarchy.

These, then, were the oppositions which structured the discourse of re-

---

[39] George Lavington, *The Moravians Compared and Detected* (London, 1755), pp. iv, xiii. A central strategy of this literature was to associate depraved sexual practices with degraded language, as if the "filthy Words" of the dissenters (in Lavington's phrase) were the literary analogue of their filthy practices.

[40] "Character of a Demagogue," *Oracle*, Oct. 15, 1795.

[41] Henry Drummond, *False Prophets* (London, 1834), pp. 4, 6.

ligion and politics in the 1790s and early 1800s: reason versus mysticism, plain speaking versus "babbling," transparency versus concealment, enlightenment versus ignorance. Despite the rhetoric of republicans and conservatives alike, however, religious visionaries did not always line up neatly on the wrong side of these oppositions. Male prophets, in particular, tried to find an uneasy middle ground between secular republican politics and the mysteries of faith. Women, on the other hand, rejected entirely the linguistic and epistemological precepts of Painite republicanism while insisting that they, too, spoke for the common people.

Paine's direct counterpart in the world of religious prophecy, a "republican prophet" if such a thing could be said to exist, was James Bicheno, the dissenting English clergyman and schoolmaster whose measured writings in the 1790s and early 1800s injected a degree of gentility and rationality into prophetic discourse. An ardent supporter of both the American and the French Revolutions, and of political reform at home, Bicheno was a consistent spokesman for the expansion of knowledge and learning throughout the European continent. Disclaiming any direct access to divine revelation ("I am no prophet" he declared),[42] he sought to provide a commonsensical "translation" of the prophetic scriptures for his readers grounded not in the scholarly efforts of learned authorities but in the exercise of his own reason. At first he "consulted commentators of the most generally approved, on the prophecies of Daniel and the Revelation of John," but found himself "still in the midst of a wilderness." "At length he determined to commit himself to his own investigations, and explore these regions of wonders, without placing implicit confidence in any guide," his editor explained. Through the use of natural reason, the "mazes of these wonderful visions may be treated with precision" and their predictions enlisted in the service of democratic reform.[43] The bulk of Bicheno's writings consisted of simple translations of the arcane symbolism of the prophecies into concrete historical and contemporary referents.

Bicheno was as disdainful of his more mystical counterparts as his republican allies, and he tried to distance himself from both the "dreams" of Joanna Southcott and the "visions" of Richard Brothers.[44] Yet he shared more

[42] James Bicheno, *The Fulfillment of Prophecy Farther Illustrated by the Signs of the Times* (London, 1817), n.p.

[43] Bicheno, *The Signs of the Times: Or the Overthrow of Papal Tyranny in France, the Prelude of Destruction to Popery and Despotism; but of Peace to Mankind* (London, 1793), n.p.

[44] Bicheno, *The Fulfillment of Prophecy*, p. 6.

with Brothers, in particular, than either man would perhaps have wished to admit. On most counts, Richard Brothers—certifiable lunatic and political cause célèbre of the 1790s—inhabited a world far removed from that of republican politics. Brothers's intemperate calls for a political revolution that would place him at the head of a reconstituted Hebrew nation as king and high priest inspired little confidence in republican circles, and his rabid hatred of the commercial classes made him an unreliable ally for those middling groups who favored a reformist agenda. Yet he drew unabashedly on the Painite tradition of plain speaking in disseminating his prophetic visions to the public. In the preface to his principal text, *A Revealed Knowledge of the Prophecies and Times*, Brothers spoke frankly of his status as the chosen one. "The following are the words which the Lord God spoke to me in a vision. . . . 'There is no other man under the whole Heaven that I discover the errors of the Bible [to], and reveal a knowledge how to correct them, so that they may be restored as they were in the beginning, but yourself.' " This heroic act of recovery was to take place not in the archaic language of the old prophets but in an entirely new vocabulary, one uniquely suited to the current times. "When I began to write, I believed it necessary to adopt the same language as the Scripture does, regularly imitating it in the words—ye, thee, and thou; but God spoke to me in a vision of the night, and said—'Write in the same manner as I always speak to you, write as other men do, write according to the Custom of the Country you live in: you will then be better attended to, and what you write will be more easily understood.' "[45]

In blunt, simple language, Brothers's writings—like those of Bicheno—laid out a prophetic key to current events which any reader could understand. Promising to "remove the Covering of secrecy" which had hitherto prevented his fellow citizens from understanding the prophetic scriptures, Brothers's pamphlets constitute a catalogue of names, dates, places, and events that are unusually specific by the standards of the genre.[46] The "loud and unusual Thunder" heard in January 1791 was none other than "the voice of the Angel" of Revelation proclaiming destruction upon the city of London; the French Revolution was a direct fulfillment of the Book of Daniel.[47] In his visions, Brothers received straightforward predictions of events to come. In one, he was "carried away by the Spirit of God to Sweden, when I

[45] Richard Brothers, *A Revealed Knowledge of the Prophecies and Times*, Second Book (London, 1794), p. iii.
[46] Brothers, *Revealed Knowledge*, First Book, p. 53.
[47] Ibid., p. 41; Second Book, p. 7.

was made to look through a window into a room: I did, and saw a man walk from the side of a great chair, leaving it empty. . . . Immediately the Angel that stood by me said, The Chair means the Chair of State; and that man you saw will make it empty; the King of Sweden is delivered over for death, and that is the very man that will shoot him."[48]

Such frank language represented the triumph of reason over priestcraft for his many admirers. Whereas "the *priests* have, as it best suited their interests, opinions or inclination, introduced a set of dogmas and abstruse, metaphysical mysteries, which the people have been wont to imagine *too sacred* for their inquiry," argued John Crease, Brothers wrote "in all the familiarity of conversation"—as one man to another.[49] His testimony was, in William Sales's view, a "plain and honest language, void of equivocation," not the "FLATTERY and FALSEHOOD" of priests and magistrates.[50] For Samuel Whitchurch, Brothers's revelations were "written as with a sun beam, in characters the most legible."[51] Critics, not surprisingly, ridiculed the very prosaic quality of Brothers's "celestial compositions." "When the final sentence of destruction against London is sealed," sneered Henry Spencer, "then the following words will appear in the Heavens, written in gigantic characters: 'IT IS DONE.' How sublimely simple the expression! how tremendously laconic! 'It is all over, my boys! you are done up.' "[52]

Even more than their British counterparts, American male prophets articulated a radical political agenda to the dissemination of plain prophetic truths throughout the reading public. Benjamin Gale, for whom "the whole tenor of Divine Revelations appears to originate from one general contest and struggle between *rulers,* for an undue extension of *power,* and the *ruled,* in order to maintain their *natural* and *constitutional rights,*" also understood this eternal political struggle of liberty against power in linguistic terms as a battle between allegorical and literal readings of the divine scriptures. "There has long been a strange disposition among men to convert some of the most plain and simple doctrines of revelation into *allegory, metaphor* and *mystery* . . . and from this source, the doctrines of revelation are often rendered *dark, intricate, mysterious* and *unintelligible,* to the great *joy* and

[48] Ibid., p. 59.
[49] J. Crease, *Prophecies Fulfilling; or, the Dawn of the Perfect Day* (London, 1795), pp. 29, 16.
[50] William Sales, *Truth or Not Truth; or A Discourse on Prophets* (London, 1795), p. 3.
[51] Whitchurch, *Another Witness!* p. 9.
[52] Henry Spencer, *A Vindication of the Prophecies of Mr. Brothers and the Scripture Expositions of Mr. Halhed* (London, 1795), pp. 28–29.

sport of *infidels*." False prophets, like tyrannical rulers, use "*unintelligible jargon*" to lead the common people astray.[53] Another ardent republican prophet, William Scales, styled himself as an American Jesus, of lowly origins and simple understanding. Disdaining the "flowery elevated stile" of the learned world, he urged his readers to "read this piece with candour . . . without quibbling, carping, or wrestling reason and scripture," for those who "are not pleased with plain language are in a state of spiritual death." Scales's pamphlet endorsed the revolutionary ideal of universal enlightenment: "I know indeed the arts of your spiritual task masters; they will, with their beguiling words . . . endeavour to keep you in ignorance. But let me beseech you to see for yourselves; don't give up your understandings to other men."[54]

The best example of this fusion of republican and millennial language can be found in the writings of David Austin. Recovering from a near fatal bout with scarlet fever in 1796, Austin—then a well-respected Presbyterian preacher in Elizabethtown, New Jersey—heard the voice of God calling him to the prophetic office. "I beheld the blessed Jesus as our *elder brother*," he recounted in his journal; "Here I seemed to stand, stripped of myself, and of all self-dependence, looking faintly at the blood which seemed to have issued from the Saviour's side." In this vision he was directed to read the third chapter of Zechariah, which "sent faintness into my soul and weakness into my bones. . . . So powerful was the impression of that chapter upon my mind . . . that it dropped me to the floor, and produced the self-abasement of which the journal hath spoken. The character and standing of *Joshua* was presented as my *own*."[55] What did it mean for Austin to take on the role of Joshua to the American people? As he describes his prophetic "office," his responsibilities were largely those of a republican publicist rather than a charismatic seer: he initiated a project to collect and publish the sermons of various evangelical

---

[53] Benjamin Gale, *A Brief Essay, or An Attempt to Prove from the Prophetick Writings of the Old and New Testament, what Period of Prophecy the Church of God is now under* (New Haven, 1788), pp. 23, 56. Most American male prophets were strict literalists on the question of prophetic interpretation; see Morgan Edwards, *Two Academical Exercises on Subjects Bearing the Following Titles: Millennium, Last-Novelties* (Philadelphia, 1788), and Benjamin Foster, *A Dissertation on the Seventy Weeks of Daniel* (Newport, R.I., 1787). As Foster declared, "The prophecy, in every particular, has been punctually, plainly, and almost in every instance, literally fulfilled" (p. 35).

[54] William Scales, *The Confusion of Babel Discovered: Or, An Answer to Jeremy Belknap's Discourse upon the Lawfulness of War* (America, 1780), pp. v–vi.

[55] David Austin, *The Voice of God to the People of the United States, by a Messenger of Peace* (Elizabethtown, N.J., 1796), pp. 36, 49. For two contemporary descriptions of Austin's prophetic career, see William Sprague, *Annals of the American Pulpit* (New York, 1859–69), 2:195–206.

clergymen (the first four volumes of the *American Preacher*) to disseminate Christian literature more widely throughout the country; he founded a magazine, the *Christian Herald, or the Union Magazine*, which became the leading periodical of millennial thought in the early 1800s; and he circulated a proposal for a national "concert of prayer" in which Americans in their individual homes and communities would pray as one at a designated hour—a perfect expression of the anonymous public sphere. Austin's claims to prophetic status thus rested on his efforts to circulate national texts and to create an imagined community of Christians via collective reading and prayer.[56]

No more stirring rendition of the "visionary republic" as a Habermasian public sphere exists than in Samuel Hopkins's learned *Treatise on the Millennium*, which was published three years before David Austin had his near encounter with death. In Hopkins's vision of the millennium, learning and print combine to create a universally enlightened society. "Those things which now appear intricate and unintelligible, will then appear plain and easy. Then public teachers will be eminently burning and shining lights. . . . And the conversation of friends and neighbors, when they meet, will be full of instruction and they will assist each other in their inquiries after the truth, and in pursuit of knowledge." Everyone will have "sufficient leisure to pursue and acquire learning of every kind that will be beneficial to themselves and to society." Universal brotherhood will be facilitated by the creation of a single universal language; "In the Millennium, all will probably speak *one language*. . . . And that language will be taught in all schools, and used in public writings, and books shall be printed; and in a few years will become the common language, understood and spoken by all." The withering away of national and linguistic differences will have the happy effect of "render[ing] books very cheap, and easy to be obtained by all." In time, this "universality of language will tend to cement the world of mankind so as to make them *one* in a higher degree."[57] Tom Paine could not have said it better.

[56] Billy Hibbard also proposed a concert of prayer in 1805; see *Memoirs of B. Hibbard* (New York, 1843), p. 257. The "concert of prayer" is described by Timothy Hall in his study of eighteenth-century itinerancy as an expression of the new community brought into being by the spread of commerce and print culture; *Contested Boundaries: Itinerancy and the Reshaping of the Colonial American Religious World* (Durham, N.C., 1994). Hall builds on the influential work of Benedict Anderson, whose *Imagined Communities: Reflections on the Origin and Spread of Nationalism* (London, 1983) explores the role of print in forging a sense of national identity.

[57] Samuel Hopkins, *A Treatise on the Millennium* (Boston, 1793), pp. 59, 75–77. Emmanuel Swedenborg, who more than any other prophet reconciled the worlds of natural philosophy and immediate revelation, also believed that "there is but one language used throughout heaven, so that all of every society, however distant, understand one another";

If the emphasis on plain language was particularly pronounced among American male prophets, it was also more closely tied to a robust tradition of oral address that persisted in America well into the nineteenth century. The "Prophet Nathan" spoke for many American writers when he issued a simple plea to his readers: "Will you suffer me, as a friend, to converse with you (if not personally, yet with my pen), about your *difficulties?*" The art of conversation, however encoded by print technology, was still the paramount ideal of communication in revolutionary and postrevolutionary America, and writers strove to simulate spoken conventions as closely as possible in their written texts.[58] Simon Hough addressed his audience through a series of imagined dialogues between himself and a "hireling" minister, enlisting both their moral and political sympathies on behalf of liberty of conscience.[59] William Scales typically addressed his readers as if they were engaged in direct conversation, posing questions and then responding to their imagined replies. David Austin, perhaps the most prolific American prophet, published numerous pamphlets in the form of epistolary exchanges which enabled him to construct a series of dialogues with real and imagined correspondents over the finer points of prophetic interpretation.

In contrast, British writers in the tradition of Brothers and Bicheno were much more self-consciously immersed in the expanding world of print culture, which formed not only the medium but the message of their republican brand of prophecy. As much as the simple language of Brothers's writings, his reliance on new modes of dissemination angered his many detractors. For his mission to succeed in the agitated days of corresponding societies and other innovations in forms of communication, oral suasion was not and could never be sufficient; Brothers was commanded by the Lord to make his writings available in published form—via "the *penny-post!*" as Henry Spencer marveled.[60] God even provided a mailing list, consisting of the king, the executive officers of the various state departments, the bishops, judges, all foreign ambassadors, the mayor and aldermen of the city of London, and members of both houses of Parliament. Circulating first among the

---

Swedenborg, *Heaven and Hell*, nos. 234–36, 239. See James Knowlson, *Universal Language Schemes in England and France, 1600–1800* (Toronto, 1975), for a broader discussion of the Enlightenment project to restore the diversity of human tongues to a single, pure language.

[58] As Jay Fliegelman notes, the elocutionary revolution of the late eighteenth century sought to "make writing over in the image of speaking." *Declaring Independence: Jefferson, Natural Language, and the Culture of Performance* (Stanford, Calif., 1993), p. 24.

[59] Simon Hough, *The Sign of the Present Time: Or, a Short Treatise Setting Forth What Particular Prophecies are Now Fulfilling in the Author's Judgment* (Stockbridge, Mass., 1799).

[60] Spencer, *A Vindication of the Prophecies*, p. 19.

highest echelons of state power and spiraling outward to the very margins of British political culture, Brothers's texts were intended for the same public then being courted by the London Corresponding Society and other radical organizations. The First Book of his *Revealed Knowledge* concludes with a graphic vision of the power of print to "open" the public sphere and make its knowledge available to all. "The night before I had finished this book for the Press, the Lord God shewed it to me in a Vision ready printed, holding it up at the same time by one leaf and shaking all the others open, while he pronounced in strong clear words, and commanded me to write them down exactly as he spoke, for universal information."[61] As scribe to the Lord, Brothers translated the oral tradition of revealed Christianity into print in the same way that the corresponding societies translated an inchoate popular radicalism into literate form. This partnership between the oral and the written, between the source of truth and its textual incarnation, was a recurring theme in much of the prophetic literature of the 1790s and early 1800s. Just as Christ "spake as never man spake," asserted John Crease in 1795, "it may without fear of contradiction be said of Mr. Brothers, that he has written, as never man wrote."[62]

Such a creative appropriation of the techniques and technologies of republican print culture was not unique to the lunatic fringe of British prophecy. Indeed, one could say that late eighteenth-century prophecy was itself the product of an expanded print culture; William Reid, for one, blamed the spread of both infidelity and religious heresy on the widespread availability of cheap print. "We have seen the principles of Infidelity transferred from *books* to men; from *dead* characters to *living* subjects; not among a few isolated or speculative individuals, but in numerous and compact bodies." The result was a flood of blasphemous literature; "Prophecies . . . teem from the British press, some of them in weekly numbers, till government, perfectly aware of these inflammatory means, prudently transferred the prince of prophets [Brothers] to a mad-house."[63] James Bicheno penned an extensive paean to the liberating effects of the print revolution in his final pamphlet, which appeared in 1817. He chose as his main text the tenth chapter of Revelation, in which an angel descends to earth holding a "little book open in his hand." For Bicheno, this was "one of the most sublime visions in all the Apocalypse. . . . It appears to me, that the least unbiased attention to

---

[61] Brothers, *Revealed Knowledge*, First Book, pp. 62–63.

[62] Crease, *Prophecies Fulfilling*, p. 4.

[63] William H. Reid, *The Rise and Dissolution of the Infidel Societies in this Metropolis* (London, 1800), pp. iv–v, 2.

the vision as a whole . . . would enable every one, at all acquainted with the symbolic language, to perceive, almost as easily as if written in alphabetical characters, that it is the *invention of printing, and the consequent revival of learning, and spread of knowledge, that is here represented.*" The print revolution had "opened" the word of God, which had been "shut for ages against the multitude by a crafty priesthood."[64]

No wonder, then, that so many male prophetic writers in England and America embraced the idea of revolution with such enthusiasm. Their vision of the millennium corresponded so closely with the vision of republican liberty espoused by political radicals that we can speak of a shared sensibility uniting men across the political and religious spectrum regardless of denominational affiliation. Deists and evangelicals made common cause to defend the emerging public sphere against its numerous enemies, political and spiritual, who would reduce the republic of letters to the Tower of Babel. William Scales, in his millenarian manifesto *The Confusion of Babel Discovered*, turned the tricks of these false prophets against themselves, and in the process offers us a wonderfully wicked counterimage to contrast to the millennial hopes of Samuel Hopkins. Sprinkling nonsensical words throughout his text, which he cleverly argued were emblematic of the "tricks of the deceivers," he showed his readers by example how a confusion of tongues, not a universal language, was the fruit of false teachers.[65]

This antirepublican vision was not a mere abstraction, a clever play of words, but was embodied in the practices and beliefs of female prophets. The writings of many female prophets suggest a partial or incomplete conversion to the world of print culture. In many of these texts the printed word appears as an object of veneration in itself. As a sacred object, books were fetishized in a manner reminiscent of pre-Reformed worship of saints' relics. The prominence of books and other printed texts as oracular signs in the dreams and visions of British prophets across the political spectrum suggests how much late eighteenth-century prophecy was still immersed in an enchanted world of supernatural portents and magical amulets.

---

[64] Bicheno, *The Fulfillment of Prophecy*, pp. 64, 69.
[65] Scales, *The Confusion of Babel Discovered*, pp. vii–viii.

A "Living Bible": Women Prophets and the Word

Sarah Flaxmer was a relatively minor prophetic figure in the 1790s, yet her one publication, *Satan Revealed,* illustrates with particular clarity the image of the Bible as a living book—an artifact of both oral and literate tradition.[66] Early in her career as a visionary she saw "a large paper book held up, with a great deal of writing in the inside of it, too small for me to discern, except a large inscription towards the top of the leaves, which a finger pointed out to me, and a voice read it aloud." In a later dream Flaxmer found herself wandering through a dark, impenetrable landscape until she stumbled upon a "dazzling," spacious house where a Christ-like figure was waiting. "He then took and wrote in my Bible in three places. . . . He turned around and took up a larger book (such a one as I never saw in my life) and opened it; he opened one part, which looked black; and opening another, it appeared white as snow, and he wrote on that in three different places; then turned round, and said, 'put your Bible now in your pocket, for it is written.' Upon my gazing at the book, he said, 'you never saw such a book in your life before.' I answered, no. He said, 'this is the book of life and the same as is written here is written in your Bible, and that brings you to this place again.' "[67] For Flaxmer, books were still mysterious things, objects of wonder whose contents were not discernable without divine assistance.

Such a talismanic worship of books helps us identify these prophets as members of a "textual community," in Brian Stock's words—a community existing at a pre- or semiliterate level in a society in which literacy is in the process of becoming more broadly established. In such a community, texts assume a cosmological and liturgical function beyond that of "bearers of the Word." One can belong to a "textual community" without, in fact, knowing how to read. "Literacy is not textuality," Stock argues; "one can be literate without the overt use of texts, and one can use texts extensively without evidencing genuine literacy."[68] There were many "textual communities" in the

[66] In important respects, the imagery of the Bible found in the writings of female prophets resembles that of the "talking book" as it was articulated by African Americans in the literature of slavery; see Henry Louis Gates, Jr., *The Signifying Monkey: A Theory of African-American Literary Criticism* (New York, 1988), esp. chapter 4, "The Trope of the Talking Book." In both cases, literacy represents the entree into a world of political and cultural legitimacy, but for the dispossessed texts "speak" in far more embodied ways than they do in the dominant culture.

[67] Sarah Flaxmer, *Satan Revealed; or the Dragon Overcome. With an Explanation of the Twelfth Chapter of Revelation* (London, 1795), pp. 6, 18.

[68] Brian Stock, *The Implications of Literacy: Written Language and Models of Interpretation in the Eleventh and Twelfth Centuries* (Princeton, N.J., 1983), p. 7. I am grateful to Martha Newman for directing me to Stock's book and suggesting that it was relevant to a study of eighteenth-century texts.

Anglo-American world in the late eighteenth century, religious societies which exhibited a profound belief in texts as sacred icons while downplaying—if not altogether discounting—the importance of literacy in gaining access to the spiritual truth contained in those texts. Edward Thompson uncovered the textuality of one such community, the Muggletonians, who existed on the fringes of the radical London underworld. Muggletonians enacted their faith through ritual encounters with texts—inscribing the works of the founding prophets in personal journals, transcribing and circulating letters from believers in distant places, and copying the sect's repertoire of sacred songs into private songbooks. By the mid-eighteenth century, Thompson writes, they were a recondite sect whose "closet and chest of manuscripts enclosed the sleeping energies of a half-forgotten spiritual and political vocabulary."[69] Eighteenth-century Moravians provide another example, with their "lots"—or strips of paper—which every believer carried as oracular aids. The leader of the sect, Count Zinzendorf, consulted his lot ("a little green book, with detachable leaves," each containing some motto or text) whenever he was in need of spiritual guidance.[70] And the Southcottian movement issued "seals" to believers—slips of paper signed by Joanna Southcott—that were endowed with extraordinary properties, including the ability to protect bearers from harm in case of foreign invasion.[71]

What these disparate sects shared was a belief in the power of texts (whether the Bible, songs, letters, "lots," or seals) to confer sacred meaning apart from the literal meaning of the words represented therein. This sacralizing of texts in effect restored to words the "mystical" power of pre-enlightened language while enveloping them in the forms of enlightened print culture. The fact that such sacralized images of texts appear more often in women's writings than in men's suggests that prophetesses as a group were more mystagogues than demagogues, and indeed this charge was leveled with particular ferocity against women like Joanna Southcott and the American Jemima

[69] Thompson, *Witness Against the Beast*, pp. 89–90. In 1772, the Church collected together all the society's manuscripts and letters, as well as books, and "from that time forward held them as Church records and library in locked closets in the public houses where they met" (p. 118).

[70] Zinzendorf wrote: "To me, the Lot and the Will of God are one and the same thing." J. E. Hutton, *A History of the Moravian Church*, 2d ed. (London, 1909), p. 274, and Hutton, *A History of Moravian Missions* (London, 1923), p. 173.

[71] See the discussion of the "seals" in James K. Hopkins, *A Woman to Deliver Her People: Joanna Southcott and English Millenarianism in an Era of Revolution* (Austin, Tex., 1982), p. 105.

Wilkinson (that "vulgar Mystagogue," as she was described by a nineteenth-century antiquarian).[72]

In retrospect it is easy to see why these female-headed millenarian sects were accused of harboring antirepublican sentiments. After all, as Ruth Bloch argues, in many respects the ideas and practices of the Shakers and the Universal Friends were diametrically opposed to that of the American revolutionary movement. Both sects rejected history and reason, even (in the case of Lee) the Bible itself, as guides to the future in favor of the word of inspired prophets who claimed to be reincarnations of Christ himself. Both rejected traditional family and gender roles, though here the androgynous persona of Jemima Wilkinson and the Shaker conception of the dual-gendered godhead complicate any straightforward association of these two sects with antipatriarchal goals. Most damning of all, both groups portrayed themselves as "otherworldly," owing allegiance to no state but to the kingdom of God.[73] As one critic of the Shakers put it in a harsh indictment, he was freed from Mother Ann's dominion only when he took up the Bible and read it for himself. "I was astonished with myself that ever I imbibed such absurd ideas; but the reason was, I never searched the scriptures to see if these things were so, but believed and received everything I heard without giving myself liberty to doubt the truth of it." Because the Shaker Elders forbid their followers to read any books, Rathbun charged, the Believers were "vicious in their natures and ungovernable."[74]

Yet this characterization of female millenarianism as apolitical and authoritarian is only a partial truth. The point is not that male prophets had fully made the transition to the Enlightenment, with its elevation of reason as the supreme human virtue and the denigration of intuition, superstition, and blind faith, while women prophets remained somehow caught in an older, pre-political moment. Rather, we need to question the presumption that mysticism was an archaic hermeneutic practice, unsuited to democratic political discourse. Female prophets enacted a very different version of the "visionary republic" in their sectarian movements, one which located spiritual and political authority not in the masculine rule of reason but in the feminine realm of mystical power. In so doing, they provide historians with

---

[72] Stafford Cleveland, *The History and Directory of Yates County* (Penn Yann, N.Y., 1873), 1:38.

[73] Bloch, *Visionary Republic*, p. 90.

[74] Reuben Rathbun, *Reasons Offered for Leaving the Shakers* (Pittsfield, Mass., 1800), pp. 16, 24.

an alternative model of democratic politics that may, in the long run, have been more appealing to a certain sector of American women (those, for instance, who would find in Spiritualism a powerful means of combating social and political ills by the mid-nineteenth century). We can see this by examining more closely the value of literacy, surely the democratic value par excellence, in the writings and practices of male and female millenarians.

Most prophets, male and female, spoke proudly of their humble beginnings and rudimentary literary achievements, distancing themselves from the world of learned discourse even while they made good use of the possibilities offered by the expansion of print culture. Illiteracy could be a badge of spiritual superiority for charismatic seers who spurned the world of men and human knowledge. But illiteracy had a different meaning for millenarian men and women. Simon Hough, a fiery lay millennialist from western Massachusetts, published several tirades against those "wavering, college learnt merchants of the gospel" who were leading good Christians down the path to spiritual death. The learned clergy tell men they cannot understand the prophetic scriptures because they are illiterate, he charged; "because men cannot go to college, and by human learning obtain this spirit of discernment, and for fear of losing their lucrative employment, [the clergy] teach the world that they cannot be understood." Acknowledging the impossibility of understanding the Book of Revelation without the "dictates of the same spirit which dictated the penning of it," that is, without an internal spiritual guide, Hough insisted that this "spirit of discernment" could be obtained by human learning. All that is needed is for men to read the Bible for themselves. "O my brethren of the laity," he pleaded, "take heed to yourselves, put no trust in man, but read your Bibles."[75] The virtue of illiteracy, in other words, did not reside in forsaking the Bible in favor of direct inspiration, but rather in rejecting the tutelage of learned men who pretend to have special knowledge of divine laws. The act of reading was, for male prophets, the supreme act of self-enlightenment, that which frees ordinary men from the dead hand of tradition and the sophistry of "hireling" ministers. "*Blessed is he that READETH*," Benjamin Gale proclaimed.[76]

The "illiteracy" of female sectarian movements was of a different order. Here American and British prophetesses diverged on one crucial point: in the United States, women like Wilkinson and Lee rejected the presuppositions of print culture altogether in reaching for a spiritual power beyond the

---

[75] Simon Hough, *An Alarm to the World: Dedicated to All Ranks of Men* (Stockbridge, Mass., 1792), pp. 8–9, 23.

[76] Gale, *A Brief Essay*, p. 54.

written word, while in England women like Joanna Southcott and Sarah Flaxmer cleverly exploited the technologies of print to proclaim a *new* Word, one rooted more in the medieval and Renaissance traditions of mystical writing than in the linguistic conventions of a Habermasian public sphere. Many, perhaps most, medieval visionaries could not read or write at all, but under divine inspiration men and women alike produced texts that were judged according to their ability to evoke the sensation of mystical union and not by the demands of logical composition. The polyglot genre of medieval visionary literature accommodated a wide range of literary styles, from the most elliptical to the classically proportioned, and women could find a niche in this tradition despite their lack of familiarity with ancient languages or stylistic conventions.[77] Illiteracy was in itself no barrier; to be "illiterate" before the advent of mass literacy in the nineteenth century meant to be unfamiliar with the learned languages of Greek and Latin, to exhibit in one's writing a residual orality and a preference for vernacular expressions—qualities valued in the mystical literary tradition as evidence of one's closeness to God.[78]

Eighteenth-century women were not so fortunate. As the standards of literary excellence narrowed to exclude the vulgar and fantastical, women's lack of classical learning became a significant liability for the first time.[79] And so some women gave up reading and writing altogether, trapped in their illiteracy. For American female sectarians, reading—of divine texts or even the words of the founder—was discouraged and at times actively suppressed; the emphasis in these movements was on oral communication, on spiritual conversation between individuals who could see and touch one another. Those who were divinely inspired had special verbal powers (recall Ann Lee's miraculous ability to speak seventy-two different languages) that both set them apart from ordinary believers and allowed them to translate the Spirit's message to their audiences. The ability to "speak in tongues" became a hallmark of Shaker worship after Lee's death, a form of supernatural communication that was understood to supersede more conventional modes of access to

---

[77] On the eclectic blend of classical and "grotesque" styles in medieval mystical writing, see Elizabeth Petroff, *Medieval Women's Visionary Literature* (New York, 1986); Laurie Finke, "Mystical Bodies and the Dialogics of Vision," in *Maps of Flesh and Light: The Religious Experiences of Medieval Women Mystics*, ed. Ulrike Wiethaus (Syracuse, N.Y., 1993), pp. 28–44.

[78] Walter Ong, *The Presence of the Word: Some Prolegomena for Cultural and Religious History* (New Haven, 1967).

[79] On the reformulation of the baroque tradition of mystical writing as vulgar in the seventeenth century, see Michel de Certeau, *The Mystical Fable*, vol. 1, *The Sixteenth and Seventeenth Centuries*, trans. Michael B. Smith (Chicago, 1992).

God's Word, including the Bible. For the Shakers, all printed texts were but false representations of the true "word" of God which could be known only in the hearts of believers. Lee herself became a kind of "living bible" to her followers ("I am Ann the Word" she declared), and she called her disciples "my epistles, read and known of all men."[80] Refusing for years to contaminate the Society's tenets and practices by committing them to print, Lee initiated a crusade in 1782–83 against formal learning that ultimately led to book-burning.[81] She left no papers of any kind for her followers. Only in 1808, more than half a century after their founding in England, did the Shakers issue a public statement of their faith. As the preface of this work stated, "in all this time of sixty years, the testimony [of the saints] hath been verbal . . . without any written creed or form of government relating to ourselves." Even now, the society insisted, "we are far from expecting, or even wishing any of our writings to supersede the necessity of a living testimony . . . for the letter killeth, *but the spirit giveth life*."[82] Lee's contemporary Elspeth Buchan (like Lee, a "living bible" to her followers) was more blunt. "Would any say, that there is one grain of life in paper and ink?" she demanded. "Would a famishing person satisfy his craving appetite by reading a well-wrote description of a dinner, without tasting the materials fitted to remove hunger?"[83]

This wholesale rejection of books and reading in favor of immediate inspiration set the Shakers and the Universal Friends apart from their male sectarian counterparts. However much they scorned college-educated ministers, no male millenarians ever extended this critique of book-learning to the Bible itself. In an age when women generally had much lower literacy rates than men, and debates over the benefits of female education still took place under the shadow of a long-standing association of learned women with sexual and moral deviance, it makes sense that some female millenarians

[80] *Testimonies of the Life, Character, Revelations, and Doctrines of Our Ever Blessed Mother Ann Lee* (Hancock, Mass., 1816), p. 26.

[81] Clarke Garrett, *Spirit Possession and Popular Religion: From the Camisards to the Shakers* (Baltimore, 1987), p. 198.

[82] *The Testimony of Christ's Second Appearing, Containing a General Statement of All Things Pertaining to the Faith and Practice of the Church of God in this Latter-Day* (Lebanon, N.Y., 1808), p. 12.

[83] Hugh White, *The Divine Dictionary; or, a Treatise Inspired by Holy Inspiration* (Dumfries, Scotland, 1785), p. 65; *Satan's Delusions: A Poem on the Buchanites* (London, 1784), p. 9. The Buchanites substituted the "living book of life, which is the love of God displaying itself through the body of a saint" for the "dead letter" of the Bible; James Purves, *Eight Letters Between the People Called Buchanites and a Teacher near Edinburgh* (Edinburgh, 1785), p. 49.

would offer a vision of the "New Jerusalem" in which literacy was irrelevant and even harmful.[84]

The alternative was to redefine literacy itself, to use the advantages of print culture to undermine the very presuppositions upon which that culture supposedly rested. This was the path that some British female millenarians pursued, with vigor and creativity. The prophetess Susan Eyre published her visions over the course of several months in 1794–95 in the London daily *Oracle*. Combative, self-assured, and never at a loss for words, Eyre was nonetheless a reluctant author. "I should not write thus, in the public papers," she confessed, "but I know people will read a newspaper, when they will not read either the holy bible or any book that talks of their God, and his wonderous words."[85] She proved an astute observer of the public mood. "You were all very still and quiet till my two Letters in the Oracle roused you, though what I did was known to no soul but myself till they were printed," she boasted.[86] By September 1795, demand for her prophecies had far outstripped the supply. "The many applications for my letters you printed for me in the Oracle, relative to Mr. Brothers and the present times, has induced me to reprint them," she explained, "with some others."[87] The very success of her mission depended entirely on her ability to place her visions where they could be most widely read. "I have so much to say . . . that must be the subject of many letters, if my country people will not be weary of hearing truths." In her case, the adage "publish or perish" took on a fresh twist, as Eyre pleaded with God to spare her life "till all my letters are finished."[88]

By exposing her dreams and visions to the dubious judgment of the *Oracle*'s readers, however, Eyre knew she was courting ridicule. "I am told my letters are too long, people will not stay to read them," she worried. Those who do persevere, she feared, will "laugh at me; yes, make a mock of me, and those letters."[89] She was right to worry. On first reading, the letters appear to be long-winded miscellanies of random thoughts arranged in no obvious order. But a closer inspection reveals how intertwined writing and knowing were for Eyre in ways that defy easy categorization. Her prophetic dreams remained but tantalizing visions, unknown and uncorroborated, until committed to

[84] For debates over the wisdom of educating women, see Linda Kerber, *Women of the Republic: Intellect and Ideology in Revolutionary America* (Chapel Hill, N.C., 1980), chapter 7.

[85] *Oracle*, Sept. 7, 1795.

[86] *Oracle*, Mar. 12, 1795.

[87] *Oracle*, Sept. 4, 1795.

[88] *Oracle*, Sept. 7 and Mar. 12, 1795.

[89] *Oracle*, Oct. 27, 1795.

print. "Were I to tell my dreams that I have had within these four months," she wrote, "they would turn your thoughts a different way: no soul on earth yet knows one word of them—two I wrote down immediately, with my own remarks on them; one is fulfilled in part, I hope the other is. I solemnly declare, I have not looked at them since the day I wrote them down, which was the morning I dreamt them, nor will I open them, but on my knees before the altar of the Most High God, in the presence of some person, where I can swear to the truth of what I there wrote."[90] As direct transcriptions of her visions, Eyre's letters retain the ragged compositional qualities that characterize ordinary speech. Marked by sudden shifts in topic, irregular voice, significant repetition, and casual grammar, the prophet's words were "as wind." The letters flirt with ambiguity and incomprehension, even while Eyre insisted that she wrote to "persuade all people to read till they find the truth." "I said in my letter, printed in THE ORACLE last December, woe to Holland, I knew she would fall, but I did not tell you why I said so," she admitted.[91] Both subject and object, the letters themselves appear as icons of power and mystery in her visions. In one of her last dreams, the devil (seated on the lap of "that wicked genius of France," the republic) is enraged by the sight of her letters: "he stormed and raved; he threatened to burn em; he wanted me to swear some words; I do not recollect what they were—my fright was beyond all description." Fortunately, one of Eyre's more provocative letters ("my second letter to Mr. Brothers") was concealed in the petticoat of the "wicked genius" and escaped detection, leaving the devil in "a great passion, to look for the shift, which I was sure could not be found but with me."[92] The passion her letters aroused in the devil had to do as much with their inaccessibility as with the prophetic messages they contained.

Though she promised to publish her letters in book form, Eyre never managed to secure a publisher for her collected visions. The unorthodox style of her letters, she complained, had caused her nothing but grief. "O! did people know what has happened to me in consequence of those letters, what would they say? How shall I tell, or to whom shall I speak? Those letters I wrote without the knowledge or consent of any living person—none knew, or even had a thought of them till they were printed."[93] Finally, in October 1795 (nearly a year after her first letter appeared in the *Oracle*), she declared,

[90] *Oracle*, Mar. 12, 1795.
[91] *Oracle*, Oct. 2, 1795.
[92] *Oracle*, Oct. 27, 1795.
[93] *Oracle*, Sept. 4, 1795.

"This is the last letter I shall write on this subject, at least for the present."[94] She was defiant to the end. "Who of you that have read my former letters, or even heard of them, but laugh at me. . . . Go on, laugh, mock, say I am mad, say any thing, you will not have long to laugh."[95] Nothing more is known about Susan Eyre, who disappeared from public view the same time as her letters ceased appearing in the *Oracle*.

Her successor, the woman who embodied antirepublican license and linguistic impropriety at its most pernicious, was far more successful. Joanna Southcott is perhaps most distinguished among her British and American counterparts by her sheer prolixity. The author of sixty-five pamphlets and thousands of pages of unpublished manuscripts, Southcott constituted a one-woman cottage industry in the world of British publishing from the time her first tract appeared in 1801 until her death in 1814. A famous engraving of Southcott (Figure 6) shows a matronly figure with a stack of heavy books on her lap, topped by the Bible, propped open for viewers to read.[96] A conservative estimate puts the number of copies of her writings published between 1801 and 1816 at 108,000—a figure well below that of Tom Paine's *Rights of Man* but substantially above most other religious and political literature.[97] Her output was not only prodigious; it represented an extended reflection on the act of reading itself that placed texts and their relation to readers at the heart of her prophetic mission.

The contemporary and historical verdicts on Joanna Southcott converge on one score: that her writings are tedious, circuitous, and maddeningly opaque. Written half in doggerel verse and half in prose, her "communications" are a crazy quilt of voices (first, second, and third person), images, and phrases that manage to be repetitive and obscure at the same time. These "rhapsodies of ignorance, vulgarity, indecency, and impiety" represented to the literary and ecclesiastical establishment not the true language of the "Spirit" (who "always speaks in good grammar and good sense") but a "farrgo of nonsense."[98] Even those scholars who accord the Southcottian movement some measure of intellectual respectability find Southcott's writings, and her peculiar relationship to the world of print culture in

---

[94] *Oracle*, Oct. 2, 1795. In fact, one more letter appeared, in the Oct. 27 issue.

[95] *Oracle*, Oct. 27, 1795.

[96] Southcott explained that she instructed the engraver, William Sharp, to have "the Bible placed before me, as opened by me promiscuously to the last two chapters of Isaiah"; *Third Book of Wonders* (London, 1814), p. 63.

[97] Hopkins, *A Woman to Deliver Her People*, p. 84.

[98] Anonymous, *A Letter to T. P. Foley* (London, 1813), pp. 36–38, 43, 45.

general, an enigma. Clearly, as J. F. C. Harrison notes, the fact that her prophecies circulated largely in print had "momentous consequences" for the success of the movement itself and for the meaning of popular literacy in an age of restricted educational opportunities.

The available evidence suggests that access to her printed works was remarkably broad, and the laborious work of copying, recopying, and indexing Southcott's manuscripts that her followers undertook in her lifetime and beyond constituted "a form of pseudo-learning" for the mostly poor farmers and artisans who made up the backbone of the movement.[99] Readers were encouraged not only to buy Southcott's writings but to actively work with them in the task of scriptural interpretation as the prophetess herself did: while rereading (something she did frequently) her account of the dispute with Satan, Joanna was "ordered" by the Spirit to "put Crosses with her pen at particular places"—and a note at the bottom of the page suggests that "It may, perhaps, be of use to the Reader if he was to mark the Crosses in their proper places in his own book."[100] A copy of a Southcottian Bible, sold at auction after her death, was "full of pencil hieroglyphic marks," suggesting again the active interrogation of texts by their readers.[101]

But precisely *how* Southcott's writings were read by her followers is a question of considerable complexity. For woven into the very substance of her prophecies was a highly systematic if idiosyncratic discourse on the practice of reading that demands closer attention. The image of the Bible as a "sealed" book whose contents can be understood only by those who have access to the words of the prophetess was the dominant motif in Southcott's writings. The Bible, Southcott told her readers, was composed of "types" and "shadows," parables whose meaning could never be discerned by human reason or scholarly investigation. The "substance" of these shadows was revealed in Southcott's communications, and in the events which these writings predicted would come to pass. Rather than urging men and women to read the scriptures in light of their natural reason, as male prophets from Brothers to Austin had done, Southcott insisted that the scriptures were and must remain a "mystery." Her deliberate obscurantism infuriated men like Robert Hann, for whom her writings were an "opium" that led readers to "prostitute

---

[99] Harrison, *The Second Coming*, pp. 88, 229. James Hopkins documents widespread ownership, or at least possession, of Southcott's pamphlets among her followers; in one congregation, for instance, the 123 believers possessed more than 1,400 copies of her works—an average of twelve per member. Hopkins, *A Woman to Deliver Her People*, pp. 115–16.

[100] Southcott, *The Answer of the Lord to the Powers of Darkness* (London, 1814), p. 56.

[101] *Independent Whig*, Jan. 22, 1815, p. 6.

their judgment, and give themselves up as willing sacrifices to delusion and imposture."[102]

Such charges of female mystagoguery had a long provenance in the history of Anglo-American dissent, but in the case of Joanna Southcott the accusation seems more than justified. Her communications were intended to confuse and unsettle—to "stumble," in her words—those who read them.[103] If believers could not arrive at spiritual truth through the usual means of enlightened reading, how then were they to be saved? Given the Southcottians' insistence that only those who had read Joanna's writings were worthy of being "sealed" for all time, an alternative practice of reading had to be devised, one that would retain the mysterious quality of the sacred texts while allowing believers some access to the divine truths contained therein. Southcott devised multiple strategies for this purpose, most prominently the age-old method of "promiscuous" reading—the random selection of passages without any preordained sequence. As generations of Christians had done before her, she read the Bible by randomly opening the book and reading the first passage that appeared.[104] As David Hall has described, such a mode of reading was commonplace in the early modern world of reformed Protestantism, where "intensive" reading—the rereading of certain key texts, "not once or twice, but '100 and 100 times' "—was still practiced. But in advocating the intensive and promiscuous reading of scripture, Southcott violated another central tenet of the reformed Protestant tradition: the belief that, in Hall's words, "the meaning of the Bible was self-evident. It was a book that made its message felt without there being any mediation—no intermediaries, no gloss, no message that called for interpretation. In the root sense of the word, the Bible was *immediately* available."[105] In Southcott's world, sacred texts (scripture and her own writings) were always and complexly mediated.

Her use of highly metaphorical forms of argumentation (the vocabulary of types, shadows, parables, dreams, and visions) placed her squarely in

---

[102] R. Hann, *A Letter to the Right Reverend the Lord Bishop of London Concerning the Heresy and Imposture of Joanna Southcott* (London, 1810), pp. 13, 7.

[103] Southcott, *A Dispute Between the Woman and the Powers of Darkness*, p. 4; and the communication of July 12, 1802, in the Notebook of Divine Communications and Letters (item 327), Joanna Southcott Collection, Harry Ransom Research Center, University of Texas, Austin.

[104] See, for example, Southcott, *Prophecies: A Warning to the World, from the Sealed Prophecies of Joanna Southcott* (London, 1803), p. 53; and Southcott, *Explanation of the Parables Published in 1804* (London, 1806), p. 51.

[105] David D. Hall, *Worlds of Wonder, Days of Judgment: Popular Religious Belief in Early New England* (Cambridge, Mass., 1990), pp. 42, 26–27.

the mystical tradition of early modern dissent, yet she also invented new methods for confounding her readers that relied heavily on manipulating the technologies of print. One of the most effective, and most provocative, was her practice of deliberately scrambling texts. She admitted in her reply to a critic, Louis Mayer, that she had reprinted his accusations not as a single block of text but broken into pieces, dispersed throughout some fifty pages of print, in order to impress upon her readers the idiosyncratic placement of truth in the scriptures.[106] On another occasion, at the Spirit's express command, Southcott ordered that the explanation of certain parables be published separately—a parable of the adulterous nation introduced by the Rev. Thomas Foley in *What Manner of Communication Are These?* was explained in William Sharp's tract, *Sharp Answer to the World*, while Sharp's parables were explained in Foley's pamphlet. The Spirit explained: "I now tell thee, these two books that I ordered to be printed in this manner, that you could not understand one without going to the other . . . perfectly so, I tell thee, stand the Scriptures of Truth!"[107]

Southcott thus offered a very archaic, and very authoritarian, understanding of literacy to the British public. Her method confounds all the tenets of a Habermasian print culture: that language is transparent; that it is impersonal—that the relationship of signs to signifiers is not secured by the personal attributes or resources of any individual or social group but by the universal recognition of "rational" correspondences; that knowledge is equally distributed throughout the population, and not the special preserve of any one person or class. Whereas republican prophets like James Bicheno believed that the language of scripture was readily accessible to people across the social and political spectrum without specialized training, Southcott insisted that only true believers could understand the Word of God, and only then after it had been channeled through the interpretive faculties of an inspired prophet.[108]

How "democratic" is such an approach to language? The labels "radical"

[106] Southcott, *Explanation of the Parables*, p. 55. See also Southcott's rendition of a vision she received in verse in 1794, in which the order of the lines was scrambled by the Spirit. "The Vision see is drawn by thee a way you don't discern." "The Vision of Candles Repeated, Numberically Arranged," Add. MSS 32,633, 1:22, British Library.

[107] Rev. T. P. Foley, *What Manner of Communications Are These?* (London, 1804); William Sharp, *Sharp Answer to the World* (London, 1806); Joanna Southcott, *On Parables* (London, 1806), p. 59.

[108] In this she departed from the linguistic practices of female Methodist preachers, who—like male prophets—adopted an "ethos of simplicity" in their spoken and written performances that affirmed Methodism's theological message of universal redemption; Christine L. Krueger, *The Reader's Repentance: Women Preachers, Women Writers, and Nineteenth-Century Social Discourse* (Chicago, 1992).

and "conservative" are not particularly helpful in trying to understand South-cottian prophecy in the context of the political struggles of the age of revolution. On the one hand, her mission was extremely autocratic. She was clearly jealous of her prophetic standing and refused to acknowledge any rivals or alternative routes to salvation save through her own writings. She was equally firm in her rejection of political radicalism, arguing that the only revolution that is needed or possible is a spiritual one. Above all, she resurrected an archaic form of Old Testament prophecy in which authority is rooted in the charismatic appeal of a single individual rather than in the collective worship of believers. On the other hand, Southcott portrayed herself as the defender of the underprivileged classes—women (especially single women) and the poor, and offered them a vision of redemption through the agency of a "poor illiterate woman."[109] She, like the Methodist clergy she so bitterly resented, was scornful of "learning" and "civilized" society, and preached the standard anticlerical message of the day—that ministers are nothing but "hirelings" and hypocrites who know less about true Christianity than their humble followers. In a strange way, it may also be that her peculiar brand of obscurantist language was a mark of rebellion: after all, women who tried to adopt the prevailing discourses of political radicalism (e.g., appeals to reason and the "universal" rights of mankind) weren't particularly successful in articulating a feminist vision of the polity in the 1790s.[110] Her retrieval of the archaic language of prophecy may, in the end, have constituted a far more effective challenge to democratic politics than the reasoned discourses of Mary Wollstonecraft or Hannah More.

A "mystical republic" thus offered powerful support to women whose inferior mental capacities and cultural "illiteracy" did not entitle them to civic or political standing.[111] What would become of the female millenarian

---

[109] Anna Clark, "The Sexual Crisis and Popular Religion in London, 1770–1820," *International Journal of Labor and Working Class History* 34 (1988), pp. 56–69.

[110] The fate of Mary Wollstonecraft's writings is a good case in point; for her reception in the United States, see Kerber, *Women of the Republic*, pp. 222–31.

[111] We can find evidence of a similar repudiation of enlightenment practices in the worship of African American slaves and their descendants well into the nineteenth century. Though the desire for literacy was an important stimulus to conversion for African American slaves in the late eighteenth century, who rightly saw in evangelical Protestantism an opportunity to capture the power of the written word for themselves, direct inspiration remained the paramount source of spiritual authority among Christianized slaves. As Albert Raboteau notes, slaves "valued the experience of God's power as the norm of Christian truth rather than the Bible"; *African-American Religion; Interpretive Essays in History and Culture*, ed. Timothy E. Fulop and Albert J. Raboteau (New York, 1997), p. 97. For a recent overview of the place of literacy in slave Christianity, see Sylvia R. Frey and Betty Wood, *Come Shouting to Zion: African American Protestantism in the American South and British Caribbean to 1830* (Chapel Hill, N.C., 1998).

tradition represented by Ann Lee and Joanna Southcott after the political storms of the revolutionary era had subsided? Ironically, it was republican prophets who found themselves pushed to the margins of Anglo-American political culture after 1815 rather than the mystagogues they so scorned. The flowering of millenarian sects in antebellum America (from the Millerites to the Mormons) represented a defiant resurgence of the mystical strand of eighteenth-century millennialism. Republican prophecy did not so much disappear as become absorbed into a potent populist brew. Paul Boyer argues that the fusion of democratic and millenarian beliefs was most complete in the Millerite movement of the 1840s. "Just as the Jacksonians claimed that any (white male) citizen could perform the duties of government, so the Millerites insisted that untutored believers could unravel the apocalyptic mysteries. Millerism heralded the full democratization of prophetic belief in the United States," he argues.[112] If Millerism represents the apogee of the republican tradition of biblical exegesis, in which Everyman could read and interpret the prophetic passages for himself,[113] it was eclipsed in importance by the stunning success of Joseph Smith and the Mormons. Drawing on diverse intellectual resonances ranging from medieval hermeticism to eighteenth-century mesmerism and Swedenborgianism, Smith's fantastic tale of buried treasure and "lost" scriptures written in ancient hieroglyphics reached an audience eager to recapture the power of the mystical word from a disenchanted world.[114] Other prophets would follow his lead, some (like the Prophet Matthias) for their own aggrandizement and some (like Matthias's most famous convert, the ex-slave Isabella Van Wagenen, who would become the abolitionist Sojourner Truth) out of genuine concern for spiritual renewal.[115] In England, the dramatic and well-publicized death of Joanna Southcott in 1814 from what she believed to be a "mystical pregnancy" dealt a serious blow to the millennial hopes of thousands of English men and women, but despite the ridicule heaped on her believers by churchmen and journalists, would-be successors to her prophetic mantle carried her message to a new generation of British millenarians. Well into the 1830s and 1840s,

---

[112] Boyer, *When Time Shall Be No More*, p. 85.

[113] David L. Rowe, "Millerites: A Shadow Portrait," in *The Disappointed: Millerism and Millenarianism in the Nineteenth Century*, ed. Ronald Numbers and Jonathan Butler (Knoxville, Tenn., 1993), pp. 1–16.

[114] John L. Brooke, *The Refiner's Fire: The Making of Mormon Cosmology, 1644–1844* (New York, 1996).

[115] Paul Johnson and Sean Wilentz, *The Kingdom of Matthias: A Story of Sex and Salvation in Nineteenth-Century America* (New York, 1994); Nell Irvin Painter, *Sojourner Truth: A Life, a Symbol* (New York, 1996).

new prophets like John Wroe and "Zion" Ward claimed to be Southcott's true "heir," the Man-child she had promised to produce in her dying days.[116] Closer in spirit to the rampant consumerism of Victorian culture than to the shabby gentility of revolutionary-era reformers, these nineteenth-century seers and their movements represent a new chapter in the history of Anglo-American prophecy.

[116] On Southcott's successors, see Harrison, *The Second Coming*; G. R. Balleine, *Past Finding Out: The Tragic Story of Joanna Southcott and Her Successors* (New York, 1956).

Chapter 5
A Rogues' Gallery:
Richard Brothers and Nimrod Hughes

A number of prophets, admittedly a small minority, were public figures of some renown, men and, less commonly, women who spoke directly to and for a promiscuous audience of skeptics, believers, and agnostics. While revolutionary-era prophets on the whole preferred the safety of the printed page to the perils of live theater, a handful of men and women braved ridicule and worse to offer themselves as living sacrifices to the public's thirst for novelty and scandal.[1] When they did so, they entered the public sphere on its own terms. The clash of cultures represented by millenarianism's encounter with the Anglo-American public produced entertaining if not always heroic stories, complete with stock characters and familiar plot twists. Two such stories are told here, drawn from opposite ends of the revolutionary era and different national contexts: that of Richard Brothers, the most famous British prophet of the 1790s, and of Nimrod Hughes, his lesser-known American counterpart who enjoyed his own fifteen minutes of fame in the winter of 1811–12.

By offering these stories as portraits in a "rogues' gallery," I am not questioning the credibility of the supernatural claims of Brothers and Hughes. Prophets they believed themselves to be, and prophets they are for

---

[1] E. P. Thompson's discussion of the "theater and countertheater" of patrician-plebeian relations in the eighteenth century provides a model for historians interested in the more subtle uses of power to define and delimit popular expression in an age in which "patrician hegemony," if tattered, was still intact. As Thompson describes it, the increasing theatricality of public contests over custom and rights over the long eighteenth century was a function of the growing autonomy of commoners from paternalist systems of rule, whether on the manor, in the church, or in Whitehall. Deprived (largely through voluntary forfeiture) of coercive means to compel obedience and exact deference, England's ruling classes entered into a social bargain with the laboring classes in which authority was maintained and contested more through symbolic gestures than through direct acts of resistance or repression. Thompson's model explains much of the studied theatricality of millenarian culture in the late eighteenth century, as well as the roots of this theatricality in the commercial and political developments of the century. E. P. Thompson, *Customs in Common: Studies in Traditional Popular Culture* (New York, 1991).

our purposes. But to most of their contemporaries they, and men like them, belonged in a much larger category of social and political disorder, that of "rogues": itinerants for the most part, the "straggling auxiliaries" of a floating underground of radical sectarians and publicists, hawkers of suspect emotional goods who were fully enmeshed in the commodity culture of late eighteenth-century Anglo-America in which people and the goods they peddled were not to be believed or trusted.[2] Enemies of enthusiasm in the 1790s and early 1800s saw a direct line of incorrigibility connecting contemporary "prophets of evil" with rogue millenarians in earlier ages, from Oliver Cromwell, "a Rogue of more talents than the contemptible lunatic[s] of the present day," to the French Prophets, those "*rogues* and *vagabonds*" driven into exile in the early 1700s.[3] The image of a "rogues' gallery" speaks more to the expectations and fears of revolutionary-era audiences than to the integrity of millenarians as messengers of God.

"King Richard Brothers . . . a Democrat and a Prophet"

In January 1795, the British monthly *Critical Review* devoted a lengthy article to dissecting the public furor caused by the penniless ex-navy lieutenant Richard Brothers, who had set up shop at 57 Paddington Street where he dispensed prophecies warning of swift destruction should England declare war against the new French republic. "That a poor madman should be under such an unhappy delusion as to believe himself inspired, is not unprecedented; but that such a man, in so enlightened a city as London, should fill for a moment the public ear, and employ the public tongue, is a humiliating consideration for those who wish to feel proud of their country, or of human nature. Whether this man be merely an enthusiast, or partly an impostor (a mixture not uncommon,) we presume not to say."[4] For several months in 1795, the Brothers affair was the talk of London. The hyperbole surrounding

---

[2] The phrase "straggling auxiliaries" is William H. Reid's, the radical apostate who in 1800 wrote a searching critique of the infidel and political societies to which he had belonged in the 1790s. These "auxiliaries" included "Mystics, Muggletonians, Millennaries, and a variety of eccentric characters of different denominations" who were active on the fringes of the London Corresponding Society and the Society for Constitutional Information. W. H. Reid, *The Rise and Dissolution of the Infidel Societies in this Metropolis* (London, 1800), p. 19.

[3] Eliza Williams, *The Prophecies of Richard Brothers Refuted* (London, 1795), pp. 13–14 (Cromwell); Joseph Moser, *Anecdotes of Richard Brothers, In the Years 1791 and 1792, with some Thoughts upon Credulity* (London, 1795), p. 11 (French Prophets).

[4] *Critical Review* 13 (Jan. 1795), p. 459.

Brothers—"the most extraordinary man this century has produced"—throws into sharp relief both the depth of public anxiety in the 1790s and the contours of the broader discourse about authenticity that shaped and constrained millenarian culture in the age of revolution.[5] As Brothers's own star rose and fell in the Anglo-American literary firmament, rival prophets emerged to challenge the self-styled "Nephew of Christ" and provide more fodder for pundits and polemicists eager to put enlightened notions of reason and revelation to the test. The origin of Brothers's visions and not their content was the focal point of debate. It was not, as we have seen, a particularly daring or novel move to see in the revolutionary events unfolding across the Channel a prophetic message about England's future. The real question was, where did such revelations come from? God himself? the disordered brain of the prophet? or from a base desire to exploit the very real fears of commoners in these days of war and want? Contra the cautious editors of the *Critical Review*, Britons across the political and social spectrum did not hesitate to venture their opinions on whether Richard Brothers was an impostor, a madman, a deluded enthusiast, or a genuine prophet of God.

In a field notable for the inflated claims of its practitioners, Brothers's career stands out as singular indeed. Like so many millenarians, his life until the point of inspiration was entirely unremarkable. By most accounts a meek man with a powerful build, Brothers was born in Newfoundland in 1757 and moved with his family to England as a boy. A child of the colonial poor, he found moderate success in the British navy where he served until 1790, when, concerned about the propriety of oath-taking, he resigned his commission in protest. His financial troubles led him first to the workhouse, then to Newgate prison, and finally (upon his release in 1792) to a boardinghouse where his prophetic pronouncements began attracting crowds of visitors. The home of this impoverished sailor was now "constantly filled by persons of quality and fortune, of both sexes, and the street crowded with their carriages."[6] His publications (the first book of his *Revealed Knowledge of the Prophecies and Times* appeared in 1794, the second in 1795) made him in-

---

[5] John Barrell, *Imagining the King's Death: Figurative Treason, Fantasies of Regicide, 1793–1796* (New York, 2000). The discussion that follows is indebted to Barrell's superb study, which goes much further than previous treatments of the Brothers affair in elucidating its central political and cultural meanings. See chapter 15, "Traitor or Lunatic: The Arrest of Richard Brothers" (the description of Brothers as "the most extraordinary man of the century" is on p. 504).

[6] Nathaniel Brassey Halhed, *A Calculation on the Commencement of the Millennium* (London, 1795), p. 28.

stantly famous: "numberless People, even of Rank and Character run in Flocks to increase the Presumption, or feed the Phrenzy of this extraordinary Man."[7] His reputation among what one critic scorned as "the Misguided Million" was due in part to the uncanny accuracy of his early prophecies: he accurately predicted the execution of Louis XVI in 1793, and the assassination of the king of Sweden that same year. Even skeptics were forced to admit that "most of the events which Mr. Brothers predicted have already been verified." (Or, as one supporter put it with considerably more legal finesse, "All those which he had recorded in print have either actually been already fulfilled, or remain in a state, of which it cannot with any propriety be asserted that their completion is impossible.")[8]

This was heady stuff for a man of "unexceptional character" who cheerfully admitted he was "illiterate and uneducated."[9] Brothers was transformed by his prophetic visions from a "peasant" to a "prince," in the honest words of one supporter—a prince, moreover, before whom royalty "trembles."[10] Brothers's "commission" as a prophet had impressive patrilineal sanction; he believed that he was the Nephew of God, descended from James the brother of Jesus. Brothers was far more than an inspired messenger in the conventional millenarian mode, however; by turns merciful and spiteful (like the God to whom he was related), he was also an active participant in the apocalyptic scenarios his visions prefigure. In his first book of prophecies, for instance, London's imminent destruction is both graphically forecast and providentially avoided by the timely intervention of the prophet himself. As the archetypal black clouds gather overhead and Satan strolls "leisurely" through the streets of London (the "Spiritual Babylon") with a smile on his face, Brothers begs God to spare the capital from the fate it so richly deserves. Out of "regard for Me, that I may be esteemed in this Country," God complies; the Lord "spoke to me from the middle of a large white cloud, and said

[7] Quoted in Barrell, *Imagining the King's Death*, p. 507.

[8] *Oracle*, Mar. 12, 1795; and Apr. 1, 1795.

[9] *Oracle*, Apr. 1, 1795; S. Whitchurch, *Another Witness! or Further Testimony in Favor of Richard Brothers with a Few Modest Hints to Modern Pharisees and Reverend Unbelievers* (London, 1795), p. 25 ("illiterate and uneducated").

[10] Nathaniel Brassey Halhed, *Testimony of the Authenticity of the Prophecies of Richard Brothers* (London, 1795), pp. 6–7 ("peasant to prince"). In a vision Brothers received in 1792 "the Lord God shewed me the present Queen of England coming towards me—slow—trembling—and afraid"; *A Revealed Knowledge of the Prophecies and Times particularly of the Present Time, the Present War, and the Prophecy now Fulfilling . . . Book the Second* (London, 1795), p. 74.

in a strong clear voice—ALL, ALL. I pardon London and all the people in it, for your sake; there is no other man on earth that could stand before me to ask for so great a thing."[11]

God would not be so merciful the next time, Brothers warned. The second part of his *Revealed Knowledge* appeared several months later and offered a much more concrete indictment of the British government and its policies. Brothers's campaign to awaken the British people to their fate and call their leaders to account led him on an unlikely journey through the halls of power. He directed that copies of his pamphlets be distributed to the king, to Prime Minister William Pitt, to the lords, bishops, judges, and foreign ambassadors, and he demanded the right to address Parliament in person. The campaign netted one notable prize: the MP of Lymington, Nathaniel Brassey Halhed, an "oriental scholar and traveller."[12] Halhed was impressed by Brothers's commission, the sheer audacity of which seemed proof of its supernatural warrant. "What shall we think of a man who has been in the habit of writing letters to the King . . . and makes the whole English nation a sort of umpire between the constituted power of the State and one obscure individual?" he wondered.[13] Through his "habit of writing letters" to important people, Brothers cultivated a familiarity with lords and magistrates that shocked even the most sympathetic observers. Joseph Moser reported a conversation with the prophet in 1792 in which Brothers casually asked, " 'if *John Pitt* had called upon me?' I answered that, to the best of my recollection, I had not the honour to be acquainted with any person of the name of *John Pitt*. 'No!' he replied, 'then you will soon! You have heard of *William Pitt*?' 'If you mean the Chancellor of the Exchequer; who has not?' 'Well, then,' he continued, 'you will soon have a visit from his brother.' 'Oh! then you mean the *Earl of Chatham*.' 'Certainly I do!' he replied; 'but as I consider titles as the baubles of vanity, I seldom make use of them.—The *Earl of Chatham*, as you call him, will soon visit you: I have wrote him a letter of *sixteen folio pages*, in which you are mentioned.' "[14] Emboldened by his successes, Brothers abandoned all pretense at persuasion in the final edition of *Revealed Knowledge* and demanded in unequivocal terms the surrender of the king. "The Lord

---

[11] Brothers, *A Revealed Knowledge of the Prophecies and Times . . . Book the First, Wrote under the Direction of the Lord God, and published by his Sacred Command* (London, 1794), pp. 45–46.

[12] "Richard Brothers," *Dictionary of National Biography*, ed. Leslie Stephen and Sidney Lee (New York, 1937–38), 2:1351.

[13] Halhed, *Testimony*, pp. 6–7.

[14] Moser, *Anecdotes*, pp. 30–31.

God commands me to say to you, George the Third, king of England, that immediately on my being revealed, in London, to the Hebrews as their Prince, and to all nations as their Governor, your crown must be delivered up to me, that all your power and authority may instantly cease." Were George to disregard the warning and bring destruction upon England, he would know that "it is for your contempt to me" that his kingdom was lost.[15]

Brothers's unwavering confidence in his own mission was matched by the grandiose nature of his vision of the millennium. Under the sure hand of God, England and its government (king and parliament) will be destroyed through the usual apocalyptic means, along with all aristocratic titles and privileges; God's chosen people—the Hebrews, both visible and invisible—will be called home to a new nation, a new land, where Brothers himself will rule supreme as the "MONARCH OF ISRAEL"; and commerce and manufacturing will flourish unhampered by national or sectarian jealousies under the "paternal government" of King Richard. No detail of this glorious new world was left to the reader's imagination: God provided the exact geographical coordinates of his kingdom, to be located somewhere in the Middle East, and a map of the capital "Jerusalem" (destined to become "the greatest emporium of the two hemispheres"), drew a picture of the national flag, supplied a long list of the tribute to be exacted from the infidel nations of the world, and spelled out in detail the various laws which would govern the lives of its inhabitants (one example: "hats and nothing else should be worn by the Hebrews," as they were "a better defence against the sun than turbans").[16] Over this busy and prosperous kingdom Brothers would rule as "an anxious father"—abolishing nunneries so that "all women may be free," ending the slave trade, reforming prisons, disbursing land in small parcels (not to exceed one thousand acres) to ensure that all "may live safe and happy in the land," and, in a sharp dig at Tom Paine, publishing "the true rights of man, according to the instruction given me from God himself, to quiet all governments and all people, to prevent all revolutions."[17]

[15] Brothers, *Revealed Knowledge . . . Second Book*, pp. 157–58.

[16] Brothers, *Revealed Knowledge . . . First Book*, p. 53 ("MONARD OF ISRAEL"); *A Letter from Mr. Brothers to Miss Cott, the Recorded Daughter of King David and Future Queen of the Hebrews* (London, 1798), pp. 81 ("paternal government"), 86 (geographical coordinates, capital as "emporium"), 88 (national flag), 105 (list of tribute), 106 (hats).

[17] Brothers, *Letter to Miss Cott*, pp. 88 ("anxious father"), 80 (land distribution); and *A Description of Jerusalem: Its Houses and Streets, Squares, Colleges, Markets, and Cathedrals, the Royal and Private Palaces, with the Garden of Eden in the Centre* (London, 1801), pp. 141 ("rights of man"), 147 (nunneries).

Brothers's plans for his reconstituted kingdom are such a mishmash of contemporary positions spanning the ideological spectrum from conservative to radical (the divine right of kings, agrarian and penal reform, commercial expansion, abolition, the natural rights of men and the social position of women), that it is no wonder his readers were confused about his true political sentiments. The anonymous pamphleteer who crowned him "King Richard Brothers . . . a Democrat and a Prophet" aptly summed up the public reaction to this theocrat who espoused democratic ideals.[18] Though this "Mysterious Prophet" may speak "the language of a downright Democrat," Henry Spencer warned, readers should not be deceived. "He speaks as flippantly of his palaces, his splendid table, his coach, his guards, and all the other trappings of Royalty, as if he had been seated on a Throne since his childhood."[19] Others, however, were just as convinced that Brothers was in league with the radical democratic societies whose calls for parliamentary reform had brought down the infamous repressive measures of the 1790s. His publisher was the noted radical printer George Riebau, himself a member of the London Corresponding Society and a man with close ties to the thriving literary underworld of republicans, infidels, and millenarians that constituted a distinct urban counterculture in the late eighteenth century.[20] Brothers's arrest in March 1795 on charges of "treasonable practices" and his subsequent incarceration in a private asylum, John Barrell argues persuasively, was symbolically important if legally questionable: by "imagining" the death or dethronement of the king, Brothers's prophecies fed public expectations of radical political change aroused by the irresponsible activities of the corresponding societies and other reformist groups. While the charge of treason proved unsustainable in the end, forcing the government into the juridically awkward position of arguing that Brothers was simultaneously a traitor and a lunatic—both in and out of his mind—that it was made at all signals the depth of the authorities' fear that fantasizing about killing kings

[18] [A Convert], *The Age of Prophecy! or, Further Testimony of the Mission of Richard Brothers* (London, 1795), p. 46.

[19] Henry Spencer, *A Vindication of the Prophecies of Mr. Brothers and the Scriptural Expositions of Mr. Halhed* (London, 1795), pp. 19, 24.

[20] Iain McCalman, *Radical Underworld: Prophets, Revolutionaries and Pornogrpahers in London, 1795–1840* (Oxford, 1993). Jonathan Mee has argued that Brothers's prophecies are rooted in a democratic vision of expanded access to the Word of God which empowers every man, however humble, to become a prophet; *Dangerous Enthusiasm: William Blake and the Culture of Radicalism in the 1790s* (New York, 1992), p. 34. James K. Hopkins also views Brothers as the man most responsible for "the fusing of radical politics and millenarian beliefs into one articulate whole"; *A Woman to Deliver Her People: Joanna Southcott and English Millenarianism in an Era of Revolution* (Austin, Tex., 1982), p. 170.

was the natural outcome of the radicals' attack on the political and social foundations of the British constitution.[21]

The charge of insanity was, however, more than a convenient cover for government panic. In fact, the question of lunacy dominated the public debate over Brothers to a far greater extent than his putative radicalism (Figure 7). Those who had visited or spoken personally with the prophet were of two minds on the subject. On the one hand, his conversation and deportment apart from the subject of prophecy betrayed no hint of derangement; "there is nothing in his conduct," claimed the *Morning Post*, "that denotes any thing like Lunacy." To their surprise, visitors were impressed by Brothers's "urbanity of manners" and the "regular congruity of sentences, apparently well digested" of his everyday speech.[22] When Moser, one of the Governors of the Poor, first met the prophet in 1792, he did not see the raving madman he expected to find. "I must confess his appearance prejudiced me greatly in his favor. He seemed about thirty years of age, tall and well formed, and in his address and manner much mildness and gentility."[23] To Henry Offley, Brothers was, in fact, the very picture of a gentleman. "Taking him in the point of view as a MAN, he is humane, generous, and polite; as a MORAL CHARACTER, he is grave in his deportment, pious in his manners and conduct, and universally beloved by those who *know* him." The prophet's conversation "always avoids running into rhapsodies, and never permits unchecked, enthusiastical disputes to take place in his presence."[24]

When this mild-mannered gentleman turned to the business of prophesying, however, his equanimity deserted him and he "wandered into all the vagaries of wildness and enthusiasm."[25] The ultimate proof of Brothers's lunacy was to be found not in his behavior, but in his writings, which were "a mass of inconsistencies and incorrectness." According to Brothers himself, the owner of the asylum to which he was confined admitted as much. "Why to be sure, Mr. Brothers, you are not insane, nor is there any thing improper in your words and behaviour: but for writing that book, you must be considered

---

[21] Barrell, *Imagining the King's Death*, pp. 504–47. As Barrell argues, the regicide imagined in Brothers's prophecies was made explicit in the hands of other radical pamphleteers; see the anonymous pamphlet *King Killing* published by the radical printer and millenarian Richard "Citizen" Lee (London, 1795).

[22] *Morning Post*, Apr. 7, 1795; *Register of the Times* 4 (Feb. 28–Mar.11, 1795), p. 43; *Register of the Times* 4 (Mar. 11–21, 1795), pp. 98–99.

[23] Moser, *Anecdotes*, p. 18.

[24] Henry Francis Offley, *Richard Brothers, Neither a Madman nor an Impostor* (London, 1795), pp. 27–29.

[25] Moser, *Anecdotes*, p. 18.

Figure 7. "The Prophet of the Hebrews,—The Prince of Peace—conducting the Jews to the Promis'd Land," 1795. Department of Prints and Drawings, British Museum. Note the ragged and fevered appearance of the prophet, dressed as a sans-culotte, leading his poor followers by the guidance of the moon (the symbol of lunacy) toward the Promised Land (in reality, the hangman's noose).

so."[26] Halhed was certain that it was Brothers's books and not the man himself who so frightened the authorities. "The man was very well, apart from his pen and ink; but when he mounted on the *Pegasus of Prophecy*, he has galloped over all our heads, at the risk, every moment, of dashing out our brains, together with his own."[27] Here we see the convergence of two strands of criticism—one focusing on the diseased imagination, the other on the diseased language of the visionary—that had been standard weapons in the learned world's arsenal against religious enthusiasm since the late seventeenth century. The conflation of mind and text as signs of prophetic madness would become complete in the vicious attacks on Joanna Southcott's writings a decade later, but in the 1790s the prophet's imagination, distempered or otherwise, was still the primary target in the ongoing war over revelation.

The political maneuvering surrounding Brothers's arrest and incarceration was, in reality, a handy smokescreen for other, less easily articulated, anxieties. No one understood this better than Nathaniel Halhed, the prophet's most prominent supporter and spokesman. In two widely publicized speeches before Parliament, Halhed undertook to present a reasoned defense of Brothers that exposed the tortured illogic behind the government's action. "All I require," said Halhed, "is to discover . . . whether this Mr. Brothers be a traitor or a lunatic. He may possibly be either: but it is morally certain he cannot be both."[28] If he was a traitor, the government would have moved to suppress the publication and dissemination of his seditious prophecies, and this it had manifestly not done. If he was a lunatic, the treasonous implications of his writings were a mere figment of his overheated imagination and hence not prosecutable. Who, Halhed argued cleverly, would believe such palpable nonsense as the visions laid out in the *Revealed Knowledge*? "If, for instance, I were to assert that on some future day, I should ascend to the top of St. Paul's, and from thence *fly over London*, and in sight of all its inhabitants, *to Westminster Abbey*, after which the king must seat me on his throne, and *kiss my great toe*, most people, I allow, would think me mad; but I should certainly not dream of being apprehended for treason."[29] There was no question, he concluded, that Brothers's prophecies were the product of dreams and visions and not subversive designs: the only real question was whether

[26] *Register of the Times* 4 (Mar. 11–21, 1795), p. 98; Brothers, "Notes, on the Etymology of a few antique Words," *Morning Post*, Apr. 18, 1796.

[27] *Oracle*, Apr. 1, 1795.

[28] *The Parliamentary History of England*, 36 vols. (London, 1806–20), 31:1424.

[29] *Parliamentary History*, 31:1417. Halhed's speech was reprinted in the *Oracle* on Apr. 1, 1795.

those visions were genuinely inspired or delusions. At issue, as John Barrell
has argued, was the "health of Brothers's imagination." Those who thought
the prophet insane attributed his visions to a diseased imagination; those
who believed him to be a true prophet accepted the notion that the imagination could be a gateway to the divine. Where some saw "the wandering of
a deranged intellect," others saw "that versatility of thought and sentiment,
which . . . is deemed one of the first essentials of genius."[30] In either case, of
course, the proper response was not prosecution but pity or belief. There
was ample evidence for the verdict of lunacy, Halhed acknowledged, in
Brothers's own writings, which certainly skirted the edge of irrationality. In
the final analysis, faith—and not reason—was the only sure ground of
belief.

In raising questions about the prophet's mental fitness while refusing to
defend in unequivocal terms the authenticity of his visions, Halhed—despite
his own unflinching support of Brothers—moved the discussion onto a plane
where it could only reinforce popular suspicions of millenarianism as an
elaborate charade rather than a legitimate enterprise. Response to Halhed's
speeches and later publications was perplexed: was he really arguing the
prophet's case or subtly lampooning the very idea of prophecy as genuine
revelation? Some thought his writings "a neat piece of irony, meant partly
to convey his political sentiments, and partly to throw contempt upon
prophecy." Others believed his defense sincere, despite the unusual (by the
standards of millenarian writing) clarity and elegance of his language, and
all the more dangerous for that. Halhed's *Testimony*, warned one reader,
"contains the whole virus of the Prophet, without any set-off on the pretext
of madness."[31] Halhed was no raving fanatic, but a gentleman of considerable learning and political acumen, and this made his support of Brothers
"one of the most atrocious acts the world has ever seen."[32] In fact, Halhed
went further than Brothers had ever done in his reading of the political import of the prophet's visions; whereas the latter consistently disclaimed any
political design, Halhed did not hesitate to acknowledge the deep political
and economic corruption implicit in Brothers's vision of London as a "spiritual Babylon." All things, including votes, were truly for sale in the British
capital—he himself, as a Member of Parliament, had "crouched behind the

---

[30] *Parliamentary History*, 31:1426. See Barrell's discussion in *Imagining the King's Death*,
p. 541.

[31] *A Word of Admonition to the Right Hon. William Pitt, in an Epistle to that Gentleman,
occasioned by the Prophecies of Brothers* (London, 1795), p. 17.

[32] *British Critic* 5 (Apr. 1795), p. 437.

Treasury Bench, with my soul in my hand, like a country girl in the market with her butter and eggs before her, anxiously waiting for the lucky moment when the Tellers would come and rid me of my burthen. And while I *did* sell my soul, it was all in the true spirit of commercial credit *that so peculiarly distinguishes this country*."[33] The tone here is difficult to decipher: was Halhed slyly endorsing the reforming political sentiments so many suspected Brothers of harboring, or ridiculing the very notion that prophecy and politics were allied by self-satire? Readers, especially those in the conservative press, could never be sure. "The shocking absurdities of BROTHERS have at last found an advocate in a GENTLEMAN who confesses himself to have *sold his soul.* . . . The good sense of mankind will, we trust, seek for the explication of *mystery* from a source less *polluted*," complained the frustrated editors of the *Oracle*.[34] Portrayed at times as a "harmless crackpot"—the "Mr. Addlehead" of a satirical novel published in 1795—at times as a clever and dangerous politician, Halhed was an enigmatic character whose ability to confound categorization seemed symptomatic of the epistemological slipperiness of millenarian culture itself.[35]

There were, of course, people who fully believed that God continued to speak in these "latter days" and who were prepared to accept Brothers, or some other contender, as a true prophet. Brothers was not without competition for the role of prophet. Some of his fellow prophets attached their wagon to his train, some repudiated his claim and struck out on their own.[36] (One, Christopher Cotter, even claimed to have received a visit from the spirit of the incarcerated prophet.)[37] The response of other millenarians to

---

[33] Nathaniel Brassey Halhed, *The Whole of the Testimonies to the Authenticity of the Prophecies and Mission of Richard Brothers as prince and prophet of the Hebrews* (London, 1795), pp. 31–32.

[34] *Oracle*, Feb. 18, 1795.

[35] Henry James Pye, *The Democrat: Interspersed with Anecdotes of Well Known Characters*, 2 vols. (London, 1795), 2:74–76. The term "harmless crackpot" is Barrell's; *Imagining the King's Death*, p. 512.

[36] A partial list of those prophets who endorsed Brothers would include Thomas Taylor, *An Additional Testimony given to Vindicate the Truth of the Prophecies of Richard Brothers . . . Dictated by the Spirit of God and Wrote by Thomas Taylor* (London, 1795); Whitchurch, *Another Witness!*; William Bryan, *A Testimony of the Spirit of Truth, concerning Richard Brothers* (London, 1795); and George Coggan, *A Testimony of Richard Brothers, in an Epistolary Address to the People of England on the Impending Judgments of God* (London, 1795). Those who challenged Brothers include Sarah Flaxmer, *Satan Revealed; or the Dragon Overcome . . . And Also, a Testimony that Richard Brothers is a Prophet Sent from the Lord* (London, 1795); Eliza Williams, *Prophecies of Brothers Refuted*; and John Wright, *A Revealed Knowledge of Some Things that will Speedily be Fulfilled in the World* (London, 1794).

[37] "Another Impostor!" *Oracle*, May 5, 1795.

the "Great Prophet of Paddington Street" tells us much about the parameters of the popular discourse on authenticity among those who remained stubbornly attached to the doctrine of immediate revelation despite a century or more of clerical opposition. The discourse *among* prophets often reproduced in ironic faithfulness the discourse *between* prophets and their literary critics about how to identify the marks of imposture. In these internecine battles over inspiration, we see once again how revolutionary-era prophets were often complicit in their own unmasking.

The pretensions to gentility among prophets and their believers were cleverly satirized in a pamphlet entitled *The Age of Prophecy! or Further Testimony of the Mission of Richard Brothers*, supposedly authored by "A Convert." Consisting of a dialogue between a believer ("Old Lady") and a skeptic ("Old Man") and dedicated to Nathaniel Halhed, MP (which, "by a happy sympathy of letters," stands for "Minor Prophet" as well as Member of Parliament), the pamphlet's real target was those misguided believers who thought modern prophecy could be defended according to the standards of polite society. The old man opens the attack in standard form by accusing Brothers of "forcing all the old women in the town . . . to go stark-mad—collecting his somniferous lucubrations into undigested, incoherent fulminations—confounding truth, and making mysteries more mysterious." Her interlocutor's tired moralizing annoys the old woman. "Don't tell me of politeness," she replies tartly: "where do we find such a word as politeness in all the Bible?" The voice of true (if deluded) enthusiasm, the old lady's impassioned defense of Brothers is more honest and penetrating than the ridiculous efforts of his more learned supporters who, ashamed of their own credulity, pass their superstitions off as reasoned opinions. "If you deny inspiration," she argues reasonably, "how would you have GOD reveal his mind? I don't set myself up for a prophetess—yet this I know, my dreams are always sure to come true, and I call them visions and revelations." The "infatuation" of the old woman (of all old women) with Richard Brothers is not "to be wondered at," the author concludes, "for she is the very essence of superstition. . . . She herself has seen armies meet, and fight horrid and bloody battles in the firmament." Honest, blunt, and utterly without affectation, the old woman is the personification of religious enthusiasm. This, the author seems to say, is the true face of prophecy—not those polite masks donned so disingenuously by converts like Henry Offley. Discriminating readers would know that old women who believe their own dreams deserve the amused tolerance of the learned classes, not their faith. "What!" cries the old lady—"not have faith in Richard Brothers. . . . If ever there were prophets, Richard Brothers is one."[38] The point exactly.

William Huntington fired back with a spirited defense of his own un-genteel version of prophecy. "There have been some warm debates lately among the wise and learned, 'Which is the greatest *enthusiast*, Mr. Brothers, for styling himself GOD ALMIGHTY'S NEPHEW, or William Huntington, for making CHRIST *his Executor*?' " he reported. (A "curious question," the *Critical Review* dryly noted.) Acknowledging that the rivalry had become a matter of sport as well as faith—"many shillings have been expended to hear this point discussed"—Huntington offered his own firm assessment of Brothers's ca-pacities. "It is no sign of a true prophet to arrogate all knowledge to himself," Huntington declared, "*as if all wisdom was to die with him*." True knowledge of God's intentions, he argued, came not from books or visions but from in-spiration; he himself "was no gentleman, Sir, nor scholar," but he knew how to interpret what he read in the prophetic scriptures by "a little supernatural light."[39] Men like Brothers were "lying prophets," so prevalent among the an-cient Jews and troublesome again in these perilous times. Among the legion of false prophets whom Huntington saw plaguing England was "that self-deifier, that enchanter," Tom Paine, and "another . . . a mere boy" who "was a lunatic from the cradle" (possibly Christopher Cotter). False prophets, in fact, were everywhere—"the nation swarms with them."[40] What, then, de-fined a false prophet? Men who serve themselves instead of God or their fel-low man. What England really needed was a true people's prophet like Huntington, the former "Coal Heaver" who came from "none of the most po-lite parts of the world" and who billed himself as a "preacher to the ignorant."

[38] *Age of Prophecy!* pp. 3–4, 15, 21, 28, 31–32, 9. So successful was the author in disguising his true views of Brothers that some historians, like contemporary readers, have assumed the pamphlet to be written by a supporter; see Mee, *Dangerous Enthusiasm*, p. 29. John Barrell argues, more persuasively I think, that the pamphlet was intended to be a satirical rebuke on Brothers's allies; *Imagining the King's Death*, p. 517, n. 46. Another satirical pamphlet also used the figure of an old woman to challenge the pretensions of prophecy; "we old women," the author proudly writes to Nathaniel Halhed, "have the honour of having you as one of our sisterhood." *A Letter to Nathaniel Brassey Halhed, from an Old Woman* (London, 1795), p. 13. Religious fanatics were commonly ridiculed as "old women of both sexes" in the eigh-teenth century.

[39] William Huntington, *The Lying Prophet Examined, and His False Predictions Discov-ered; Being a Dissection of the Prophecies of Richard Brothers* (London, 1795), pp. viii–ix, 2, 87; *Critical Review* 15 (Oct. 1795), pp. 219–20.

[40] William Huntington, *A Watchward and Warning from the Walls of Zion* (London, 1798), pp. 41–43.

By his own account "harsh and uncouth," Huntington was nonetheless confident that he was a better representative of God than the deluded Richard Brothers.[41] Huntington was not unique in putting his populism to the service of monarchy, though he did so in a uniquely acerbic style that was reminiscent of that "devil in human shape," Tom Paine. Both monocrat and democrat, Huntington was, in fact, a prophet very much in the mold of his nemesis Richard Brothers. He, naturally enough, rejected the comparison. "And now, reader," he concluded grandly, "as I have set aside Mr. Brothers's relationship to GOD ALMIGHTY . . . he can stand no longer as a competitor with me."[42]

Other prophets engaged Brothers more directly on the terrain of revelation. Sarah Flaxmer and Joanna Southcott believed that Richard Brothers had indeed been the recipient of supernatural revelations. If Brothers had not "had some visitation from the Lord," he "could not have foretold the things" he did in 1791 and 1792, Southcott argued.[43] But the Paddington prophet, "heavy laden with the burden of his own mind," overreached: Brothers's arrogance was his real undoing. Once he was imprisoned, the "Powers of Darkness" began to "work hard upon him," to "load him with pride and envy" against God's true emissary—namely, Southcott herself.[44] Throughout the remainder of the 1790s and into the 1800s Southcott repeatedly issued demands for Brothers's release, which earned her the gratitude (and ultimately the loyalty) of many of his followers. Her fellow prophetess Sarah Flaxmer was less generous in her assessment of Brothers. Whereas Southcott believed that Brothers had initially enjoyed the gift of revelation, only to lose it through his own vanity, Flaxmer thought that the prophet's "visitation" had been demonic from the beginning. "Satan's angels" have "visited the Lord's prophet, RICHARD BROTHERS," Flaxmer proclaimed, "and have caught him by their spirit."[45] Neither Southcott nor Flaxmer doubted Brothers's sincerity, only his ability to distinguish divine from demonic reve-

---

[41] William Huntington, *The Sinner Saved; Or, Memoirs of the Life of the Rev. W. Huntington, the Coal Heaver* (London, 1813), pp. 10, 22. Jonathan Mee provides a good overview of Huntington's career, including his stormy relationship with Brothers, in "Is There an Antinomian in the House? William Blake and the After-Life of a Heresy," in *Historicizing Blake*, ed. Steve Clark and David Worrall (New York, 1994), pp. 43–58.

[42] Huntington, *Lying Prophet Examined*, p. 87.

[43] Joanna Southcott, *An Answer to Mr. Brothers' Book, Published in September* 1806, *And Observations on his Former Writings* (London, 1806), p. 16.

[44] Joanna Southcott, *A Communication Given to Joanna, in Relation to Mr. Brothers's Last Book, published the End of this Year,* 1802 (London, 1802), p. 11.

[45] Flaxmer, *Satan Revealed*, p. 9.

lations. Hubris (the classic flaw of ancient heroes), not imposture, was the prophet's real sin in the eyes of these women. This jockeying for position among rival millenarians was nothing new in the 1790s—by its very nature, prophecy was a singular gift that could not be shared—and accusations of demonic influence had a long provenance in the battles over revelation that Anglo-American visionaries had been waging for two centuries. But Satan himself was a shadowy presence in the arguments of the 1790s, really a metaphor for spiritual pride rather than an agent of evil—and pride meant the defects of sense and sensibility rather than the self-glorifying ambitions of princes and minor gods. When Southcott and Flaxmer dismissed Brothers as an unworthy rival, they did so in the vocabulary of eighteenth-century polite discourse rather than in the language of heroic or cosmic contests. He was a simple man who thought too highly of himself, nothing more, nothing less. In so diminishing Brothers, they risked diminishing all prophets who spoke as common men and women.

The most daring critique of Brothers was offered by a rival millenarian, Susan Eyre, in the pages of the London daily *Oracle* over a span of several months in late 1794 and 1795. Eyre neither forsook the path of genuine inspiration nor tried to hedge it about with damning qualifications, but matched Brothers vision for vision. God's voice, she told her readers, could be heard loud and clear in the present age to those still willing to listen, and he spoke not as a gentleman or a republican but as the avenging king Brothers described in his pamphlets. As for Brothers himself, Eyre believed that the self-declared "Nephew of Christ" did have a prophetic role to play, but not the one he envisioned for himself. "My devoted country, hear—think not that I will deceive you—I pledge my life to prove that RICHARD BROTHERS is a liar, a false prophet; yes—the Antichrist!"[46] Rather than the deliverer of God's people, Brothers is in fact their destroyer. "Brothers is the man, I know, that was foretold by our Lord—the false prophet, that by his signs and wonders was to deceive even the Elect," Eyre informed her readers.[47] Any diligent reader of the Book of Revelation would know Brothers for what he was: the false prophet foretold in chapter 13, whose appearance signals the resurrection of the Beast and his terrible reign on earth. "Jesus Christ told us, such a man was to come on the earth, and warned us near two thousand years ago to beware such a man."[48] The false prophet's fatal alliance with the Beast—Bonaparte, in Eyre's reading—would be the downfall of England: "this *false*

[46] *Oracle*, Nov. 18, 1794.
[47] *Oracle*, Apr. 2, 1795.
[48] *Oracle*, Mar. 12, 1795.

prophet persuaded you to make peace with those beasts of French; but I can prove whoever makes peace with them are undone. What a harvest the devil will have on the Continent; for they certainly will make peace with the French, and then what Brothers has said will be fulfilled," she warned.[49]

In contrast to her contemporaries, then, Eyre viewed Brothers not as a cipher to be decoded by the political and cultural conventions of the day but as a genuine prophetic figure. Eyre was contemptuous of those who thought Brothers could be defeated by the spurious claims of superior learning or worldly authority. "*I admire the profound sagacity of our learned Phyicians who have pronounced Brothers insane,*" she wrote sarcastically in an open letter to the archbishop of Canterbury. Only those "too *wise* and too *learned* to believe our Saviour's words" would "treat the false prophet as a madman."[50] To those who thought the established authorities should display better sense than the infatuated Nathaniel Halhed, she was scornful. "You are astonished that a Member of Parliament should defend BROTHERS.—What is a Member of Parliament more than any other man?"[51] Against these men of reputation and sense, Eyre argued for the authority of revelation alone. "I will answer for him," she asserted repeatedly, for she was like him—or rather, she was what he pretended to be. Reverting to the archaic language of the Old Testament, Eyre essentially challenged Brothers to a prophets' duel. "Why don't thou not come out of thy hole, art thou afraid of a woman? I challenge thee in this public manner—Either thou or myself must be of the devil."[52] Only a true prophet could know a false one.

The combativeness of Eyre's writings and her self-designation as the "Woman of Revelation" have led historians to read her prophecies as evidence of a protofeminist millenarianism.[53] There is considerable evidence to support this interpretation. Let "all *our wise and learned men give their opinion first,*" she concluded her defiant letter to the archbishop, "and then a woman, a *fly* may speak." Eyre spoke as a woman, to women: "it is not from men but my country-women that we must expect a reformation, as I shall be able to shew, if I live till all my letters are finished."[54] Addressing her "country-women" directly, she scolded them for their addiction to fashion and luxury

---

[49] *Oracle,* Apr. 2, 1795.

[50] Ibid.

[51] *Oracle,* Mar. 12, 1795.

[52] *Oracle,* Apr. 2, 1795.

[53] Anna Clark makes this argument in "The Sexual Crisis and Popular Religion in London, 1770–1820," *International Journal of Labor and Working Class History* 34 (1988), pp. 56–69.

[54] *Oracle,* Apr. 2, 1795.

and their wastrel ways, warning that just as Eve had brought sin into the world through her disobedience to God, women would be the cause of England's downfall today—or the means of her regeneration if they heeded the prophet's call. This was a charge that millenarian women had sounded since the early 1700s, when one M. Mercin published two prophetic pamphlets addressed to "The Good Women" of England, but it was a message sharpened by new social and political anxieties about women's role that surfaced in the revolutionary era.[55] Despite the feminist overtones of Eyre's prophecies, however, it would be a mistake to read her challenge to Brothers as rooted in the semiotics or sociology of gender opposition. Eyre confronted Brothers as one prophet to another, not as woman to man. "To whom do I speak? To whom do I talk—to whom do I tell these things?" she asked; "who can understand me?" Not just or even primarily women, but "All those who know their God, their Saviour."[56] Those who "know God" include the poor and unlettered, men and women without degree or pedigree who labored in England's urban wasteland. Eyre's championing of her "country-women" (laced at all times with a heavy dose of condemnation) was a championing of all those dispossessed by arrogance or the pretensions of caste and culture. Her readers understood this: "woman" was still a relatively elastic category in the late eighteenth century, a positional rather than psychosexual identity that bespoke structural inferiority rather than innate deficiency—the status of a "fly."[57] One consequence of this disinterest in Eyre's sex is that, in contrast to her contemporary Joanna Southcott, we know almost nothing about her as a person.[58] She was simply an "oracle" whose predictions circulated, fittingly, in the anonymous pages of a semireputable daily.

The response to Eyre among male millenarians was swift and predictable. Samuel Whitchurch, one of Brothers's many admirers and a prophet in his own right, dismissed Eyre as "that 'female bedlamite of Cecil Street,' the raving productions of whose distempered brain, have been inserted in

---

[55] M. Mercin, *Good News to The Good Women, And to the Bad Women too that will grow better; The like to the Man. But here the* WOMEN *are put in the first place (the which is now out of the place) because this Book chiefly treats of the Women* (London, 1701); and M. Mercin, *Two Remarkable Females of Womankind, Fore-Prophecied in the Scriptures, and Given as Signs of the Times* (London, 1701). My thanks to Tim Hitchcock for directing me to these pamphlets.

[56] *Oracle*, Sept. 7, 1795.

[57] Anthony Fletcher, *Gender, Sex and Subordination in England, 1500–1800* (New Haven, 1995); Thomas Laqueur, *Making Sex: Body and Gender from the Greeks to Freud* (Cambridge, Mass., 1990).

[58] Of all those who have written about Eyre, for example, only John Barrell has identified her first name; she is referred to simply as "Mrs. S. Eyre," the name by which she signed her *Oracle* letters.

the paper called the *Oracle*."[59] Harsh words indeed, from a defender of a man whose own sanity had been savagely attacked in the penny press. The discourse on authenticity with which we began this discussion has thus come full circle, back to the terrain of "distempered brains" and "raving productions." The alternatives available to believers intent on making a principled and genuine defense of prophecy in the revolutionary era were few, and self-defeating. Prophets were either lunatics or cheats, to be pitied in one case and silenced in the other, but never to be taken seriously. A vicious and self-fulfilling cycle of discursive associations ensnared would-be prophets: extraordinary revelations lifted them above the world of ordinary men and women, but the more extravagant their visions, the more delusional they appeared; and the more they tried to temper their visions by adopting the language of gentility, the more designing they seemed. No prophet in the revolutionary era was able to break out of this discursive dead end, not even in self-defense. Richard Brothers would spend eleven years in confinement. When he was released in 1806, few noticed or cared.

Nimrod Hughes, "the Democrat's Devil"

In contrast to his British cousin, Nimrod Hughes was a far more shadowy figure in the world of Anglo-American prophecy. Born half a generation later in a place far removed from the radical urban milieu that nourished Brothers, Hughes was in every way a product of his own peculiar time and place—a period of rapid commercial and national expansion, and lingering anxiety over the price of independence. Where Brothers was a mild and polished man who had once occupied a respectable profession in the British empire, Hughes was a scrappy ex-felon who lived a peripatetic existence amidst the new republic's outcasts. Both men gained enormous if fleeting popularity, but where Brothers seems to have had a constituency among the well born and well placed, Hughes's following was primarily limited to "women and children." Where Brothers proclaimed a grand millennial vision of a rejuvenated and powerful kingdom with himself at its head, Hughes offered only nihilistic visions of death and destruction rooted in a personal vendetta against those he blamed for his own failures. Both men spoke in times of war and distress, and both were used as pawns in the partisan bickering that reached new levels of nastiness in their respective eras, but where

---

[59] Whitchurch, *Another Witness!* p. 23.

Brothers adopted the Painite language of frank speech, Hughes spoke in the splenetic vocabulary of personal grievance. Where Brothers engaged the most pressing political issues of his day in productive if unorthodox fashion, Hughes raged against enemies largely unseen. Incarceration was the price of one man's visions and the cause of the other's. And yet the two men shared an essential identity as rogue prophets which allows us to explore further the tangled connections among millenarian politics, gentility, and the culture of consumerism in the revolutionary era.

Nimrod Hughes published only one pamphlet in his lifetime. *A Solemn Warning to All the Dwellers Upon Earth* first appeared in the fall of 1811 as America teetered on the brink of war with its former colonial master and partisan feelings ran high among the nation's embattled Federalists and resurgent Republicans.[60] The pamphlet was an instant best-seller. The *Trenton Federalist* carried an advertisement on December 2, 1811, which breathlessly hailed this "extraordinary prophet, whose writings have excited the curiosity and attention of the public for a considerable time." Hughes's *Solemn Warning* was "eagerly sought after from every quarter, and the printers are hardly able to keep pace with the uncommon demand. Five or six editions have already been disposed of and others are now preparing for the press."[61] Most newspapers were more restrained in their response. The *Weekly Museum* reported the publication of this pamphlet which "has excited no small degree of wonder among our women and children" (and even some "weak-minded" men), lecturing its readers that "the worst thing that the people can do is purchase such vile impositions" even while advertising its availability.[62] The *Alexandria Daily Gazette* was even more dismissive. A letter to the editor noted, "I saw an advertisement in the Trenton Federalist of 2d instant, headed *Hughes' Prophecy*: and as we have not been in the habit of hearing of many miracles since the Apostles time, my attention was attracted to read it." The writer was not impressed: "It appears that one *Nimrod Hughes* has found out that the trade of *prophesying* is easier & more lucrative

[60] The full title of Hughes's pamphlet is *A Solemn Warning to All the Dwellers Upon Earth, Given Forth in Obedience to the Express Commands of the Lord God, as Communicated by Him in Several Extraordinary Visions: And Miraculous Revelations, Confirmed by Sundry Plain but Wonderful Signs, Unto Nimrod Hughes, of the County of Washington, in Virginia. Upon whom the Awful Duty of making this Publication has been Laid and Enforced, by many Admonitions and Severe Chastisements of the Lord, for the space of Ten months and Six Days of unjust and close Confinement in the Prison of Abingdon* 2d ed. (New Jersey, 1811).
[61] *Trenton Federalist*, Dec. 2, 1811; the same notice appeared in every issue of the newspaper through the month of December.
[62] *Weekly Museum* (New York), Feb. 22, 1812.

than *hoeing*, and that any capacity is equal to the task, which only requires a disbelief or indifference about the denunciations pronounced against *false prophets*, and sufficient impudence to declare the visions were from Heaven;—and the work is done. Any tale which borders on the miraculous, and has a hardy wretch to step forward and aver to its truth, is sure to be greedily sought after by a vast proportion of the 'dwellers upon earth.' "[63]

Hughes was not entirely an unknown quantity when he published *A Solemn Warning*. Several months before the pamphlet appeared, he had made quite a stir in the port city of Alexandria, Virginia, by taking his prophetic message to the streets at the peak of summer. Memories of Hughes's visit to Alexandria in August 1811 divided as sharply as did reactions to his pamphlet. The *Trenton Federalist* applauded the dignified response of the prophet to the abuse he encountered among the "unthinking people" of Alexandria who threatened him with "imprisonment as a vagrant and blasphemer." "Hughes mildly reproached them for their persecution," it reported approvingly, "assuring them he had no earthly interest in the promulgation of his prophecy; believeing it to be his duty and the command of the Almighty to proclaim an awful denunciation." Nonsense, retorted the *Alexandria Daily Gazette*. "I have now some recollection that a miserable dirty looking creature passed through this town last summer," the paper's correspondent replied, "which probably was this Hughes; his uncouth appearance soon gathered a retinue of more than a hundred children; but I am far from believing that any of them offered the least violence."[64] Even the *Daily Gazette* was forced to acknowledge the prophet's considerable influence among the provincial folk, however; "A Lady from the country told me some time ago, that this prophecy had such weight in her neighborhood, that many of her neighbors had determined not to sow a kernel of small grain! Many indigent families must suffer in consequence," deplored the editor. Those most susceptible to the prophet's charms were thus the usual suspects in cases of excess credulity: women, children, and rubes.

And what of the controversial pamphlet itself? The central message of *A Solemn Warning* was clear and uncompromising: one year hence, Hughes declared, God would destroy one-third of mankind and subject the rest to "such troubles as never was before." The exact date for this day of reckoning was the result of a preternatural confluence of numerical patterns. "Let no

---

[63] *Alexandria Daily Gazette*, Dec. 12, 1811.
[64] *Trenton Federalist*, Dec. 2, 1811; *Alexandria Daily Gazette*, Dec. 12, 1811.

one presume to slight this warning, for it is determined and will positively take place upon that very day appointed, that is June 4th 1812; That is from the birth of our Lord one thousand eight hundred and twelve years, five months and ten days . . . from the author's birth, forty years, three months and ten days; and four years from the day he was condemned to prison." As this passage suggests, Hughes's incarceration was the source of the outrage that fueled his apocalyptic visions. "On the fourth day of June, 1808," he recalled with unconcealed bitterness, "being then 36 years and 99 days old, I was condemned to the prison of Abingdon, on the charge of being guilty of a charge which I detested, and of which I was totally innocent. Yet here I was constrained to remain in false imprisonment for the space of ten months and nine days before my innocence could be made to appear, and the depravity of my malicious accusers made manifest." During his term in prison "the Lord did not forsake me; but made the day of my age and the days of my captivity, signs to me of what he purposed to do; and there he revealed to me many things which hereafter shall come to pass." The preoccupation with numbers and their hidden meanings is a signature of the pamphlet—could it be a mere coincidence, Hughes asked, that Christ was crucified at the age of 33 years and 99 days while he himself was thrown into prison at the age of 36 years and 99 days? "Even the numbers of the books, the numbers of the chapters, the numbers of the verses, even the numbers of the letters contained in each word; but especially the initial letters, were said to have their uses for various purposes," Hughes instructed his readers. Skeptics might attribute his peculiar interest in numerology to the ancient cabalistic tradition of assigning magical properties to words and letters, but Hughes insisted he relied "upon the truth of *revelation* and not *calculation*."[65] In truth, revelation and calculation were intertwined in Hughes's writing. Appropriately enough for a "calculating people" such as Anglo-Americans had become by the early 1800s, God himself spoke to Hughes not in the archaic biblical language of types and shadows but in the modern vernacular of what Patricia Cline Cohen calls "republican arithmetic." God's plan for his people, like the ledgers and account books of the nation's shopkeepers, was to be reckoned in the steady passage of simple linear units of time (and money).[66]

Hughes did not elaborate on the charges against him, which one newspaper reported to be "stealing bacon, and setting fire to a barn"—charges of

---

[65] Hughes, *A Solemn Warning*, pp. 5–6, 19, 24, 27.

[66] Patricia Cline Cohen, *A Calculating People: The Spread of Numeracy in Early America* (Chicago, 1982).

which he was ultimately acquitted, though "it is generally believed that he was guilty."[67] But the litany of sins which he singled out for condemnation in his pamphlet bespeaks Hughes's conviction that he had suffered a lifetime of persecution. The "earth is full of iniquity and violence, deception, fraud and blasphemy," he railed, "with every species of pollution and uncleanness, so that it has been only typified by ancient Babylon." Where Brothers located Babylon in the brick-and-mortar city of London, Hughes believed it to be an emblem of the widespread spiritual corruption infecting all of God's earth. The leisured classes came in for special abuse: "what will avail your strong and comfortable dwellings, your rich furniture, your extensive freeholds, your numerous slaves, your honorable connections, your wealthy stores, your brilliant genius, your eloquence, learning, or philosophy," he demanded. Everywhere, he suggests, men in power cheat and lie to men like Nimrod Hughes. The "detestable crime" of perjury is "now so general on this earth," he complained, especially among "our great men, our rulers, governors, legislators, judges, lawyers & magistrates." Merchants are guilty of "fraudulent overreaching" in business, retailers perpetrate "direct fraud" on their trusting customers, so-called gentlemen "defile" their "neighbour's wife, or use any means to seduce her, or any other woman from her duty." And, when the wicked third have been destroyed and God returns to reign in peace on earth, the arbitrary and oppressive instruments of man's justice shall be destroyed: "the laws shall be few, and those who compose them shall be few, and those who administer them shall be few."[68] The voice of outraged populism that narrates *A Solemn Warning* would be heard even more loudly in the 1830s as prophets like Joseph Smith and Robert Mathews made this critique of America's new commercial and social order the cornerstone of their millenarian movements. Losers all in the scramble for prosperity and position that drove ordinary Americans after the Revolution, this new generation of millenarians took up the gauntlet thrown down by earlier visionaries like Nimrod Hughes in representing the disaffected laborers and farmers whose economic and political grievances had been simmering since the 1780s.[69]

1811–12 was a singularly unsettled time in America's postrevolutionary history. A series of calamities, recounted in gory detail in the newspapers

<hr/>

[67] *Weekly Museum*, Feb. 22, 1812.

[68] Hughes, *A Solemn Warning*, pp. 6, 16–17, 24–25.

[69] On the populism of Joseph Smith, see Nathan O. Hatch, *The Democratization of American Christianity* (New Haven, 1989), pp. 113–22; on Robert Mathews, see Paul Johnson and Sean Wilentz, *The Kingdom of Matthias: A Story of Sex and Salvation in Nineteenth-Century America* (New York, 1994).

and magazines of the new republic, seemed to confirm the general sense of a world spiraling out of control. Earthquakes, hurricanes, eclipses, comets, hailstorms, homicides, suicides, riots, and fires all seemed to occur with frightening regularity as relations with Great Britain deteriorated and politicians began to talk of war. "Overwhelming Calamity" blared the *Alexandria Daily Gazette* on December 28, 1811, as news of the terrible fire in the Richmond theater that killed sixty people, including the governor of Virginia, first hit the country. "In the whole course of our experience, we have never taken our pen under a deeper gloom than we feel at this moment. It falls to our lot to record one of the most distressing scenes which can happen in the whole circle of human affairs." Worse, however, was yet to come. "More Conflagrations!" cried the *Columbian* the next month as its continuing coverage of the Richmond tragedy turned up fresh cases of fire. "Our wounds have not time to cicatrize, before some new blow opens them afresh." The Richmond fire "appears to have been but the forerunner of a chain of disasters," the *Daily Gazette* gloomily concluded. "Ever since that mournful era, the appalling cry of 'FIRE!' has resounded throughout Virginia."[70] Nature, too, conspired to terrify America's citizens. An earthquake felt from Washington to Charleston, South Carolina, on December 17, 1811, was "preceded by a blowing noise, resembling that made by smith's bellows," and created great "consternation" among the inhabitants.[71] "Another Earthquake!" proclaimed the *Weekly Museum* two months later. "The frequent repetition of this awful visitation had ex[c]ited the utmost anxiety in the minds of our citizens. This is the tenth distinct shock which we have felt in this city since the 16th of Dec. last, and was stronger than any that had preceded it."[72] "EARTHQUAKES" screamed another headline as the *Trenton Federalist* bemoaned the "frequent recurrence within a few months past of earthquakes, storms, and whirlwinds, with other awful and disastrous phenomena."[73] Shaken by this chain of tremors, the citizens of the coastal cities were told that "There have been no such instances of such continued and repeated shocks recorded in the history of this country."[74]

To many Americans, there could be only one explanation for this crescendo of disaster. The vulgar "superstitious" recognized in these events

[70] *Alexandria Daily Gazette*, Dec. 28, 1811 and Apr. 24, 1812; *Columbian* (New York), Jan. 23, 1812.

[71] *American Mercury*, Jan. 1, 1812.

[72] *Columbian*, Feb. 10, 1812; *Weekly Museum*, Feb. 22, 1812. Notice of the publication of Hughes's *Solemn Warning* appeared in the same issue of the *Weekly Museum*.

[73] *Trenton Federalist*, Mar. 30, 1812.

[74] *Columbian*, Feb. 10, 1812.

the awful "signs of the times" predicted in the prophetic scriptures. "These are indeed times of wonder," declared the *New-York Herald* in mock horror. "Comets—eclipses—tornadoes—earthquakes—in the age of superstition, these were held to be portentous signs. Powers of the physical world are yet not satisfied? Are not your omens already out?—Does not the conflagration of the theatre verify your superstitious auguries?—Are not the ashes of our citizens enough?—But this is the language of superstition." Enlightened readers should reject such nonsense. "Away with all the dregs of those 'degenerate days.' Whether they are the tales of the nursery or of old women; whether we are told of the fate of nations in an eclipse or of a friend's death in the winding sheet of a candle; whether it be a dream, or the vision of a bigot, just let loose from prison, they are equally at war with the lessons of philosophy."[75] Ordinary people, however, continued to look to their Bible rather than to the nation's literary elite for guidance. When the earthquake of February 14, 1812, was felt as far south as Raleigh, North Carolina, "the timid took to prayer, expecting every moment (as they say) to hear the sound of the last trumpet."[76]

The appearance of a comet in the eastern sky in the fall months of 1811, in particular, inspired apocalyptic visions in a number of citizens. The *Weekly Museum* noted, in its advertisement for *A Solemn Warning*, that "there have been four or five different prophecies since the appearance of the comet," though none were "so artful, so wicked, or so dangerous as Nimrod Hughes's."[77] The comet arrived at a perilous moment in the nation's psyche. "Notwithstanding the repeated 'rumours of war' with which our newspapers have been lately filled, this celestial stranger has attracted considerable attention," noted the *Alexandria Daily Gazette*. "To people in general, it is an interesting spectacle, as one of the magnificent works of the creation." But to others, "it is viewed with the trembling eye of ancient superstition, as the precursor of desolation and bloodshed. Among the latter we find a prophet who signs himself '*Christ. McPherson, a man of color, alias Ross's Kitt, formerly of the Elk Horn Store, Petersburg, Virginia.*' "[78] Comets had a long and illustrious history as apocalyptic signs in Anglo-American Protestantism. As Perry Miller long ago remarked, "Comets had always figured prominently in the panorama of conflagration, if only because for centuries they had been

75 *New-York Herald*, Feb. 8, 1812.
76 *Alexandria Daily Gazette*, Feb. 14, 1812.
77 *Weekly Museum*, Feb. 22, 1812.
78 *Alexandria Daily Gazette*, Oct. 17, 1811. The article links the approach of the comet to the predictions of Hughes as well.

the most charmingly lawless of actors in the cosmos." These "blazing stars" with "long bloody hair" had captured the imagination of poets and seers as far back as Pliny and Seneca, and early Puritans looked to the skies for a glimpse of falling stars whose appearance signaled imminent change if not always disaster.[79] The 1811 comet inspired contemporary readers to recall earlier instances of superstition, such as William Whiston's famous prediction in 1712 that "the return of a Comet" meant "a total dissolution of the world by fire . . . on the Friday following." Terrified Londoners had taken Whiston seriously. "Before noon, the belief was universal, that the day of judgment was at hand," recounted the *New-Jersey Journal* in a tongue-in-cheek article entitled "Ludicrous Effects of the Appearance of a Comet." "The South Sea stock immediately fell 5 cents, and the Indian to 11. . . . Three maids of honour burnt their collections of novels and plays. . . . The run upon the Bank was so prodigious, that all hands were employed from morning till night in discounting notes," and "considerably more than 7000 kept mistresses were legally married."[80] Modern readers should beware such fanciful illusions: "As what has been done *once*, but be done *again*—as indeed the Comet which is now in our sky, begins already to scare all the old women over 80 and young children under a twelve month—as even some wiseacres say that our present spell of warm weather is owing to its influence."[81] In the end, the *Columbian* noted gleefully, the comet came and went without incident. In its honor the paper published a doggerel verse dedicated to "The Departing Comet":

Eccentric stranger! tell us why
You came so near, yet pass'd us by?
Had you been fraught with vengeful ire,
You might have set our world on fire.
Methinks I hear the Comet say—
"I knew your fears, and kept away."[82]

Comets were not the only "eccentric strangers" to appear in these years. An eclectic array of human and natural oddities was paraded before the readers of the nation's newspapers alongside accounts of such rogue phenomena

[79] Perry Miller, *Errand into the Wilderness* (Cambridge, Mass., 1956), p. 229; David D. Hall, *Worlds of Wonder, Days of Judgment: Popular Religious Belief in Early New England* (Cambridge, Mass., 1989), p. 78.

[80] *New-Jersey Journal*, Oct. 15, 1811. The same article appeared in the *Alexandria Daily Gazette* on Oct. 17, 1811.

[81] *Alexandria Daily Gazette*, Oct. 18, 1811.

[82] *Columbian*, Jan. 22, 1812.

as fires, earthquakes, and falling stars. Child prodigies were discovered in unlikely places—Zerah Colburn, the boy mathematician born with "a fifth finger on each hand" whose father was determined to "make a public and indiscriminate spectacle of him for money"; and "*master Smith*, a bashful infant of six years old" whose talents on the piano and violin were deemed "musical genius."[83] Deformed creatures of every species—a "Horned Cock," a "serpent of extraordinary size," a "Mermaid," a newborn (a "sport of nature") whose face "bears the marks of extreme old age, with the strongest resemblance of a Mamoset"—turned up on the same pages as these boy wonders.[84] Tales of curious and inexplicable events provided comic ballast to the more serious political fare dished up by the nation's partisan press: the "strange and uncommon spectacle" of a farmer riding a cart drawn by four large hogs, the "very singular Phenomenon" observed by several bemused citizens of kettles that rattled mysteriously; ghostly "apparitions" that turned out to be nothing more than wandering cats.[85] These were stories that skirted the line between farce and satire, designed for a quick laugh and a knowing look shared between men of taste and sensibility. Occasionally the moral of the tale was driven home, as when past instances of primitive superstition were dredged up as cautionary tales. The *New-York Weekly Museum* retold in gothic terms the story of an "Extraordinary Instance of Superstition" in which a young woman drives four large nails through the corpse of her dead lover ("What agitated feelings! what chilling perspiration!") to escape the unwelcome nightly visitations of his ghost, marveling at the potent mixture of "courage, superstition, and love" displayed by the young heroine who dared to defy the supernatural.[86] But more often than not the point was to laugh, not moralize.

While the tone in these articles was for the most part light, another series of articles pointed to a more worrisome streak of overcredulity in the national character. The belief in supernatural lore was one thing, charming in its own way; the gullibility of Americans when faced with the dizzying array of con men who plagued the new republic in the early 1800s was quite

[83] "Extraordinary Powers of Calculation in a Child," *Richmond Enquirer*, Feb. 9, 1811, and Feb. 22, 1811; "A Musical Prodigy," *Columbian*, Dec. 23, 1811.

[84] "The History of a Horned Cock," *Alexandria Daily Gazette*, June 13, 1811; "A Monster," *Richmond Enquirer*, June 28, 1811 (serpent); "A Mermaid," *Richmond Enquirer*, June 21, 1811; "Prodigy," *Richmond Enquirer*, June 4, 1811 ("sport of nature").

[85] "Curious Novelty," *New-York Herald*, Jan. 15, 1812 (hog-drawn cart); *New-York Herald*, Feb. 1, 1812 ("singular phenomenon"); *Alexandria Daily Gazette*, Feb. 3, 1812 (ghostly apparition).

[86] *Weekly Museum*, June 20, 1812.

another. A range of human predators took their place alongside these natural prodigies in the nation's press: counterfeiters, thieves, forgers, quacks, charlatans, extortionists, and corrupt politicians. The exploits of the notorious Stephen Burroughs, the picaresque confidence man whose bold reinventions made him a household name in the early 1800s, were chronicled, as were those of lesser known counterfeiters and forgers such as Hezekiah Wadsworth and Homes Bostick.[87] A "female swindler" was uncovered in Liverpool, and in New York "a *woman*, calling herself Mary Davidson, was detected in passing counterfeit money near this town."[88] Petty criminals were not the only ones preying on America's innocent citizens—professional politicians and journalists alike conspired to defraud the public. "Mr. Madison has once more consented to serve the people in the capacity of political *pimp* to Thomas Jefferson," charged the federalist *New-York Evening Post*, while its republican rival the *New-York Herald* complained of "More Humbugging!" in March 1812. "It will be seen from our Congressional report this day, that another electioneering trick has been played off at Washington."[89] In a country where rhetoric seemed to count more than results, the unholy alliance of politicians and their editorial mouthpieces came in for special cynicism—even in the pages of the partisan press itself. A "mercenary writer" is nothing more than a "political vagabond, without a place of legal settlement—a hireling scribbler, who writes for pay, and who libels for bread," complained the *Columbian*.[90] Politics in the early republic seemed to be all heat and no light, a situation ripe for exploitation by unscrupulous men with quick tongues and empty souls. This hollowness at the very core of

---

[87] "Stephen Burroughs!!" *Richmond Enquirer*, May 14, 1811; "Extensive Forgeries Detected," *New-York Herald*, Jan. 15, 1812; "Counterfeiters Disconcerted," *New-York Herald*, Feb. 12, 1812 (Hezekiah Wadsworth); *New-York Herald*, "A Swindler Taken," Oct. 15, 1811 (Homes G. Bostick). Burroughs published his own memoir, *The Memoirs of Stephen Burroughs*, in 1798, a modern edition of which is edited by Philip F. Gura (Boston, 1988). One of the most successful examples of the genre known as the traveling rogue tale, Burroughs's memoir (and life) has been the subject of literary interest ever since; see Daniel Cohen's discussion in *Pillars of Salt, Monuments of Grace: New England Crime Literature and the Origins of American Popular Culture, 1674–1860* (New York, 1993), pp. 155–62; Christopher Jones, "Praying upon Truth: The Memoirs of Stephen Burroughs and the Picaresque," *Early American Literature* 30 (1995), pp. 32–50; and Daniel Williams's work on rogue tales, "Rogues, Rascals, and Scoundrels: The Underworld Literature of Early America," *American Studies* 24 (1983), pp. 5–19, and "In Defense of Self: Author and Authority in *The Memoirs of Stephen Burroughs*," *Early American Literature* 25 (1990), pp. 96–122.

[88] *New-York Weekly Museum*, Feb. 13, 1813 ("female swindler"); *New-York Herald*, Feb. 21, 1812 (Mary Davidson).

[89] *New-York Herald*, Mar. 14, 1812.

[90] *Columbian*, Dec. 10, 1811.

democratic politics was exposed by the *New-York Herald* in a mock dialogue between a "Great Man" and a "Sycophant." "The nation are becoming sick of words," worries the Great Man, "and I fear they'll vomit up long speeches as squeamish children throw up nauseous drugs. That, you know, will destroy our talking plan." Not to worry, replies his sidekick *"Supple."* "We'll change names, alter labels, and so work the business, that like vendors of quack medicines, we'll make whole communities gulp down the very same sort of doses they already puked up. Your excellency will recollect, *always*—that *our* people are most easily bubired of all people on earth."[91]

No wonder, then, that Americans were such easy prey for men like Nimrod Hughes. If we can learn something about the public perception of Hughes by looking at the company he kept in the pages of the nation's newspapers, he appears to be a cross between a prodigy and a confidence man, with the emphasis distinctly on the latter. Like the comet whose appearance frightened so many old women and children, Hughes was "charmingly lawless." Like the political hacks whose job it was to whip up public frenzy on a regular basis, he represented "men without mind . . . the mere scrapings of society, and the very dregs of vulgar profligacy and impudence."[92] Like the smooth-talking Stephen Burroughs, he was adept at exploiting the insecurities of America's provincial citizens caught between the vanishing comforts of pastoral life and the hard realities of the new market economy. Like the "counterfeiters and Swindlers" who operated with impunity in the anonymous spaces of the urban republic, he passed false coin (superstition) for true faith. He was truly "the democrat's devil" as one Federalist paper put it, the seducer of innocence and the tool of designing men impatient with the slow pace of America's fitful emergence onto the world stage as a mature republic.[93]

The threat posed by these various con men to the republic's fragile identity had become deadly serious by 1811 as the decade-long quasi-war with Great Britain neared its final denouement. Reports of atrocities committed by British ships against American sailors filled the pages of the nation's press, creating an atmosphere of collective paranoia almost unmatched in the history of the United States. Continental hostilities spilled over into the Americas during the first decade of the 1800s. Hobbled by its losses during the Napoleonic wars, the Royal Navy in 1803 had begun impressing American sailors from merchant vessels, a practice that ultimately netted

[91] *New-York Herald*, Jan. 4, 1812.
[92] *Columbian*, Dec. 10, 1811.
[93] "The Democrat's Devil," *New-York Herald*, Feb. 19, 1812.

several thousand desperate men, while harassing commercial vessels bound for Europe and the West Indies. After 1807 both England and France declared open season on American ships, forcing Jefferson to impose the infamous embargo in a vain attempt to bring the belligerent powers to their knees. The effect, of course, was calamitous for American commerce, which reached a state of near-paralysis by 1808. To add insult to injury, Great Britain redoubled its efforts in the American interior to build a new coalition with its former Indian allies to attack the vulnerable republic from the western front. A series of skirmishes with western tribes proved the alliance to be a potent if disorganized force, capable of inflicting real devastation on backcountry settlements from Ohio to Pennsylvania. The rise of nativist prophets like the Shawnee Tenskwatawa and the Seneca Handsome Lake coincided with the renewal of British military agitation in the region, producing a deadly confluence of spiritual, ethnic, and political enmities that would help inflame the passions of war. By the summer of 1811, war with Great Britain seemed inevitable and victory by no means assured. The covert war that the two countries had been waging for a decade became open hostilities on June 1, 1812.

The War of 1812 has always been something of a puzzle to American historians. The battles were few and far between, and of little consequence (with the notable exception of the burning of Washington in 1814). Nevertheless, the actual events of the war pale in significance next to the public mood of hysteria which turned every skirmish on the high seas into a morality play of good and evil. The nation entered war bitterly divided, with partisan rancor at a level of intensity rivaling the poisonous 1790s. Federalists charged Republicans with being grasping and self-serving demagogues who had bullied the country into a debilitating war they could not hope to win, while Republicans cried treason at every hint of dissent from a party whose craven fidelity to its former imperial master threatened to emasculate the republic itself. Partisan animosity ran so high, cooler heads worried, that civil war was not an impossibility—and indeed, disgruntled Federalists would make a serious bid for secession two years later at the Hartford convention of 1814. In hindsight, the frenzy seems out of proportion to the political realities of the time: few in either party deserved the label of hypocrite or traitor, and the stability of the federal government and the party system itself was never seriously endangered. But deeper issues were at stake, and ideologues in both camps were responding to the real fear that America faced a peril far more dangerous than the Royal Navy, Indian warriors, or even corrupt politicians—namely, its own inability to restrain the centrifugal tendencies of its expansive and volatile political and commercial culture. The republic, it was feared, would disintegrate into a thousand particles of disaffection under the twin anvils of war and internal dissent, with citizens cut loose from all meaningful social and political bonds to pursue in reckless fashion their own puny interests. Every con man who swindled a farmer out of his savings, every quack who impersonated a professional doctor or lawyer to cheat a trusting client, every politician who sold his vote to fatten his purse, and every religious impostor who exploited real terrors for false ends was contributing in a small way to the massive erosion of republican confidence and character evident in all spheres of American life.

Demagogues who covered their own ambitions in the lofty language of prophecy were considered the worst offenders of all. One opposition politician, complained the Republican *Columbian*, had resorted to "puerile" rhapsodies to argue his position. " 'We should go to war (says he) under the ominous auspices of eclipses, comets, earthquakes, and the most desolating visitations of God, which are fit harbingers of that disastrous event!' " Such infantile "incantations" were more suited to a primitive age, though even "Cromwell, with all his hypocrisy and fanaticism, never resorted to a more gross or fulsome play upon the weakness of bigotry and superstition, than that exhibited in the above quotation" the paper argued. "But it would seem, that in politics as well as theology, the present time is to be distinguished by the rage of a *mania*, as disgraceful to true religion and philosophy, as it is repugnant to every principle of candour and humanity."[94] The *New-York Herald* published a long rant on the eve of the declaration of war against that "species of political quacks which, quite as much as any other, characterizes the present age: I mean that of prophets." Ever since "the volcano of the French revolution burst upon the world, these tutelary seers have started up in every country," the paper complained. "We have at the present day a great number of prophets in this country, mostly however, as is usual of the gloomy kind; for alas! who would venture to predict peace, prosperity and happiness to our country, in its present miserable and degraded state? Our total ruin has been boldly announced for the fourth day of June next. . . . It would seem that our administration were in league with the prophet to blast our only hope of safety." However compelling they might be to frightened readers, such prophecies were nothing more than the "sickly forebodings of disappointed ambition," the "consolation" of sore losers who would "fain avenge themselves on posterity by the indulgence of their spleen or resent-

[94] "Monkery," *Columbian*, Jan. 28, 1812 (a reprint of an article that originally appeared in the *Albany Register*).

ment." Prophecies like those contained in *A Solemn Warning* were thus "a stale story," one told countless times by desperate men to redeem their own "incapacity or depravity."[95] Men like Nimrod Hughes were, in the words of another correspondent, modern-day Jacobins, constitutionally hostile to the tenor and accomplishments of modern democratic life. "A JACOBIN's picture is easy to draw," suggested the paper.

His manners unsocial, his temper unkind,
He's a *Rebel* in conduct, a *Tyrant* in mind.
He is envious of those, that have riches and power.
Discontented, malignant, implacable, sour;
Never happy himself, he would wish to destroy
The comforts and blessings which others enjoy.[96]

This was stern stuff, and not surprising coming from the pen of the literary elite who fancied themselves modern men living in a new age of democratic promise. The very tone of biblical prophecy—dark and foreboding—offended the modern sensibilities of these men of letters who looked for, and found, signs of progress everywhere in the new republic. What is perhaps more surprising is the total absence of support for Nimrod Hughes among his fellow millenarians, of whom (as the *New-York Herald* acknowledged) there were supposedly many in 1811–12. No prophet came forward, as legions had in Richard Brothers's day, to lend his or her spiritual or hermeneutic authority to Hughes's apocalyptic vision. No prophet offered an alternative reading of the "signs of the times," at least not in the pages of the nation's newspapers and periodicals. Prophecy had been driven largely underground by 1812, continuing to express itself powerfully in the daily visions and dreams of numerous believers, especially those of an evangelical bent, but rarely surfacing in visible ways that we can track in the burgeoning print culture of the republic. Where were the voices of men and women like Henry Offley, Thomas Taylor, Sarah Flaxmer, or Susan Eyre? No voice is more conspicuous in its absence than the voice of polite society: there was no Nathaniel Brassey Halhed to step forward and shelter the prophet's visions under his own capacious legitimacy in 1812. Even the millenarian wing of the evangelical movement repudiated Hughes: a notice in the *Herald of Gospel Liberty*, the leading periodical of mainstream millennialism, chastised believers who foolishly chose to heed *A Solemn Warning*. "We are told that many in different

[95] *New-York Herald*, Apr. 15, 1812.
[96] "Portrait of a *Jacobin*," *Alexandria Daily Gazette*, Feb. 19, 1811.

parts of the country believe this prophet, and are looking for the awful *fourth day of June*, when one third of each family on earth must be buried by the remaining two thirds," the magazine reproved, even though the author "acknowledges that his Prophecy is delivered in a dark and mysterious stile, and some things in an unintelligible manner, which he is not allowed to explain."[97] The silence in the pages of the other evangelical periodicals that flowered in the early 1800s was deafening.

The only alternative prophets available were Indian ones, Indians moreover in the pocket of the marauding British, or African American ones like the mysterious "Christ. McPherson" mentioned briefly by the *Alexandria Daily Gazette*. No trace of McPherson's actual prophecies survives; the book he intended to publish apparently never materialized.[98] While Anglo-American prophets were well aware of their Native and African counterparts in the revolutionary era, there are only tantalizing hints of a shared visionary world among red, black, and white millenarians. Francis Asbury, having heard that "there is a prophet risen up among the Indians" in 1807 (most likely Tenskwatawa), showed little curiosity to meet him.[99] There were, to be sure, striking parallels between Native American, African American, and evangelical Anglo-American spirituality in the early nineteenth century: the reliance on dreams and visions as means of spiritual communication, the embodied nature of religious worship, the reciprocal dance of individual expression and communal discipline enacted in rites of worship, the porous and well-traveled boundary between the supernatural and natural worlds.[100] But however well certain elements in evangelical Protestant, African, and Native symbolism meshed, their eschatological traditions were not easily assimilable. African and Native American religious systems had no concepts compa-

[97] *Herald of Gospel Liberty*, 4 (Apr. 24, 1812), p. 384.

[98] *Alexandria Daily Gazette*, Oct. 17, 1811.

[99] Elmer T. Clark, ed., *The Journal and Letters of Francis Asbury*, 2 vols. (Nashville, Tenn., 1958), 2:555.

[100] The literature on the syncretism of white and black religious beliefs in colonial and antebellum America is extensive; see Sylvia R. Frey and Betty Wood, *Come Shouting to Zion: African American Protestantism in the American South and British Caribbean to 1830* (Chapel Hill, N.C., 1998); Mechal Sobel, *The World They Made Together: Black and White Values in Eighteenth-Century Virginia* (Princeton, N.J., 1987); Albert Raboteau, *Slave Religion: The "Invisible Institution" in the Antebellum South* (New York, 1978); and Donald G. Mathews, *Religion in the Old South* (Chicago, 1977). On the cross-cultural sharing of symbols and beliefs between Christian and Native American religions, see Jane Merritt, "Dreaming of the Savior's Blood: Moravians and the Indian Great Awakening in Pennsylvania," *William and Mary Quarterly* 3d ser., 54 (Oct. 1997), pp. 723–46; Harold W. Van Lonkhuyzen, "A Reappraisal of the Praying Indians: Acculturation, Conversion, and Identity at Natick, Massachusetts, 1646–1730," *New England Quarterly* 63 (1990), pp. 396–428.

rable to the Christian notions of sin and hell—the idea of eternal damnation carried little meaning to peoples who already inhabited a living hell and felt no need to imagine another waiting beyond the borders of this world. Without the idea of the wages of sin as a goad, scenarios of divine retribution made little sense. Those enslaved and Native Americans who accepted the rudiments of Christian belief were certain that God would avenge sin, but not their sins and not any time soon. The day of judgment seemed too far away in postrevolutionary America to serve as a reliable guide to action in the here and now. There is scant evidence of pervasive millenarian belief among enslaved African Americans until the 1830s when Nat Turner's bloody raid shattered the complacency of white Christians about their slaves' capacity to suffer quietly. Black Christians in the revolutionary era looked for a Moses to lead them out of captivity rather than for a Messiah to overturn the world.[101]

Indian prophecy is another story. Nativist renewal, often expressed in the visions of charismatic prophets, had been endemic since the 1760s, and the brutal invasion of the interior by hordes of newly independent white farmers in the 1790s and early 1800s ignited a new "Age of Prophecy" among the western tribes that lasted until the defeat of the Indian-British alliance in 1814.[102] Indian prophets shared certain characteristics with their Anglo-American counterparts: they were men and on occasion women of obscurity, whose dreams catapulted them suddenly from the fringes of Native society onto center stage. Their visions combined elements of political and cultural protest with idiosyncratic references to personal troubles, and helped create a common language of grievance and redress among men and women of widely scattered ethnic and tribal identities. Their careers were marked by swift ascendance and sudden eclipse, much like the comets that streaked across the American sky in these years. Unlike Anglo-American millenarians, however, Indian prophets attached their visions to concrete political and social programs of reform: they told their followers not only to await the avenging Spirit but to stop drinking, stop trading and intermarrying with whites, avoid intratribal violence, return to a subsistence economy, and shun all white ways. And their believers listened, creating pan-Indian alliances with other tribes in pursuit of these goals, even taking up arms in response to

---

[101] Eugene Genovese, *Roll, Jordan, Roll: The World the Slaves Made* (New York, 1972), pp. 233–55, 271–79.

[102] Gregory Dowd, *A Spirited Resistance: The North American Indian Struggle for Unity, 1745–1815* (Baltimore, 1992); Anthony Wallace, *Death and Rebirth of the Seneca* (New York, 1969); R. David Edmunds, *The Shawnee Prophet* (Lincoln, Neb., 1983).

the prophet's call for renewal. The fusion of visionary and military aims made the Indian Age of Prophecy a far more potent political force than any movement headed by an Anglo-American in these years. But more than politics separated Indian prophets like Tenskwatawa from millenarians such as Nimrod Hughes, despite the efforts of the nation's journalists to couple them as renegade elements in the pages of the newspapers.[103] By 1800, the language of racial destiny had become so all-encompassing, so indelible as to vitiate the meaning of other ways of connecting human beings, including religion. An enormous gulf separated red, black, and white by the early 1800s, hampering the development of a truly syncretic religious worldview among peoples who shared a history of suffering but not a common understanding of the roots of oppression or a common solution to its historical and theological presence or even a common identity as children of the one God.

An impressive isolation from other prophetic worlds, in other words, surrounded Nimrod Hughes in 1812. His *Solemn Warning* stands as a monument to his own sorry history, unsupported by fellow visionaries, white or red, or by respectable society. When the fourth of June came and went without incident, the public took no notice. Hughes himself disappeared entirely from view, and no trace of his subsequent career exists in the public records or the newspapers. We cannot even be sure he existed in the first place; his name alone suggests an apocryphal identity that cannot be denied or confirmed by the facts. Were it not for historical hindsight, we might be tempted to conclude that the vein of prophetic thinking represented by *A Solemn Warning* was millenarianism's last hurrah, a gloomy vision of biblical retribution out of step with the aggressively modern tenor of postrevolutionary American life. But a brief reference to another shadow prophet in the pages of the nation's press reminds us that, however quiescent millenarianism might have appeared in the aftermath of the War of 1812, it would burst again on the literary and cultural scene twenty years later with a vengeance. The *Alexandria Daily Gazette* published a piece on August 29, 1811, calling for more information about one "pretended *Reverend*, Mr. William Miller." "Much enquiry was in vain bestowed by us in tracing who this personage might be, and though he was extremely notorious as the hero of handbills, and the saint of the Whig and other democratic papers, it was not till Saturday that we were able to discover any more of his character and properties, than those veracious vehicles had thought fit to disclose." Who was this mys-

---

[103] Articles on Tenskwatawa appeared in the same papers that covered Hughes's meteoric rise to popularity; see *Columbian*, Dec. 26, 1811; and the *New-Jersey Journal*, Jan. 14, 1812.

terious preacher? A man of suspect political convictions, apparently, since the reverend declared in conversation that the real beast of Revelation was Napoleon Bonaparte, and the followers of the beast—those who had received "a mark in their right hand, or in their forehead"—none other than "the democrats." Thus was Miller "held up in his true character, a changeling of no respectability."[104] Historians of antebellum America know William Miller well, as one of the most influential of the prophets who, along with Joseph Smith, inaugurated a new era of millenarian zeal in the 1830s and 1840s.[105] In 1811, however, he was—like our friend Nimrod Hughes—a "changeling, of no respectability." Such was the contemporary verdict on prophets in postrevolutionary America.

Richard Brothers and Nimrod Hughes were two men who traveled remarkably similar paths to an ignoble end. Little changed in their worlds as a result of their prophetic interventions. Britain declared war on France despite Brothers's warnings and paid the price for the next twelve years as political unrest surged at home, prices skyrocketed, and commerce stagnated, leaving thousands of poor farmers and laborers in real distress and poisoning the partisan well for decades to come. The United States declared war on Great Britain on June 1, 1812, ignoring Hughes's dire prediction that one-third of humanity would be crushed by sword and fire three days hence, and emerged triumphant two years later with its position as an independent nation and commercial power secure. The terror both men inspired was real enough, and we can glimpse the depth of popular anxiety beneath the cavalier treatment both received by the literary elite. In the end the forces of skepticism and scorn were too strong to overcome, even by determined messengers inspired with a holy zeal, and both men sank into an obscurity from which it has been difficult to rescue them ever since.

Thanks to Nathaniel Brassey Halhed we know much more about Richard Brothers than about his American cousin, who had no such powerful supporter to galvanize public opposition. Halhed himself retreated into private life after Brothers' incarceration, his career and personal life in tatters. Forsaken by his friends and mercilessly ridiculed by his enemies, the former MP became a recluse and pariah "waiting for the millennium to

---

[104] "The Reverend Mr. Miller, Answer to Your Name," *Alexandria Daily Gazette*, Aug. 29, 1811.

[105] On Miller, see *The Disappointed: Millerism and Millenarianism in the Nineteenth Century*, ed. Ronald Numbers and Jonathan M. Butler (Knoxville, Tenn., 1993); and Hatch, *Democratization of American Christianity*.

begin," in the words of his biographer. His hopes would be answered when a new prophet came knocking at his door in 1804 seeking his support. Nathaniel Halhed came to believe that Joanna Southcott was Brothers's prophetic successor, gratefully telling the prophetess that "he had been a prisoner ten years and was ordered not to go into any persons house but his own before she came to free him." Released from his self-imposed captivity by his belief in Southcott's mission, Halhed sought to rejoin the world of writers and politicians who had repudiated him after his disgrace in 1795—writing poems and satirical essays which he circulated to a close circle of friends. But the world was not interested in Nathaniel Halhed anymore. Few returned his letters and his essays, and gradually he stopped writing them. He lived another quarter century in a state of genteel poverty, though many believed he had died years before.[106]

Joanna Southcott was not the savior of Nathaniel Halhed. But she inspired more devotion and enthusiasm among the British poor than any prophet since Richard Brothers. Her story is told in the next chapter, along with that of the most famous American millenarian of the revolutionary era, the ex-Quaker Jemima Wilkinson, whose dramatic appearance on the public stage in the 1770s and 1780s parallels the career of her countryman Nimrod Hughes some thirty years later. These prophetesses, both of whom claimed to be the "Woman clothed with the sun" foretold in chapter 12 of the Book of Revelation, inspired similar hopes but different anxieties in their audiences than their male counterparts. Not rogues in the eighteenth-century sense of the word, a term conventionally reserved for male forms of cultural and political transgression in the Anglo-American world, they were subject to a more searching critique of their visionary claims that attacked their inner selves as well as their public representations. Women prophets did not fit as comfortably into the established categories of social commentary as did male prophets. The various scoundrels to whom men like Brothers and Hughes were compared—rogues, confidence men, quacks, swindlers, counterfeiters— all achieved notoriety for their actions in the *public* sphere, for crimes against that sphere. A man who cheated in private was still a cheat, but he was not a confidence man. A man who pretended to be something he was not to his intimates was despicable, but he was not a quack. The assorted "women of Revelation" were harder to classify because women in general occupied a much more ambiguous place in the Anglo-American public sphere in the

---

[106] Rosane Rocher, *Orientalism, Poetry, and the Millennium: The Checkered Career of Nathaniel Brassey Halhed, 1751–1830* (Delhi, 1983), pp. 192–209 (quotes on pp. 193, 196).

revolutionary era.[107] Uneasily skirting the porous and ever-shifting boundary between the private and the public, women prophets found themselves facing an array of questions about their private behavior (were they chaste? did they drink or wear outlandish clothes? what sexual and domestic sins lay in their past?) that male prophets rarely encountered. At the same time, they were forced to defend their public conduct in much the same terms as their male counterparts, as accusations of deceit and imposture dogged their heels as well. Rather than inhabiting a recognizable category of social and political disorder, in other words, women prophets were located betwixt and between competing categories—cultural hermaphrodites. We shall see that the gender identity of women prophets floated indeterminately while critics scurried to find the best way to attack and discredit their visionary claims.

[107] Susan Kingsley Kent, *Gender and Power in Britain, 1640–1990* (New York, 1999) offers a superb synthesis of the literature on women's shifting public role in Great Britain; on the American side, see Rosemary Zagarri, "The Rights of Man and Woman in Post-Revolutionary America," *William and Mary Quarterly* 3d ser., 55 (1998), pp. 203–30; Mary P. Ryan, *Women in Public: Between Banners and Ballots, 1825–1880* (Baltimore, 1990).

Chapter 6
Women of Revelation:
Jemima Wilkinson and Joanna Southcott

While Richard Brothers languished in a private asylum and Nimrod Hughes was still a twinkle in the eye of America's neophyte urban press, an unlettered seamstress from England's provincial southwest was beginning her remarkable rise to fame as the revolutionary era's premier prophet. Alone among her peers, Joanna Southcott has been the recipient of serious scholarly as well as popular interest in the nearly two centuries since her death; alone among her peers, she continues to be a living presence in the contemporary world of Anglo-American millenarianism, as offshoots of her enormous following dispersed throughout the English-speaking world in the 1830s and 1840s, spawning numerous local societies who today trace their lineage back to the Devonshire prophetess in a series of generational and theological "dispensations."

While Southcott has garnered the lion's share of historical attention, much of it negative, her popularity in fact was built on the backs of hundreds of obscure men and women who kept the flame of millennial hope alive in the inhospitable climate of the late eighteenth century. We can trace a direct line of connection from Richard Brothers to Southcott through figures like Nathaniel Brassey Halhed and the engraver William Sharp, but even more important in creating a mass audience for Southcott's millenarian message were her fellow "women of revelation" who embodied in their very persons the biblical promise of violent regeneration. Women like the Philadelphian Jane Lead (whom we encountered in Chapter 3), the renegade French Prophets Hannah Wharton and Mary Plewitt, the Shaker Ann Lee, along with a host of lesser lights like Mary Mercin, Sarah Flaxmer, Elspeth Buchan, and Dorothy Gott, constituted a distinct female tradition of British millenarianism whose roots lay in the radical sectarian challenges of the 1640s. The female prophets of the Civil War era were true women warriors, fearlessly attacking the very foundations of the British ecclesiastical and civil order with bold gestures of contempt.[1] Revo-

---

[1] Phyllis Mack, "Women as Prophets During the English Civil War," *Feminist Studies* 8 (Spring 1992), pp. 19–45; Keith Thomas, "Women and the Civil War Sects," *Past and Present* 13 (1958), pp. 46–62.

lutionary-era female prophets were a remarkably tame group by the standards of the seventeenth century, but they did not entirely repudiate the aggressive iconoclasm of their forebears. Women had a unique role to play in the apocalyptic script, foreshadowed by the ancient Hebrew prophetesses, and Southcott, like her predecessors, was determined to carry out this mission. "Is it a new thing for a Woman to deliver her people?" she demanded. "Did not Esther do it? Did not Judith do it?"[2]

The women of revelation faced a new set of political and cultural barriers, however, that their Civil War counterparts were spared. The "patrician hegemony" of church and state, so vulnerable in the 1640s, had been secured by a hundred years' offensive against the forces of disorder (dissenters, republicans, infidels), a campaign that blended appeasement and repression in a disarming mix.[3] Men and women were freer to express their opinions and air their discontents in the eighteenth century than they had been before 1688, even to congregate in dissenting societies and petition for collective redress, but in an important sense their opinions mattered less. Firebrands, whether religious fanatics or political radicals, were (for the most part) no longer imprisoned or punished for blasphemy or sedition, but neither did they inspire revolutionary movements on the same scale as the Levellers, Diggers, and Commonwealth men. The government had learned an important lesson: it was better to laugh at than to hang heretics, to provide just enough latitude for malcontents to harangue themselves into cultural oblivion. By providing commoners relatively unfettered access to the world of cheap print and easing the restrictions on heterodox religious worship, England's governing elite achieved what Parliament had been unable to do without bloodshed 150 years before—quiet the voices of anger and despair before they exploded in violence. It was a remarkable achievement, given the depth of popular grievance, and one that would ensure the security and power of the propertied classes well into the nineteenth century.[4] Religious dissenters were partially complicit in this extralegal disarming of the "mob," and the radical wing of Protestant dissent—including millenarians—paid a high price for their acquiescence. What women prophets faced in the late eighteenth century was a formidable alliance of writers, critics, and politicians

[2] Joanna Southcott, *A Warning to the World: Joanna Southcott's Prophecies* (London, 1804), p. 52.

[3] J. C. D. Clark, *English Society, 1660–1832*, 2d ed. (Cambridge, 2000).

[4] On the triumph of conservative ideology in the face of considerable popular pressure, see H. T. Dickinson, "Popular Conservatism and Militant Loyalism," in *Britain and the French Revolution, 1789–1815*, ed. H. T. Dickinson (London, 1989), pp. 103–26.

with the will and resources to bury genuine discontent under an avalanche of hearty condescension. Against such a protean and ubiquitous enemy, their chances of success were slim.

Women, of course, were not alone in this battle. Male prophets too endured stinging critiques of their visions and dreams from a broad array of opponents. But the contempt directed at female prophets was different in kind and magnitude from that faced by men like Richard Brothers and Nimrod Hughes. Men at least had a recognizable place in the public sphere as thinkers and writers, however eccentric or crazy their opinions. And male prophets did not surrender this advantage cheaply: as we saw in Chapter 4, they labored to speak and write within the acceptable parameters of polite discourse, even if their efforts were frequently ridiculed. Skeptics might debate whether Richard Brothers was a lunatic or an impostor, or even a traitor, but they rarely questioned his right to exercise a public voice in a forum of his own choosing. Many even accorded him the status of a "gentleman," at least as far as his manners and public demeanor were concerned. Coarser specimens like Nimrod Hughes did not enjoy the protective covering of a (perhaps superficial) gentility, but even Hughes was not without cultural resources. Every newspaper that mocked his pamphlet also advertised its availability for purchase and gave implicit support to his alarmist views by printing his prophecies alongside breathless warnings of other imminent disasters. Women prophets enjoyed few such advantages. Most received no recognition, either positive or negative, in the popular press, and the few who did appear in print were subjected to vicious commentary that denied the very possibility that a woman might legitimately act or speak for others, God included. As one discerning journalist said in mock defense of Southcott, "Why should the old lady be silenced, when W. Huntington, S.S., was permitted to rave[?]"[5] This chapter contrasts the reception that two of the more visible women of revelation received in their respective communities: Jemima Wilkinson, the only woman to achieve a public following in revolutionary America, and Joanna Southcott—the most famous, and last, prophet of them all. One left barely a trace in her native society; the other was the object of fanatical devotion. The careers of both exemplify the intractable hostility of Anglo-American men of letters toward women in public.

[5] *Morning Chronicle,* Aug. 24, 1814, p. 4. The comparison is to the millenarian William Huntington, S.S. (or Sinner Saved, as he designated himself).

Jemima Wilkinson, the "Publick Universal Friend"

In 1776, a strange tale unfolded in a small town in Rhode Island. A young Quaker, Jemima Wilkinson, took to her bed in the midst of a lingering illness, appearing several hours later with a miraculous tale of death and rebirth. She had, so her followers claimed, died and been reincarnated as the Second Coming of Christ—a transfiguration so complete that she refused from that point on to answer to the name Jemima Wilkinson. Rising from her bed, the "Publick Universal Friend," as she insisted upon being called, began a long career as a preacher and prophet that would take her from the cozy villages of New England to the wilds of New York's Indian country. A new prophet had been born, or rather, reborn.[6]

Wilkinson's ministry coincided exactly with the opening skirmishes of America's colonial rebellion, and her message clearly resonated with a people on the brink of war. In the words of Ruth Pritchard, "The Friend of Sinners began to serve In the year 1777 When this Nation was still in arms and America had embroiled her hands in human blood." Rhode Island declared its independence from Britain in May 1776, and within months British troops occupied the town of Newport, a strategic post they would not relinquish for three years. When the British finally left, the French moved in, making Newport their headquarters in North America until 1781. For most of the war, then, Wilkinson's native state was under foreign occupation and its population subject to the worst indignities of war—prisoners in their own homes when not reluctant combatants in what many regarded as (in the words of one of her followers) an "unnatural war."[7] Wilkinson's sermons fit the unquiet tenor of the times. Abner Brownell, a believer who later wrote a critical account of his mentor, faithfully recorded the Friend's sermons in the diary he kept before his apostasy. His record gives us a good glimpse into the artful weaving of apocalyptic and martial themes in Wilkinson's oratory. On November 9, 1779, the Friend preached on the Old Testament story of the prophet Samuel's confrontation with King Agag. "And Samuel hewed Agag in pieces before the Lord in which was shewn to them (by way of a Parable) that as it was now about the time that the British Troops had Evacuated and

---

[6] An old but still useful biography of Wilkinson is Herbert A. Wisbey, Jr., *Pioneer Prophetess: Jemima Wilkinson, the Publick Universal Friend* (Ithaca, N.Y., 1964). More recently, Catherine Brekus has explored Wilkinson's theology and her struggles as a female preacher in an era of changing gender norms in *Strangers and Pilgrims: Female Preaching in America, 1745 to 1845* (Chapel Hill, N.C., 1998), pp. 80–97.

[7] Diary of Abner Brownell, 2 vols., 1:3, American Antiquarian Society, Worcester, Mass.

Left Rhodeisland, that Now they thought that the Difficultest and most Distressing time was over, but it was told them, that if they did not Now repent of all their abominations and Evil ways, as Killing and Destroying one another and Committing all manner of Immoralities and going on in all manner of Wickedness, Like Sodom and Gomorrah . . . that God would eer long bring on Some more heavier Judgment, and make them Examples of his Vengeance."[8] Wilkinson's sermons were fairly bloody by the standards of the day—"She Preaches up Terror very alarming," noted a supporter.[9] "Behold the day of the Lord cometh," she warned, "cruel both with wrath & fierce anger, to lay the land desolate; and He will destroy the sinners thereof out of it."[10] The list of targets whom God will "number to the Sword" was long— "the fearfull and unbelieving and abominable & Dogs & Sorcerers & Whoremongers and all Lyers shall have their part in the Lake that Burns with Fire & Brimstone"—though she singled out a range of Old Testament evildoers for special punishment: witches, whores, fornicators, "painted Jezebels."[11] Not exactly the language of "civil millennialism" or "Christian republicanism" or even republican motherhood, Wilkinson's "fire and brimstone" oratory was relatively untouched by the more genteel versions of evangelical rhetoric then circulating in the republic of letters.[12]

As we might expect from a prophet so steeped in the language of the Old Testament, Wilkinson displayed a fondness for regal imagery that further complicates her relationship to the revolutionary movement unfolding around her. Like Richard Brothers, the Friend often imagined herself in the role of a king or royal avenger. In one particularly dramatic vision, the Friend and her company, "ranged along as it were in martial order in Twelve Columns," defeat a rich and powerful emperor (whose cloven foot reveals his

[8] Brownell Diary, 2:31.

[9] Quoted in Wisbey, *Pioneer Prophetess*, pp. 18, 28.

[10] Ruth Spencer's Sermon Book, 1795, Jemima Wilkinson Papers, 1771–1849, Department of Manuscripts and University Archives, Cornell University Library, Ithaca, N.Y. (hereafter JW Papers).

[11] [A Universal Friend to All Mankind], *Some Considerations Propounded to the Several Sorts and Sects of Professors of this Age* (Providence, 1779), p. 82; Friend to Sarah Richards, Mar. 11, 1787, JW Papers.

[12] On "civil millennialism," see Nathan O. Hatch, *The Sacred Cause of Liberty* (New Haven, 1977); on "Christian republicanism," see Mark Noll, "The American Revolution and Protestant Evangelicalism," *Journal of Interdisciplinary History* 23 (1993), pp. 615–38; on republican motherhood, see Linda K. Kerber, *Women of the Republic: Intellect and Ideology in Revolutionary America* (New York, 1980). All three phrases connote the taming of evangelical language by its incorporation into the language of civic republicanism during the revolutionary movement.

true identity) on a desolate battlefield. As "Smoke of a purple Couler" issues from her mouth, the triumphant Friend and her band of warriors "[walk] on the men, Stamping them small with their feet, small as the dust of the earth."[13] While some listeners heard treason in her denunciations of those who "have persisted in rebellion against the King of heaven," many appreciated the urgency of her message as yet another call to arms.[14] True, she made no attempt to choose sides in the rebellion, and patriots and loyalists alike flocked to her banner, but it would be a mistake to see Wilkinson's career as detached from the political currents swirling around her. With the air full of prophetic warnings, the addition of her particularly strident voice contributed to the general feeling in the mid-1770s that Americans faced a decision of apocalyptic import. Those who heeded the Friend would most likely find themselves on the side of rebellion.

Still, scandal and charges of political disloyalty followed the Friend wherever she went. As Brownell noted, "The Manner, Appearance and Method of her coming forth as a Preacher different from all other Sects or Denominations of People" created an "Abundance of strange Reports spread abroad concerning her, some false and some true, which produces Abundance of Spectators and Enquirers."[15] She was accused of a variety of fanciful crimes, most patently absurd even to those who invented them—seducing her most prominent supporter, an elderly judge; inducing her female followers to leave their husbands and abandon their children; covering up a pregnancy which resulted from an illicit affair with a British officer—as well as blasphemy and imposture. As the crowds grew, so too did public hostility. Wilkinson was a bold and charismatic performer, riding into town with an entourage of two dozen attendants that never failed to attract attention. "Saw Jemimy Wilkerson the Imposter," the Reverend John Pitman noted in his diary on September 22, 1783, "with a number of Deluded Creatures that go about with her standing &c. in the Road about 4 1/2 Miles from Providence."[16] Beginning in the 1780s, Wilkinson widened the scope of her ministry to include Pennsylvania as well as her native New England, a move that backfired. In the Quaker capital, the crowds turned violent, throwing "brickbats" and other debris at her company outside their lodgings and interrupting her assemblies with noisy demonstrations. A rumor that one of her

---

[13] "Religious Allegory," undated, JW Papers.

[14] [A Universal Friend], *Some Considerations*, p. 90.

[15] Abner Brownell, *Enthusiastical Errors, Transpired and Detected* (New London, Conn., 1783), p. 8.

[16] Quoted in Wisbey, *Pioneer Prophetess*, p. 54.

closest followers, Abigail Daton, had tried to murder a young woman in her sleep received wide coverage in the local press. The Friend's letters show her mounting frustration. "I have Been very much troubled about thee for fear of Treacherous Dealers," she wrote Sarah Richards in 1787. "I have been to Philadelphia more than once, and am Some acquainted with people there and their ways & their Doings—And due know if it were possible they would Deceive the verry Elect. . . . I do Know that you are Sent fourth as lamb Among Wolve[s]. . . . I Believe that the wicked will find some other Business to due before it is long Besides publishing me and them that Desire to due well in News Papers."[17]

Finally, in 1790, the Friend made the decision to give up her public ministry and retreat to a place of refuge. "I have long prayed that there might be a peaceful habitation for me & my friends to dwell somewhere," she wrote a trusted adviser in 1788. "I am determined not to dwell with revilers for I am weary of them that hate peace."[18] As so many religious seekers did in the late eighteenth and early nineteenth centuries, she and a small band of believers relocated to western New York and founded a community she named "Jerusalem." Scores of letters survive from her beleaguered followers during the years on the road, in which they speak longingly of their desire for the Friend. Having made the painful decision to "[leave] Father and Mother, Brother and Sister, according to the Flesh, which was a day of great Sorrow and Trouble" to join the Friend, her followers too often found themselves abandoned during the itinerant years of her ministry, thrust into a kind of spiritual purgatory they found unbearable.[19] Mary Brannel was "sick for want of seeing the Friend." Sarah Richards, a widow who was Wilkinson's second-in-command and an epileptic, was often distraught over her separation from the Friend. "If I may only see the Friend's face once more in Time," she wrote in 1790. "Oh my ailing heart, I will write no more. I pray the Friend to remember me for my trouble on the Friend's account can't be told." Ruth Spencer turned to the lyrical prose of the Bible to express her longing. "I would follow no Voice but Thine. . . . O Blessed Friend, Entreat me not to leave Thee . . . for where Thou goest I will go."[20] The reunification of the scattered community in New York was thus both a practical and emotional necessity for a people who had renounced all that was familiar and dear

---

[17] Letter from Friend to Sarah Richards, Mar. 11, 1787, JW Papers.
[18] Friend to James Parker, 1788, JW Papers.
[19] Brownell Diary, 2:49.
[20] Sarah Richards to Friend, Oct. 1787; Sarah Richards to Friend, Aug. 3, 1790; Ruth Spencer to Friend, n.d., JW Papers.

(including, for many, marriage and family) for an uncertain and dangerous future. One convert, William Carter, was imprisoned by his "most intimate friends" when he "declar[ed] my Selfe a Friend." He pleaded to be allowed to join Wilkinson in Jerusalem; "I can say although at a great distance, yet my Heart is with thee and the dear friends in the western World, and I hope it may be the divine [will] to permit me soon to leave this Wicked Country."[21] By 1800, the settlement had some 260 inhabitants, and the Friend had become deeply involved in local affairs, from mediating disputes between white settlers and the resident Indians (who called her Squaw Shinnewanagistawge, or "Great Woman Preacher") to attacking slavery. This utopian experiment did not long survive her death in 1819 at the age of sixty-seven; within two decades the sect had entirely disappeared, leaving behind a complicated legal tangle over property claims and an unsavory regional reputation.

To understand Wilkinson's relationship to American millenarian culture, we need to look beyond the dynamics of personal charisma to examine her as a public figure. In contrast to Richard Brothers or even Nimrod Hughes, the substance of her prophecies was never the focal point of public debate. Indeed, in comparison with these two millenarians, her prophecies had very little substance: although Abner Brownell suggests that she believed the world would end on May 19, 1780—the infamous "Dark Day" that spawned apocalyptic fears throughout New England—she for the most part avoided making the kind of specific readings of the prophetic scriptures that were the bread and butter of so many other millenarians.[22] When "the time expired and nothing happen'd" in May 1780, "that doctrine seem'd to die away, and there wasn't much said about it afterwards, only it would be in the Lord's own time, &c." More typically, her sermons offered only vague warnings of generic judgments. "After she has taken a text," Brownell explained, "she never expounds or explains much upon it, but leaves it as abstruse as it was before, and then goes on mainly to set forth what she calls the present dispensation . . . so she speaks, unto a dying world, and so she will generally entertain people with a long discourse, in which will be many entertaining and

---

[21] William Carter to Friend, Feb. 25, 1791, JW Papers. By his own account he remained in prison for "more than three months."

[22] The "Dark Day," on which the sun disappeared and all of New England was plunged into darkness around mid-morning, was not an eclipse but the result of the common practice of burning fields to clear the brush more effectively, which produced a coating of ash that blotted out the sun for a period of hours. To many frightened farmers, it was a clear sign that the last days were at hand; see *Some Remarks on the Great and Unusual Darkness that appeared on Friday, May 19, 1780* (Danvers, Mass., 1780), by "A Farmer," for one example of the popular response to this event.

necessary instructions that are very applicable."[23] Such abstruseness was characteristic of much millennial writing in the late eighteenth century, as we saw in Chapter 4, but in Wilkinson's case the attention of her audience was never on the content of her message in the first place. As one observer recalled some years later, "What she said, or of the subject matter, nothing is remembered; but her person, dress and manner is as palpable . . . as though she thus looked and spake but yesterday."[24] What people saw when Jemima Wilkinson took to the pulpit made a greater impression than what they heard.

Popular perception of Wilkinson went through several shifts during her own lifetime and beyond. Questions of identity were at the heart of the public discourse about the Friend, whose legitimacy as a prophet was inextricably bound up with questions about her spiritual and sexual identity as a woman whose body housed the spirit of a man. Brownell tells us that the rumors swirling around Wilkinson began with the curious tale of her rebirth. He first heard of this "remarkable Person of a Female Preacher from a back Town of Providence, call'd Cumberland" in 1778, when a report of "something very remarkable and extraordinary" caught his ear—people said, he recounted, "that she was a Person that was said had been dead for the Space of an Hour, and by the mighty Power of God had been rais'd immediately to a State of Health, and had an immediate call to appear in public Testimony to preach to the People."[25] There were several competing accounts of her "reincarnation" circulating in the 1770s and 1780s, in which her illness was variously ascribed to a high fever, hysteria, or cold-blooded deceit. The prominent Rhode Island merchant Moses Brown thought "Her Case was Like one other he knew of that the fever being Translated to the head She Rose with different Ideas than what She had when the fever was General, and she Conceived the Idea that she had been Dead and was raised Up for Extraordinary Purposes, and got well fast." Other commentators were less generous. David Hudson, who wrote a scathing exposé in 1821, believed she had faked the entire episode.[26]

It was left to nineteenth-century historians to make the case that Wilkinson was in fact crazy; in contrast to the public debate over Richard

[23] Brownell, *Enthusiastical Errors*, p. 15.

[24] Quoted in John F. Watson, *Annals of Philadelphia and Pennsylvania in the Olden Days* (Philadelphia, 1870), p. 554.

[25] Brownell, *Enthusiastical Errors*, pp. 4–5. Brownell provides a less sensational account of his first meeting with the Friend in his unpublished diary; see Brownell Diary, 1:2.

[26] David Hudson, *History of Jemima Wilkinson, A Preacheress of the Eighteenth Century* (Geneva, N.Y., 1821).

Brothers, lunacy was rarely mentioned during her lifetime as the explanation for her vision. The Wilkinson family genealogist grudgingly conceded that his infamous ancestor might well have been the victim of mental illness. "If any one feels disposed to throw the mantle of charity over her strange life, that of mental derangement induced by febrile decease and religious excitement is the only one that would seem to be available." Her most recent biographer endorses this diagnosis, believing that "the fever was part of, or brought on, a mental disturbance that left the young woman under the influence of a form of megalomania."[27] Among those who actually met her, only Ezra Stiles, the president of Yale College and an astute observer of heterodox practices, attributed her illness to "temporary Insanity or Lunacy, or Dementia quo ad hoc." In fact, women prophets in general were rarely accused of lunacy in the revolutionary era, in sharp contrast to their male counterparts, who were far more likely to find themselves at risk of incarceration in an asylum. There were easier, and perhaps less costly, ways to discredit the visions of women than allowing them to pass into the respectable realm of medical diagnosis.

Wilkinson's own "memorandum" of her illness, found tucked into her Bible, identified the "fatal fever" as the "Columbus fever: since call'd the Typus, or malignant fever" and traces its source to a "Ship of War" which appeared in Providence harbor in 1776. This "Awful, and allarming disease," the memorandum continued, "spread more universally across the Country," and struck the Wilkinson household in early October. "On the fourth Day of the 10th Month, on the Seventh Day of the weak, at night, a certain young-woman, known by the name of Jemima Wilkinson was seiz'd with this mortal disease. And on the 2d. Day of her illness, was render'd almost incapable of helping herself."[28] Whatever its origins, the disease reached a crisis point on October 10. "And the fever continued to increase untill fifth Day of the Weak about midnight, [when] She appear'd to meet the Shock of Death."

What happened next was the subject of dispute during the Friend's lifetime. Wilkinson's account is ambiguous enough to leave plenty of room for conflicting interpretations.

The heavens were open'd And She saw too Archangels descending from the east, with golden crowns upon there heads, clothed in long white Robes, down to their feet. . . . And the Angels said, The time is at hand, when God will lift up his hand, a second time, to recover the remnant of his People, whos day is not yet over; and the Angels

---

[27] Rev. Israel Wilkinson, *Memoirs of the Wilkinson Family in America . . . 1645–1868* (Jacksonville, Ill., 1869), p. 437; Wisbey, *Pioneer Prophetess*, pp. 10, 14.

[28] "A Memorandum of the Introduction of the Fatal Fever," undated, JW Papers.

said, The Spirit of Life from God, had descended to earth, to warn a lost and guilty, perishing dying World, to flee from the wrath which is to come; and to give an Invitation to the lost Sheep of the house of Israel to come home; and was waiting to assume the Body which God had prepared, for the Spirit to dwell in. . . . And then taking her leave of the family between the hour of nine & ten in the morning dropt the dying flesh & yielded up the Ghost. And according to the declaration of the Angels,—the Spirit took full possession of the Body it now animates.

Clearly, a death of some kind occurred, and a spiritual transformation of some kind took place as a result. But was Wilkinson really claiming to be the Messiah, come "a second time"? James Manning, president of Rhode Island College, believed she "pretended to be Jesus Christ in the form of a woman," arguing that "when Jesus Christ first appeared, he came in the flesh of a man, but that he is now come in the flesh of a woman."[29] His colleague Ezra Stiles agreed; "she died & is no more Jemima Wilkinson. But upon her Restoration, which was sudden, the person of Jesus Christ came forth & now appears in her body with all the miraculous Powers of the Messiah."[30] Another observer thought there was some ambiguity about the exact nature of the "spirit" who now inhabited the body of Wilkinson. "It is not quite clear," wrote a French visitor, "whether this soul is an emanation of the Virgin Mary or of Jesus Christ himself, and the inspired woman is very reserved in her answers on this point."[31] A convoluted, though not implausible, explanation supposedly given by one of her followers suggests the creative redrawing of the boundary between body and soul within the epistemological orbit of evangelical religion that we explored in Chapter 3. "Some of the society, when asked to explain themselves, do it after the following manner; 'That the name of persons most properly belongs to the soul; but while body and soul are in union, the body may also be called by the name of the soul; but when a person dies and the soul leaves the body, the body then can no more be called by its former name:—now some years ago, there was a person by the name of Jemimah Wilkinson, but she died, and her soul went to heaven, after which the divine spirit re-animated the same body, and it arose from the dead; now the divine inhabitant is Christ Jesus our Lord, the friend to all mankind, and gives his name to the body to which he is united, and therefore body and soul, conjointly, are the universal friend."[32] This long-winded ex-

[29] Quoted in Wilkinson, *Memoirs*, p. 421.
[30] Quoted in Wisbey, *Pioneer Prophetess*, p. 20.
[31] *Our Revolutionary Forefathers: The Letters of François, Marquis de Barbe-Marbois*, trans. and ed. Eugene Parker Chase (New York, 1929), p. 163.
[32] "Account of Jemimah Wilkinson," *American Museum* 1 (Feb. 1787), p. 151.

planation shows just how difficult it was to restore the psychosomatic unity of body and soul whose unraveling had led so many eighteenth-century believers to declare war on the flesh. Wilkinson's solution to the problem—a kind of transplantation of the soul from one host body (Christ's) to another (hers)—was unique.

Or was she, as many sincere believers insisted, a messenger, a prophet in the Old Testament mold? Christopher Marshall believed that "in all the ages of the world God hath had some Special Friends, though perhaps hidden for the most part from the world, because 'they were not of it' with whom in a more familiar and Intimate manner he hath chosen to converse and manifest himself," and that Wilkinson was "one of that happy number."[33] Ezra Stiles recounted in his diary that Wilkinson told a colleague of his that she was not the Messiah but "one raised up by God to give comfort to his people."[34] Wilkinson's own writings, while opaque, offer some clues. The anonymous pamphlet published under the name "A Universal Friend to Mankind" (largely copied verbatim from the *Works* of the Quaker Isaac Pennington though widely believed to be written by Wilkinson) makes a circumstantial case for her divinity. The greatest obstacle to belief in the days of the ancient Jews, the pamphlet argues, was "Christ coming in a way that they looked not for him. They had concluded from the scriptures how Christ must appear; and he coming in a far different manner, they could not own him, but looked upon him as a deceiver." As in Christ's day, so too today. Jesus appeared "in that body of flesh" to the disbelieving Jews, and he appears "(in spirit) in this age."[35] When we add to this Wilkinson's early attempts at faith healing and miracle-working, including an ill-fated attempt to raise a believer from the dead in 1780, the conclusion seems inescapable that the Friend had messianic ambitions.

The question of Wilkinson's true identity—messiah or prophet?— would not have attracted so much attention had she not presented such a striking figure to her audiences. Abner Brownell was startled by his first glimpse of the Friend. Her "outward Appearance seem'd to be something singular and extraordinary, appearing in a different Habit from what is common amongst Women, wearing her Hair curl'd in her Neck, without any other Covering on her Head, except it was when she travel'd out, she put on a Hat much like a Man's, only the Brim flap'd down."[36] Draping herself in

---

[33] Christopher Marshall to Friend, Jan. 28, 1789, JW Papers.
[34] Wisbey, *Pioneer Prophetess*, p. 20.
[35] [A Universal Friend], *Some Considerations*, pp. 8, 41.
[36] Brownell, *Enthusiastical Errors*, pp. 4–5.

severe clerical garb (long black robes unadorned with accessories save a plain black hat and a white neckcloth), forbidding her followers to address her in gendered pronouns, Wilkinson presented a tantalizing if ambiguously gendered persona. Even the most sympathetic observers conceded that her dress was provocative, a loud "call or proclamation to the people at large to 'come, see, and hear.' "[37] (When confronted by a "gentleman" who cautioned her that "the singularity of her appearance would excite many remarks," including "some indecent ones," the Friend retorted, "There is nothing indecent or improper in my dress or appearance; I am not accountable to mortals, *I am that I am*.")[38] The question "messiah or prophet?" often became coded in gendered terms—male or female?—by those who witnessed the Friend's transformation.

Wilkinson's supposed transfiguration was the subject of a lively and occasionally heated exchange in contemporary newspapers and pamphlets from 1783 to 1787 in which her unusual physical appearance was subjected to intense scrutiny. From tip to toe, every aspect of her distinctive dress was noted, analyzed, ridiculed, and rebuked. The descriptions we have are remarkably consistent in the particulars, and, more important, in the sheer level of detail: according to one account, Wilkinson wore a "light cloth Cloke with a Cape like a Man's—Purple Gown, long sleeves to Wristbands—Mans shirt down to the Hands with Neckband—purple handkerchief or Neckcloth tied around the neck like a man's—No Cap—Hair combed turned over & not long—wears a Watch—Man's Hat."[39] The effect was to transpose her spiritual hermaphrodism into the more familiar category of transvestism: "As she is not supposed of either sex, so this neutrality is manifest in her external appearance."[40] Her costume, in fact, presented ambiguous clues that left many viewers puzzled. One described her as "habited partially as a man."[41] Another recalled that "she appeared beautifully erect, and tall for a woman, although at the same time the masculine appearance predominated; which, together with her strange habit, caused every eye to be riveted upon her." Even her underclothes were cause for speculation; "Under [her robe], it is said, her apparel is very expensive; and the form of it conveys the same idea, as her external appearance, of being neither man nor woman."[42] The

[37] *American Museum* 1 (Mar. 1787), pp. 253–54.
[38] *American Museum* 1 (Apr. 1787), p. 335.
[39] Wisbey, *Pioneer Prophetess*, p. 25.
[40] *American Museum* 1 (Feb. 1787), p. 153.
[41] Quoted in Watson, *Annals of Philadelphia*, 1:553.
[42] *American Museum* 1 (Feb. 1787), p. 153.

long dark gown fascinated because of what it concealed rather than what it revealed. "It falls to the feet, without outlining her figure," one disappointed observer wrote, "and its sleeves reveal only the tips of her hands."[43]

What viewers hoped to glimpse beneath the long robe of the Friend was some hint of sexual corruption. The suspicion that women who took on the appearance of men did so to satisfy perverse desires was a long-running theme in the literature on transvestism in the eighteenth century, but Wilkinson's critics were frustrated by the modesty of the prophet, which by all but the most malicious accounts was unquestioned.[44] "She lives soberly, her conduct is good, and her morals are irreproachable," admitted one reluctant admirer.[45] Her harshest critics found little to disapprove of in her personal life, though not for lack of trying. "Whatever obloquy may justly rest on Jemima as an impostor, claiming the gift of prophecy, and the power of performing miracles, or however culpable she may have been in attempting to exercise superhuman authority, or imposing her pretensions on a weak and credulous people, there is no just cause for imputation on her moral character."[46] Frustrated in its attempts to pin any real crimes on Wilkinson, the urban press turned to rumor and innuendo in its eagerness to associate the Friend with the disorder of sexual license. A letter to the *Freeman's Journal* in 1787 ridiculed the supposed modesty of Wilkinson and her female disciples; like Jezebels, the female Friends "paint" their minds as well as their faces and "anoint" their bodies with "nasty stuff" which makes them "smell rather disagreeable" (a hint of venereal disease, perhaps?).[47] The reluctance of one disciple, Abigail Daton, to spell out the word "bed pan" in a letter to the paper in which she defended the Friend as a caring leader provoked ribald scorn; "You call it, I believe, the bed-p——. But what does p— stand for? I thought the Spirit which inspires you never spoke with *dashes*. If I am not mistaken, that *p* means something rather unbecoming the gravity of a prophetess, and you

---

[43] *Our Revolutionary Forefathers*, p. 164.

[44] On tales of transvestism, see Dianne Dugaw, *Warrior Women and Popular Balladry, 1650–1850* (New York, 1989); Julie Wheelwright, *Amazons and Military Maids: Women Who Dressed as Men in Pursuit of Life, Liberty, and Happiness* (London, 1989); Daniel Cohen, " 'The Female Marine' in an Era of Good Feelings: Cross-Dressing and the 'Genius' of Nathaniel Coverly, Jr.," *Proceedings of the American Antiquarian Society* 103 (1994), pp. 359–95.

[45] *Our Revolutionary Forefathers*, p. 166.

[46] Wilkinson, *Memoirs*, p. 438. The local historian Stafford Cleveland, who in general viewed Jemima Wilkinson as a "vulgar Mystagogue," reluctantly agreed that the "nobility and integrity of her character" were undeniable. *History and Directory of Yates County*, 2 vols. (Penn Yann, N.Y., 1873), 1:79.

[47] "To the Most Holy Sybil, Abigail Daton, a Fool by birth and a Prophetess by Profession," *Freeman's Journal*, Aug. 29, 1787.

must have made a sweet figure in the act of performing that charitable office. I would give twenty pounds to have seen you at that precious moment, provided the spirit had not moved you to throw the contents of what you held in my face."[48] Wilkinson and her female followers were really no better than prostitutes, the press implied, unclean in body and habit, even if they assumed the airs of a lady.

Observers were genuinely confused over the sexual nature of this hermaphrodite figure, whose masculine dress disgusted some but whose feminine beauty captivated others. The Marquis de Barbe-Marbois, secretary of the French legation in Philadelphia, was clearly charmed by the prophetess. "This soul sent from heaven has chosen a rather beautiful body for its dwelling," he enthused. "Jemima Wilkinson, or rather the woman whom we call by that name, is about twenty-two years old. She parts her hair on top of her head, and lets it fall onto her shoulders. Her only care for it is to wash it every day in fresh water; she never powders it. She has beautiful features, a fine mouth, and animated eyes." The marquis, a man who prided himself on his superior breeding and cultivation, was bewitched. "If she had been born in France, I imagine she would have played the part of Madame Geoffin [a noted salonnière]. In Italy, she would have improvised verses and belonged to all the academies. They would have burned her in Spain and Portugal."[49] Another eyewitness praised her "glossy black hair" which "fell in profusion around her neck and shoulders, seemingly without art or contrivance—arched black eyebrows and fierce looking black eyes, darting here and there with penetrating glances."[50] Others found her coarse and unattractive, though undeniably still a woman. Wilkinson was "about the middle size of women, not genteel in her person, and rather awkward in her carriage." When she spoke, it was "not in such a way as becomes a meek and good woman" but in a "masculine, authoritative tone of voice," a voice "very grum and shrill for a Woman."[51] The indeterminacy of her gender was the strongest proof available, in the eyes of her many critics, that Jemima Wilkinson was a fraud. Had she and her followers dared to "openly profess to the world who they are in their own imagination, or pretend they are, they would be universally detested." Instead "they go to work more ingeniously . . . by hints and innuendos" that left plenty of room for doubt.[52]

---

[48] Ibid.

[49] *Our Revolutionary Forefathers*, pp. 163–64, 166.

[50] Watson, *Annals of Philadelphia*, p. 554.

[51] *American Museum* 1 (Feb. 1787), p. 152; ibid., p. 338; Brownell, *Enthusiastical Errors*, p. 5; Watson, *Annals of Philadelphia*, p. 554.

[52] "Further Account of Jemimah Wilkinson," *American Museum* 1 (Apr. 1787), p. 334.

This confusion extended beyond the Friend to her closest disciples, many of whom were portrayed in the press as characters of indeterminate spiritual and sexual status. A nineteenth-century biographer credits Wilkinson with bestowing the names of ancient prophets on her inner circle (Sarah Richards was the prophet Daniel, another woman was the prophet Enoch, and a third John the Beloved)—a claim that has some contemporary support.[53] Ezra Stiles, who was no friend of enthusiasts but nonetheless curious enough about Wilkinson to invite her to tea, recalled Alice Potter Hazard telling him, "That the Univ. friend has anointed her (Alice Haz'd) to be a prophet, and accord'y she predicts the day of Judgt. to come in half a year."[54] These satellite prophets were as ambiguously gendered as their mentor. Sarah Richards "would be a comely person, were she to dress as becomes her sex. But as she imitates the person they call the friend, in her external appearance and particularly in wearing her hair down like a man, she is by that means somewhat disfigured. It is said she is now clothed in what they call sackcloth (that is mourning), in which she is to fulfill the days of her prophecy." James Parker, on the other hand, was "artful, conceited, and illiterate," a man so inept at the art of prophecy that he had to resort to trickery to persuade people he was really the prophet Elijah. According to Thomas Morris, Parker "would, before prophesying, wear around the lower part of his waist, a bandage or girdle, tied very tight, and when it had caused the upper part of his stomach to swell, he would pretend to be filled with prophetic visions."[55] If Wilkinson and Richards were women masquerading as men, the men in their society were described as weak and effeminate. They wore "large round flipped hats, and long flowing straight locks, with a sort of melancholy wildness in their countenances, and an effeminate dejected air." By "general assertion," reported another visiting Frenchman, they were believed to have "literally followed the precept of 'making eunuchs of themselves for Christ's sake.' "[56]

Wilkinson's gender identity thus floated somewhere in between two cultural types that would come to embody the moral ambiguities of post-revolutionary America, the "confidence man" and the "painted woman." As a symbol of both imposture and seduction—vices that blended masculine power and feminine guile into a dangerous mix—Jemima Wilkinson became

[53] Wilkinson, *Memoirs*, p. 432.
[54] *The Literary Diary of Ezra Stiles*, 3 vols. (New York, 1901), 2:381.
[55] *Freeman's Journal* 1 (Feb. 1787); Morris quoted in Wisbey, *Pioneer Prophetess*, p. 180.
[56] Marquis de Chastellux, *Travels in North America in the Years 1780, 1781, and 1782*, trans. Howard C. Rice, Jr., 2 vols. (Chapel Hill, N.C., 1963), 1:322.

a focal point for republican anxieties about the precarious nature of civic and familial bonds in a world of uncertain sexual boundaries.[57] The debate over her dress took place in the context of a sustained conversation among literate Americans about the nature of social and national identity after the Revolution. The new urban press, in which most contemporary observations of Wilkinson appeared, engaged its readers in serious and thoughtful inquiries into the latest scientific and philosophical traditions emanating from Europe.[58] Lockean sensationalist psychology, modified by commonsense thought, provided a new paradigm for understanding the role of environment in shaping the individual (and the national) character.[59] Samuel Stanhope Smith's essay on "the causes of the variety of complexion and figure in the human species," serialized in the periodical press, surveyed the entire sweep of human history to conclude that "the features of the human countenance are modified, and its entire expression radically formed, by the state of society. . . . Every passion, and mode of thinking, has its peculiar countenance."[60] Social states were, so to speak, marked on the body in ways that both thrilled and discomfited postrevolutionary Americans. The debilitating social effects of monarchy and aristocracy (effeminacy and enervation) could be erased by the institution of republican forms of government, but by the same token the republican polity was itself in danger of being deformed by the corrupting influence of "others" (blacks, Indians, women, the poor) in the population. It was feared that the "poor labouring classes" would mark their social superiors with the same depravity that they exhibited in their "coarse ruddiness" if allowed to participate fully in political life, and—more ominously—the white skin of southern planters was in danger of being permanently darkened by constant exposure to the vicious habits of their slaves.

[57] Karen Halttunen, *Confidence Men and Painted Women: A Study of Middle-Class Culture in America, 1830–1870* (New Haven, 1982); Jan Lewis, "The Republican Wife: Virtue and Seduction in the Early Republic," *William and Mary Quarterly* 3d ser., 44 (1987), pp. 689–721.

[58] For an overview of these magazines, see Frank Luther Mott, *A History of American Magazines, 1741–1850* (Cambridge, Mass., 1930); and James Playsted Wood, *Magazines in the United States*, 3d ed. (New York, 1971). The Philadelphia magazine *American Museum*, in which most of the articles about Jemima Wilkinson appeared, was the largest of these new urban periodicals, with a subscription list of about 1,250 (Mott, p. 101). See also David Paul Nord, "A Republican Literature: Magazine Reading and Readers in Late-Eighteenth-Century New York," in *Reading in America*, ed. Cathy N. Davidson (Baltimore, 1985), pp. 114–39.

[59] Jay Fliegelman, *Prodigals and Pilgrims: The American Revolution Against Patriarchal Authority, 1750–1800* (New York, 1982).

[60] *American Museum* 6 (Sept. 1789), p. 186; Samuel Stanhope Smith, *An Essay on the Causes of the Variety of Complexion and Figure in the Human Species*, ed. Winthrop D. Jordan (Cambridge, Mass., 1965; orig. pub. 1787).

"A dark colour, once contracted," warned one writer, "will be many ages before it can be entirely effaced. . . . The negro colour may, by the exposure of a poor and servile state, be rendered almost perpetual."[61]

The moral and physical boundaries of the self were thus conceived of as permeable and malleable in the new scientific discourse of the late eighteenth century. The environment imprinted its features on the bodies and souls of its inhabitants through the benign influence of climate or the more invidious influence of social custom. The physical alteration observed in the pigmentation of white southerners was a consequence both of the tropical climate of the region and the moral erosion of civilized values by the proximity of brutish slaves. On occasion, this fantasy of altered bodies took on a macabre quality, as in Francis Hopkinson's grotesque account of the "Dialogues of the Dead" in an early issue of the *American Museum*. "Bodies have no palpable outlines," the Pennsylvania doctor insisted. "There is not to be found in all nature a truly solid body. [When] bodies lie so near each other, their atmospheres interfere, there must be actual intercourse of parts between them . . . and by a communication of parts, sentiments may be conveyed from one incarnate body to another." By this logic even the line separating death from life was breachable—in Hopkinson's nightmarish vision of postrevolutionary society, dead bodies conversed with one another and with the living as their essences were dispersed into the "atmosphere."[62]

That such an insidious process of assimilation across racial, class, and gender boundaries was already in progress was all too evident to the editors and contributors of these (mostly conservative) periodicals. The urban press provided numerous examples of mutant bodies and sudden transfigurations, in response to an apparently insatiable appetite among postrevolutionary Americans for stories about the bizarre and the inexplicable. "Motley coloured" or pye negroes, mermaids, and remarkable "alterations" of color in both Africans and Indians appear regularly in the pages of the *American Museum* and the *Columbian Magazine* in the 1780s and 1790s, juxtaposed with lengthy essays on the merits of the new federal constitution and the need to stamp out religious fanaticism.[63] A graphic description of two mulatto children exhibited at the American Philosophical Society in 1784 was provided

---

[61] *American Museum* 6 (Aug. 1789), pp. 125, 276.

[62] "Some Account of a New Work, Entitled Dialogues of the Dead," *American Museum* 1 (Mar. 1787), pp. 257–58.

[63] For example: "Account of a Remarkable Alteration of Colour in a Negro Woman," *American Museum* 4 (Dec. 1788), pp. 501–2; "Remarkable Change in the Complexion of an Indian," ibid., p. 558; "Account of an Extraordinary Lufus Naturae," *American Museum* 6.

for the voyeuristic pleasure of the *American Museum*'s subscribers in 1788, followed several issues later by a detailed account of the physical deformities of the "free-martin" and other "mutilated animals" whose genitals exhibit "an equal mixture of both sexes."[64]

Social hermaphroditism was also a recurring motif of essays on the pernicious habits of urban men and women in the new republic. A satirical poem celebrating the appearance of such hybrid creatures as the "Man-Milliner" praised the "strange reverses" taking place in American homes.

Husbands the distaff take—wives seize the club,
At home their Hercules to drub.
While *sir* appears so feminine and trim,
And *madam* looks so masculine and grim,
You scarce know *him* from *her*, or *her* from *him*.[65]

The magazines chided men for assuming female manners, and women for acting like men; "governing women" and "submitting husbands," both abominations of nature, had become all too common in domestic parlors, while a new category of "social being" made its appearance in the leisured spaces of the new city—the "*ambosexual* order of tatlers."[66] Examples of the barbarous gender customs found abroad (especially in the "savage" continents of Africa and Asia) reinforced the moral lesson; in the archipelago island of Metelin, "manly ladies seem to have changed sexes with the men. The woman rides astride—the man sits sideways upon the horse."[67] In post-revolutionary America, it was genteel men in particular ("ye macaronies of the age") who were in danger of losing their masculinity altogether in the presence of greedy women of leisure who consumed sex and foreign luxuries in equal measure. "The nearer a man assimilates himself to female manners, capacities, and softness, the more acceptable [to the fair sex]," complained

---

(Nov. 1789), p. 350; "Account of a White Negro," *American Museum* 5 (Mar. 1789), p. 234; "Account of Turtle with Two Heads," *American Museum* 8 (Aug. 1790), p. 85; "Account of Mermaid," *American Museum* 8 (Oct. 1790), p. 192. See Joanne Pope Melish, *Disowning Slavery: Gradual Emancipation and "Race" in New England, 1780–1860* (Ithaca, N.Y., 1998), for a superb discussion of these stories of racial transfiguration.

[64] "Some Account of a Motley Coloured, or Pye Negro Girl, and Mulatto Boy," *American Museum* 3 (Jan. 1788), p. 38; "An Account of the Free-Martin, or Hermaphrodite Cow," ibid., p. 521. See also another "Account of the Free-Martin" in *Columbian Magazine* 1 (Sept. 1787), pp. 651–52.

[65] "Prologue to the Man-Milliner," *New York Journal*, Feb. 8, 1788.

[66] *Columbian Magazine* 2 (Aug. 1788), p. 449.

[67] "Singular Customs at Metelin," *American Museum* 12 (Oct. 1792), p. 230.

one writer. "On no other principle can we account for the effeminacy, lepidity, and languid lassitude of our modern beaux."[68] The term "coxcomb" came to describe, not a flirtatious woman as prior usage would suggest, but increasingly a man who forfeited the rights of masculinity by "assimilating" to femininity.

One could be tempted to dismiss these accounts of bizarre deformities as evidence of the vulgar popularizing of literary tastes in the age of "democratic eloquence," were it not for the undercurrent of political anxiety which runs through these reports.[69] Wilkinson appeared at a particularly anxious moment in the history of American gender politics, a moment when, in the words of the *Worcester Spy*, Americans had "broken the line that divided the sexes."[70] Women were drawn into the war against Britain in a variety of capacities—as camp followers who serviced the troops in the field, as spies and informants, as local enforcers of nonconsumption agreements, as "Daughters of Liberty" who staged public demonstrations, and as consumers and producers both in the vital economic battles that constituted a highly effective second front during the war. Highly visible in their local communities, women patriots found it difficult to translate the moral authority gained as guardians of the home front into concrete political gains as they faced a determined consensus among the rebel leaders about the unsuitability of women for public service. With no conceptual space in which to formulate a persuasive theory of female citizenship, women who aspired to a greater role beyond that of "republican motherhood" were labeled "amazons."[71]

The Revolution, in other words, had created social forms "which nature never intended to create."[72] Among the mutant offspring of the political experiment undertaken so rashly in 1776 were women warriors, and men who changed political positions as well as races or genders with bewildering ease. In an age of "changes and revolutions," man is the most "variable" being on earth. "He is a creature perpetually falling out with himself, and sustains two or three opposite characters every day he lives."[73] The fierce, overwrought

[68] *American Museum* 10 (Appendix 1, 1791), p. 8; *American Museum* 3 (Mar. 1788), p. 267; *American Museum* 3 (June 1788), p. 508; *American Museum* 6 (Sept. 1789), p. 240.

[69] Kenneth Cmiel, *Democratic Eloquence: The Fight over Popular Speech in Nineteenth-Century America* (New York, 1990).

[70] *Worcester Spy*, Apr. 24, 1788.

[71] On women's role during the revolutionary war, see Mary Beth Norton, *Liberty's Daughters: The Revolutionary Experience of American Women, 1750–1800* (Boston, 1980); Kerber, *Women of the Republic*.

[72] *American Museum* 1 (Jan. 1787), p. 54.

[73] *American Museum* 1 (June 1787), p. 559.

debates over growing partisanship in the late 1780s and 1790s provided a troubling glimpse of the protean nature of personal and political identity in postrevolutionary America. A man who was as variable in his political opinions as in his fashion habits, who changed his character to suit the prevailing political winds, was—like Wilkinson herself—a "mongrel form," as a fable about treason put it.[74] As a woman who violated most conventional categories of being (sacred and profane, body and soul, male and female, even life and death), Wilkinson thus represented everything the new republic most detested and feared. It was this ambiguity of sexual status more than her masculine appearance that most unsettled her audiences, and they responded by attempting to fix her identity via a searching examination of the external signs of dress, voice, gesture, and demeanor.

Above all, Jemima Wilkinson was, most emphatically, not a "natural" woman. The urban press devoted a great deal of energy to delineating the attributes of this sublime if elusive figure. One exemplar, the apocryphal "Louisa," "is (what nature intended her to be) wholly a woman. She has a quality, that is the direct opposite to manliness and vigour. Her voice is gentle; her pronunciation delicate; her passions are never suffered to be boisterous; she never talks politics; she never foams with anger; she is seldom seem in any masculine amusements. . . . I will venture to prophecy, that she will never canvass for votes at an election. I never saw her in an unfeminine dress, or her features discomposed with play."[75] On every score, Jemima Wilkinson was the perfect antithesis of "Louisa." And unnatural women—like the unnatural governments they were thought to give birth to—were creatures marked for extinction in republican America.[76]

In the nineteenth century, Wilkinson's media image underwent a curious metamorphosis from antirepublican harpy to barren spinster. Her self-imposed exile in western New York improved neither her appearance nor her reputation, according to a steady stream of visitors who traveled to Jerusalem

[74] "The Birds, the Beasts, and the Bat," *Columbian Magazine* 1 (Mar. 1787), p. 346. In this fable, written during the revolutionary war in 1778, the bat—"half-bird, half-beast"—cannot make up its mind which side of the battle between the birds and the beasts to support, presenting himself first in one form and then another. In the end, his "mongrel form" leads to political exile as he is not accepted by either camp.

[75] *American Museum* 11 (May 1792), p. 195.

[76] As Carole Pateman and Joan Landes have argued, Lockean political theory was predicated on a reformulation of the categories of "nature" and "society." Characteristics (including gender) that had previously been part of the social order were reassigned to nature and thereby newly authenticated by Lockean liberalism; see Pateman, *The Sexual Contract* (Stanford, Calif., 1988); and Landes, *Women and the Public Sphere in the Age of the French Revolution* (Ithaca, N.Y., 1988).

to see this strange man-woman for themselves. A travel piece published in the literary magazine *Portfolio* in 1810 described the elderly prophetess in unflattering terms, as "a corpulent woman, masculine featured, her hair (nearly gray) combed back," whose conversation betrayed the coarsening effect of social isolation. "Neither her tone of voice nor manner bespoke much intercourse with the world, and nothing with the polite part of it."[77] Another visitor to Jerusalem in the final years of the Friend's reign likewise found her "illiterate in her conversation, and so ignorant of worldly concerns as scarcely to be enabled to understand a common newspaper."[78] Where spectators in the 1780s saw a raven-haired beauty who dressed provocatively and had a sharp tongue, those who saw the prophetess in her later years found her dull and unattractive.

As the years passed, Wilkinson diminished even further in stature, betrayed by both her aging body and the greed of her followers. An article on "Jemima, the Friend" published in the mid-twentieth century told a cautionary tale of a haughty woman brought low by her own ambition. Once "easy to look at," with "raven hair of great luster, and dark hypnotic eyes," the Friend "grew more dictatorial" as her community prospered. "The former little Quaker girl had learned to like luxury and she showed it, living on the backwoods frontier like an Oriental queen." Near the end of her life, she had become a repulsive figure—"fat and ugly with dropsy." "Her marvellous beauty deserted her swiftly, and she died in 1819 an embittered old woman."[79] Another modern rendition of the story—a piece in the *New Yorker* on "The Woman Who Died Twice"—was equally cruel in its assessment of the Friend's last days. Bloated with dropsy, "The Friend was distressed, less with the disease than with her loss of physical charm. She became sterner in her insistence on chastity, more wrathful when her disciples gave unmistakeable proof of their sins by having children." Surrounded by "younger and prettier women," her power waning, the Friend grew jealous and despondent.[80]

These contemporary versions emphasized Wilkinson's fading beauty rather than her hermaphrodism in order to make a fairly conservative point about the superiority of modern over primitive times. Once a "winsome woman," a "famous and fascinating beauty" who was "the toast of the local

[77] "A Ride to Niagara," *Portfolio*, Sept. 1810, p. 235. This and other articles can be found in the file of newspaper and magazine clippings about Wilkinson and her society housed at the Yates County Historical Society in Penn Yann, N.Y.

[78] John W. Barber and Henry Howe, "Jemima Wilkinson," *Historical Collections of State of New York* (New York, 1844), p. 605.

[79] "Jemima, the Friend," *American Mercury*, July 4, 1947.

[80] "The Woman Who Died Twice," *New Yorker*, May 9, 1936, p. 47.

lads and the despair of the Cumberland lasses," Jemima Wilkinson became to these modern writers a pathetic symbol of the poverty of religious fanaticism.[81] Readers fortunate to live in more enlightened times could be grateful that such childish fantasies of supernatural power were no longer in fashion. "Were Jemima Wilkinson living in our day, we should doubtless hear of her as a successful 'spirit-medium,' " an essayist for the *Newport Mercury* wrote in 1882. "Yet how distant seems the time when claims such as hers, or such as were advanced by Ann Lee, or still later, by Joanna Southcote, were heard and received. How great a change has been effected in the popular habits of thought by the free press and the common school."[82] Commentators at the time noted the striking similarities between Wilkinson and her fellow "women of revelation," all of whom practiced celibacy and endorsed some vision of female divinity.[83] Though there is no evidence that Wilkinson and Lee ever met, the Friend was aware of her rival's existence: a vision by "M.T." found in her papers describes the appearance of two "full moons" which represent "those two Persons that caused so much talk in the world"; one "had the face of the son of God in it" while the other was "a plane moon."[84] Her followers believed that Lee was "preparing the way for a higher dispensation," and messengers were dispatched to the Shaker communities to "lay a foundation for their receiving the Friend" in the 1790s.[85] To the revolutionary generation, Wilkinson and Lee were serious rivals for the allegiance of America's disoriented religious seekers, two in a crowded field of fanatics and impostors tramping the American countryside sowing chaos and disorder.[86] To a later generation, they were embarrassing reminders of a bygone era, a time when citizens newly emancipated from the shackles of colonial dependency had still not liberated themselves from the tyranny of superstition.

[81] "Women in Our Past," *Providence Journal*, Jan. 3, 1966 ("winsome woman"); "Rare Pamphlet Recalls Beauty, Who Founded R.I. Sect," news clipping from unknown source, Nov. 28, 1930, in Yates County Historical Society, Penn Yann, N.Y. ("famous beauty"); "Preacheress of the Jemimakins," *Yankee*, June 1963 ("toast of local lads").

[82] "Passages from the History of East Greenwich," *Newport Mercury*, Jan. 28, 1882.

[83] For contemporary linkings of Wilkinson to Lee, see Wisbey, *Pioneer Prophetess*, pp. 69–73.

[84] "Vision or Dream of M.T.," JW Papers.

[85] William Carter to Friend Botsford, Mar. 14, 1799, JW Papers.

[86] See Hannah Adams, *An Alphabetical Compendium of the Various Sects Which have appeared in the World from the beginning of the Christian Era to the Present Day* (Boston, 1784), for a survey of these radical sects, ranging from the Dunkers, French Prophets, Sandemanians, and Hopkintonians to the Shakers. Adams included a description of the Universal Friend in the appendix.

The threat that "unnatural" women like Jemima Wilkinson posed to the new republic seemed in the end to have been safely defused by the joint efforts of moralizers and the urban press to strip her character bare, to lay before the American reading public a near-clinical dissection of the forms of deceit possible when faith put on the wrong clothes. Faced with this onslaught of public ridicule she retreated, hoping that once out of sight, her community would be left in peace to pursue its own path to salvation. But she had not counted on the power of public opinion to continually revisit the objects of its fascination. Wilkinson became a living legend, remembered in Yates County well into the twentieth century as a "shrewd, unscrupulous impostor whose tricks won her fleeting notoriety but whose false pretensions ultimately brought on her downfall." When the New Milford Historical Society wanted to erect a historical marker in her honor in the late 1930s, the trustees demurred for fear that it would be defaced or destroyed.[87]

Joanna Southcott, the "Woman Clothed with the Sun"

There was never any doubt that Joanna Southcott was a woman. Not just any woman, but a famous and (among the biblically literate) an easily recognizable one—the woman "clothed with the sun, and the moon under her feet, and upon her head a crown of twelve stars," whose appearance in chapter 12 of the Book of Revelation prefigures the downfall of the Beast. A figure of majesty and power, the "woman of Revelation" was sent to complete the work begun by her biblical ancestors, Eve and Mary. Eve had first introduced sin into the world, Mary had produced the first Christ, whose resurrection signaled the end of sin, and the "woman clothed with the sun" would finish the work of redemption begun by Christ's birth and death by bringing a new savior into the world—the "man-child" destined to "rule all nations with a rod of iron." In this female-centered salvation cycle, women's sexuality is credited with both the creation of evil in the first place, and its eradication at the end of time. God's warning to the serpent who seduced Eve in the Garden of Eden—"I will put enmity between thee and the woman, and between thy seed and her seed. It shall bruise thy head, and thou shalt bruise his head"—was interpreted by a long line of woman prophets in the eighteenth century to mean that God would choose a woman (the "second Eve") to save

[87] Wisbey, *Pioneer Prophetess*, pp. 182–83.

mankind from the first Eve's folly.[88] Southcott was one of many claimants, though certainly the most formidable, to the title of "Woman of Revelation" in the late eighteenth century.

Southcott was born in 1750 in Taleford, Devon, daughter of a tenant farmer whose deep bitterness over a lost inheritance cast a shadow over the entire family. Each child of William Southcott "was to inherit this sense of lost gentility," Joanna most of all, writes James Hopkins.[89] After a youth marked by minor rebellions against authority and a series of failed love affairs (each of which the prophetess would periodically revisit in her communications), Southcott settled into an unremarkable routine as a domestic servant and, later, upholsterer, dependent on the good will of others for her livelihood. In 1792, while working in the market town of Exeter, she had a startling vision. "One night I dreamt I saw men in the air, who pitched with their horses upon the earth. The horses fought furious, and the men fought furious, and so frightened me that I awoke, and thought the French would land." This first prophecy was followed by other visions, and Southcott began hearing "Voices" which later resolved themselves into ongoing "communications" from a "Spirit."[90] It would be another ten years or so before Southcott was confident enough of her prophecies to publish them, though she carefully saved handwritten copies of these early visions for later verification. Her first book, *The Strange Effects of Faith*, was published in 1801, and the flow of publications (sixty-five titles in all) continued at a remarkable pace until her death thirteen years later.

The same questions about the nature and origins of the "Spirit" who animated Jemima Wilkinson's body were raised about Southcott's visitations. Robert Hann, one of the prophet's most prolific critics, argued that Southcott, like Wilkinson, promoted the "heretical" doctrine that "Christ has changed his sex, and is come in the form of a woman." The verse, "My spirit is already come/ You'll find me in the woman's form," found in her *Divine and Spiritual Letters*, he interpreted to mean that Southcott was claiming a

---

[88] For an early example of this reasoning, see the two pamphlets by M. Mercin, *Good News to the Good Women, And to the Bad Women too that will grow better* (London, 1701); and *Two Remarkable Females of Womankind, Fore-Prophecied in the Scriptures, and Given as Signs of the Times* (London, 1701); other prophets who made similar arguments include Susan Eyre, Dorothy Gott, and Sarah Flaxmer. See Anna Clark, "The Sexual Crisis and Popular Religion in London, 1770–1820," *International Journal of Labor and Working Class History* 34 (1988), pp. 56–69.

[89] Hopkins, *A Woman to Deliver Her People*, p. 5.

[90] Joanna Southcott, *Strange Effects of Faith, Second Part; With Remarkable Prophecies* (London, 1802), p. 86.

messianic identity: "The spirit that is represented as dwelling in Joanna, in the woman's form, speaking with *her* mouth, writing with *her* hands, and walking with *her* feet," is "CHRIST" himself. "If it should be asked if any one has seen this strange woman, that was once a man, this female Messiah? The answer is plain. Hast thou seen Joanna? Thou hast seen this metamorphosed Christ also." Hann imagined an interior dialogue in which Southcott, assessing the marketability of her message, plots her deception. "What can I do?" the prophetess asks herself. "I cannot say that I am the Christ, because I am a woman, and Christ is a man. I have but one thing to choose: a metamorphose must take place, either with Christ or me. I must pretend, either that I am changed to the form of a man, or that Christ is changed to the form of a woman; now, which of these two will be the most feasible, and least detectable? If I say, I am made a *man*, the cheat will soon be discovered"—a lesson her American cousin learned the hard way.[91]

Hann was too clever by half; his was a willful distortion of Southcott's position, a barefaced attempt to spark the same kind of gender-bending debate that swirled so maliciously around Jemima Wilkinson in the 1780s. Southcott, unlike Wilkinson, never claimed to embody or regender the spirit of Christ. "Where is thy accuser, that can prove my sex was altered, by my visiting thee in the Spirit?" was God's indignant reply to Hann's pamphlet.[92] Rather, the Spirit spoke to her in words "as distinct to my hearing as if they were spoken in an audible voice."[93] Sometimes she felt the presence of the Spirit so powerfully that she was physically shaken: "All of a sudden, the Spirit entered in me with such power and fury, that my senses seemed lost; I felt as though I had power to shake the house down, and yet I felt as though I could walk in air, at the time the Spirit remained in me; but did not remember many words I said, as they were delivered in such fury that took my senses; but as soon as the Spirit had left me, I grew weak as before."[94] However visceral the encounter, Southcott's relationship with the Spirit was primarily a linguistic, not an incorporative, one. She practiced a form of spiritual ventriloquism, in other words, not spiritual transfiguration. When the Spirit left her, all that remained were the words he had spoken—with the prophetess herself (her thoughts, feelings, desires, and opinions) scrupulously

---

[91] R. Hann, *A Letter to the Right Reverend the Lord Bishop of London concerning the Heresy and Imposture of Joanna the Prophetess* (London, 1810), pp. 9, 16, 25.

[92] Southcott, *Controversy of the Spirit with the Worldly Wise* (London, 1811), p. 37.

[93] Southcott, *A Continuation of the Controversy with the Worldly Wise* (London, 1811), p. 36.

[94] Southcott, *Copies and Parts of Copies of Letters* (London, 1804), pp. 80–81.

elided from these "communications." Snippets of her life story appear in her writings as parables or "shadows" of general social problems, but the prophetess was adamant that her role as an oracle did not encompass her thinking, feeling self.

Nonetheless, Southcott's ventriloquism was not a simple reprise of the trance preaching popularized by the French Prophets a century before. The "divinized speech" of the Camisards was firmly located within the body of the prophet; convulsions and twitchings preceded the appearance of the Lord's voice, which was manifestly different in tone and timbre from the prophet's natural voice. Trance preaching was a form of spirit possession for these early eighteenth-century visionaries, in which the natural self was displaced by a supernatural presence: for a moment, at least, the prophet's self was entirely dissolved in the act of hosting the spirit of God. We spoke earlier of the French Prophets as transitional figures, men and women whose visionary exercises were halfway between the somatic transfiguration of medieval and early modern saints and the theatrical performances of eighteenth-century visionaries. Neither fully possessed by God nor self-contained, the Camisards were demigods, sporting in the demimonde of Restoration London. Revolutionary-era prophets had a difficult time calibrating the ontological boundary between the body and the spirit in an era of shifting physiological paradigms, as we saw in Chapter 3, a dilemma that neither Jemima Wilkinson nor Joanna Southcott ever resolved to their own or their believers' satisfaction. The approaches they took were dramatically different, though rooted in the same paradox: how to be a vessel of God without entirely abandoning the core of one's subjectivity. Southcott spoke for, not as God; she was the empty shell through which flowed the unimpeded voice of the Spirit. Nothing of her true self was implicated or altered in the process. In this way she could claim both the authority of divine inspiration and the credibility of a simple woman who spoke for the dispossessed of the earth.

Her printed "communications," moreover, provided the main link between Southcott and her numerous followers (estimated at the height of her popularity at between 10,000 and 100,000 people), most of whom never saw their leader in person. Southcott was not the mesmerizing preacher that Jemima Wilkinson was, nor the intimate "mother in Israel" that her predecessor Elspeth Buchan was to her Scottish flock in the 1780s. She had no personal relationship of any kind with most of her followers beyond that of author and reader, and even that relationship was attenuated by her insistence that the words she spoke were not hers, but God's. She was, like Susan Eyre ten years before, an "oracle"—not a miracle-worker or suffering martyr.

Southcott's insistence that she was merely a passive "ear" did not entirely persuade. Her readers questioned whether her "communications" flowed from the mind of God or her own perverted imagination. Believers had no doubt who was speaking. "I have lived two years in the same house with her," Thomas Foley assured skeptics, "and can assert with Truth and Confidence, that she has had no assistance whatever, from Men, Books, or any other Sources, but the Invisible Spirit that directs her."[95] Others were equally confident that the "voice" of God was none other than her own thwarted desires. When she spoke of feeling "the hand of the Lord upon her . . . as perfect as ever woman felt the hand of her husband," was this not just "the delirium of sensuality . . . gratified under the imagination of spirituality"? Dismissing her visions as the "witless effloresences of a distracted old woman," scoffers placed the blame squarely on her deformed imagination which was, explained Hann, "a receptacle for vapours."[96] In this critique, standard since the time of the French Prophets, the imagination—or, more precisely, the pathological imagination—has replaced the body as the source of enthusiastical disorders. This trend had been evident since the last decades of the seventeenth century as more secular-minded philosophers began to consider supernatural revelation a "malady of the imagination," but by Southcott's day the critique had reached a level of popular vulgarization that suggested just how successful was the Enlightenment campaign against all forms of "wonder" (including the miraculous). As Lorraine Daston and Katharine Park argue, enlightened intellectuals "did not so much debunk marvels as ignore them. On metaphysical, aesthetic, and political grounds, they excluded wonders from the realm of the possible, the seemly, and the safe." Only the "vulgar"—the ignorant and credulous—continued to believe in, or at least to be entertained by, tales of the marvelous and the fantastic.[97]

Safely consigned to the roomy category of the "vulgar," women like Southcott and those who believed in her mission were the very antithesis of the Enlightenment. "Old, vulgar, and illiterate," the prophetess was the butt of many jokes among educated Englishmen who had one eye nervously

[95] Thomas Foley, *An Answer of the Rev. Thomas P. Foley to the World* (London, 1805), pp. 4–5.

[96] D. Hughson, *The Life of Joanna Southcott: Illustrative of her supposed Mission; Her Erroneous Opinions, and Delusive Prophecies* (London, 1814), pp. 4, 88–89; R. Hann, *The Remarkable Life, Entertaining History and Surprising Adventures of Joanna Southcott, the Prophetess* (London, 1810), p. 31.

[97] Lorraine Daston and Katharine Park, "The Enlightenment and the Anti-Marvelous," chapter 9 in *Wonders and the Order of Nature, 1150–1750* (New York, 1998), quotes on pp. 341, 361.

cocked at the irritable lower orders and the other on their cosmopolitan peers abroad who might be tempted to use the Southcottian delusion to make some anti-British jokes of their own. "The foreign journals cast a stigma on the English, for a credulity which they do not possess," warned R. S. Kirby. " 'Are these the people,' they cry, 'who would beat us in arts as well as arms—who now shape their political projects according to the silly garrulity of an infatuated old woman and her followers[?]' "[98] National pride in England's vaunted achievements in an era of great scientific and intellectual advances was at stake; "However distinguished we may be, in comparison with our ancestors, for general information and science, we scruple not to say, that the darkest period of our history can scarcely furnish a parallel instance to the credulity and blindness that prevail amongst the followers of this woman."[99] As William Cobbett said in 1813, the Southcottians were "a gross and outrageous insult to common sense, and a great scandal to the country. It is in vain that we boast of our *enlightened state* while a sect like this is increasing daily."[100]

Despite such constant sniping from above, Southcott doggedly pursued the path laid out by her spiritual guide for twenty years, a path bordered on one side by an unapologetic vision of redeemed womanhood, and on the other by an almost pathetic desire for public acclaim and respectability. Three times over the course of her career Southcott arranged for public "trials" of her writings, hoping to enlist the support of prominent clergymen and magistrates for her prophecies. Each time she was bitterly disappointed. A few ministers were converted to her cause, but most remained hostile or (worse) aloof, not caring to sully their reputations or the reputation of the church they served by association with a local prophetess. Dictatorial and demanding within her own society, Southcott could be downright servile when soliciting the favor of important men. The woman who confidently proclaimed *"This is a New thing Amongst mankind, for a woman to be the Greatest Prophet that ever came into the World"* spent years in futile pursuit of one minister who spurned her overtures.[101] Southcott's sensitivity to learned

---

[98] R. S. Kirby, *Kirby's Wonderful and Eccentric Museum: or Magazine of Remarkable Characters*, 3 vols. (London, 1820), 1:348.

[99] *Bell's Weekly Messenger*, Aug. 7, 1814, p. 6.

[100] *Political Register*, June 12, 1813.

[101] Joanna Southcott Collection, 340, June 3, 1802, f. 61, Harry Ransom Research Center, University of Texas, Austin. Southcott's pursuit of the Rev. John Pomeroy, which led to a state of virtual war between the two that spilled over into the newspapers and coffeehouses of Exeter, is chronicled in several of Southcott's publications; see the *Divine and Spiritual Letters of Prophecies* (London, 1801), and *The Book of Wonders, Marvellous and True* (London, 1813).

opinion, so unusual among the millenarian crowd, who for the most part scorned the educated and high-born as pharisees, can be traced to her unusual dependence on the world of print. By offering herself as an inspired author rather than a "living Bible" as her contemporaries Ann Lee and Elspeth Buchan did, Southcott and her writings became part of the bourgeois public sphere, subject to its laws and standards. It was a risky enterprise for a woman of such limited literary talents, and Southcott paid the price.

Her prose style was the subject of withering criticism by the British literary and ecclesiastical establishment, which accused her of foisting "delectable doggerel" upon a weak-minded public. These "rhapsodies of ignorance, vulgarity, indecency, and impiety" could only have proceeded from one source, "AND THAT SOURCE IS THE FILTHY AND VULGAR VOCABULARY OF JOANNA SOUTHCOTT!" The "trash" she published in her voluminous tracts was a "nauseous mixture of blasphemy and insanity."[102] Deriding the illiteracy of Southcott and her "petticoat republic," critics compared Southcott's writings to the Bible (as she herself advocated) and declared the former a bastardized version of divine language. There is "no good reason why these *Communications* should not be made in the *usual style and language* of the Spirit of God," one critic complained, "always the language of good grammar and good sense." As a clergyman assured William Sharp, one of Southcott's closest confidantes, "he had no opinion of a Holy Ghost who could not write grammar."[103] Holy men and women in the past had also presented themselves as "ignorant and illiterate," the *Times* noted, but true prophets like the Apostles "were enabled by the holy spirit to speak all languages; whereas no spirit enables these wretches even to speak their own grammatically."[104] Even a former devotee complained that "she could not write for any one to read; neither could she spell a word of two syllables, nor indeed many monosyllables."[105]

Such attacks eventually took their toll. To those who complained that "the complete jumble of nonsense, so conspicuous in your writings" had "hitherto sheltered you from controversy," she could only reply in exasperation, "whatever my writings may be, they have not screened me from controversy."[106] The only way to redeem her "communications" from the ridicule of

[102] *Bell's Weekly Messenger*, Aug. 7, 1814, p. 1.

[103] Anonymous, *A Letter to T. P. Foley* (London, 1813), pp. 36–38, 43, 45; *Sharp Answer to the World* (London, 1806), p. 16.

[104] *Times*, Jan. 12, 1815, p. 3.

[105] Elias Carpenter, *An Apology for Faith and Detection of Existing Errors Subversive of the Truth* (London, 1814), p. 35.

[106] Joanna Southcott, *The Long Wished-For Revolution Explained* (London, 1806), pp. 49–50.

the learned world was to turn word into flesh as God himself had done. In one of the most bizarre turns in the history of Anglo-American millenarianism, Southcott abruptly abandoned her role as a prophet of the written word in 1814 and announced to her public that she was pregnant with Shiloh, the son of God. (The parallel with the Virgin Mary, if not intentional, was duly noted at the time.)[107] Her followers could not have been more stunned. The literary elite, who had tormented the prophetess for her ungainly writings for two decades, were delighted. "If the dome of St. Paul's had fallen in, or a quarter of the Metropolis been swallowed up by an earthquake, it is scarcely possible that the awful event could have occasioned more general conversation. In every street, alley, court, and house, nothing was heard but the name of Southcott, coupled with expressions of astonishment, disappointment, or profane ridicule," marveled the *Sunday Monitor*.[108]

The absurdity of her "pregnancy" has hovered like a black cloud over Southcott's reputation, blocking any serious consideration of the prophetess as an important public figure. The prominent exception is James Hopkins's scholarly biography, which, despite its evenhanded treatment of the prophet and the social and religious milieu which nourished her movement, still characterizes her visions as fantasies born of a stunted psychosexual development, a diagnosis to which her mystical pregnancy lends a certain credibility.[109] Part of the fascination with what experts at the time and since have termed Southcott's "hysterical pregnancy" had to do with her age and marital status—she was, after all, nearly sixty-five years old in 1814 and unmarried; and no small part was due to the thirst of the London press for scandal of any kind, as coverage of Southcott's pregnancy fed into a general war of words between the respectable *Times* and its less reputable competitors over the norms of civil discourse in the metropolis. But the public reaction—in which accusations of avarice and fraud mingled with an almost voyeuristic fascination with the physical details of Southcott's changing body—reflects

---

[107] William Blake, who disapproved of celibacy on spiritual grounds, penned an unflattering epigram entitled "On the Virginity of the Virgin Mary & Johanna Southcott." For a more sympathetic comparison of Southcott and Mary, see Daniel Roberts, *Observations Relating to the Divine Mission of Joanna Southcott* (London, 1807), p. 26.

[108] *Sunday Monitor*, Nov. 6, 1814.

[109] Hopkins, *A Woman to Deliver Her People*; see chapter 1 in particular. Most recent treatments have been far less generous; Don Herzog refers to her briefly as that "dotty religious enthusiast" in his wide-ranging discursive tour through the underside of British political culture after the French Revolution (Herzog, *Poisoning the Minds of the Lower Orders* [Princeton, N.J., 1998], p. 301), and W. H. Oliver puzzles over the success of this "obscure Devonshire countrywoman" and her "preposterous publications" (Oliver, *Prophets and Millennialists*, p. 154).

as well the widespread repudiation of millenarian thinking evident by 1815 in the aftermath of revolutionary upheaval, political repression, and continental war. It had simply become inconceivable to large numbers of Christians that God would come again, in this way, to an "antiquated virgin."[110] It was very nearly inconceivable (in both senses of the word) to the prophetess herself, who was profoundly disoriented by this latest "visitation" from a Spirit who had been her faithful companion for twenty years.

"It is now Four Months since I felt the powerful Visitation working upon my Body," Southcott wrote uneasily to a friend in February 1814; "to my astonishment, I not only felt a power to shake my whole Body, but I felt a Sensation that is impossible for me to Describe upon my Womb; This alarmed me greatly, yet I kept it to myself."[111] Despite her fears, Southcott was "ordered" by the Spirit to publish the news of her condition in two pamphlets. As word of her pregnancy began to spread in the fall months of 1814, she secluded herself with a handful of followers in a London house and ceased all public appearances. Thousands of the curious and faithful made their way to London, flocking to her residence each day in hopes of a glimpse of the prophetess. Expensive gifts, including a satin-lined crib embroidered in gold valued at a whopping £200, were stockpiled for the baby Shiloh, and enterprising shopkeepers sold "Joanna Southcott's Cradles" complete with miniature doll.[112] News of her pregnancy traveled far abroad, as papers in Europe and North America picked up reports from the London dailies about this latest craze. "The French Editors have taken notice of the noise which this imposter makes in England, and have copied the description which our papers have published of the cradle intended for the young Messiah."[113]

At some level, Southcott knew her pregnancy was a desperate gambit from the start. What strikes one most in reading her pamphlets is the tone of doubt and fear with which she relates the events surrounding her miraculous conception. "All my nerves shook, my head was like the rivers of water. . . . My spirits were so confused, that I could scarcely speak."[114] (This from a woman who had famously talked down the devil himself in one of her earlier

---

[110] *Observer*, Aug. 21, 1814, p. 4.

[111] "The Conception Communication given to Joanna, addressed to George Turner," Feb. 25, 1814, Joanna Southcott Collection.

[112] For descriptions of the crib, see *Bell's Weekly Messenger*, Aug. 7, 1814, p. 6; and *Morning Chronicle*, Aug. 2, 1814, p. 3.

[113] *Bell's Weekly Messenger*, Sept. 4, 1814, p. 6.

[114] Southcott, *The Second Book of Wonders, More Marvelous than the First* (London, 1813), p. 5.

spiritual encounters.)[115] Throughout the long months of her pregnancy Southcott was never able to determine to her own satisfaction whether this was a divine or a diabolical intervention. According to several accounts, she "professed her conviction, that she had either been visited by a *good* or *evil spirit,* and that her womb contained a *living* creature of *divine* or *wicked* origin"—a "devil's imp."[116] She feared at times that she had "*a wolf in her insides.*"[117] So strong were her doubts that she instructed her followers to allow an autopsy to be performed in case of her death to determine if she had in fact been deluded. Perhaps even more surprising was her willingness to allow a troop of (mostly male) medical practitioners to examine her body and publish their findings in the weekly press, a task which they undertook with little scruple for the modesty of their elderly patient. London readers were entertained for several months by accounts of these examinations, which suggested at least the possibility of pregnancy to seventeen of the twenty-one physicians called in. They learned that Southcott's breasts, "which she said had been flabby and shrivelled, with the nipple drawn in" were now "plump, the veins large and visible, the nipple red and protruded . . . the areola pale, partly covered with a little whitish scurf";[118] that her belly "had grown to a prodigious size" and her loins "had become thin"; that "there appeared to be a solid tumor, reaching not far above the pubes" which exhibited a "kind of undulating motion, appearing and disappearing in the same manner as a foetus."[119]

In fact, Southcott was dying. After months of speculation and feverish anticipation, the *Sunday Monitor* rushed into print on January 1, 1815, with the first news of the prophetess's death. As the disapproving *Times* sniffed, "the scandalous delusion which has for several months disgraced the metropolis, and even the character of the times we live in, is now at an end."[120] Such high-handed sentiments were, of course, rank hypocrisy to many read-

---

[115] Southcott, *A Dispute Between the Woman and the Powers of Darkness* (London, 1802). "What room have I to speak, if thy tongue runs on so fast?" Satan protested (in vain); "All men are tired of thy tongue" (pp. 25, 32).

[116] *Independent Whig,* Jan. 8, 1815, p. 6; *Times,* Jan. 2, 1815, p. 3; *Observer,* Aug. 28, 1814, p. 2.

[117] P. Mathias, *The Case of Joanna Southcott, as Far as it came under his Professional Observation* (London, 1815), p. 7.

[118] *Morning Chronicle,* Sept. 5, 1814, p. 3.

[119] These quotes are taken from two pamphlets, both of which were excerpted in the newspapers before publication: Richard Reece, *A Correct Statement of the Circumstances that attended the Last Illness and Death of Mrs. Southcott* (London, 1815); and Mathias, *The Case of Joanna Southcott.*

[120] *Sunday Monitor,* Jan. 1, 1815; *Times,* Jan. 1, 1815.

ers. The press came in for its fair share of criticism in the public outrage which erupted after Southcott's death; had publishers been less greedy, more responsible in sifting out the outrageous from the legitimate in their coverage of Southcott's pregnancy, her influence would have been confined to the lunatic fringe of British popular culture. Respectable papers like the *Times* were just as much to blame as the tabloids they so disdained. For all its ridicule of the *Morning Chronicle* as a paper "which has for some time past degraded itself into the vehicle of this poor wretch's infatuation or imposture, for the sake of selling a few copies to those very silly people who will buy such trash," the *Times* had shown no squeamishness about profiting from the public curiosity about Southcott.[121] "The more this imposture is brought forward, particularly in respectable papers, like your's, the greater attention does it excite, till at length many weak persons, whose hearts are better than their understandings, begin to wonder and to become credulous," scolded one letter to the editor. "It is a fact, that, in consequence of what the newspapers have for some time been relating about this woman, shoals of enthusiasts, with more money in their pockets than brains in their skulls, are now pouring into London and its vicinity, to behold this chosen vessel!"[122]

The medical profession was not spared in the posthumous condemnation of those learned authorities who had led the public astray to line their pockets or gratify their egos. The physicians who had been so eager to encourage the prophetess's delusions of pregnancy for the publicity backpedaled furiously after her death to explain this appalling lapse in judgment. Her symptoms, they explained, using the language of nerve psychology, were the result of overstimulation. "I am inclined to believe," wrote one physician, "that the sympathy which naturally exists between the uterus and the diaphragm and abdominal muscles is so much increased by morbid irritation in the uterus, that on pressing this organ externally, spasmodic contractions of the diaphragm and abdominal muscles takes place, giving the idea of the motion of a fetus in the woman."[123] Such excessive sympathy between body parts indicated that the prophetess had a "distempered brain," caused by "distension of the blood vessels."[124] Others were less generous, accusing Southcott of deliberate imposture. The tumor in her belly was in reality a bladder "distended by urine, retained on purpose," while "the breasts had

[121] *Times*, Dec. 28, 1814, p. 3.
[122] *Times*, Sept. 2, 1814, p. 2.
[123] *Sunday Monitor*, Dec. 17, 1814.
[124] *Observer*, Oct. 30, 1814, p. 72; Richard Reece, *A Correct Statement*, p. 93.

been enlarged by the irritation of suction," produced by "artificial means."[125] Either way, these medical experts belatedly argued that Southcott was in fact suffering from involuntary or self-inflicted "irritation" of the brain and reproductive organs and not from a miraculous conception. Their post hoc justifications did little to soothe public animosity. Dredging up past instances of supposed medical "miracles" that had turned out to be hoaxes, letter-writers and cartoonists pointed the finger squarely at the duplicity of doctors who had traded their scientific credibility for fleeting fame (Figures 8, 9). "Those of your readers who are acquainted with the history of impostors, will recollect that *Mary Tofts*, the rabbit-breeder of Godahning, would not have gone on so long as she did, had it not been for the ridiculous part which some medical men took on that occasion," reminded one letter to the *Times*.[126] "That some medical men have been so mistaken, so imposed upon, and so instrumental in imposing upon others" is "a thousand times more wonderful, than all Johanna's wonders of wonders!" declared another.[127]

But for all the anger directed at learned men who should have known better, it was the poor—Southcott's "enduring constituency"—who were the subject of savage contempt in the nation's papers.[128] "Our rural friends hardly know what idiots London contains," the *Times* reproved in an article ridiculing such urban legends as that of "a woman, with a strangely deformed face, resembling that of a pig," currently making the rounds in the metropolis. "The pig's face is as firmly believed in by many as Joanna Southcott's pregnancy, to which folly it has succeeded." The fact that similar rumors of "pig-faced" women and other wonders had been around for more than fifty years was proof of the intractable foolishness of the urban poor, a credulity that persisted like a chronic disease despite the best civilizing efforts of the press. "Does any one think that the wretches who worshipped that monster are half such savages in ignorance as those whom we have seen

[125] Reece, *A Correct Statement*, pp. 96, 101.

[126] *Times*, Sept. 2, 1814, p. 2. Other examples of past medical hoaxes included an eighty-three-year-old woman who supposedly gave birth to a child in 1768, a woman who "laboured twenty-seven years" before finally producing a "fleshy mass" weighing forty-two pounds, and the Duchess of Parma whose hysterical pregnancy was endorsed by a panel of midwives and physicians in 1731. See *Morning Chronicle*, Sept. 17, 1814, p. 3; Oct. 11, 1814, p. 4; Oct. 29, 1814, p. 4.

[127] *Times*, Jan. 12, 1815, p. 3.

[128] Hopkins, *A Woman to Deliver Her People*, p. 139. Hopkins reconstructed the social profile of Southcott's followers from surviving lists of those who received her "seals"; of the 7,249 names that appear on these lists, the "overwhelming number" were "humble souls, many living in impoverished conditions" (p. 80).

Figure 8. "The Imposter, or, Obstetric Dispute," ca. 1814. Department of Prints and Drawings, British Museum. The physicians huddle together in self-protection while the prophetess, brandishing one of her books, fends off an angry mob.

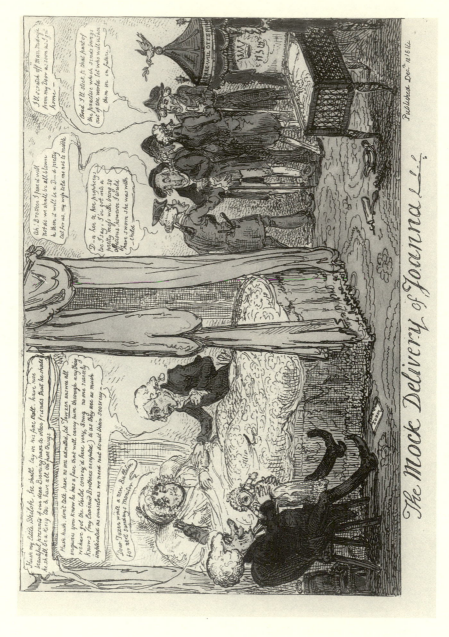

Figure 9. "The Mock Delivery of Joanna!!!" 1814. Department of Prints and Drawings, British Museum. Note the self-serving excuses of the physicians conspiring at the foot of Southcott's bed.

worshipping the fat and flatulence of a flasty old woman, here at home?"[129]
The "present miss piggy" (Southcott) was a fitting ambassador to the poor,
whose "swinish" inclinations were a favorite object of satire among the literary elite in the revolutionary era.[130] The denigration of the poor as a "swinish
multitude" had become so commonplace by the late eighteenth century, Don
Herzog notes, that radical pamphleteers had even begun to appropriate the
term for themselves in order to expose the hypocrisy of the enlightened
classes who mouthed republican pieties while despising the common people
they professed to serve. The list of contributors to the radical periodical *Politics for the People* (1794) included "A Ci-Devant Pig, Brother Grunter,
Gregory Grunter, Porkulus, Gruntum Snorumn, Old Bristle-Back, A Young
Pig, A Liberty Pig, A Pig with One Ear, The Learned Pig, and more"—all
proud spokesmen for the piggish underclass.[131] The metaphor worked on
several levels, linking the urban poor with a range of social pathologies
rooted in an inability or unwillingness to restrain their grossest appetites.
The "swinish multitude" wallowed in filth of its own making, too lazy to ex-
ert itself economically or politically, too stupid to realize it was being fleeced
by clever tricksters like Joanna Southcott.

Southcott herself ("this swinish female") was accused of encouraging
the worst habits of her working-class constituency by pandering to their desire for easy wealth. An aversion to hard work was probably the defining
characteristic of the underclass in the eyes of their social betters, a trait
shared by Southcott and her followers alike. "Suffice it to say," charged one of
the doctors who examined her, "that her complaints appear to have origi-
nated in fat and idleness. . . . Early in life, when she should have laboured
diligently with her needle, in an upholsterer's employ at Exeter, she found it
much easier to talk nonsense by the hour, than to work hard by the day."[132]
To her believers, she held out a tantalizing vision of a redeemed world without work. An "itinerant cobbler" who preached in one of Southcott's chapels
promised that, when the millennium arrived, "a poor man [would] get bread
without the sweat of his brow."[133] James Hopkins finds a consistent message
of sympathy for the suffering poor and outrage at the indifference of the
propertied classes in Southcott's pamphlets, coupled with vague assurances

---

[129] *Times*, Feb. 16, 1815, p. 3.

[130] *Times*, Feb. 16, 1815, p. 3; Feb. 17, 1815, p. 3

[131] Herzog, *Poisoning the Minds of the Lower Orders*, p. 513; Herzog traces the literary career of this popular phrase in chapter 12, "The Fate of a Trope."

[132] *Times*, Jan. 12, 1815, p. 3.

[133] *Times*, Aug. 30, 1814, p. 3.

of better times to come. She lashed out repeatedly at the "luxury and extravagance" of the rich, whose dissolute habits had ruined not only themselves but
also "the poor, honest, industrious tradesmen" who depended on their patronage for survival.[134]

The misery Southcott deplored in her pamphlets was real enough; during the dark years of the war with France, which seemed to drag on forever,
poverty blighted the lives of many working men and women.[135] Genuine
famine threatened in the crop failures of 1795–96 and 1800–1801, taxes were
driven relentlessly upward by the high cost of war, and soaring prices se-
verely limited the ability of many poor households to support themselves
without the humiliation of poor relief. "The Prospect on every side is gloomy
for the unbelievers. Trade ruined, Scarce any employment for the Poor in
the manufacturing Towns." By 1800, the price of corn and meat had risen
300 percent, a crippling blow to households that typically spent more than
80 percent of their income on food.[136] Work itself was one of the casualties of
war: "labour that was then plenty for the Poor had been taken from their
hands." The poor, Southcott concluded bitterly, were "born to be the negroes
here."[137]

Southcott's miraculous conception itself became a metaphor for greed,
for an appetite that could not be satisfied by normal channels. Famously
stigmatized by E. P. Thompson as an icon of the "chiliasm of despair" that
seemingly drove working Englishmen and women into sterile fantasies of
supernatural deliverance after the political repression of the 1790s, the
prophetess was caricatured by the press as a bloated Jezebel exploiting the
natural credulity of her moral peers for her own gain.[138] Money flowed into
Southcott's hands as quickly as publishers could print her books and the infatuated could empty their pockets. "It should never be forgotten that whatever other *labours* this woman may be engaged in, that of filling her pockets
is constantly going on, and proceeds the faster the more noise made about
her."[139] A ballad composed in the same doggerel verse she used in her communications gleefully thanked the "male old women, toddlers, dupes" whose
appetite for "super-human babies" had been so profitable.

---

[134] Hopkins, *A Woman to Deliver Her People*, pp. 137–48.

[135] John Rule, *The Labouring Classes in Early Industrial England, 1750–1850* (London, 1986).

[136] R. A. E. Wells, *Wretched Faces: Famine in Wartime England, 1793–1803* (London, 1988); John Rule, *Albion's People: English Society, 1714–1815* (New York, 1992).

[137] Hopkins, *A Woman to Deliver Her People*, p. 141.

[138] E. P. Thompson, *The Making of the English Working Class* (New York, 1963), pp. 382–87.

[139] *Morning Chronicle*, Sept. 3, 1814, p. 4.

What have I fleeced you finely, hey?
Bamboozled, bubbled, bit—nay, nay—
Discard your fuming passion,
Why am I worse than other folks,
When every season has its hoax,
And quackery its fashion?[140]

In another satirical verse, the prophetess is plied with "a thumping glass or two" of "spirits" to fortify her nerve as her chief priests gloat over the spoils of their scam—the expensive gifts piling up for the baby Shiloh. "Well I'm a great man grown, that's sure," boasts one, "No longer scorn'd, no longer poor." " 'Tis a good trade—God bless the day," his co-conspirator agrees; "Aye, this is profitable work,/ And makes me richer than a Turk."[141] The conflation of sex and commerce in the public representations of Southcott's unnatural pregnancy was a twist on a commonplace rhetorical strategy in the eighteenth century, an era in which cycles of economic fecundity produced "bubbles" of speculative fever that burst as disastrously as Southcott's visions of a miraculous conception. But in this version, it was the vicious poor who were responsible for the country's financial peril, represented so graphically by the prophetess' swollen belly.

The arrival of peace brought some surcease to the sufferings of the poor, but did little to abate the deep anxiety that eleven years of hardship and bloodshed had hardened into a state of national paranoia. In 1814, as the long wars with France were coming to an end and Britain was finally beginning to emerge from the political funk it had been plunged into by the loss of the American colonies, the reading public was in no mood to humor anyone who reminded them of the bullet they had just dodged. "No sooner than a political war was successfully brought to a conclusion, but a religious one commenced—I mean relative to the *blasphemous* doctrine of Joanna Southcote," complained one critic; "now the effusion of blood hath ceased to flow, England has apparently sifted this woman out for her revenge."[142] The limited tolerance accorded to a prophet like Richard Brothers was noticeably absent in the 1810s.

Had she not ended her career in such spectacular fashion, it might have been easier for historians to see Southcott as a crucial link between popular visions of apocalyptic renewal in the eighteenth century and the reformist movements of the nineteenth century which inspired a new generation of

[140] "An Appeal from Joanna's Ghost," *Morning Chronicle*, Jan. 9, 1814, p. 3.
[141] Peter Pindar, Esq., *Physic and Delusion! or, Jezebel and the Doctors! A Farce, in Two Acts* (London, 1814), pp. 7, 9, 14–15.
[142] *Morning Chronicle*, Aug. 11, 1814, p. 4.

British radicals—a link readily apparent in the 1830s, as the lyrics of a popular song about the abolitionist Frances Wright attest: "She beat Jemima
Wilkinson/ Joana Southcote quite,/ E'en mother Lee was nothing to/ Our little Fanny Wright."[143] As it stands, however, redeeming this particular com-
moner from the "condescension of posterity" has proven a challenging task.
And, without question, Southcott did not make it easy for those of us who
wish to see in her voluminous writings a critical and discerning (human)
intelligence at work. As we explored in Chapter 4, her "communications" follow no linear path through the mazes of scriptural and prophetic interpretation but meander seemingly without direction or design through the
personal details of her private life, the lives of her family and friends, and her
idiosyncratic reaction to the events unfolding around her. The heterogeneous jumble of facts, warnings, vague predictions, scriptural allusions,
and diatribes against disbelievers that constitutes her writings makes for difficult, and tedious, reading. To argue, as some historians have tried, that her
prophecies harbor a protofeminist or protodemocratic message is ingenious
at best, delusive at worst.[144]

But just as we were able to discern a particular if idiosyncratic hermeneutic in the structure of her written publications, we can discern patterns of
cultural meaning in the discordant elements of her personal story. The tra-
jectory from inspired author to miraculous savior that she attempted to
complete was both a reversal of the dominant eighteenth-century pattern of
millenarian behavior and a foreshadowing of the Victorian fascination with
supernaturalism that her successors would exploit, with great effect. The
awkwardness of her prophetic persona is symptomatic of her role as a transitional figure straddling two very different eras of spiritual renewal. One in-
triguing piece of evidence comes from her own testimony. Although we have
no way to know what Southcott really thought of her condition, the most
suggestive is her conviction—repeated several times—that the child would
be born not in the usual manner but from a hole in her side. "Two days before her dissolution," Richard Reece reported, "on awakening in great pain
from one of her dying fits, she loudly exclaimed that the child was making its
way through her side." Her chief disciple also declared his belief that "the
child is to be cut out of her side."[145]

We seem, with these statements, to be thrown back to another era
altogether—to the days of those renowned late medieval saints Catherine of

[143] Wisbey, *Pioneer Prophetess*, p. 185.
[144] Clark, "The Sexual Crisis and Popular Religion."
[145] Reece, *A Correct Statement*, p. 82; *Times*, Jan. 2, 1815, p. 3.

Siena and Theresa of Avila, who gloried in the grotesqueness of such paramystical behaviors as weeping rivers of blood. In late medieval sanctity, the "grotesque body" (to borrow Bakhtin's phrase) was a powerful model of mystical union for a handful of women whose physical excesses provided a point of phenomenological contact between believers and Christ, bleeding on the cross. We cannot know for sure whether Southcott was consciously reaching back to an older model of mystical experience with its unnatural openings and strange productions to explain what was happening to her, but we do know that this was a model that was inappropriate to her time and place.[146] The medicalization of childbirth and the disciplining of the female body through the rationalizing discourses of civility and enlightened piety effectively foreclosed the possibility of resurrecting a fully embodied version of spiritual communion.

Even Southcott's closest followers were confused over the meaning of her pregnancy. Some believed she would indeed give birth to the messiah as promised, a flesh-and-blood child. The Rev. Hoadley Ashe reportedly vowed that "unless Joanna Southcott had a child born and sucking at her breast on or before the 12th instant, he should be solemnly bound never to preach" again.[147] Others believed she would fall into a "trance" instead and return four days later to proclaim a new dispensation, while still others believed the promised Messiah was to be a spiritual heir only.[148] In the end, all were disappointed as the autopsy of Southcott's rapidly decomposing body yielded only a shrunken uterus and "intestines much distended by flatulency."[149] The official verdict was dropsy, the same disease that felled Jemima Wilkinson. Southcott was buried quickly and in secrecy, while effigies of the prophetess were burned throughout Great Britain.[150] Within weeks some of her chapels were dismantled, their contents "exposed to sale by public auction in the

[146] In Bakhtin's reading of early modern cultural representations, the "grotesque body" is marked by multiple points of ingress and egress from which fluids (blood, milk, excrement, sweat) flow in unnatural quantities; Mikhail M. Bakhtin, *Rabelais and His World*, trans. H. Iswolsky (Cambridge, Mass., 1968). For discussions of the "grotesque" body of the medieval female saint, see Elizabeth Petroff, *Body and Soul: Essays on Medieval Women and Mysticism* (New York, 1994); and Laurie Finke, "Mystical Bodies and the Dialogics of Vision," in *Maps of Flesh and Light: The Religious Experiences of Medieval Women Mystics*, ed. Ulrike Wiethaus (Syracuse, N.Y., 1993), pp. 28–44. The heuristic value of comparing Southcott's pregnancy with the somatic expressions of late medieval piety is elaborated further in Susan Juster, "Mystical Pregnancy and Holy Bleeding: Visionary Experience in Early Modern Britain and America," *William and Mary Quarterly* 3d ser., 57 (April 2000), pp. 248–88.

[147] *Independent Whig*, Jan. 15, 1815, p. 8.

[148] *Bell's Weekly Messenger*, Jan. 1, 1815, p. 4.

[149] *Times*, Jan. 2, 1815, p. 3.

[150] For details of the burial, see the *Times*, Jan. 9, 1815. For accounts of the burning of effigies, see *The Fifth Book of Wonders* (London, 1814), p. 16.

open air"—a fitting end for a mission mired in charges of greed and fraud from the beginning. "The bubble having burst, and the Society being dissolved, seats, curtains, cushions, chandelier, *Bible*, &c. all fell under the auctioneer's hammer," reported the *Independent Whig*.[151] The cruelty of the public response can startle, even across a divide of some two centuries. A believer described one scene, which disgusted even the participants: "a horse and cart with a gallows in it and Buonparte tied on one side, and an effigy of our Dear Mother on the other, big with child" was paraded through the village, where the effigy was stabbed in the belly by the hangman, "saying she was with child of a baboon." From there the procession continued on to the Market House, where "every obscene thing was done. . . . The effigy . . . was, by a doll put for the purpose, delivered before them all . . . even some of their own vulgar women cried shame. Then they were hung, shot for hours, and then burned."[152]

The ritual defilement of Southcott's body, like the examination of Ann Lee's body for signs of criminality and sexual deviance, stands as a fitting symbol of the fate of prophetic women in the age of Enlightenment. Yet here too, we should note the progression from actual to vicarious violence in millenarian culture: Lee and Mother Buchan were assaulted physically in the 1780s, dragged through the streets by mobs of angry young men, while Southcott endured the indignity of a posthumous desecration only. By the end of the revolutionary era, women's bodies—alive or dead, empty vessels or living incarnations—did not register the same metaphysical challenges that the somatic exercises of earlier female visionaries posed. Southcott's pregnant body was an ungainly burden for all concerned: for the elderly prophetess herself, for her confused disciples, and for her unforgiving critics. But it was not in itself a threat. In the end, her books were more important than the phantom Shiloh, and their survival ensured the prophetess's relevance to a new generation of English millenarians.

In the final analysis, I think Southcott's story is both more complex and more tragic than that of Jemima Wilkinson. Both endured very public assaults on their character and teachings during their lifetime, but whereas Wilkinson was able to escape to a place of sanctuary when her public turned hostile, Southcott lived out her full career as a prophet in the very heart of Anglo-America's thriving commercial culture, a sacrificial lamb to its lust for entertainment and scandal. Her story provided plenty of both to the avid

[151] *Independent Whig*, Jan. 22, 1815, p. 6.
[152] Quoted in J. F. C. Harrison, *The Second Coming: Popular Millenarianism, 1780–1850* (London, 1979), p. 105.

consumer of wonder tales in fin-de-siècle London. On the other hand, if residents of New York's Finger Lakes region dimly remember Wilkinson as a historical anachronism, there are those today who continue to believe that Joanna Southcott was an inspired "messenger" sent by God in a direct line of succession stretching from the 1790s to the present to warn his people that their days are numbered. A box of her prophecies, sealed until God reveals the proper time for its opening, resides somewhere, awaiting a new messenger to begin the final chapter in the Southcottian story.

Epilogue

Looking back in the 1850s over a long and productive career as an itinerant Methodist preacher, Peter Cartwright saw a long chain of enthusiasm and imposture linking the eclectic prophets of the early republic who had so bedeviled him to the organized millenarian movements of antebellum America. The prophets of the 1790s "would even set the very day that God was to burn the world, like the self-deceived modern Millerites. They would prophesy, that if any one did oppose them, God would send fire down from heaven and consume him, like the blasphemous Shakers. They would proclaim that they could heal all manner of diseases, and raise the dead, just like the diabolical Mormons. They professed to have converse with spirits of the dead in heaven and hell, like the modern spirit rappers. Such a state of things I never saw before," he concluded, "and I hope in God I shall never see again."[1]

What, apart from the hostility of mainstream evangelicals, connected revolutionary era prophets to their more famous antebellum progeny? The current historical wisdom tends to credit Peter Cartwright's assessment of the Millerites, Shakers, Mormons, and "spirit rappers" as direct lineal descendants of Richard Brothers and company. John Brooke, Clarke Garrett, E. P. Thompson, and Leigh Eric Schmidt, among others, have made a strong argument for the existence of a shared intellectual tradition linking radical Protestant dissenters across two centuries and two continents.[2] In Brooke's magisterial account of the roots of Mormon cosmology, the potent blend of medieval hermeticism, alchemical magic, and religious primitivism that an

---

[1] Peter Cartwright, *Autobiography of Peter Cartwright, the Backwoods Preacher*, ed. W. P. Strickland (New York, 1856), p. 52.

[2] John L. Brooke, *The Refiner's Fire: The Making of Mormon Cosmology, 1644–1844* (New York, 1994); Clarke Garrett, *Spirit Possession and Popular Religion from the Camisards to the Shakers* (Baltimore, 1987); E. P. Thompson, *Witness Against the Beast: William Blake and the Moral Law* (New York, 1993); Leigh Eric Schmidt, *Hearing Things: Religion, Illusion, and the American Enlightenment* (Cambridge, Mass., 2000); Stephen A. Marini, *Radical Sects of Revolutionary New England* (Cambridge, Mass., 1982).

obscure seeker named Joseph Smith put together in 1830 can be traced directly back to the radical sectarians of the 1640s, the French Prophets of the early 1700s, the assorted continental pietists of the mid-eighteenth century, and the millenarians of the 1790s. The affinities among the various spiritualist movements of the seventeenth, eighteenth, and early nineteenth centuries are real enough, centered in an unshakable belief in God's indwelling presence in man. An antipathy to learning and the intellect, to church structure and to hierarchy in general, an openness to the spiritual gifts of outsiders and outcasts, a primitive desire to restore man to his prelapsarian purity and the true church to its pentecostal origins, and a deep suspicion of wealth and birth as markers of spiritual worth—all these elements can be found, in various combinations, in the dissenting sects of the Radical Reformation.

But in temperament and cultural disposition, Smith and his antebellum peers seem to me of a different type altogether than the republican prophets of the late eighteenth century. Their profound alienation from the structures of modern life registers the extent of the social, economic, and political changes that transformed a proto-revolutionary society perched precariously on the threshold of modernity into a liberal democratic colossus. Too much separated the religious and intellectual culture of the early Victorians from that of the revolutionary generation—too many paths not taken and journeys aborted for those Anglo-Americans still searching for tangible evidence of God's ongoing presence in the world.

One path that proved a spiritual dead end was the Enlightenment faith in pure reason and the transparency of truth. As we have seen, reason proved an especially unreliable ally in the prophet's drive for respectability; the more reasonable his or her demeanor, the more suspicious his audience that deception was at work. Antebellum prophets saw little benefit in adapting their message to the language and forms of the Anglo-American public sphere. Reason, they concluded, had led sincere Christians astray, first down the treacherous path of deism and infidelity, and then, for an unfortunate few, down the path to disbelief itself. At the end of the journey of discovery, which enlightened scientists and philosophers promised would bring truth and justice to a benighted world, lay the self, not God, a self moreover stripped of charisma, the very thing that made it possible to see God in man.

The tradition of rational dissent was stronger and politically more potent in Great Britain than in the American republic, and rationalists did not retreat as quickly from the field of political and intellectual contest in the face of the resurgent evangelical movement of the early nineteenth century. Evangelicalism itself retained a far more conservative cast in Britain after the death of Wesley in 1791, though it was hardly (as some have argued) the handmaiden of political and economic repression, and its millenarian off-shoots tended to be less exotic than in the American case. Comfortably ensconced in the historicist tradition of biblical scholarship, millennialists in Britain continued to write learned treatises on the prophetic scriptures that did not differ markedly in tone or content from those penned in the 1780s. Men like George Stanley Faber and James Bicheno, genteel representatives of the millenarian wing of rational dissent, would have felt very much at home in the prophecy conferences which were convened regularly by Anglican ministers beginning in the late 1820s.[3] Nonetheless, the model of the "gentleman prophet" who not only wrote learned treatises but who lent his intellectual authority to popular speculation about the end times did not long survive the death of revolutionary hopes in 1815. The bifurcation of millenarian culture into the respectable and the chiliastic was never as complete as some English historians would have us believe, but the gap separating learned from popular expressions of prophecy clearly widened in the nineteenth century.

On the whole, millenarian culture in England and the United States took a decidedly populist turn after 1815. The "antinomian" spirit that Edward Thompson and others have identified as the lifeblood of radical religious dissent in the seventeenth and early eighteenth centuries revived in the mid-nineteenth.[4] "Mechanick-preachers" and itinerant prophets, many as illiterate as their impoverished followers, moved from the margins to the center of the radical evangelical world. The reasons for this vary by national context, but a new brand of religious primitivists in Britain and the United States shared a disdain for law, history, and education that went far beyond the tepid populism of a Brothers or a Southcott. Late eighteenth-century prophets worked for the most part with the Bible, for instance, using the Books of Daniel and Revelation as holy scripts. Their mission was to fulfill the promises of the Old and New Testament, to follow in hermeneutic paths laid out by the ancient prophets. At most, they proposed to supplement the Bible with their own writings, as in the case of Southcott, or to embody the truth of the Bible in their own persons, as in the case of Ann Lee.

The most radical nineteenth-century prophets, on the other hand, threw out the Bible altogether and proclaimed an entirely new dispensation, often complete with new sacred texts (the Book of Mormon) or, more dar-

[3] Ernest R. Sandeen, *The Roots of Fundamentalism: British and American Millenarianism, 1800–1930* (Chicago, 1970).
[4] Thompson, *Witness Against the Beast.*

ingly still, devoid of any textual basis whatsoever. The primitivism of these new prophets took believers back to the heady days of the apostles, before the foundational books of the New Testament had been written, before there was even a church or a canon. They promised not to fulfill but to rewrite sacred history. And this time, outsiders—the seekers, despised and ignored within their own society—would come out on top. William Miller came to millenarianism after a brief flirtation with deism, inspired, he said, by his fury at the "history of blood, tyranny, and oppression" that was the legacy of the modern church, "in which the common people were the greatest sufferers."[5] Literary and psychological analyses of the Book of Mormon reveal it to be a kind of populist manifesto, filled with righteous anger at the hypocrisy and greed of contemporary money-changers.[6] Drawing their adherents from the most desperate classes in postrevolutionary society (debtors, landless laborers, homesteaders and migrants, the flotsam of the early industrial revolution), the millenarian sects of the 1830s and 1840s tapped into a deep well of economic frustration and social alienation. Failure was the common denominator in the lives of antebellum prophets, almost all of whom were men and women of truly marginal existence, and failure was the bond they shared with their followers. The eighteenth-century faith in the uplifting power of reason shriveled in the face of such intractable poverty—poverty of body and soul.

Not all nineteenth-century prophets adopted the antinomian distrust of reason. William Miller declared the Bible to be a "feast of reason," and offered his followers a fairly traditional form of biblical exegesis in which simple numerical calculation and commonsensical translations of obscure passages led the diligent reader to the truth of revelation. After two years' intensive study of the Bible, a book he had once despised in his deistical youth for its contradictions and inconsistencies, he found that "all that was dark, mystical, or obscure, to me, in its teachings, had become dissipated from my mind before the clear light that now dawned from its sacred pages."[7] There is little to separate Miller's brand of numerology from that practiced by Nimrod Hughes thirty years earlier, or by generations of seers before him. As did Hughes, Miller calculated the exact date on which the world would be

---

[5] Joshua V. Himes, *Miller's Works*, 3 vols. (Boston, 1842), 1:9.

[6] Nathan O. Hatch, *The Democratization of American Christianity* (New Haven, 1989); Fawn M. Brodie, *No Man Knows My History: The Life of Joseph Smith, the Mormon Prophet*, 2d. ed. (New York, 1985).

[7] Quoted in Wayne R. Judd, "William Miller: Disappointed Prophet," in *The Disappointed: Millerism and Millenarianism in the Nineteenth-Century*, ed. Ronald L. Numbers and Jonathan M. Butler (Knoxville, Tenn., 1993), p. 33.

destroyed—originally 1843, later revised to October 22, 1844—using a simple day-year formula, though in his case grand historical events (like the fall of the Persian empire) rather than his own personal life provided the referent points. Such numerical reckoning was commonplace in the eighteenth and nineteenth centuries; one compilation of prophetic timetables lists nineteen British and American millenarian tracts published between 1768 and 1831 that also identified 1843 as the fateful date.[8] The Bible remained the cornerstone of Miller's apocalypticism, and reason his guide through its figurative mazes. Yet his rational biblicism was packaged with a thriving folk supernaturalism that was far more appealing to a certain sector of radical believers. The prophetic charts and colorful illustrations that were the hallmark of Millerite culture transformed the Bible from an authoritative text to an occult aid, akin to an astrologer's chart.

Reason, it was clear, would not by itself lead Anglo-America's Christians to the promised land. Civility—reason's external face—was no help, either. The "civilizing process" of which sociologists and literary critics alike speak so fondly had, if anything, proved even more destructive to true faith; reason might, eventually, lead man to God (or, at least, to God's plan as revealed in nature and history), but civility could never be anything but a false God. Civilized man values himself and his comforts most of all, and seeks his true happiness in the ephemera of the world—its well-appointed parlors, polished manners, polite conversation, venues of urban sociability (the coffee-house, debating society, gentleman's club) where the polite and the respectable met to admire one another. Everything that conferred status in this world was anathema to the true prophet. Those prophets who aspired to gentility were fated to insignificance, fools in the eyes of their contemporaries, and perhaps in our own as well. We prefer our religious enthusiasts raw and unbound, not decked out in the gilded trappings of metropolitan culture: the Quaker Sarah Goldsmith naked except for a sackcloth, her hair smeared with ashes, holding silent vigil in front of the market cross in Bristol, rather than

---

[8] Leroy Edwin Froom, *The Prophetic Fate of Our Fathers*, 3 vols. (Washington, D.C., 1946–54), 3:404–5. See the discussion of prophetic timetables in David Rowe, *Thunder and Trumpets: Millerites and Dissenting Religion in Upstate New York, 1800–1850* (Chico, Calif., 1985), pp. 12–13. The year 1843 was arrived at by using the prophet Daniel's revelation that 2,300 days (years) would elapse between the fall of the Persian empire and the fall of the fourth beast (widely assumed to be the Roman Catholic Church), and that the fourth beast would reign for 1,260 days (years). Subtracting 457 (the year in which the Persian empire fell) from 2,300 yields 1,843, as does adding 1,260 to 583 (the year in which the Roman Catholic church began its reign).

portly Joanna Southcott with her bonnet selling books to the London poor.[9] The former seems genuine, if kooky; the latter suspiciously calculating. The fact that we credit more extreme forms of religious fanaticism with greater authenticity (Joseph Smith's status as a prophet is unquestioned, whereas Richard Brothers is considered an amusing footnote to the history of British radicalism) is a prejudice born of the nineteenth century's insistence that true religious belief is beyond comprehension or analysis. "True" prophets, we tend to believe, do not aspire to be judged by the standards of the profane world, only by the ineffable marks of genuine inspiration found solely in the realm of feeling and experience. But that is a conceit we inherited from the Victorians, who were more adept than their eighteenth-century forebears at compartmentalizing their lives into separate spheres, thus facilitating our own analytical predisposition to do the same.

Culturally, the antebellum prophets are closer in spirit to the fanatics of the 1640s than their counterparts in the 1790s in their extravagant disregard for the niceties of civil society and their insistence on speaking the word of God unvarnished. Their distrust, even hatred, of city life was a central tenet of their populism, one that separates them definitively from their eighteenth-century peers. Revolutionary-era prophets thrived in the city: the urban milieu, with its expansive social venues and unrivaled print offerings and its graphic representation of all the vices associated with modern commercial life, made it the ideal staging ground for millenarian culture. British prophets, in particular, had a symbiotic love-hate relationship with London. The urban behemoth that was the British capital personified all that was evil in the world—the modern Babylon—and its destruction by fire and sword was the first sign of the coming apocalypse in most millenarian scenarios. Richard Brothers's vision of blood in the streets was repeated a hundred times, in varying detail. But cities not only were evil, they also provided the best means of combatting evil with their newspapers, chapels, markets, coffeehouses, reading rooms, and public squares. Confronting the beast in his lair meant that prophets, whatever their social origins (and a sizable number hailed from the provinces), had to make the pilgrimage to the nearest metropolis, whether London or Edinburgh or Philadelphia or New York. Some fled as soon as they could to a rural retreat, but removal from the urban environment where they had first tasted success almost always meant a loss in status and influence.

[9] For a description of Goldsmith, see Phyllis Mack, *Visionary Women: Ecstatic Prophecy in Seventeenth-Century England* (Berkeley, Calif., 1992), p. 168.

Nineteenth-century prophets, in contrast, turned their backs on the city and embraced a militant vision of rural simplicity. "Our cities and villages," William Miller wrote in despair after he visited New York City in 1842, "of every class, present scenes of awfully blackened depravity. It walks at noon day—it is dressed in the richest attire—it assumes the more refined culture—it sits in the most fashionable circles." Cities, to Miller, were the seat of economic and political corruption, home to the anonymous institutions (banks, insurance companies, business corporations) that the rich used to "grind down the poor."[10] His contemporary, Robert Mathews, who called himself the Prophet Mathias, was a broken and bitter man after three years' hard toil in New York and returned to his rural roots determined to re-create himself and the spiritual community he gathered in the image of his austere Scots-Irish forbears.[11] The Mormons' heroic pilgrimage west to the promised land was but the most spectacular example of the general antebellum retreat into an imagined pastoralism in which the vices of the modern world were held at bay and powerful fathers ruled over "peaceable kingdoms."[12] These examples are all drawn from the American side of the Atlantic, and in fact British millenarians never embraced the pastoral ideal with the same fervor as did their American cousins. The greater attachment of British prophets to the city is one of the more pronounced differences between British and North American millenarian culture. In the revolutionary era, British prophets were both more urban and more urbane than their American counterparts, and they continued to draw inspiration and outrage from the metropolis throughout the nineteenth century.

Unburdened by the need to appear respectable as well as authentic, nineteenth-century prophets resurrected earlier forms of supernaturalism that had been declassé in the revolutionary era. Miracles were once again in vogue in the 1830s and 1840s. Ezra Stiles's confident prediction in 1773 that occult knowledge was dead or dying, "the Vessel of Sorcery shipwreckt, and only some shattered planks and pieces disjoyned floating and scattered on the Ocean of . . . human Activity and Bustle," proved wildly inaccurate.[13] Cunning folk had never entirely disappeared from the Anglo-American

[10] Quoted in Rowe, *Thunder and Trumpets*, pp. 76–77.

[11] Paul E. Johnson and Sean Wilentz, *The Kingdom of Mathias: A Story of Sex and Salvation in Nineteenth-Century America* (New York, 1994).

[12] See Charles Sellers, *The Market Revolution: Jacksonian America, 1815–1846* (New York, 1991), on rural antinomianism. The phrase "peaceable kingdoms" comes from Michael Zuckerman's study of the New England town ideal; *Peaceable Kingdoms: New England Towns in the Eighteenth Century* (New York, 1970).

[13] Quoted in Brooke, *Refiner's Fire*, p. 50.

landscape, of course, and the occult arts (both black and white) which revolutionary-era prophets for the most part disdained reemerged in the 1830s and 1840s with some creative twists. The quiet wonders performed by Ann Lee and a handful of other spiritualist votaries in the eighteenth century were replaced by flamboyant spectacles of miracle-working, designed as much to awe the unconverted as to reward the faithful. Faith-healing, a perennial favorite of the spiritually gifted, continued to be practiced by a new generation of seers who imported scientific theories of animal magnetism to boost their healing powers. Andrew Jackson Davis, the "Poughkeepsie Seer" and disciple of Emmanuel Swedenborg, was a popular clairvoyant healer in the 1840s and 1850s whose performances helped popularize mesmerism for American audiences.[14] Edward Irving, the irascible Scottish prophet and faith healer, also encouraged his poor London congregation to speak in tongues as had the apostles; according to his friend Thomas Carlyle, "the 'Gift of Tongues' has fairly broken out among the crazed and weakliest of his wholly rather dim and weakly flock," and soon a national revival of pentecostal gifts was under way.[15] The public exorcism and levitation of a young convert, Newell Knight, in 1830 inaugurated a burst of popular interest in magic within Mormonism that soon threatened to eclipse even Joseph Smith's considerable charismatic powers.

Angels and other supernatural visitors returned in force to the villages of Anglo-America, and even the devil himself made an encore appearance, in somewhat domesticated form, in the massive frontier revivals of the early American republic.[16] A gifted visionary such as Betsy Babcock, the heroine of the "Angel Delusion" of 1806–11 in Vermont, might see or speak to an angel once in a lifetime; a new generation of visionaries, following the lead of the Fox sisters, made spirit conversations so commonplace as to seem ordinary.[17] At the height of Spiritualism's popularity in the mid-nineteenth century, the

[14] Andrew Jackson Davis, *The Magic Staff: An Autobiography of Andrew Jackson Davis* (Boston, 1857). See also Robert W. Delp, "Andrew Jackson Davis: Prophet of American Spiritualism," *Journal of American History* 54 (June 1967), pp. 43–56; and Robert C. Fuller, *Mesmerism and the American Cure of Souls* (Philadelphia, 1982).

[15] Sandeen, *Roots of Fundamentalism*, pp. 23–29 (quote on p. 26). See also W. H. Oliver, *Prophets and Millennialists: The Uses of Biblical Prophecy in England from the 1790s to the 1840s* (Auckland, 1978), pp. 126–27; and Margaret O. W. Oliphant, *The Life of Edward Irving*, 2 vols. (London, 1862).

[16] Christine Leigh Heyrman, *Southern Cross: The Beginnings of the Bible Belt* (New York, 1997).

[17] Susan Juster and Ellen Hartigan-O'Connor, "The 'Angel Delusion' of 1806–1811: Frustration and Fantasy on the Northern Frontier," *Journal of the Early Republic* 22 (Fall 2002), pp. 375–404.

parlors and sitting rooms of the British and American middle classes were crowded with spirits who carried messages from dead loved ones and provided an important phenomenological link between this world and the hereafter. True, the seances performed by spiritualist mediums were civilized affairs, or at least conducted with enough decorum to appeal to the most ambitious consumer of middle-class culture, but civility was beside the point. Spiritualists wanted to break down the artificial barriers that separated human beings—barriers of taste, class, gender, even race.[18]

If reason and civility were dead ends, commercialization was a more promising path, pursued clumsily in the 1790s and early 1800s, and energetically after 1830. Revolutionary-era prophets for the most part limited their commercial offerings to print, the first sector of the burgeoning leisure economy to reach a mass audience in the eighteenth century.[19] (All of those Shiloh dolls and cradles being peddled at the height of the Southcottian "delusion" in 1814 were sold by opportunistic shopkeepers, not by Southcott or her disciples.) Southcott herself was the queen of print, but while unsurpassed in the sheer quantity of pamphlets she published, she was not the first or only prophet to recognize the possibilities of widespread literacy and the advent of the daily newspaper and penny tract for disseminating her message beyond those in immediate earshot. Far more than earlier generations of Anglo-American visionaries, from the French Prophets to the early Methodists, revolutionary-era millenarians exploited the technologies of print to great effect after 1780.

Early Victorian-era prophets certainly did not abandon print, but they did expand dramatically the repertoire of commercial tools available to spread the word of God. The Millerites were particularly innovative in this regard. Tracts, periodicals, colorful illustrated charts, and handy visual aids poured from high-speed Millerite presses in the 1840s, supplemented by prophecy conferences and tent services large and entertaining enough to rival any secular amusement. Miller was the first prophet to entrust his mission to

---

[18] Bret E. Carroll, *Spiritualism in Antebellum America* (Bloomington, Ind., 1997); R. Laurence Moore, *In Search of White Crows: Spiritualism, Parapsychology, and American Culture* (New York, 1977); Ann Braude, *Radical Spirits: Spiritualism and Women's Rights in Nineteenth-Century America* (Boston, 1989); Alex Owen, *The Darkened Room: Women, Power, and Spiritualism in Late Nineteenth-Century England* (Philadelphia, 1989); Robert S. Cox, "Without Crucible or Scalpel: A Sympathetic History of American Spiritualism," Ph.D. diss., University of Michigan, 2002.

[19] J. H. Plumb, "Commercialization of Leisure," in *The Birth of a Consumer Society: The Commercialization of Eighteenth-Century England*, ed. Neil McKendrick, John Brewer, and J. H. Plumb (Bloomington, Ind., 1982), pp. 265–85.

a professional promoter, Joshua V. Himes, whose entrepreneurial skills transformed an obscure rustic seer into a national sensation. Himes founded Millerite newspapers and periodicals in most of the leading cities, created book clubs (the Second Advent Book Depots) in select urban areas to distribute tracts and pamphlets, and commissioned the construction of the "great tent" (supposedly the largest of its kind ever seen in rural America) which became the leading attraction in Millerite camp meetings. Some 4,000 people fit comfortably under the roof of the great tent, where they were entertained by lecturers, songs, and booths selling everything from Bibles to handheld charts.[20] The phenomenal success of Himes's commercial strategy turned Millerism into the first mass millenarian movement in American history, with 50,000 avowed converts and thousands more willing spectators.

Such commercial saturation carried the potential for fraud, always a concern in millenarian culture, to a new level in the nineteenth century. In John Brooke's words, the "cunning folk" of early modern Anglo-America had become the "conning men" of the Victorian age.[21] As religion itself became more and more a commodity to be packaged and sold like any other form of entertainment, the line between legitimate expressions of faith and cynical manipulation was considerably blurred. A story recounted by the famous nineteenth-century huckster P. T. Barnum in his autobiography may be apocryphal, but it illustrates the extent to which millenarian culture had become just another show. Calling upon the head of the Mormon church with some friends, Barnum was received "with a smile" by Brigham Young, who asked the entrepreneur, "what will you give to exhibit me in New York and the Eastern cities?" "Well, Mr. President," Barnum replied, "I'll give you half the receipts, which I will guarantee shall be $200,000 per year, for I consider you the best show in America."[22] An alliance between Barnum, the master of humbug, and the Mormon leader would have been an unholy one, to say the least, but not one without cultural precedent. Barnum made a career fooling his customers, usually with their tacit approval, by means not far removed from the occult practices of early Mormonism.[23] Joseph Smith made a career for himself before his reincarnation as a prophet as a local diviner,

[20] David T. Arthur, "Joshua V. Himes and the Cause of Adventism," in *The Disappointed*, pp. 36–58.

[21] Brooke, *Refiner's Fire*, p. 104.

[22] Quoted in R. Laurence Moore, *Selling God: American Religion in the Marketplace of Culture* (New York, 1994), p. 118.

[23] James W. Cook, *The Arts of Deception: Playing with Fraud in the Age of Barnum* (Cambridge, Mass., 2001).

promising to find buried treasure in the earth by magical methods of detection, and his youthful fascination with the supernatural carried over into his discovery of the famous gold plates which became the foundation of the Mormon church. Mormon cosmology was a curious blend of the old and the new: the folk magic of rural healers and the black arts of witches and sorcerers, the divining cults of the American backcountry and the counterfeiting rings of the early republic that turned dross into gold. And the Mormon prophet was not an isolated case. The 1830s and 1840s abounded with con men of every description who sought to harness the popular fascination with the occult to their own money-making schemes. Whatever we think of Smith himself, his success in forging an entire cosmology out of the cruder elements of folkloric supernaturalism and economic desperation was imitated by other, perhaps less pure souls.[24]

No figure better captures the transformed millenarian spirit of the mid-nineteenth century, in fact, than Joseph Smith. Smith's personal journey from village diviner to inspired prophet to *magus* neatly summarizes the history of millenarian culture more broadly between the seventeenth and the nineteenth centuries. The transformation of the prophet into a "Christian-hermetic *magus*," a divinized being with supernatural powers, opened the way for a radical democratization of notions of the self.[25] Ironically, in the figure of the *magus* we can see the ultimate fulfillment of a process begun in the mid-eighteenth century by savvy itinerants such as George Whitefield of exploiting the iconoclastic potential of commerce for very human ends. Whitefield, the "peddlar in divinity," pioneered the modern practice of selling God in a largely deregulated market, and though his motives were pure, his methods carried a subversive message that future hawkers of religion would exploit to good effect. For in the end, it was Whitefield himself, not his "product," that was glorified by the process of commodification. Whitefield and his fellow itinerants became the first modern celebrities in Anglo-American culture, their exploits known to and emulated by thousands.[26]

What the itinerants began, the philosophes finished. The unstated promise of the scientific and intellectual achievements of the eighteenth cen-

---

[24] Alan Taylor, "The Early Republic's Supernatural Economy," *American Quarterly* 38 (1986), pp. 6–34; Kenneth Scott, "Counterfeiting in Early Vermont," *Vermont History* 33 (1965); Brooke, *Refiner's Fire*, pp. 121–28.

[25] Brooke, *Refiner's Fire*, p. 4.

[26] Harry S. Stout, *The Divine Dramatist: George Whitefield and the Rise of Modern Evangelicalism* (Grand Rapids, Mich., 1991); Frank Lambert, *"Peddlar in Divinity": George Whitefield and the Transatlantic Revivals, 1737–1770* (Princeton, N.J., 1994).

tury was the deification of the self. From seeing man as an imperfect reflection of God, the boldest of enlightened thinkers had come to see man as God's equal. It was left to the radical spiritualists of the nineteenth century to turn man into a God by endowing him with the kind of supernatural powers that the revolutionary generation by and large rejected as superstition. The irony would surely have been appreciated by an enlightened believer like John Wesley, whose own forays into supernaturalism were always kept carefully in check by a humble appreciation for man's fallen nature. Wesley saw no *magi* in his Methodist bands, only sinners struggling mightily to transcend their own frailty.

From *magus* to magician was a relatively small step. The rise in popularity of what James Cook calls "the arts of deception" in the antebellum period, aimed primarily at the new middle classes, registers a new stage in the cultural history of illusionism. Performances like Barnum's offered to the middle classes what antebellum prophets offered to the desperate classes: an escape from the privations and banalities of ordinary life into a magical realm of miracles and dreams come true. The social bifurcation of antebellum cultural performances was less pronounced in the late eighteenth century, where millenarians made a conscious effort to appeal to believers from all classes. The more socially heterogeneous audience for prophecy in the revolutionary era goes some way toward explaining its hybrid intellectual and cultural nature—its appeal to reason *and* faith, enlightened notions of human ability *and* primitive fears of human futility in the face of real evil.

But we shouldn't go too far down this road. Millenarian beliefs have never been the exclusive preserve of a particular social class or social agenda, even at their most chiliastic. Rather than seeing the hybrid quality of prophecy in the age of revolution as the product of its mixed social base, it is better to locate its origins in the flexible intellectual environment of the late eighteenth century. The revolutionary era was a moment in which much creative thinking about man and God was possible—when no hard and fast lines were drawn around the "spiritual" and the "secular," when old paradigms of nature and the human body coexisted with newer formulations, when far-reaching changes in the way societies and governments were organized did not seem hopelessly utopian. The Victorians were more cynical than their eighteenth-century forbears about the possibilities for genuine communication across the barriers separating science from religion, a cynicism we tend to read as cultural maturity. If we can look beyond their skepticism for a moment, we might be able to see Richard Brothers, Joanna Southcott, and company as more than amusing eccentrics. They may not have set the world on fire, but their careers illuminate a corner of the Anglo-American world that would otherwise remain a "mystic land" of primitive fears and desires, best forgotten by those who think they have moved on to surer ground.[27]

---

[27] In the words of an early Methodist preacher, "One thing is certain: There is little space between us and the unknown world, and we sometimes receive impressions from that mystic land." Quoted in Donald E. Byrne, Jr., *No Foot of Land: Folklore of American Methodist Itinerants* (Metuchen, N.J., 1975), p. 42.

Index